TOKUGAWA IDEOLOGY

TOKUGAWA IDEOLOGY

EARLY CONSTRUCTS, 1570-1680

Herman Ooms

PRINCETON UNIVERSITY PRESS

PRINCETON, NEW JERSEY

Published by Princeton University Press, 41 William Street, Princeton,
New Jersey 08540
In the United Kingdom: Princeton University Press, Guildford, Surrey

Library of Congress Cataloging in Publication Data will be found on
the last printed page of this book

ISBN 0-691-05444-4

Publication of this book has been aided by a grant from the Publications
Program of the National Endowment for the Humanities

This book has been composed in Monophoto Baskerville

Printed in the United States of America by Princeton University Press,
Princeton, New Jersey

Frontispiece: *Kei*, respect, reverence, by Asami Keisai. From the collection
at the Keisai Shoin in Ōta (Takashima-gun, Shiga Prefecture).

For Emily

Contents

Preface

THIS study was originally meant to focus on Yamazaki Ansai (1618–1682), the founder of the Kimon School of Neo-Confucianism. In a previous work on the leader of the Tokugawa bakufu's Kansei Reform, Matsudaira Sadanobu (1758–1829), my attention had been drawn to the ideological importance of Ansai's school.[1] As I began reading, however, it soon became clear that I was facing a complex enterprise.

The political points made by Yamazaki Ansai, like those of most other writers of the seventeenth century, are few and rather predictable. These writers enjoined their audiences to accept the new system of domination that centered on the Tokugawa bakufu. Yet they filled numerous volumes in their efforts to communicate that simple message to their audiences. It seems that what they had to say could not be said often enough or in sufficiently variegated ways. Yamazaki Ansai was no exception.

To establish the conceptual framework of Ansai's teachings required a familiarity not only with his own voluminous written legacy but also with that of his immediate disciples (Satō Naokata, Asami Keisai, and Miyake Shōsai) and even some of their disciples, such as Wakabayashi Kyōsai. Kyōsai's teachings, for example, jotted down by one of his disciples, often include sayings by Ansai that Kyōsai had heard from his own teacher, Asami Keisai. Furthermore, Ansai grounded his teachings in two traditions at once, namely, Neo-Confucianism and Shinto.

I had initially assumed that an analysis of Yamazaki Ansai's teachings, however complex the sources, would provide an avenue to understanding early Tokugawa ideology, for he served for seven years (1665–1672) as mentor to the bakufu leader Hoshina Masayuki (1611–1672). But by Ansai's time the bakufu had already survived four shoguns under a Neo-Confucian ideology established by Tokugawa Ieyasu (1542–1616), the founder of the Tokugawa dynasty. An adequate understanding of Ansai's formulation of early Tokugawa ideology thus required a preliminary study of the writings of that ideology's "founding fathers," Fujiwara Seika (1561–1619) and Hayashi Razan (1583–1657).

While I was conducting the research for the now wider project in

---

[1] Ooms, *Bureaucrat*.

Japan in 1976–1977, Naitō Akira published his sensational reconstruction of Oda Nobunaga's Azuchi castle. That article made it evident that many elements of this bakufu ideology predated by several decades Tokugawa Ieyasu's ascendance to power in 1600. The study was thus widened to include the first of the three so-called unifiers, Oda Nobunaga (1534–1582). Along the way, now stretching from Azuchi to Ansai, it also became necessary to expand the scope of the investigation beyond written texts to politics, policies, and ritual, which also embodied ideological messages.

Moreover, I was gradually forced to come to terms with the phenomenon of ideology itself. This concept proved to be a portmanteau in which scholars have packed a number of varying interpretations. To refer to a political doctrine simply as an ideology explains nothing. Rather, one must specify how a doctrine becomes an ideology, how it informs and legitimizes action, and how it comes to bear upon the power structure of a society. Indeed, to understand the historical construction and establishment of an ideology more deeply than the conventional functionalist interpretations of that process allowed, a number of problems had to be addressed.

In formulating my own interpretation of the formation of early Tokugawa ideology, I have relied on a broad range of theoretical writings on the problem of ideology. Instead of synthesizing these theoretical approaches in an introductory chapter, I have worked them into the analytical essays that constitute this book. The opening chapter, nevertheless, without being a theoretical discussion of ideology, offers some historiographical considerations. The purpose of this study is not to illustrate a single interpretation of ideology through a discussion of a particular historical period, but to come to an understanding of a specific historical discourse. Elsewhere I have discussed more succinctly the contours of the problem concerning the formation of ideology and its links with Neo-Confucianism in the early Tokugawa period.[2] In that same essay, I discuss the implications of the interpretive language one chooses in describing and explaining these matters. There the reader can find a concise statement of the concerns and theoretical strategies that inform the present work.

During the course of my research, I discovered that my subject

---

[2] Ooms, "Neo-Confucianism."

kept evading my grasp, moving into more distant fields whenever I approached it, its boundaries receding over the horizon. Thus the presentation of what I learned remains affected by the way in which it was learned. The progressively widening scope of this inquiry has guided the organization of this book. If the traditional assumption that Tokugawa ideology encompassed only Neo-Confucianism had proved correct, I might have organized the exposition as a sequence of narratives on the lives and thought of a number of Confucian intellectuals, or I could have proceeded immediately to a structural analysis of this ideology. Either format would have been appropriate.

The terrain of ideological investments, however, turned out to be vast and variegated: politics, ritual, legislation, and texts not only of the Neo-Confucian tradition but of Shinto and Buddhism as well. Given this multiplicity of ideological expression, I could have opted for parallel chronological coverage of the topics that seem to divide this field of study almost naturally. Such a choice, I decided, had several drawbacks. A presentation of this kind would introduce such sharp and artificial expository divisions that the unity of the phenomenon under study would have been lost. One could argue that the uncritical acceptance of such ready-made organizational units of exposition has prevented past historians from surveying the whole ideological landscape. Furthermore, such a format would sacrifice structure to development.

Having discovered the heterogeneity of ideological formations, I wished to preserve the totality, to lose neither the process of their construction nor the homologous character of the end products. Hence the mixture of diachronic narrative and synchronic analysis in each chapter and some necessary overlap in subject matter from one chapter to the next. This approach also accounts in part for the "essayistic" quality of several of the chapters.

The first chapter, "Beginnings," provides my answers to the twin questions of locating a chronological beginning for the phenomenon under study and forming a proper vantage point for the exposition that follows. The epistemological question dominates the discussion and it is only within this framework that reference is made to previous work on Tokugawa ideology. Epistemology, I believe, is the level at which scholarship and methodology show their colors.

Chapters 2 and 3 trace the articulation of a new political discourse as predominantly a religious one that sacralized the rulers and the polity. Within this perspective, a general chronology of the whole period under study is sketched. The first step was taken by the rulers. The medium they chose was ritual, their purpose was self-deification. Next, a written discourse was formulated in a number of texts that seem to have been produced without any directives from above. The predominant features of these writings are analyzed here, and the point is made that this discourse was rooted in not one but a number of traditions.

The very structure of Chapter 4 highlights the manifold manner whereby the Tokugawa bakufu was acquiring ideological significations. The teachings of Fujiwara Seika, the founder of Tokugawa Neo-Confucianism, are examined next to those of Suzuki Shōsan, a Zen preacher. The thrust of their thought is very similar, and, moreover, Shōsan's teachings gain new concrete significance when juxtaposed to Tokugawa legislation. The first popular defense of Neo-Confucianism, the *Tale of Kiyomizu*, further illustrates the plurality of initiative that generated ideological constructs. Although the ideas were disseminated from such divergent points, they nevertheless mutually reinforced one another.

Chapter 5 makes another diachronic sweep, this time of the institutional and ritual arrangements that effected a recentering of all public symbols around the new focus of power in Edo. The place of the emperor was central to these symbolic negotiations. Within this context early Tokugawa historiography is also examined for what it reveals both about the emperor-shogun relationship and about the construction of the new divine-ruler figures.

Early Tokugawa writers are repetitious and unoriginal to a very high degree. Not only do they stress the same values but they do it with the same bits and pieces of data, mainly from the Neo-Confucian and Shinto traditions. Yamazaki Ansai, however (chronologically the last of the teachers whose writings are examined in this study), seems to bring it all together in a new synthesis. Chapter 6 and the greater part of Chapter 7 analyze his writings. The very nature of his thought requires that one both disentangle the Shinto and Neo-Confucian elements and demonstrate their mutual articulation. The particular synthesis he constructed, however, did not last beyond his lifetime. His school split into Suika Shinto and Kimon Neo-Confucianism, both of which retained the values, dynamism, and power of Ansai's ideology. The second half of Chapter 7 explores this aspect of the most powerful construct of early Tokugawa ideology, which, through the Suika and Kimon schools, had a profound impact on Japanese history until very recent times.

In the final chapter, I come back to the way in which this study reconstructs early Tokugawa ideology and discuss the validity of my approach. I also present the hypothesis that the ideology constructed during the period under study here represents the first articulation of a fully closed ideology in Japanese history.

Acknowledgments

IN THE research and writing of this study, I have benefited from the knowledge, active interest, and support of many whom I would like to thank here.

I conducted the basic research for this book while on sabbatical leave from the University of Illinois at Chicago during the 1976–1977 academic year. A research grant from the Japan Foundation as well as supplementary funding from the Joint Committee on Japanese Studies, of the American Council of Learned Societies and the Social Science Research Council, and the American Philosophical Society enabled me to spend the year in Japan. While there, I consulted with a number of scholars who generously shared their expertise with me: professors Bitō Masahide, University of Tokyo; Kondō Keigo, Kanazawa University; Suzuki Hankyū, Rikkyō University; and Tani Seigo, Kōgakkan University in Ise.

My research led me to numerous libraries and collections whose facilities were graciously put at my disposal: the Cabinet Library of National Archives, the Diet Library, Kokugakuin University Library (including the Nihon bunka kenkyūjo), and the libraries of Kyōiku University, the University of Tokyo (especially the Department of Religious Studies), Waseda University, and the University of Kyoto. The collections at the Mukyūkai, the Seikadō bunko, the Tōyō bunko in Tokyo, the Ōkura seishin bunka kenkyūjo in Yokohama, and the Hōsa bunko in Nagoya also provided rich material.

I am also grateful for the opportunities I was given to share some of my interpretations before putting them into print. Such occasions were provided when I was invited to read papers at Duke University, Princeton University, the Regional Seminar in Neo-Confucian Studies at Columbia University, and the Workshop on Responses to Neo-Confucianism in Tokugawa Japan, held at St. John's University, New York, April 3–5, 1981. During this workshop, the comments from professors Wm. Theodore de Bary (Columbia University) and Matsumoto Sannosuke (University of Tokyo) were especially helpful, but I am most grateful to Kate Wildman Nakai (Sophia University, Tokyo) whose detailed comments and criticism helped me to fine-tune the final draft. The careful readers for the Princeton University Press also deserve special thanks, as does the text editor, Margaret Case, whose highly professional skills have greatly contributed to the readability of my prose.

At the University of Illinois in Chicago, I was fortunate to find a group of bright undergraduates with whom I could discuss my ideas and who enthusiastically tackled the theoretical writings that gave shape to them. They are Agostino Cerasuolo, Steven Diamond, Carl Harper, Marshall Johnson, and Andrea Sorensen.

My warmest words of gratitude are reserved for my wife, Emily Groszos Ooms, to whom this work is dedicated. This book owes much to her editorial assistance in the final stages of writing, but I am most grateful for her intellectual companionship which sustained, inspired, and enriched me throughout an otherwise solitary enterprise.

TOKUGAWA IDEOLOGY

One. Introduction: Beginnings

Strange though it may sound, in all "science of morals" hitherto the problem of morality itself has been *lacking*: the suspicion was lacking that there was anything problematic here. What philosophers ... sought to furnish was ... only a scholarly form of *faith* in the prevailing morality, a new way of *expressing* it, and thus itself a fact within a certain morality, indeed even in the last resort a kind of denial that this morality *ought* to be conceived as a problem.—*Nietzsche*[1]

All Japanese historians locate the birth of a new political order in the opening years of the seventeenth century. With his military victory at Sekigahara in September of the year 1600, Tokugawa Ieyasu forged a lasting peace out of war. To consolidate this peace, it is said, Ieyasu borrowed a body of Chinese learning known as Neo-Confucianism and prescribed this political doctrine as an ideology for this new society. Historiographical tradition thus suggests that a discussion of Tokugawa ideology should start in 1600 and take Neo-Confucianism as its subject.[2] Before following this path, however, it is advisable to examine what is involved if one accepts a given beginning as one's historiographical point of departure.

NOTHING seems more reasonable than to begin at the beginning, especially for historians. We study phenomena as they appear and develop in time. Mankind, societies, institutions, movements, personalities—all lend themselves to a preoccupation with beginnings, if for no other reason than that they were not always there. To begin at the beginning is thus not only reasonable but natural, because one retraces a natural developmental sequence. When reason follows nature this closely, one claims objectivity.

Beginnings always present themselves as fully objective, for if they do not, they are discarded and replaced by other beginnings or, if unknown, are assumed to lie silently awaiting identification and vivification. To doubt their objective character is contradictory because it would undermine the very reality of what is being

---

[1] *Beyond Good and Evil*, translated by R. J. Hollingdale (New York: Penguin Books, 1973), p. 91 (original emphasis retained).
[2] Even Maruyama Masao's classic and original study starts this way: *Studies*, p. 15.

studied. Beginnings may raise problems but, as such, they seem unproblematical.[3]

Upon reflection, however, any beginning has to shed its simple naturalness and objective factuality for human artificiality and historical contingency. Beginnings pertain to an epistemological order rather than to the order of things. To talk of a beginning is to engage in a highly interpretive discourse, and a very problematical one.

The identification of a beginning does not have the simplicity of marking a cellular point of departure for later more complex developments. It is, rather, similar to the creative work of fashioning a structured identity whose features, clearly delineated, regulate the future fate of that identity. Maruyama Masao, for example, sets up a seamless seventeenth-century orthodoxy to have his hero, Ogyū Sorai (1666–1724), break it down in the early eighteenth century.[4] Discussion of beginnings is an arbitrary and deterministic intellectual exercise which to various degrees marshals notions of intentionality or causality (some agency, circumstance, or personality is posited as begetter), identity, irruption, and continuity (something that was not there appeared at one point, continued or unfolded, grew and spread). For Wm. Theodore de Bary, early Tokugawa Neo-Confucianism had an identity that was pluralistic rather than monolithic, the result of a gradual unfolding of all its conceptual potential; of shifts in the balance between the polarities that marked the boundaries of the field of Neo-Confucian discourse.[5]

Another problem with beginnings is that only very rarely are they intended or seen as such at the time of their alleged occurrence. Thus, one question that arises is whether Ieyasu *meant* to establish Neo-Confucianism as the official bakufu ideology when, two weeks after his victory at Sekigahara, he invited Fujiwara Seika to join his service and when, five years later, he hired Hayashi Razan. Most often, it is only in retrospect, after irruptive events have solidified into continuities, that one talks of them as beginnings and recognizes in them the lasting features of an identity that seems to have maintained itself over time. Thus it is the

---

[3] These reflections on historical and historiographical beginnings owe much to the first two chapters of Said, *Beginnings*.

[4] Maruyama, *Studies*, ch. 2.

[5] de Bary and Bloom, *Principle*, pp. 28–30, 156, 167, 174; see, however, also p. 32 for difficulties with defining such boundaries. See also de Bary, *Unfolding*.

official Tokugawa history (*Tokugawa jikki*, True Tokugawa Records, a text to be discussed later), compiled in the early nineteenth century, that provides the *locus classicus* for the assertion that Ieyasu promoted Chinese learning for political purposes. One searches in vain for similar statements during the first half-century of the Tokugawa period. Beginnings thus mark retrospective victories of identities over time and history. But lasting features, such as those that turn a philosophy into an ideology, are only abstracted aspects with which one selectively builds or typifies identities, and which themselves are nothing but perspectival products of reflective minds. Even the view that Neo-Confucianism was perceived as a separate tradition in the early 1600s (let alone one supported as such by the bakufu) cannot be taken for granted and must be examined. Looked at in this way, beginnings, or even the phenomena they are supposed to be the beginnings of, are in no way naturally given. They are all perception; they are all of the mind.

Locating beginnings, however, entails more than bringing clarity to a diffuse past. There is no innocence about such an undertaking. The project of going back to a beginning is engaged in only because a pressing present has drawn singular attention to some item of the past. The execution of such a project accordingly bestows even more importance upon that particular reality. The *Tokugawa jikki* were compiled after Matsudaira Sadanobu's 1790 Ban on Heterodoxy, when the question of a bakufu-sponsored orthodoxy had become a genuine political issue.[6] Phenomena for which a beginning is projected increase in reality, and are not simply spoken of more easily because of their clearer identity. They may acquire an identity because they have been assigned a beginning. They are thus spoken of differently. Authorized more fully, such phenomena have a thicker layer of legitimacy.

A discourse of beginnings always produces a force akin to that generated by mythological origins. Thus it appears that beginnings are often not "real" beginnings but real talk about beginnings. Such talk of beginnings often serves concrete interests and is thus itself ideological. As will become clear later, it was only in the 1660s that the Hayashi scholars, for very specific reasons, found it advantageous to project back to 1600 a tradition of bakufu orthodoxy; which in turn served different bakufu interests after 1800.

[6] Ooms, *Bureaucrat*, ch. 6.

   The historian who unreflectingly engages in an effort to locate a beginning or who subscribes to a traditionally given beginning follows the same ideological path with all its unexamined assumptions as those who spoke of that particular beginning in the first place. Believing that he has isolated a fact, he is unaware that he is the last in a long line of victims of a particular ideological project. Rather than repeating the "mythologizing" talk of a beginning or rephrasing it as an objective "fact," one ought to question the talk about beginnings, examine the significance of such talk when it occurred. And having thus exploded the discourse of one beginning, one ought to reexamine the substance of what had thus originated, and perhaps locate and disentangle the many strands that had been covered and fused by the myth of this one single beginning: rediscover the multiple and contingent history of the one "natural origin."

   HISTORIANS need a rhetorical entry into their subject, and they usually find one that strengthens their conscious or unconscious identification with their subject. In structuring the case they want to make, they often play out one historical personality against another, one Zeitgeist against another. Michel Foucault's foil for his study of the emergence of modern man in Europe was the *prose du monde* (prose of the world) of the sixteenth century: a beginning that was dictated by his whole project.[7] When Maruyama Masao, years earlier, studied the emergence of modernity in Japan, he used seventeenth-century Neo-Confucianism as the point of leverage for a dialectic centered around Ogyū Sorai. His beginning, Neo-Confucian orthodoxy as a political ideology, betrayed the intention of his project: to equate the disintegration of that orthodoxy with the emergence of modern thought. In his manipulation of contrasts, however, Maruyama separates himself from earlier historians only by chronologically displacing that irruption. The standard treatment of this period pits the new spirit of the seventeenth century against the obscurantist, medieval, and clerically dominated society that preceded the Tokugawa order. For Maruyama, the watershed lies not around 1600, but roughly one century later. His dark ages include most of the seventeenth century, which he sees as medieval and without any early-modern features.

---

[7] Foucault, *The Order of Things*.

The historian's free hand in stressing or even creating cultural contrasts—the early modern rationalism of seventeenth-century Neo-Confucianism against the religious thought of the previous centuries, or Sorai's secular pragmatism against the metaphysical thinking of the same century—should come as no surprise. Doing history is an exercise in interpretation, involving *prises de position* that affect the construction not only of beginnings but also of linkages to what follows. And yet, ironically, change, the very stuff of history, is precisely what most often escapes the historian. Change is usually captured under the guise of difference. Historians often punctuate time by noting differences (just as they mark a beginning point), and then bridge the differences by postulating transformations within an essence said to retain its identity. Change is thus mortgaged by sameness: differences become aspects or characteristics of a persisting substance.

Scholars most explicitly interpret societies in the past when they attempt to describe a culture in a very general way—whether they speak of dialectical moments, Zeitgeists, or value systems. Culture is presented as an integrated whole, nearly stagnant. In such an interpretation the flow of time is frozen into structures often defined as the fundamental and immutable core of a particular society. Robert N. Bellah's *Tokugawa Religion* is cast in such a functionalist mode.[8] In such accounts, society and culture become atemporal, without process. The stress on patterns of integration gives the impression that nothing is produced, that everything just "is."

Often, however, time is reintroduced surreptitiously, by contrasting one structure with a later one and thus obfuscating the problem by assuming precisely that which begs explanation: namely, the transformation of one such hypothesized historical constellation into the next one. This approach to the past is obviously more anthropological than historical and avoids the problem of time. Data are organized in blocks of sameness or continuity (which dissolves time), or discontinuities (which obscures the transforming process of time). This historiographical genre produces selected units and then extrapolates interpretively to the whole of society. Thus, Bellah's work conveys the impression that all religious values during the Tokugawa period were supportive of the polity. The tendencies to withdraw from the polity,

[8] Bellah, *Tokugawa Religion*.

expressed by new religious movements in the early nineteenth century, are not even mentioned. The suppression throughout the period of certain groups deemed a threat to society is not given its due weight.

Those who take a second general approach are skeptical about the oneness of a culture or society because they see only plurality, variety, and variability in the phenomena they study. In this perspective, society always seems to realize, somewhere, all of its potentialities. The historian's capacity to order and interpret empirical data in terms of larger patterns or systems is paralyzed through the attention paid to difference and variation.

Conclusions phrased in the static, structural, or essentialistic vocabularies of the first general approach belie the unceasing process of cultural productivity, even if that productivity merely reproduces or reappropriates tradition. In the second approach, however, the historical process, which constantly provides new variables without entirely canceling old ones, is invoked against structures—but only polemically. It is not given the central analytical place it deserves. Respect for the unceasing historical process is thus invoked as precluding a general anthropology of wholes, units, or cultures—which leaves only one way out: empirical case studies or specific ethnographies, biographies, and so on.[9] Neither genre solves the serious difficulties involved in incorporating time into the study of cultural or social wholes. Historical time, if taken seriously, seems to dissolve any coherence of a larger whole.

These problems are particularly acute in the practice of intellectual history. The generalists, whether dialecticians or structuralists or both, as was Maruyama, seem to make light of historical time, yet provide us with thick meaning. They deal with contiguities, congruencies, and contrasts, yet do so in time-stills, because only in that way can they treat the larger totalities that are their primary interest. It is as if latitudinal scope can only be obtained by damming up flow and movement. Historians, on the other hand, who focus on the transformations (and transmogrifications) of ideas over time face the problem of spreading their nets wide enough to take in the larger surrounding world (Umwelt) and root these ideas in their contemporary context. The problem

[9] Robert J. Smith, an anthropologist sensitive to the formative impact of the past on present practices, uses history precisely in such a way in his *Ancestor Worship in Contemporary Japan* (Stanford: Stanford University Press, 1974); for a discussion of this work from this point of view, see my review in *Japanese Journal of Religious Studies* 2 (1975), 4: 317–22.

an intellectual historian faces is thus the problem of anchoring ideas (texts) in an Umwelt that consists of other ideas (other texts) and a political, social, and biographical world (context).

One is thus confronted with a set of dilemmas: between generalization and particulars, history and anthropology, time and cultural construct, text and context. These seemingly irreducible choices involve more than personal taste; they concern the organization of understanding, the achievement of meaning, and degrees of persuasiveness and plausibility. In other words, the problem is epistemological: how can one responsibly achieve a meaningful integration of a number of items, the so-called historical data?[10]

Michael Polanyi has argued from a Gestalt-theoretical perspective that achieving understanding, even at the most specific level, involves bringing to bear on a focal target a number of items or particulars. In other words, understanding consists of the construction of a "from-to" relationship that transforms the status of these particulars from one of independence to one of subordination to a focus. This transformative process consists essentially of interpretation, because the focal target on which these particulars come to bear constitutes the meaning of these particulars (which turns them into subsidiaries). Thus for Maruyama, individual Tokugawa thinkers line up in a progression that is identified with the (abortive) modernization process of Japanese thought. His focus, as is apparent from the introduction to the English translation of his work, is the ambivalent status of modernity in the nationalistic Japan of the 1940s. In de Bary's work, Neo-Confucian thinkers are given a place within the logical and almost necessary possibilities of the original Sung synthesis.

Conversely, the moment we redirect our attention to a subsidiary, the meaning it had acquired as a subsidiary is wiped out, although it can in turn become a focus that provides meaning for other data (which thus become *its* subsidiaries). In Matsumoto Shigeru's study of Motoori Norinaga (1730–1801), the latter's psycho-biography provides the organizing focus for Motoori's texts—an organization that precludes a possible explanatory status for other data (social, political, discursive) for these texts.[11] One can thus see that the dilemmas of the historian are inherent in the nature of interpretation and understanding: the meaning a

---

[10] The discussion of knowledge that follows was inspired by Polanyi and Prosch, *Meaning*, pp. 70–72, 79, 82, 144. For a similar view, see Barthes, *Mythologies*, p. 123.

[11] Matsumoto, *Motoori Norinaga*.

focus such as biography or modernization provides for subsidiaries (texts) seriously hampers the possibility of giving these texts—social vehicles of meaning for a past audience—their full due as foci themselves of meaning to other items.

The historian provides the focus, the integrative perception, that ties particulars to itself. Such integrations, by their very nature, are partial perspectives and thus subjective. As such they escape "objective" control and restraint. The only requirement they must fulfill is plausibility. Plausibility, however, is also a matter of judgment. On the surface, it seems that we are caught in Sorai's absurd "the mind chasing the mind":[12] the subjective work of the imagination is controlled by another subjective standard—plausibility, also a product of the mind.

The historiographical imagination may indeed operate solipsistically, but the demand to build plausible relations involves the historian's audience and activates a social standard in the form of a flexible convention that is softer than empirical measures, but far harder than whimsical arbitrariness. Plausibility may be undemonstrable and the criteria may change over time, but there are real constraints within which the historian has to work in order to be credible and reach an audience. In this respect, the position of the historian is parallel to that of the producers of the texts he studies: they too had to meet standards of plausibility to reach their audiences. This parallel, however, entails two differences.

One, the focus is different. The authors of the texts had to make sense about their society for their contemporaries. The historian in his own writings has to make sense of the sense made by the authors in their texts. Hence the constraints of plausibility that govern these two sense-making operations are different. The meaning provided by the authors is controlled by an order acceptable to their readers. The historian cannot simply display that same meaning but has to engage in an interpretation of that meaning, bringing out its significance, in a framework acceptable to his own readers.[13] He cannot simply let the texts speak for themselves, because the decoding keys applied to the text by the historians's present audience and the past audience of the texts are not the same. Yet, in the mediation between a past text and his present

---

[12] Ogyū, *Bendō*, p. 88; for the Japanese text, see NST 36: 27–28 (for abbreviations, see the Bibliography).

[13] On the difference between meaning and significance, see Hirsch, *Validity in Interpretation*, p. 8; quoted by Horton, *Interpreting*, pp. 128–29.

audience, the historian has to remain true to the original meanings of the texts. If the historian uses present-day concepts such as modernization or scientific rationality to explicate the texts to his readers, he cannot help but lose the significance the texts had in their own time.

This brings us one step closer to a formulation of the historian's task as I understand it. The particulars that the intellectual historian, especially one who addresses the problem of ideology, has to bring to bear on the meaning *that is already locked* in a text lie in the contemporaneous context of that text. A procedure that from the outset introduces a chronologically, let alone culturally, extraneous focus shatters historical meaning and precludes an understanding of the process of text production and through it the reality that was converted into texts when they were produced. In retrospect, particular ideas or concepts may seem to correspond to modern ones, but in their own time they could not have been so conceived. Even if these texts addressed universal problems, or were part of a larger tradition such as Neo-Confucianism, their thrust and orientation—to avoid the ambiguous term of intentionality[14]—certainly did not lie in the future but in their own context.

Some of these past utterances may cast a pleasing light on our own concerns ("they are already modern, like ours") or offer cures for our problems ("they provide meaning we are short of").[15] If they are marshaled for such purposes, however, then they are deflected from what they were trying to communicate when they were brought forth. This anachronistic "foregrounding" of texts ultimately belittles these texts (under the guise of enhancing their relevance), because such foregrounding can do no more than make these texts appear to stammer about things we today know how to speak of eloquently.[16] It is the task of the historian, then, to locate those particulars that are plausible subsidiaries for the meaning that is already provided by the texts. The message of these texts,

[14] For a discussion of intentionality, see Horton, *Interpreting*, pp. 103–104.

[15] Bellah's two interpretations of the significance of Ishida Baigan are good illustrations of both. In his *Tokugawa Religion*, written in the 1950s, Bellah portrays Baigan as a rationalizer and modernizer of Japanese thought who helped make Japan's modernization a success. This was much in tune with the optimistic hopes of the 1950s in modernization as the salvation for mankind. In a reinterpretation of Baigan, written twenty years later in the 1970s, when the excesses and ill effects of modernization were all too visible, Bellah turned Baigan into a different kind of hero, one whose teachings held cures for modernity ("Baigan and Sorai", pp. 137–52).

[16] On "foregrounding," see Horton, *Interpreting*, pp. 23–24, 77.

being conditioned by time and place, is particular and contemporaneous no matter how universal, abstract, or borrowed the content. Thus, one of the questions that requires serious examination is why Neo-Confucianism came to be given the status of an ideology—if that is what took place under Ieyasu—when it had been available in Japan, albeit in a limited way, for several centuries, and why one speaks so easily of a Tokugawa ideology but never of a Kamakura or Ashikaga ideology. Reference to a doctrine as a public ideology automatically makes texts the focus of the social and political world surrounding them.

ONE must also consider that the audience gives particular meaning to the message—an audience that may not be, and indeed in premodern times never was, the whole of society. Furthermore, as Sally F. Moore argues, ideologies are never invoked *in toto* all the time; such invocation is always a piecemeal matter.[17] Audience and circumstance therefore fix limits to the import of a particular communication in a given population. What, in the complex teachings of Neo-Confucianism, was meant for whom?

The audience, in fact, conditions both the form and the content of the message. The author has to share style, assumptions, and expressive formulae with the world in which he operates. And the way things are said limits *what* can be said, because not everything would make sense everywhere and at all times.

Ironically, this particularization forces the historian to attend to those things beyond the text that effect this particularization. Historical interpretation is thus driven out of the text and its contextual subsidiaries into a discussion of silences: who does not participate in the formulation of a discourse, and what is left unsaid? Ultimately, it may turn out that these questions have to be rephrased as: who is excluded from the discourse and what silences are purposeful?[18] Indeed, it is only the latter formulation of the question that is historiographically responsible, because it is only when one can document exclusion from participation and an imposition of silence that one is dealing with a historical reality. In

---

[17] Moore, "Uncertainties in Situations," p. 236.

[18] Richard E. Palmer writes: "Every interpretation must do violence to the explicit formulations in the text. To refuse to go beyond the explicitness of the text is really a form of idolatry, as well as of historical naïveté" (*Hermeneutics*, p. 148; quoted in Horton, *Interpreting*, p. 30).

other words, one should be careful not to impute to people who had no such desire an urge to speak, or hypothesize as unsaid what would make no sense at a given time and place.

Context also involves alternative texts and traditions. In the early Tokugawa period, besides Neo-Confucianism, these include Shinto and Buddhist as well as eclectic and folk traditions. In the face of this plurality, it is possible to decide on a most "representative" tradition and let it speak for the whole society, thus obscuring the importance or even existence of the other traditions. In the discussion of early Tokugawa political thought, political thought has usually been equated with official ideology, and the latter with Neo-Confucianism, in the silent understanding that this tradition held a monopoly on political discourse and legitimizing strategies. Alternatively, one may take on the role of an ethnographer of ideas or genealogist of schools, giving them all equal time and losing expository and explanatory cohesion in the process.

In view of the social character of texts, however, especially texts said to carry an ideology, another possibility presents itself. Intellectual concerns in any given period may be clearly marked by overriding problems to which men in different traditions direct their thoughts and words. Witness today's preoccupation with language in the disciplines of anthropology, history, psychology, and literary criticism: in the works of Foucault, Said, Lévi-Strauss, and Geertz, the distinctions between these fields are blurred. Such concerns may be shared by many, although formulated in languages that appear to divide the epistemological field into different conceptualizing traditions. This perspective can account for both unity and diversity: unity of concerns, unity or plurality of messages, and diversity in formulations. It is possible that there is an all-encompassing similarity in the scope of things that can be said. This analytical approach may, for instance, discover a unity of discourse under a variety of conceptualizations, which reduces the relative importance of preoccupations with the new versus the old, marginal versus mainstream, pure versus eclectic or transformed traditions. New concepts may be applied to a not-so-new problematic, and old traditions may from hidden recesses provide answers to new questions. They may all contribute to the same discourse, but one must still specify in what ways such a discourse constitutes an ideology. This approach enables one to circumvent the dilemma of having to talk about a culture either as totally cohesive (a Cartesian temptation) or as never making sense, (whereby the historian's role is reduced to picking through a pile of ideological debris).

One final remark on the arena where a discourse may play itself out. Texts are not the only access to a particular historical problem. Actions, policies, and legislation also mediate meaning, and can, by their public and symbolic character, display meanings that, as eloquently as words, contribute to a discourse or formulate an ideology that sets the parameters within which people conduct their lives. They further expand our field of investigation and interpretation, and enable us to come to a responsible understanding of what is going on epistemologically in a given society.

The above considerations call into question the assumption that early Tokugawa Neo-Confucianism (an alien, novel, secular, and rational philosophy, as the stereotype goes) acquired a new space in the intellectual and political field, presumably displacing Shinto and Buddhism in the process, because only Neo-Confucianism could fulfill specific needs of the time. In recent years, Japanese historians have begun to point out that the intellectual turnabout was far less radical than this.[19] Religious concerns were still paramount, even within the new Neo-Confucian tradition. Scholars attacked spiritual rather than rational shortcomings when they criticized colleagues, calling them "rotten" or "vulgar" Confucians. It is also clear that Neo-Confucianism, rather than simply rationalizing and secularizing traditional thought, provided many scholars with a privileged medium to pursue religious quests outside clerical bondage.[20] Conversely, answers to the twin problems of establishing political legitimacy for the new warrior class and of putting into operation an "ideology" were available in the old Shinto and Buddhist traditions. Ieyasu and his immediate predecessors and successors were deified in Shinto style. It was a Buddhist monk, Suzuki Shōsan (1579–1655), and not a Confucian scholar, who was dispatched by the bakufu to reform the seditious peasants of Amakusa following the Shimabara rebellion of 1637–1638. Moreover, the harmonious coexistence of the three

[19] For a critique of the prevailing interpretations in the writings of Maruyama Masao, Bitō Masahide, and others, see Ōkuwa, "Bakuhantaisei to Bukkyō." See also Watanabe, "Tokugawa zenki Jugakushi."

[20] De Bary highlights this aspect for China in *Unfolding*, pp. 13–18; for Japan in de Bary and Bloom, *Principle*, pp. 4–5. Concrete examples are Nakae Tōju's religious thought (see de Bary and Bloom, *Principle*, pp. 307–35) and Fujiwara Seika and Yamazaki Ansai, discussed in the present work.

teachings was at least as strong an intellectual current as the militant reaction against one of them (Buddhism). It should also be noted that the new regime had a variety of means at its disposal, such as the ritual display of foreign relations, to surround itself with an aura of legitimacy.[21]

The thesis concerning Tokugawa Neo-Confucian ideology is commonplace. When reading about the ideological fit between this doctrine and the Tokugawa social and political order, however, one wonders how a philosophy, capped with an elaborate metaphysical panoply and with no practical base in Japan, could generate sufficient persuasive power to serve as the ideological underpinning for the complex society that took shape in the early seventeenth century. On first reading, much of the discourse of the time, Neo-Confucian and other, seems to lack political necessity and strikes one as academic, arbitrary, and irrelevant.

One of the difficulties is that the writings of the time do not convince us through critical analytical demonstration. Rather, they attempt to persuade the reader or reinforce his personal convictions and emotional commitments by appealing to apparently unquestioned symbolic assumptions. They rely on seemingly uncontrolled concatenations of analogical concepts and unexamined metaphors that rest in a shared symbolic universe taken for granted by many at the time.

This universe constitutes for Maruyama a metaphysical orthodoxy that by and large dominates seventeenth-century pre-Sorai thought. Other scholars have labeled it as medieval, a leftover of religious thought. Whatever its origins or subsequent fate, this philosophy cuts across schools and traditions. At the most general level one is dealing with a philosophy of "anthropocosmos," one that is centered on both man and cosmos.[22] It presents an elementary but widely ramified doctrine about man, and specifically about his psyche and mind, because it was through his mind that the individual had to fit in the polity. This political psychology was reinforced by an all-embracing cosmology. The practical world of political society, power, economics, and history had no legitimate autonomy, but was absorbed and dissolved into the two poles of man and the cosmos. The intellectual responses to the concrete problems of the new Tokugawa society were thus minimally practical, and not in the least programmatic. Although meant to be

[21] Toby, "Reopening the Question of *Sakoku*."
[22] Durand, *Nouvel esprit*, pp. 37, 50, 52.

about human affairs, Tokugawa thought was not a simple mirror reflection of it. Thought, as Roland Barthes has argued, is reality converted into speech through human history.[23] The mode of this conversion is defined by discursive conventions that condition not only the expression of what is observed but perception itself. They stipulate the range and structure of what are plausible and responsible perceptions and utterances. They determine that things be seen and said only in a certain way, and thus define the texts both in their style and content.

The partitions between doctrines were very porous for one more reason. Most scholars were eclectic in one way or another: they all were tradition-hoppers (the sequence usually being Buddhism, Neo-Confucianism, and then, sometimes, Shinto) but some also combined traditions (the mix consisting of a recasting of Shinto teachings in Neo-Confucian categories). It thus seems unwarranted to limit a study of early Tokugawa ideology to Neo-Confucianism, or to begin with Fujiwara Seika's audience with Ieyasu in 1600.

Politically, the period under investigation covers slightly over a century, from the time Oda Nobunaga came to power in the 1570s to the reign of Ietsuna, the fourth Tokugawa shogun, who died in 1680: the gestational, formative, and maturing period of the Tokugawa order. If the political order took that much time to settle, it should not be surprising that political discourse about that order evolved over a similar time span. Adopting for convenience the traditional standpoint that analyzes political thought or ideology through the thinkers that produced it, the attention will be on those writers who were most closely associated with the Tokugawa bakufu (Fujiwara Seika, Hayashi Razan, Suzuki Shōsan, and Yamazaki Ansai). By now it should be clear, however, that the analysis will encompass a number of other items that qualify as ideological constructs.

This leaves out other figures of obvious importance in a general history of Tokugawa thought—men such as Nakae Tōju (1608–1648), Itō Jinsai (1627–1705), Kumazawa Banzan (1619–1691), and Yamaga Sokō (1622–1685). Although all of these men also talked about what one may call political psychology, they were either not related to the power structure (Tōju and Jinsai) or were in the service of daimyo and were censured by bakufu leaders (Banzan and Sokō). Such was not the case with the four teachers

[23] Barthes, *Mythologies*, p. 110.

considered here. They were all sought out by the bakufu, although they related in different ways to the bakufu and society.

Fujiwara Seika was consulted by Ieyasu, but declined the offer to enter his service. He distanced himself from the power-conscious society he observed at close quarters and became a cultured recluse. Razan, his disciple, parted ways with his mentor and grasped every opportunity to advance his bureaucratic career under the new rulers. He helped codify some of the new regime's laws and regulations. He also founded his own school with financial support from the bakufu. Shōsan, unlike the other three, who started as Buddhist monks, was a warrior-turned-monk. As a *Buddhist* he became the bakufu's ideological mouthpiece in the critical situation after the Shimabara Rebellion of 1637–1638. Finally, Yamazaki Ansai, mentor and advisor to the shogunal regent Hoshina Masayuki, claimed to teach a purer Neo-Confucianism than Razan's, while maintaining that his teachings were completely harmonious with Shinto. It seems, then, that these schoolmen in the entourage of the rulers rummaged rather freely over the intellectual landscape.

For the rulers of the century under review, the ideological question, seen as a choice between specific doctrines, was rather blurred—possibly even irrelevant. Their most pressing problems, especially from Oda Nobunaga until Tokugawa Ieyasu, had to do with a military and political balance of forces, the management of power in a hostile and fragile world, and later the preservation of a political *modus vivendi* that was still in danger of collapse as late as 1638. Economic and fiscal questions were not as prominent then as they would be from the Genroku period (1688–1704) on; neither were social problems (peasant disturbances) that would require close attention from the mid-eighteenth century on.

The preoccupations of these rulers were preeminently political, and therefore included a concern with the justification and acceptance of the new power distribution by all politically relevant sectors of society. In the next chapter we will examine the attempts by those at the pinnacle of power, starting with Oda Nobunaga, to transform their power into a legitimate authority and to ground it, beyond their military might, in symbolic—often religious—terms.

Two. Trajectory of a Discourse: Transfiguring Warlord Power into Sacred Authority

Warriors are like dogs or beasts; victory is their business.
—*Asakura Norikage, daimyo, c. 1550*[1]

Vassals (*fudai*), for better and for worse, are the dogs of the house.
—*Ōkubo Tadataka, vassal, c. 1625 reporting a conversation of c. 1575*[2]

The traditional thesis concerning Tokugawa ideology presupposes a problem for the early Tokugawa center of power; a problem said to have been solved with the adoption of Neo-Confucianism by Ieyasu, the last of the three "unifiers." The inquiry here will thus begin with the concerns that preoccupied these centralizing power holders in the last three or four decades of the sixteenth century.

In the late 1560s, before Oda Nobunaga began making some progress toward the realization of his vague but grandiose ambition to pacify and unify the whole country, military power and political authority in Japan were practiced in a rudimentary and experimental fashion. Effective central authority, whether imperial or shogunal, was nonexistent. In the provinces, the old *shugo* (provincial protector) military families had disappeared during the Ōnin War (1467–1477). Locally, the *shōen* (manor) system of land rights and land management was collapsing in the chaos of incessant warfare. Viewed from the top, the country must have appeared in an extreme state of fragmentation in the absence of any central government.

The only rulers in control of circumscribed territories were a newly emerging class of independent and contentious warlords, the daimyo. Their struggles had been tearing up the country for nearly a century. Yet even they did not know how to secure stability for very long. Victory one day was never assurance against defeat the next; peace was never more than a lull between military campaigns; order was merely a temporary compromise with anarchy. In the words of one daimyo around 1550: "warriors may be called

---

[1] *Asakura Sōteki waki* (c. 1552), in NKB 5: 127.
[2] *Mikawa Monogatari*, in NST 26: 118.

dogs or beasts, but no matter what, victory is their business," or, according to another daimyo: "no matter how powerful you are, there is always someone more powerful."[3] One hundred years later, as we shall see, these self-confessed subhumans would pose as exemplars for mankind. Moreover, they would be accepted and recognized as such, their virtuous status firmly secured. They would be said to dispense benevolence from the tip of the sword. The self-representation of the warrior class, in these one hundred years, underwent a total turnabout.

The survival of the warlords was constantly threatened by two unpredictable risks—defeat by rivals and defection by vassals: "only to be feared by one's vassals is no good; one has to be held in awe to the point of drawing tears, otherwise they will not throw their life away and will be of no use to the lord."[4] And there were no sure remedies. Tactical superiority often bought only a temporary advantage. Oaths of loyalty seldom proved to be stronger than the crude opportunism of vassal or ally.

If tactics and oaths failed to achieve security, the teachings of Confucianism were equally ineffective. *I-ching* diviners "assisted" the daimyo in coming to decisions on the battlefield. Of all the classics, the *Book of Changes*, as a divination manual, was the one lectured on most in the Ashikaga College for Confucian studies in the Kanto. Generals always had a vassal-diviner, a graduate from the college, at hand. In 1600 at Sekigahara, Ieyasu could even afford a very famous one in the person of the Zen monk Sanyō (Kanshitsu Genkitsu; 1548–1612), the ninth rector of the college.[5] (After Sekigahara, Ieyasu put Sanyō in charge of his printing press, a novelty at the time, as printing presses had been introduced in Japan only a few years earlier.)

Confucianism was also of some use to certain daimyo as a literary tradition that could provide style and occasionally substance in their efforts to formulate regulations for their vassals. A small number of daimyo, concerned with the loyalty and solidarity of their vassal bands, drafted house rules for regulating the life and behavior of their followers, some in the minutest detail—a practice that went back to at least the thirteenth century but was perfected

[3] See above nl; *Tako Tokitaka kakun* (c. 1544), in Kakei, *Chūsei* ("Shiryō-hen"), pp. 305–307.
[4] Asakura Norikage, in *Asakura Sōteki waki*, p. 129; on the importance of securing vassal loyalty, see Steenstrup, "Imagawa," p. 313.
[5] Wajima, *Chūsei*, pp. 250–51, 256, 258; Haga, *Chūsei Zenrin*, pp. 85–89.

during the sixteenth.[6] These house rules were a mixture of didactic sermonizing (increasingly in a Confucian rather than Buddhist vein) and haphazard attempts at articulating maxims of managerial wisdom.[7] In the second half of the sixteenth century, one comes across a few instances of daimyo holding Confucian ceremonies or hiring scholars versed in matters other than divination, but they must have been as rare as those that patronized missionaries from the West: colorful oddities in strange and turbulent times.[8]

Confucianism was helpless with regard to the central issue that gave the sixteenth century its mercurial quality: power—how to maximize, maintain, and manage it. No rules, conventions, or authority restrained the growing application of sheer military might. The sixteenth century was an age in which coercive power, naked, was unashamed to show itself or speak for itself. Authority had disintegrated in the face of military might that felt no need to hide behind a screen of legitimacy. Power did not seek another name to obfuscate its true nature, neither did it refer to "sources" other than itself:[9] emperor, shogun, shugo were useless to the daimyo who were attempting to break down local resistance to their armies, and who survived by their own cunning in their battles against one another.

Although in the first half of the sixteenth century sheer force, apparently self-sufficient and comfortable with itself, felt no compulsion to transfer its burden of guilt outside itself and thus apologize for its existence, voices were being heard that started to envelop it in a new vocabulary. This conceptualization gained momentum as power expanded in a way unheard of in the history of Japan and as it came to pressure the center. A discourse was

[6] For references as early as 1260, see entries 10, 46, 91, 97 in Steenstrup, "Gokurakuji." Of the twelve house rules extant today, ten date from after the Ōnin War. See NST 21: 499.

[7] See Steenstrup, "Imagawa;" *Asakura Toshikage 17 kajō* in NST 21: 350–52, or Kakei, *Chūsei* ("Sankō-hen"), pp. 48–49; *Tako kakun*, in *id.*, *Chūsei* ("Shiryō-hen"), pp. 249 ff.

[8] Kakei, *Chūsei* ("Kenkyū-hen"), p. 266; Wajima, *Chūsei*, pp. 196–97, 207–10, 262.

[9] A brief note on style is in order here. I am well aware that human actors were involved in applying coercive power, dismantling traditional authority and building it anew, and constructing a discourse that made this possible. In a discussion of ideology, however, the three realities of power, authority, and discourse constitute the centers around which the analysis must orbit. I have adopted an anthropomorphic style in speaking of these realities because it keeps alive the awareness that what is presented here is an analytic interpretation. Strictly speaking, such statements should be introduced with the words "it is as if." The role played by conscious will and subjective motivation in these developments will be discussed in due course.

spun, a conceptual cocoon in whose dark center power could hide from view. Thus power came to be accepted almost unknowingly, because it had found a way to maintain itself behind a new symbolic language that gave it legitimacy.

This process of ideation started in earnest with Oda Nobunaga. The unprecedented accumulation of power by this daimyo brought into sharp focus questions of its preservation, management, and concentration. Only *aufgeheben* or overtaken by something else—a new kind of authority—could it continue its awesome exercise. It had to die to survive—differently. Power had to be converted into distorting speech.

Before Oda Nobunaga's rise to prominence in the 1560s, effective political authority did not exist apart from direct local control. From the fourteenth century on, sequestration from the top and direct local management had increased through *ikki* organizations. The earliest ikki were local leagues of warriors (*gokenin*) seeking a direct alliance with the Ashikaga shoguns in defense against the shugo.[10] The fifteenth century saw the development of *tsuchi-ikki* or village ikki in the Kinai region, which periodically forced shogun or shugo to cancel debts or lift toll barriers, and often usurped the authority of shōen proprietors. In the cities from around 1500, defense of self-interest in the face of political anomie led to the establishment of similar autonomous governments (*machishū* in Kyoto).[11]

In the feudal hierarchy, fissures opened between the top echelons of shogun and shugo and the lower ranks, splits that also cut the provinces loose from the center. Provincial warlord-proprietors (*kokujin*) more and more aligned their interests with those of the increasingly autonomous villages, where they came to exercise gentry power, and not with the original shōen proprietors and shugo, whose legal rights they usurped and replaced with their own *de facto* control.[12] Military power was doing away with the legal order.

This gravitation toward localism from the mid-fifteenth century on tore at the cohesion of the traditional shogun-shugo centered

[10] The Ōtomo in 1347; the Shinano kuni ikki in 1400; Mori in the fifteenth century. See Davis, "Kaga," p. 223; Kawai, "Shogun and Shugo," pp. 80–83.

[11] There were *tsuchi-ikki* in the years 1428, 1441, 1457, 1485; see also Davis, "Kaga," p. 224. Hayashiya, "Kyoto in the Muromachi Age," p. 30.

[12] Kawai, "Shogun and Shugo," pp. 74–81; Miyagawa, "From Shōen to Chigyō," pp. 90, 97.

vassal system, ultimately replacing it with a new hierarchy. The end of this process came when, in the "sword hunts" of the last quarter of the sixteenth century, a new kind of powerful daimyo, strong warlord-proprietors who had drawn weaker daimyo into their vassal ranks, succeeded in forcing the yet undecided ones to choose between becoming cultivators or warriors.

By far the most dramatic instance of ikki power was the *Ikkō-ikki* that controlled the entire province of Kaga for almost a century until Nobunaga's victory in 1580. The Ikkō sect, headquartered in the Honganji, first in Kyoto and after 1532 in Ishiyama (later Osaka castle), provided organization, leadership, and effective control over a wider territory and for a longer period than any other ikki, such as Yamashiro kuni ikki of 1485–1493. The sect appeared as a serious alternative to the collapsing shogun and shugo system, and proved to be Nobunaga's most persistently threatening foe. More pertinent to the present discussion, however, is the impact this ikki had in shaping Nobunaga's exercise of power and conception of authority—its ideological role.

In one sense this ikki was a marginal phenomenon because it ultimately lost to the new daimyo power. From another point of view, Honganji played an ambivalent role as an anti-warrior center that came to structure its own authority in feudal ways.[13] There were minor ways in which ikki structure influenced Nobunaga's (and later the Tokugawa's) military organization of bannermen or liege vassals (*hatamoto*) and brigades (*kumi*).[14] But according to Asao Naohiro, the Ikkō sect's historical impact, far from being negligible, was of great significance because it transformed the character of Nobunaga's rule.[15] The Buddhist Ikkō sect was an important contributor to the emerging discourse on power and authority.

[13] Honganji's directives and representatives in Kaga (in many respects ruled like a warlord domain) and attempts to expand its power into Echizen were often criticized and resisted by the sect's followers. See Shingyō, "Ikkō ikki," pp. 269, 276 n31.

[14] Davis, "Kaga," p. 135. *Hatamoto* (bannermen) and *gokenin* (housemen) were liege vassals; only the bannermen enjoyed the privilege of attending shogunal audiences.

[15] Asao, "Kinsei hōkenseiron," p. 6; *id.*, "Bakuhansei," p. 197. In 1981 two works appeared in English containing pieces that relate to the material of this chapter. On *kōgi* in general, see Asao, "Shogun and Tennō;" and Sasaki, "Daimyo Control." On *tenka* and Nobunaga's politics in Kyoto, see Fujiki, "Oda Nobunaga." On Azuchi castle, see Elison, "Cross," pp. 62–65; Wheelright, "Eitoku's Lost Paintings." On Nobunaga and Hideyoshi, see Elison, "Cross;" and *id.*, "Hideyoshi." See also Mary E. Berry, *Hideyoshi* (Cambridge: Harvard University Press, 1982) and my critique of this work in *Journal of the American Oriental Society* 104 (1984), 2: 351–55.

The significance of Nobunaga's conceptualization of power under Ikkō pressure can be seen more clearly against the background of other attempts by the daimyo and Nobunaga himself to regularize the political management of their vassals and the people. The problem had already been perceived, although mentioned as such only in passing, by Ryōshun, shugo and author of the famous *Imagawa Letter* (1412), which became well known as a *vade mecum* for daimyo government from the 1570s throughout the Tokugawa period. What makes one a warrior, Ryōshun wrote, is expertise in the martial arts, but what makes one outstanding is an altogether nonmilitary skill, namely, one's capacity for management.[16] All warrior rules, starting with the earliest ones, spelled out in meticulous detail ritual etiquette. For example the *Gokurakuji Letter* of about 1260 prescribes, among other things, the proper way to pour *sake* and how to shake the water from one's leather leggings after wading through a river; it prohibits chewing with the mouth open, using a toothpick, spitting, dozing, and so on in the presence of one's lord.[17] The fifteenth-century shugo, however, faced the substantive problem of consolidating their hold on great numbers of warriors and large populations. Administrative regularity had virtually disappeared by the end of the century, as the shōen system, the legal and economic underpinning of warrior rule, fell in disarray. It became evident then that those among the militarily powerful shugo and daimyo who perceived their difficulties in clear managerial terms and responded skillfully had a considerable edge over their rivals. Two house rules exemplify this new consciousness very well: *The Seventeen Articles of Asakura Toshikage* (1428–1481) and the *Tako Tokitaka House Code* (c. 1544).

On several points, Toshikage's prescriptions have more in common with those of the daimyo of the Momoyama and Tokugawa period, a hundred or more years later, than with contemporary practices. Toshikage recommends, for instance, that posts be given to able men from any vassal family rather than be fixed to elder families; he forbids his vassals to live in fortifications other than the central castle town; he uses *metsuke* (spies) to gather information from the countryside, and professes care for equitable government for all classes of people within the provincial

---

[16] Kawazoe, *Imagawa Ryōshun*, p. 252; for the English translation, see Steenstrup, "Imagawa," pp. 299–316, esp. p. 306.

[17] Steenstrup, "Gokurakuji," pp. 10, 31, 32; see also the very long seventeenth rule of the *Tako House Code* in Kakei, *Chūsei* ("Shiryō-hen"), pp. 281 ff.

domain.[18] The concern with establishing locally a centralized power structure and converting it into a government for all is evident in this document. In addition, there is an implicit assumption that the right to govern rests with the ruler and does not stem from proprietary rights.

The *Tako House Code* includes a rarity for the sixteenth century: extended disquisitions on the nature of society. This document discusses the principles of successful government, and puts forward some philosophical arguments that are in tune with certain innovative strains in *late* Tokugawa thought (such as Kaiho Seiryō's principle of the measurability of all phenomena, including virtues such as loyalty, and the bakumatsu stress on *jinzai*, talent).[19]

According to Tako Tokitaka, the central quality that is needed in the age is *sanyō*, "calculation." Trustworthiness alone is insufficient. Loyal servants have to be able to calculate things, resources, and talent; otherwise it is impossible to move great masses of people. Without this ability one cannot order society, give a place to all the people, shape human ethics, and organize the realm.[20] Practical knowledge is necessary for the functional arrangement of society. Society is seen as a whole to be constructed, an enterprise to which any skill not only can but should contribute. The assumption is that all elements in society are part of a total design, and hence should be incorporated: separateness is seen as illegitimate. All vassals should learn skills that make them useful in a specific way. Quite naturally, the simile of a house is invoked, where the lord is the roof, his immediate relatives the beams, elders the pillars, servants the gate, peasants the tatami floor, and so on.[21] The image stresses the imbricated character of society, the functional interdependence of all, from the lord to the least of his subjects. This resulting unity, however, is a construct, an artifact of the ruler: the simile is the building of a house, a work of engineering, not the still harmony of nature. The vision is constructivist, dynamic, not simply structuralist. It is interesting to note that one

---

[18] Kakei, *Chūsei* ("Sankō-hen"), pp. 48–49.

[19] For Kaihō Seiryō (1755–1817), everything is a commodity that is interchangeable and has a price, including warriors and feudal service: see Tsunoda et al., *Sources* 1: 488–93. On *jinzai*, see Harootunian, "*Jinsei, Jinzai* and *Jitsugaku*." As will become clear later, the Tokugawa political discourse appropriated many elements from pre-Tokugawa writings. In pre-Tokugawa times, however, one searches in vain for elaborate discussions on the nature of society. The only exception I know of is the *Tako House Code.*

[20] Kakei, *Chūsei* ("Kenkyū-hen"), pp. 262–66, 279–80.

[21] Kakei, *Chūsei* ("Shiryō-hen"), pp. 291–95, 297; ("Kenkyū-hen"), pp. 283–86.

of the central points of Ogyū Sorai's philosophy (the contingent, man-made character of society), for which he argues elaborately, is presented here unceremoniously.[22]

If one wants to become a lord, one has to qualify oneself by living with the people, crying and rejoicing with them and being useful to them in a private and public way: one needs the people, how else can one be a lord? A ruler can justify his position only because he succeeds in coopting his subjects' needs and functions (Sorai's "small virtues").[23] Everyone in society has a (ranked) political function.

A metaphysical grounding for such an encompassing view of society was also available. Calculation and quantification are at the heart of Heaven and Earth: there are twelve months in a year, thirty days in a month, and so on. The administration of districts, villages, fields rests on this calculation. Trade, all occupations, and even religion are based on it: rebirth presupposes calculation, because one's heart will unredeemably wander astray if one follows one's desires without figuring out where the limits are. Sanyō, calculation, thus offers an insight into the principles that govern things (*dōri*). Desires (*yoku*) are all-pervasive. One finds them even among the gods and Buddhas. To stress one's own *kuni* (province) over another, one's *ujiko* (shrine members) over another, even to pray—all are inspired by desires.[24] Sanyō is equally universal, and although sanyō in and of itself offers no salvation, it is an indispensable element in the way to salvation. Parts are always pitted against each other through desire; only sanyō can overcome particularisms because it can arrange them so that they become structural elements that recompose the lost totality. In order to achieve this integration, however, sanyō has to be total, has to extend to everything.

This view holds not only a program for rebuilding society: it presents a fundamental metaphysics. The inner-outer dichotomy of Confucian categorization is used, but the original ethical content is transformed into a sociological one: man has a jewel within himself, which is his capacity for calculation, and a jewel outside himself, consisting of other men with whom to build society.[25]

---

[22] For Sorai's category of "invention," see Maruyama, *Studies*, pp. 189–238.

[23] Kakei, *Chūsei* ("Shiryō-hen"), pp. 307–309; Oygū, *Bendō*, pp. 62, 68, 76–78, 94 (for the Japanese text, see NST 36: 22–24, 29).

[24] Kakei, *Chūsei* ("Shiryō-hen"), pp. 249, 257, 329.

[25] *Ibid.*, p. 331.

In this text then, society is discussed in functional terms, and even religion is subjected to rational discourse. One hundred years later, there will have been a total reversal in which religious and spiritual concepts have been mobilized for the construction of a discourse on society. The Tako document identified a crucial social and political problem and talked about it in straightforward, constructivist terms. The same problem is recognized in early Tokugawa society, but its texts formulate a discourse that is oblique, elaborate, and spiritual if not religious.

OFFICIALIZING STRATEGIES

Pragmatic, secular, and functional, the two texts just discussed reflect a preoccupation with the best way a daimyo could reconstruct a shattered society. One finds no further discussion of the sources of power or attempts at legitimizing it. Power (and authority) seemed to have been available to anyone who succeeded in making a new whole out of all the parts.

Elsewhere, however, one also finds vague references to something beyond power: *kōgi*, public good, and *tenka*, the realm. At first, such references may seem to be stylistic formulae that in another age carried more political meaning but whose symbolic content had since shriveled to empty form. Indeed, the authorizing symbolism of kōgi and tenka may very well have faded in the face of the uninhibited exercise of military power. But although in the second half of the sixteenth century techniques of social and political control were being refined to provide a tested structure to the Tokugawa, the question of power—what to call it, how to refer to it obliquely so that it becomes acceptable—could not be avoided. It was as if authority as distinct from military force was again seeking a name under which it could occupy, or pretend to occupy, its own place in the political field. And, after a few false starts under the old guises of kōgi and tenka, it found a fitting symbolic language.

Nobunaga's final formula was truly novel, but he came to it gradually. Any cognitive development of this kind obviously does not occur in a vacuum. The impetus for this process of symbolization came from pressing realities in the present, but it was past practice that initially provided inspiration and cognitive context. The intellectual operation at work here is thus one of appropriation. The signifying power (however weak) of available concepts is transferred to new realities.

Kōgi, literally "public ceremony/affairs," was one such term that a number of daimyo, like the Mōri or Rokkaku, started to use in the mid-sixteenth century in reference to the purpose of their rule (*kōgi no tame*). These warlords were not merely posing as selfless servants of the "public good/benefit," as the new use of the term certainly also implied, playing on a traditional opposition between private benefits and public duties (*kōmu*) (as had been done much earlier, for instance, in the *Imagawa Letter*). Still earlier, in the fourteenth century, kōgi had referred to the affairs or ceremonies of the imperial or shogunal court.[26] The daimyo, by speaking of kōgi in the context of their own particular regimes, arrogated for themselves a semblance of legitimacy, if only by mental association with the two traditional sources of ruling authority: the emperor and the shogun. (It is also interesting to note in passing that some daimyo, for example Asakura Toshikage and Tako Tokitaka, composed their house rules in seventeen articles, at the price of logic or stylistic balance, no doubt having in mind some prestigious precedents produced at the center of power, such as Shōtoki Taishi's *Seventeen Article Constitution* and the *Kenmu Formulary*.)[27]

Tenka, the realm, also provided a handy referent to give an official aura to decrees. Here, the appeal was explicitly to the whole that was supposed to make the particular (psychological and geographical: desires and domains) acceptable by pointing out that particular interests were not what they appeared to be but were conditioned, and therefore transformed, by a holistic focus.

In their attempts to legitimize their efforts to unify or pacify the whole of Japan, Nobunaga and his successor Hideyoshi fully utilized both concepts. Indeed, "pacification" was itself a term that transformed selfish and violent efforts at conquest, efforts that were divisive, particular, and segmental, into selfless duty toward the whole—integrated, harmonious, and organic. This tactic of "officializing" his position, however, was only the beginning of Nobunaga's legitimizing strategy.[28]

The struggle for conquest that was taking place in the remotest corners of Japan did not become a struggle for legitimacy until control of the traditional center of authority became a possibility. Oda Nobunaga understood Kyoto's importance very well, and his

[26] Fukaya, "Kōgi," p. 153; Steenstrup, "Imagawa," p. 301; Asao, "Bakuhansei," p. 209 n2.
[27] Kakei, *Chūsei* ("Kenkyū-hen"), pp. 272–73.
[28] On "officialization" as a legitimizing tactic, see Bourdieu, *Outline*, pp. 21–22, 40.

whole career was one long endeavor to draw on imperial and shogunal authority. He feigned submission, but in fact bypassed and controlled the emperor and shogun, thus subjugating them to the new authority with which he was investing himself.

Nobunaga's centralist ambitions may have started in 1564, when he received a secret imperial invitation to assist the court in a variety of matters, including palace repairs. At the end of 1567 he was further encouraged when the court requested him to restore imperial estates in Owari and Mino, and expressed the hope that he would continue to expand his territory.[29] At that moment Nobunaga was already engaged in the battle for the Inaba fortress, the last obstacle on his route to the capital—the center where his imperial sponsor was waiting, but also the arena that provided him with the opportunity to exploit shogunal politics. The next year Nobunaga entered Kyoto and restored his own candidate, Ashikaga Yoshiaki, to the shogunal office. It is after the fall of Inaba that Nobunaga grafted a new plan on his drive for power: the military pacification of Japan. His new seal from then on proclaimed his program on all his official documents: it read *tenka fubu*, "overspreading the realm with military might." He acted like a shogun, yet would have no part of the shogunal structure. Nobunaga encouraged other lords to strive for tenka, but repeatedly refused Yoshiaki's offers to become vice-shogun.[30]

In 1570 Nobunaga clearly took control by coercing the shogun into issuing a decree whereby all matters of the realm would henceforward be handled directly by himself and all shogunal orders would require his countersignature. Thus Nobunaga gave himself the equivalent of kōgi, specific shogunal authority, in the name of something bigger yet: tenka. Two years later, in 1572, in a letter to the shogun that he circulated widely, Nobunaga accused him on seventeen accounts—again the number seventeen—of breaking the earlier agreement.[31] The bakufu had outlived its usefulness for Nobunaga. The next year he sent Yoshiaki into exile.

Nobunaga never seems to have been interested in occupying the shogunal office himself. This would have made him the emperor's servant. He apparently had grander ambitions. To Jesuit missionaries he boasted about himself as a king and emperor, and even as a god.[32] Emperor Ōgimachi must have sensed the danger, and

---

[29] Okuno, "Oda," pp. 35, 38; *id.*, *Oda Nobunaga*, 1: 93–94; Asao, "Bakuhansei," p. 194.
[30] Okuno, *Oda Nobunaga* 1: 169.
[31] *Ibid.*, pp. 343–45, 565–76.
[32] Okuno, "Oda," pp. 38–39.

within a year after the shogun's exile he tried to domesticate Nobunaga by granting him court rank. Nobunaga complied, but avoided the trap. He rose from third rank in 1574 to senior second rank in 1578, at which moment he suddenly resigned. He must have been secure and shrewd enough by then to reject the limitation that an outside legitimizing authority imposes on power. Such legitimacy is needed up to a point because it increases acceptance of one's power by others, but it gives away the autonomous and total character of that power for a defined authority. This Nobunaga did not want. Rather he sought to use his power to circumscribe existing authority, which could only be done if he created for himself his own legitimacy without any reliance on traditional authority.

After resigning his court titles, Nobunaga started to deploy strategies to control the court. He presented Nijō castle, which he had originally built for the now exiled shogun and had furnished with a special chamber for imperial visits, to the crown prince, whom it was rumored he had adopted. In 1581, a few days after the emperor had been duly impressed by a military parade of Nobunaga's vassals from the five neighboring provinces, the court offered him a new title. Nobunaga replied that he would accept the honor if the emperor abdicated and left the throne to the prince, Nobunaga's protégé. The emperor refused, and the next year played his last card by offering Nobunaga the post of shogun (although the exiled shogun was still alive). Nobunaga did not even deign to reply.[33]

COOPTING A RELIGIOUS WORLD VIEW

The imperial and shogunal institutions did not provide Nobunaga with the right idiom in which to speak of his power. Symbols expressing notions of shared or delegated power were not what he sought. Yet even autonomous power needs a name and a base. What Nobunaga had in mind became clear shortly before he was killed in 1582. The idiom he then revealed as his own was religious, and the referent for his power, himself—not as a general but as a divine ruler. Self-validating, Nobunaga the power holder became the source of his own authority through new symbolic and ideological manipulations. Generator and recipient at the same time of his own legitimacy, he nullified the external referent or-

[33] For this whole development, see Asao, "Shogun kenryoku (2)."

dinary political legitimacy usually points to. He could do so only by an idiomatic transposition of political discourse into an absolute mode.

There was no precedent for this formula in Japan's political past, nor did Nobunaga hit upon it all at once. Beneath his confrontations with the shogun and emperor, one can detect in many of his directives the first murmurs of this new language. Initially, however, Nobunaga did not use it in his struggles with the center but in his wars against the Ikkō-ikki. Nobunaga's father had already fought the sect, and Hideyoshi, after Nobunaga, would still have to deal with it. In 1580, after ten years of virtually uninterrupted campaigns, Nobunaga finally eliminated the most formidable obstacle to his plans for a pacified Japan. Indeed, many historians argue that most of Nobunaga's new policies (policies that later became permanent features of the Tokugawa system) took shape as anti-ikki policies.[34]

It is also worth noting that the case for class conflict that many Japanese historians indiscriminately and almost routinely make for any period of Japan's past is most convincing in explaining certain confrontations in the second half of the sixteenth century. New military men, aspiring to lordships and seeking to centralize their power, faced strong resistance from their would-be subjects, other warriors and peasants. In principle, one may object that it is difficult to distinguish between warriors and armed peasants. Around Oda Nobunaga's time, however, it became clear that warriors were competitors for centralized power (even at some local level) and as such were in some way brothers-in-arms. Defeated warriors were often incorporated into the victor's band. The peasants, on the other hand, often took up arms in order to protect their local autonomy against warrior bands. They recognized the new exploitative nature of the emerging order.[35] The staunchest resistance came from those ikki with an articulated world view. The Ikkō-ikki did not always follow the official doctrine of Ishiyama Honganji, but they put it to use when it could help them defend their interests. The Honganji leadership, on its part, wielded doctrinal weapons to sharpen the spirit of its followers.

Nobunaga's battles against the Ikkō-ikki stand out as particularly bloody and cruel in character. Enemy daimyo and warriors

[34] Asao, "Bakuhansei," p. 197.
[35] Fujiki, "Tōitsu seiken," pp. 34–37.

were often spared, but warfare with the ikki was total and victories were often followed by extermination campaigns. Nobunaga's most innovative and lasting institutional measures took shape in the wake of his victories over the ikki. The year 1575 was important in this respect. In the eighth month of that year, after his 30,000-man army reportedly slaughtered an equally great number of ikki followers in Echizen and systematically killed the higher bonzes, Nobunaga left the region in charge of Shibata Katsuie and ordered him to do the following: seek and destroy seditious elements and secure from village headmen proof that their villages had abandoned the Ikkō faith (1575/10); conduct a sword hunt (1576/1); forbid movement to the peasants and impress upon them that their sole occupation should be to till the soil (1576/3); and conduct land surveys (1577).[36] All of these new institutional arrangements that originated as responses to the ikki (and other measures such as the granting of fiefs as rewards to loyal vassals, the frequent transfers of vassals, and the destruction of secondary fortifications) are readily recognizable as typical of the later Tokugawa system.[37] As early as Nobunaga's regime, therefore, we find ourselves in an era where Japan's so-called early modern features were being fashioned.

Nobunaga's experimentation and its importance for the future, clear as it is at the institutional level, is equally crucial in the area of legitimacy, authority, and ideology that form nodal points of what can be called a discourse on power. Nobunaga was prompted to transpose the score of political discourse by his experience with the ikki. His ikki opponents—mostly peasants and warlord-proprietors (*kokujin*) in Kaga and Echizen, but also people of various occupations such as miners, blacksmiths, woodworkers, fishermen, boatmen in the Kawachi region[38]—had organized themselves into autonomous temple towns, villages, and districts under the umbrella of Ishiyama Honganji. The Honganji provided this *résistance* with an organizational network and guaranteed privileges of immunity. Most important, the sect's leadership offered not simply a rationale but a full-fledged world view that legitimized in the eyes of the Ikkō followers the stance they took against the new daimyo power.

The ikki members considered themselves royal subjects (*ōson*, "royal descendants"), or peasant-servants of the court (*kōgi no*

---

[36] *Ibid.*, pp. 55–56.
[37] *Ibid.*, pp. 66, 72–73.
[38] *Ibid.*, pp. 39–46.

onbyakushō)—a view strikingly similar to the one held by the late
Tokugawa rebel Ōshio Heihachirō—and rejected the warriors as
illegitimate interlopers. They declared themselves ready to kill all
warriors and make the saintly rulers of Honganji kings of the
country (*kokuō*). This world, they argued, is Buddha's realm and
ought to be ruled by the reincarnations of Shinran and Rennyo.[39]
The Ikkō followers refused to recognize any intermediaries between the very highest authority, the emperor or the Honganji
high priest, and themselves. In Echizen in 1575 they resisted even
the Honganji's attempt at posting powerful bonzes in their midst
who would function like daimyo deputies. One can therefore ex-
trapolate that, in their view, there was properly speaking no
political hierarchy in society, since authority had only one place: at
the top. This political order would free them from all intermediary
powers and safeguard their autonomy—a view remarkably akin to
peasant consciousness in the bakumatsu-early Meiji period.[40]

The Honganji, on the other hand, had increasingly absolutized
its own idiom of authority (not always with total success, especially, as Shingyō Norikazu points out, when it ran counter to
peasant interests). Amida had come to be regarded not only as a
guarantor of rebirth in the Pure Land after death, but (contrary to
Asao Naohiro's claim of an exclusively otherworldly interest) as
the savior in this life. All things in this world were considered to
belong to *buppō*, the Buddhist order, not to individuals. To use
things that were properly Buddhist for secular or individual purposes was condemned as misuse. This theory could easily benefit
the peasants in their attempts to defend their own interests.
Moreover, the Honganji, when it developed in the first half of the
century into a full-grown ecclesiastical power, increased its efforts
at strengthening its authority in matters of doctrine. Heretics were
expelled from the church, death penalties issued, and some members were even excommunicated *post mortem* and thus denied rebirth in the Pure Land. In the final battles against Nobunaga,
absolute obedience was demanded from the followers. Nobunaga
was cast as an enemy of the faith (*hōteki*). The battle itself was seen
as a religious act of gratitude toward Amida and Shinran in

[39] *Ibid.*, pp. 34, 55; Asao, "Kinsei hōkenseiron," p. 5; *id.*, "Shogun kenryoku (1)," p. 74.
The classic texts for these statements are to be found in NST 17: 230, 338. Also see Kuroda,
Chūsei no kokka, p. 338.

[40] According to Ozawa Hiroshi, the "living gods" of the new religious movements of late
Tokugawa justified separation from the established order: "Bakumatsuki ni okeru minshūshūkyō undō," p. 105.

protection of Buddhism. Absolute loyalty and death in action constituted sure guarantees for salvation. Ikkō members who refused to respond to this call for a holy war were excommunicated.[41]

Nobunaga had experienced the formidable effects of this novel source of power, a religious doctrine, on the battlefield. He recognized its particular nature and the necessity of fighting it on its own terms. He must have sensed that brute force and extermination of the leadership could not dislodge this world view from the new space it had created in the realm of politics, and that he had to adopt the same language in order to turn this new power, redeployed, to his own benefit. Ultimately, this discourse was not simply a weapon in a struggle for power: it became the issue of the struggle, with mastery over it as the reward for the victor.

Nobunaga strove to deflect from the Ikkō world view all crucial elements of this discourse so that it would speak of his own power, his own legitimacy, and his own authority. Accepting the language of the Ikkō rebels and their leadership, he subverted it by inserting himself into it at strategic points. He neutralized the peasants' argument that they were public "citizens" of the realm, and not the property of private power, by posing as the protector of the emperor and identifying himself with the realm. Nobunaga became tenka, which not only justified his stance toward the shogun and his assumption of public responsibility in Kyoto and the surrounding provinces but also legitimized his subjugation of the ikki in 1575/11 and 12. As early as 1570 he had mobilized forces against ikki in northern Omi by demanding support "for tenka, for Nobunaga." Contributors to Honganji were castigated as accomplices to anti-tenka plots (1572). On 1575/10/25, in a letter to the father of Date Masamune, Nobunaga admitted that few survived the slaughter in Echizen, but that the rebels had to be suppressed, lest the harm to the realm be incalculable.[42] More and more, tenka came to be equated with Nobunaga.[43] In a nineteen-point decree of 1580/5, when Honganji's power was finally broken, the standpoint of tenka was taken to discuss contributions to the war (arts. 4, 10) and to objectify his expectations for his warriors (arts. 2, 5, 13).[44]

---

[41] Shingyō, "Ikkō ikki," pp. 269, 272, 276; Kasahara, *Shinshū*, pp. 110–11, 117–19, 174, 215, 219; Asao, "Kinsei hōkenseiron," p. 6; *id.*, "Shogen kenryoku (3)," p. 26.

[42] Okuno, *Oda Nobunaga* 1: 389, 549; 2: 124, 125, 159, 161.

[43] For examples in 1578 and 1579, see *ibid.*, 2: 389, 417.

[44] *Ibid.*, 2: 531–33.

Nobunaga arranged the final surrender of Kennyo, the head of Honganji, through imperial emissaries, giving Honganji's defeat the appearance of submission to imperial will and not to his own forces. Far from being an enemy of the law, of faith, of the public order, Nobunaga instead posed as its defender. *Ōbō ihon*, the official Ikkō doctrine that upheld respect for the secular order (*ōbō*) as fundamental, was subsumed under the new equation that identified ōbō with tenka, with Nobunaga.[45]

Nobunaga did not stop there, however. He absolutized his own power, like Honganji, arrogating for himself even religious authority to bestow divine blessings and salvation after death. Following the defeat of the Echizen ikki in 1575/9, he issued nine guidelines for his *chargé d' affaires* Shibata Katsuie that demanded not only respect and total obedience—"to follow Nobunaga in all matters"—but veneration (*sūkei*), and promised divine protection (*myōga*) and long life to his samurai. In a 1579/9 letter to Kitabatake Nobuoki, he assured him in the same way that obedience would benefit him in this life and the next.[46]

With no further evidence, one might be tempted to brush these formulations aside as empty phrases and epistolary conventions of the time. They were not. They were specifically Nobunaga's attempts to ground the unprecedented power he had acquired in an equally unprecedented way. During these same years, he laid the foundation for a visible expression of the new legitimacy he had centered on himself. Through ritual celebration he planned to institutionalize this new concept of authority. He converted his private musings about power into a novel public discourse on authority, expressed in new symbols with himself as their referent.

Nobunaga had always taken great care to increase his symbolic capital with each new victory. In 1564, in his battles against Saitō Tatsuoki, grandson of Dōsan, an oil merchant-turned-daimyo who claimed descent from the Fujiwara, he changed his own Fujiwara name, used since 1549, into Heike, thereby magnifying a local confrontation to national relevance through historical associations connected with the Heike name.[47] When, three years later, he took the Saitō fortress, the route to Kyoto lay open, and Nobunaga converted his victory into a declaration of a program for the whole nation. From now on his victories would not simply be conquests

[45] Fujiki, "Tōitsu seiken," p. 76.
[46] Okuno, *Oda Nobunaga* 2: 87–89, 460; Asao, "Kinsei hōkenseiron," p. 6.
[47] Okuno, "Oda," p. 37.

but steps toward the unification of the country. The campaign would start from Inaba mountain where the Saitō fortress was located, and he gave the place a new name: Gifu ("Gi mountain") after the name of the mountain whence the legendary sage-king Wen unified the Chou kingdom. At the same time Nobunaga chose his new seal, *tenka fubu*, "overspread the realm with military might." (It was unusual in that it was composed of four characters, which was a Ming fashion.)[48]

Once in Kyoto, Nobunaga very astutely used the prestige-granting centers of emperor and shogun without getting caught in the nets that sources of legitimacy throw around those who seek it. This adroit avoidance of political bondage was, however, only the negative side of his self-image as ruler. Already he had begun to speak of himself to outsiders as an emperor or god. With the construction of Azuchi castle, Nobunaga was to give a dramatic and visible expression to his view of his hegemony.

He revealed his first plans for building this fortified palace in 1576/1 (only a few months after his victory over the Echizen ikki) and work began three months later. Construction of the central keep began in 1577/8 and, although it was far from finished, Nobunaga used it as his base of operations from 1578/1 on, but did not formally move in until 1579/11, an auspicious day—his birthday.[49] Azuchi castle, however, was more than a fortress. It was a formula; not simply a grandiose architectural display of Nobunaga's enormous power, but a carefully planned ritual setting for the enactment of a new authority. Azuchi was to be the new center toward which traditional authority would pay tribute: a chamber for imperial visits was provided. Its structural design and interior decoration embodied symbols of religious and cosmic centrality and dominance. Through this monumental architectural medium, Nobunaga was making an overpowering political statement: his regime was to be a divine autocracy.

The castle, in the form of a seven-story, 150-meter-high keep, provided Nobunaga with the functional space of waiting rooms and audience halls for his vassals (on the first two floors). Its design was more than functional, however. Visitors entering at the ground-level basement under the first floor were confronted with a Buddhist stupa, placed in the center of an open space that reached up to the third floor. The stupa was in honor of a Buddha men-

[48] Tsuji Zennosuke, *Nihon Bukkyōshi* 5: 179.
[49] Naitō, "Azuchi-jō," 1: 10–14; 2: 47.

tioned in the Lotus Sutra, Prabhūtaratna, who arose from underground and represents the center of the cosmos. This centrality was to be all-comprehensive and include the great traditions. The decorations of the two top floors pictured key figures, respectively, of the Buddhist and Confucian traditions (in the latter case, the sage kings, Confucius and his main disciples). The first floor also contained a room dedicated to a popular Shinto deity, Bonsan, represented by a mound of pebbles. Yet, as Father Frois who visited the castle writes, these stones were not the *shintai* or embodiment of the deity, because "Nobunaga declared that he himself was the very *shintai* and living *kami* and *hotoke* [god and Buddha] and that there was no other lord of the universe and author of nature above him." [50]

Nobunaga had arranged a stage from which he could preside over and dispense the Way of Heaven. The Japanese term for castle keep is *tenshu*, "Heaven's keeper," and according to Naitō Akira the term seems to have originated in reference first to the Nijō-jō and then to Azuchi-jō. The term may very well owe an intellectual debt to all religious traditions of the time, including Christianity (*Tenshu-kyō*; Teachings of the Lord of Heaven), but it primarily embodies the concept of harmonious coexistence of all traditions, the Way of Heaven, *tendō*. It is worth noting in this context that Nobunaga had friendly contacts with the Jesuits who had been allowed to build a seminary in the castle town of Azuchi, which he honored with a visit in 1582. Nobunaga also had several temples moved to the new town. [51] This apparent ecumenism points to the prominence of religious matters in Nobunaga's overall scheme for political hegemony. From this tendō platform, Nobunaga arrogated for himself adjudicative powers in the realm of religion and ideology.

Nobunaga's first public act, two weeks after he formally moved into his tenshu, demonstrated this to the world. On 1579/5/27, he organized a public debate between two Buddhist sects, the Pure Land and the Hokke branch of Nichiren Buddhism. A street fight had broken out in Azuchi between preachers of the two sects, and Nobunaga ordered a debate, seizing the occasion to force the Hokke sect, whose growing power was based on a militant proselytism, into humiliating submission to his authority. The Hokke

[50] *Ibid.*, 1: 65–68; 2: 23–35, 47; Cooper, *They Came*, p. 102.
[51] Naitō, "Azuchi-jō," 1: 14–16, 2: 47–62; Cooper, *They Came*, pp. 93–106, 131–35, 377–79.

debating team consisted of three learned monks from well-established temples. Nobunaga quite arbitrarily declared them losers and forced them to sign an oath whereby they admitted defeat and swore to abandon attacks on other sects. At the time Nobunaga was about to launch his final campaign against the Ikkō sect, which had shown a tenacious strength in a number of provinces. He wanted to prevent the Hokke sect from becoming a similar threat, and for this he held the Hokke higher bonzes responsible.

The temples whence the debators came were not particularly active, and relied on a stable base of members who were traditionally associated with these temples. But Nobunaga's arbitrary decision on the outcome of the debate, the imposition of the oath, and the several days these learned monks spent locked up after their defeat convinced them that their survival depended upon their ability to control the radical elements in their own sect. Nobunaga himself unambiguously showed them what was at stake: he executed the two Hokke preachers involved in the street brawl and also a third one, Fuden, who was not involved in the incident and was not even in Azuchi at the time.

Fuden was possibly the most zealous, effective, and well-known Hokke missionary of those days. Although his association with the Hokke sect seems to have been brief and somewhat obscure, throughout his peregrinations he had built, unlike the Kyoto scholars, a broad popular base in several provinces. Hokke teachings, even more exclusivistic than the Ikkō sect's, projected the future unity of society as a Buddhist nation.[52] In their holistic vision there was no room for secular rulers. All authority other than Buddha's was seen as an usurpation of Buddha's divine kingship. (One radical fundamentalist branch of the Hokke developed as a separate sect, Fujufuse, after 1595 and banned all interaction—*fujufuse* means "no receiving and no giving"—with nonbelievers, including the authorities.) The Hokke sect was strongest in Kyoto, but seemed to be gaining influence in the provinces through men like Fuden. It was this shady religious populism with radical anti-establishment tenets not unlike the Ikkō sect's that Nobunaga sought to eradicate, and for which he enlisted the cooperation of the Hokke traditional leadership.[53] Secular authority had started to regulate the world of Buddhism, and its target was Buddhist

[52] Fujii Manabu, "Kinsei shoki kokka ishiki."
[53] Nakao, "Azuchi shūron."

political philosophies. This regulatory policy was continued in the Tokugawa temple and sect legislation and in bans against the Ikkō and Fujufuse sects.

In 1582, Nobunaga finally began to implement his plans to give proper ritual expression to his divine autocracy. At the New Year, Nobunaga's son, followed by all the daimyo owing him allegiance, formed a procession and made a monetary offering to Nobunaga as to a living god. The emperor was not present, but when the visitors were shown the lodging set aside for imperial visitors, the implication was clear that he too would be expected at some point in the future to express obeisance to Nobunaga.[54] In 1582/3, after pacifying the Kanto region with the help of his son, Nobutada, he entrusted Kyoto to him, probably in order to concentrate his attention on consolidating and giving shape to his regime.

The whole of Japan was not yet under his control, however. An appeal for help from his general Toyotomi Hideyoshi. locked in battle against the Mōri in western Japan, made him leave for Kyoto to make preparations for his new campaign. There, on 1582/6/2, Nobunaga and his son Nobutada were betrayed by Akechi Mitsuhide, a daimyo who was to join with him against the Mori, and they perished in the blaze of the Honnōji, the temple where they were staying. Nobunaga was forty-eight when he died. He had set Japan on a new course but had not been granted the time to fulfill his dreams of conquest. These dreams did not stop at bringing the whole of Japan under his rule, but as a letter from Frois written several months after Nobunaga's death indicates, included the subjugation of China. On 6/14–15, less than two weeks after Nobunaga and Nobutada had died, Azuchi castle also went up in flames. Nobunaga's successors were not far away. Tokugawa Ieyasu had witnessed the glory of Azuchi only one month earlier, on 5/15. Toyotomi Hideyoshi rushed back from his Mori campaign, but arrived one day too late in Azuchi, only to find the smoldering ruins of the keep.[55]

We have a final word on Nobunaga's vision for his new regime from the same letter of Father Frois, dated 1582/11/5. Frois reports how eighteen days before Nobunaga met his end—a date that should coincide with Ieyasu's presence in Azuchi—he decreed that he be worshiped over all Buddhas in the Sōkenji, one of the temples that had been moved to Azuchi. Nobunaga vowed that worship of

[54]Okuno, "Oda," p. 50.
[55]*Ibid.*, p. 51; Naitō, "Azuchi-jō," 1: 20; 2:39.

him would bring wealth to the rich and poor; descendants to the heirless; and long life, health, and peace to all. The wicked and unbelievers would be condemned to hell in this life and the next. Nobunaga declared, in addition, that his birthday would mark a special day of celebration in this new cult. The missionaries were horrified: their patron had turned into a new Nebuchadnezzar.[56] Nobunaga, however, had finally resolved his problem of legitimacy. His successors now had a model, for Nobunaga had outlined the possibilities of a new political discourse.

BURSTING THROUGH TRADITIONAL AUTHORITY STRUCTURES

The careers of Toyotomi Hideyoshi and Tokugawa Ieyasu follow a path quite similar to that of Nobunaga. These two generals did not simply pick up where their respective predecessors had left off, but ran again the same course that Nobunaga had traveled, amplifying some of his institutional arrangements, executing unfinished plans, and groping in similar ways to transform their military power into political authority. Both, like Nobunaga, eventually chose self-deification as the ultimate statement of their political personae.

There are several reasons for these historical reenactments. The heirs of Nobunaga and Hideyoshi were unable to take over immediately after their fathers' death: Nobunaga left two quarreling sons, ages twenty and twenty-four, and a two-year-old grandson whom Hideyoshi decided to sponsor; Hideyoshi left a five-year-old son. In this situation of uncertain succession, power reverted to the one who was able to assert his will over the regency councils set up by a group of generals: Hideyoshi after Nobunaga and Ieyasu after Hideyoshi. This also meant, however, that they could not automatically take over the authority left by their predecessors. They both began by holding temporary fiduciary powers, while kōgi (official authority) lay with the young heirs. Although they controlled more military power than Nobunaga had, they still had to struggle to vest it with legitimate authority. Nobunaga had pro-

---

[56] Naitō, "Azuchi-jō," 2: 46, 47; Cooper, *They Came*, pp. 27, 101–102; Crasset, *Histoire*, pp. 486–87. George Elison rejects Frois's letter as untrustworthy and considers the report of Nobunaga's action of establishing this cult a fabrication by Frois ("Cross," pp. 74–75, 301–302 nn62, 63.) For the reasons why I cannot accept Elison's argument, see my "Neo-Confucianism," n41.

vided them with a number of successful formulae in administrative and political matters. It was up to them to apply these formulae to the achievement of their own goals.

As early as the spring of 1583, less than a year after Nobunaga's death, Hideyoshi had firmly established his position of preeminence among the daimyo. He controlled thirty provinces, ten more than Nobunaga ever had, and was able to concentrate his efforts on giving shape to his rule. In this respect, Nobunaga's career and vision served as his textbook. In that year, Hideyoshi began to reshuffle the domains of his vassals, to dismantle castles in the various provinces, and to talk of ruling the whole of Japan. On the spot where the Ishiyama Honganji had once stood, construction was started the same year (and completed in 1590) on his enormous Osaka fortress; the circumference around the outer courtyard measured eight miles.[57] Hideyoshi intended it to be the new center of power, no doubt modeled after Azuchi. Daimyo would have their residences there, and it was rumored that Hideyoshi even had plans to move all the main Kyoto temples (including the Gozan and a Christian church) as well as the imperial court to Osaka.[58]

The emperor was quick to understand that Hideyoshi represented another power that needed regulation and domestication, and therefore granted him a modest court rank several months after Nobunaga's death. Hideyoshi, who came from a peasant family, gratefully seized the opportunity to acquire prestige. This, he increased to a national scale when, in 1585/7, he was appointed *kanpaku*, regent to the emperor. Hideyoshi transformed this office into a platform from which to speak to all the lords of the land, although not always successfully—some daimyo, like Shimazu Yoshihisa, merely scoffed at his new title. Two months after his appointment as kanpaku, Hideyoshi made public a plan for the invasion of Korea, which, when implemented in 1591, increased considerably his authority over the daimyo. During the next few years he issued a number of laws for the whole country, including the famous sword hunt decree, the decree restricting change of status and residence, persecution degrees against Christians, and laws against piracy. Hideyoshi thus turned the kanpaku office into a seat of legislative authority. In the same unprecedented manner he also used it to push his national land survey, which he had already initiated in his own provinces ten years earlier (in 1582; it

[57] Boscaro, *101 Letters*, Letter 7, p. 11; Cooper, *They Came*, p. 146.
[58] Asao, "Toyotomi seikenron," *Shokuhō seikenron*, p. 148.

was completed in 1598, the year he died).[59] It should be noted that the land survey and population census (1592), although conducted by the daimyo, were registered and computed by district and province: Hideyoshi pretended not simply to be wielding his private feudal authority, but to be acting as an official administrator within traditional structures.

At the beginning of his first Korean campaign, in 1591/12, Hideyoshi left the kanpaku office to Hidetsugu, his nephew and newly designated heir, and took for himself the title of *taikō* or retired kanpaku. Military necessity or an attempt to secure proper succession probably prompted this move. In the light of the distance Nobunaga had built between himself and the court, however, it makes sense to interpret Hideyoshi's action, as Asao Naohiro does, as signifying political distance, as well. Taikō, unlike kanpaku, is a title that does not carry official responsibilities toward the court. He retained, however, the title of Dajōdaijin (Prime Minister) that he had received in 1586. This highest of all court titles was also devoid of administrative responsibilities.

It seems, then, that Hideyoshi was seeking a formula to convert his power into authority on a national scale. He apparently was not interested in the shogunal office, perhaps because he correctly perceived that the shogunal title in the past had never, either in principle or in reality, been associated with a nationwide authority. Even so, he already wielded more power than any shogun ever had. Hideyoshi thus reached for those titles that signified, if not the highest authority, at least the highest prestige in the land. His achievement, however, created an unprecedented situation because he was a *military* kanpaku and a *military* taikō.[60] Moreover, like Nobunaga, he may have felt uncomfortable with the service to the court that the kanpaku title, more than the other titles, entailed. His abandonment of the kanpaku office can thus be seen as an attempt to break through these traditional constraints.

Hideyoshi, even more than Nobunaga, was fond of marking turning points in his career with monumental constructions. Osaka castle, built in 1583–1590, was the largest fortress in Japan at the time, even larger than Azuchi had been. In 1586–1587, after he became kanpaku, Hideyoshi built a Kyoto residence, the sumptu-

[59] *Ibid.*, pp. 149–52.
[60] Jien (1155–1225), in his *Gukanshō*, argues precisely that the solution to the political problems of his time lay in the combination of the offices of shogun and kanpaku in one person. See Brown and Ishida, *Future and Past*, p. 418.

ous and impressive Jūrakudai castle-palace, which was surrounded by a moat and thick walls, and occupied almost as much space as the Imperial Palace grounds. There, in 1588, Hideyoshi realized another of Nobunaga's fantasies: playing host to the emperor.

The only previous time an emperor had paid a visit to a warrior residence was in 1408, when emperor Gokomatsu had been entertained for three weeks by the Ashikaga shogun Yoshimitsu, an extraordinary political event. This was a sumptuous display of Yoshimitsu's kingly powers. He disported himself as the Emperor's equal: he had his consort given status equal to that of the emperor's mother and his favorite son treatment comparable to that of the crown prince.[61] Hideyoshi's five-day-long lavish entertainment of the emperor spoke as eloquently as Yoshimitsu's of the unprecedented pretentions of his power. On the second day of the festivities, in the presence of the emperor, over twenty of the leading daimyo were sworn in as protectors of the court and servants of the kanpaku. The first Tokugawa shoguns continued to feel the need for these imperial settings, both as a support for and as a display of their new authority. The imperial visit in 1626 at the rebuilt Nijō-jō, hosted by Iemitsu, was preceded by two years of preparations and extensive renovations and expansion of the buildings. This political game ended in 1634, when Iemitsu paraded an army of 307,000 men through Kyoto—the grand finale to imperial politics that had started with Nobunaga.[62] For the next two hundred thirty years, no shogun would again set foot in Kyoto or even know what the reigning emperor looked like, while every year an imperial delegation would undertake a pilgrimage of obeisance to the mausoleum of Tokugawa Ieyasu in Nikkō: the imperial form of the daimyo's alternate attendance. The shogun thus had succeeded in monopolizing public authority. The imperial visit of 1588 was an unmistakable expression of kōgi authority that Hideyoshi had already been invoking regularly (in his 1583 campaign against Shibata Katsuie, in his 1587 persecution decree, and again in his 1589 campaign against the Hōjō).[63]

The Jūrakudai was handed over to Hidetsugu together with the kanpaku office. Hideyoshi, having become taikō, then built another colossal castle-palace in Fushimi, south of Kyoto (1592–1594),

---

[61] I owe this detailed information to Kate Wildman Nakai. See also Sansom, *A History of Japan, 1334–1615*, p. 157.

[62] Asao, "Shogun seiji no kenryoku kōzō," p. 13.

[63] Fukaya, "Kōgi," p. 157; Asao, "Bakuhansei," p. 201.

for his own retirement. In 1593, however, a son was born to Hideyoshi. Two year later Hidetsugu was made to step down from his kanpaku office, sent into exile, and forced to commit suicide on Mount Kōya. Hideyoshi further had all of Hidetsugu's descendants exterminated. The Jūrakudai was razed.

Scholars have presented various interpretations of Hidetsugu's cruel fate, which is as notorious as the forced suicide, four years earlier, of Sen no Rikyū, Hideyoshi's famous tea master and diplomat. The birth of Hideyoshi's son had certainly made Hidetsugu superfluous, but Asao Naohiro thinks that Hidetsugu and Rikyū fell victim to a policy dispute about the further consolidation of Japan. In a similar vein, Miki Seiichirō has argued more recently that the kanpaku's power had grown too independent of Hideyoshi and that Hidetsugu controlled the only fiefs that were outside the taikō's control.[64] All these factors may have played a role, but it is certain that Hideyoshi had found it impossible either to share his power with or to delegate it to a traditional court office, no matter how the office had been modified. He found himself, just as Nobunaga had toward the end of his life, groping for an adequate seat for the enormous power that he had acquired.

Ever more extravagant fortified palaces were being built and destroyed in and around Kyoto at a dizzying pace: Nobunaga's Nijō palace in 1569 was followed by those in Azuchi, Osaka, Kyoto (the Jūrakudai), Fushimi, and finally Ieyasu's Nijō-jō in 1603 and Iemitsu's expansion of it in 1624–1626. Considerable armies of laborers were mobilized, and enormous contributions exacted from the daimyo. Scores of the best artists of the time saw their works destroyed, then found themselves reemployed at another site. These palaces were thus the visible, colossal signs of the authority and power that their builders had won at one point or another, and they lasted no longer than the political base they were meant to symbolize. Their owners held traditional offices granted by the emperor, but the new military and feudal character of the officeholders had forced them to burst beyond the traditional framework. The new power of Nobunaga and Hideyoshi resembled that of kings, and when in 1603 Ieyasu finally became shogun, the authority that he exercised was of an altogether different order from that of past shoguns.

After his victory over the Hōjō at Odawara in 1590, Hideyoshi

[64]Asao, "Toyotomi seikenron," *Shokuhō seikenron*, pp. 153–54; *id.*, IKNR (1963) 9: 196–210; Miki, "Taikō-kenchi," pp. 104–107.

could claim that pacification had been achieved, even though it took the form of a military truce and was by no means firm. The daimyo's participation in the Korean campaigns constituted a public ratification of Hideyoshi's authority as Japan's overlord. The new war, a prelude to the conquest of China, one of Nobunaga's dreams, was a most dramatic enactment of Japan's new military unity. The symbolism and ritual that surrounded the campaign were national in character. Ceremonies were held at shrines to the war god Hachiman, who was in fact emperor Ōjin, with whom Jingū kōgō was pregnant when she invaded Korea around 400 A.D., as the *Kojiki* relates. Victories were hailed as blessings sent by the gods of Japan. Heads of the slain were lined up, the ears cut off, pickled, and shipped to Hideyoshi's headquarters in Nagoya, Kyūshū. The bloodshed was orchestrated as a sacrifice or blood festival (*chimatsuri*) in honor of Hachiman.[65]

The careers of both Nobunaga and Hideyoshi are among the most dazzling in Japanese history. They captured not only the popular imagination, but their own as well. Nobunaga was the son of a small territorial warlord with no more than two or three thousand warriors under his command. Little is known about Hideyoshi's background except that he was the son of a peasant. Nobunaga came to hold military control over twenty provinces. Hideyoshi was recognized as the supreme daimyo. He mustered over 150,000 men for the siege of Odawara and sent an invasion army of the same size to Korea, backed by a reserve force of another 100,000 men in Kyūshū. A quick comparison will put these numbers in proper perspective. At the heyday of their power, the Ashikaga shoguns commanded an army that "rarely exceeded several thousand mounted men."[66] The French army in 1640 did not exceed 100,000 troops, and neither did Wallenstein's twenty years earlier. When Charles V, who ruled most of Europe, abdicated in 1558, he had an army of 60,000 men and 80,000 garrison troops. For the siege of St. Quentin in 1557, one of the largest military events of sixteenth-century Europe, Phillip II used 53,000

[65] Nagura, "Hideyoshi no Chōsen shinryaku," pp. 31–33. Sacrifice was never, in fact, part of any religious tradition in Japan. For Shinto, blood was polluted. The gods purified men and women polluted through contact with bloodshed. Any occupations that involved the killing of animals was impure and its practitioners were outcasts (*eta*). The celebration of bloodshed as a festival to Hachiman is perhaps an illustration of how far the reinterpretation of tradition, under the pressure of overwhelming political events, can go.

[66] Grossberg, *Japan's Renaissance*, p. 119.

men.[67] Whatever measure one uses, the military machine at the disposal of Japan's rulers from Oda Nobunaga through Tokugawa Iemitsu was impressive.

In the past, historians have often spoken of Nobunaga and Hideyoshi as cruel megalomaniacs, especially toward the end of their lives.[68] Whatever the state of their minds, however, these were shrewd and thoroughly political men whose "megalomania," because it culminated in conscious efforts to achieve self-deification, had great political significance.

APPROPRIATING SHINTO FOR A POLITICAL CULT

Hideyoshi, like Nobunaga, was preoccupied with the public presentation of his authority. Coming as he did from a humble background, Hideyoshi's career clearly resembled that of some Chinese dynasts. And he used a similar legitimating rationale by portraying himself as the instrument of a higher authority: Heaven, *tendō*. He himself writes that his rise to power was nothing short of miraculous and was not due to his own strength, but to Heaven's selection of him for the special mission to rule Japan, China, and even parts of Asia farther west.[69] He writes to the governor of the Philippines that the sun had entered his breast when he was born, thus predestining him to rule East and West.[70] Hideyoshi obviously relished the lore that had built up around him, and was not above using it in his international correspondence.

When, as Japan's overlord, he had to assume national leadership vis-à-vis the outside, Hideyoshi adopted a Shinto idiom. To the missionary Coelho he boasted that "the lords of Japan are the true *kami* (gods), deserving worship by the people for their victories and exploits." In his 1587 edict expelling the missionaries, he argued

---

[67] For these figures, see Delbrück, *Geschichte der Kriegskunst: IV. Neuzeit*, pp. 261 (France), 255 (Charles V), 221 (St. Quentin); Redlich, *German Military Enterpriser*, 1: 156 (Wallenstein).

[68] Cooper, *They Came*, p. 101; Sansom, *A History of Japan, 1334–1615*, pp. 367–71. For a critique of Elison's pyschologizing interpretations, see my "Neo-Confucianism," n41.

[69] See Hideyoshi's public proclamation of 1589 against the Hōjō: Kōmoto, "Ieyasu to Bukkyō," p. 44. For his letters to the governor-general of the Philippines in 1591, 1592 and 1593, see *Ikoku*, pp. 29, 51, 59.

[70] *Ikoku*, p. 59; For other such tales, see Toyoda, "Eiyū to densetsu," p. 22. In Chapter 5, I shall return to this question.

that Japan is the Land of the Gods.[71] Further elaboration on this theme occurs in two letters addressed to the Portuguese viceroy of the Indies in Goa (1591) and the governor-general of the Philippines (1597).[72] In these letters, Hideyoshi poses as the defender of Japanese values, invoking Shinto theology to legitimize two major policies: foreign conquest and a tightening of domestic control. His arguments are ideological in both cases. They intend to represent his exercise of power as something else.

Japan as the Land of the Gods is contrasted with the pernicious *senmon* or exclusivistic, fanatical doctrine of the West. Appropriating the teachings of Yoshida Shinto, Hideyoshi writes that

Ours is the land of the *kami*, and *kami* is mind (*kokoro*), and the one mind is all-encompassing. No phenomena exist outside it. Without *kami*, there would be no spirits or no Way. They transcend good times of growth and bad times of decline; they are yin and yang at the same time and cannot be fathomed. They are thus the root and source of all phenomena. They are in India under the name of Buddhism; they are in China under the name of Confucianism; they are in Japan where they are called Shinto. To know Shinto is to know Buddhism and Confucianism.

Hideyoshi thus spells out the ideological whole of the world he is about to unify under Japan. The Korean invasion becomes an exercise in *kultur politik*: the realization of a unity that is already there and only calls for implementation. Hideyoshi has found in Shinto the ideological leverage that Nobunaga had found in tenka.

Hideyoshi elaborates on the political aspects of this East Asian cultural sphere. Here, he says, proper social hierarchies are upheld between rulers and the people, fathers and sons, and so on because they are based on adherence to the principles of *jin* and *gi* (humaneness and righteousness). On the other hand, "in your country [that is, the Indies and the West in general] you teach an exclusivistic doctrine (*senmon*) that ignores *jin* and *gi* and is subversive because it does not respect the gods and Buddhas and does not maintain a separation between the rulers and the people." Christianity is pernicious because it is fanatical, exclusivistic, and potentially subversive of the new social order.

The term *senmon* is a synonym for *senshū*, the label that characterized the world view of the Ikkō and Hokke sects. In his expulsion

---

[71] Boscaro, *101 Letters*, p. 37 n26; Elison, *Deus Destroyed*, p. 115.
[72] *Ikoku*, pp. 26–28, 78–79. For a free translation of the former, see Tsunoda et al., *Sources*, 1: 316–18.

edict, Hideyoshi had clearly equated the Christians with the Ikkō sect because they had established, in a very similar way, enclaves in Japan (in Nagasaki) that escaped incorporation into the new order.[73] The problem with the Christians was the same as that with the Ikkō and Hokke sects: they stood for separateness where Hideyoshi was fighting for a new whole; they were obstacles to national integration; and the source of their power was a religious world view.

In 1597, Hideyoshi argues similarly that "from the time that Heaven and Earth were separated at the beginning of the world, the country of Japan has venerated its gods and rulers through Shinto," a statement that leaves the impression that the gods are the rulers of Japan and vice versa. The virtue of these gods is the source of regularity and order in nature and of distinctions between people, but the "bateren [Padres, Fathers] that came from your country are destroying the government of our country. . . . Would you be pleased if Japanese were to come to your country, spread Shinto doctrines and mislead the people?"

Compared to the daimyo house codes of fifty years earlier, the argument has shifted from a vision that provides a functional place for all parts within a total unity to stress on a hierarchical distinction between ruler and ruled that partakes of the sacred. *Shinkoku*, the Land of the Gods, had come to be used as Japan's new identity in the world at large. In 1605, Ieyasu would write: "ultimately, our country is the Country of the Gods and what you call 'idols' have been respectfully venerated by our ancestors."[74]

Buddhism also held an important place in Hideyoshi's plans for the nation. He ingratiated the Buddhist establishment by restoring and supporting the centers of Hiei, Kōya, and Honganji, whose power had been broken by Nobunaga, and issued laws regulating temple and shrine affairs for the whole country.[75] Hideyoshi, moreover, in order to break the last peasant resistance, coopted the popular Buddhist world view.

In 1586 Hideyoshi issued, without much success, a law to tie the peasants to the soil. The land surveys he had ordered in his new territories also met with strong local resistance. Ikki such as the one of 1587 in Higo province flared up everywhere. Clearly, before any further headway could be made in tapping the tax potential of the

[73] Elison, *Deus Destroyed*, p. 118.
[74] *Ikoku*, p. 91.
[75] Asao, "Bakuhansei," pp. 201, 208; *idem*, "Kinsei hōkenseiron," p. 8.

provinces, the peasantry had to be disarmed. Hideyoshi's well-known national sword hunt decree of 1588 provided the solution to this problem.[76]

It is important to notice the conscious use of religious arguments Hideyoshi makes in this decree. The purpose of the decree is unambiguously stated in the first article: to prevent resistance to tax levies and the fomenting of ikki. Concentration on agricultural pursuits will bring well-being to the people (art. 3). This alone will not work, however, as Hideyoshi seems to admit. In China, he writes, the sage ruler Yao, after pacifying the realm, converted swords into agricultural implements. "This, however, should not be attempted in our country (*tameshi aru bekarazu*)." Surrendering their weapons will benefit the people in this life and provide salvation in the next (art. 2) because it will be an act of devotion: the metal of the weapons will be used as nails and bolts in the construction (underway since 1586) of the Great Buddha in Hōkōji. Thus Hideyoshi coopted peasant Buddhist beliefs to make his power effective in the countryside. These policies were a success: he overcame the last ikki power that had drawn so strongly on Buddhist doctrine. But once overcome, that world view had to remain suppressed. Tokugawa Japan would have its *kakure* (underground) Buddhists next to its *kakure* Kirishitan (Christians).

Hideyoshi's image as a unifier was much better served by the Shinto tradition. He relied on the symbols it provided not only to represent Japan in his dealings with foreigners, but also to bolster his domestic authority; the posthumous shrine he had built for himself was a Shinto shrine.

Very early, Hideyoshi paid an unusual amount of attention to the Ise shrines. As early as 1583, when campaigning in Ise, he had made contributions in preparation for the ritual rebuilding of the shrines, and even settled matters in disputes between the Inner and Outer Shrine concerning this all-important ritual. In the end, he provided sufficient funds to conduct full-scale renewal ceremonies, as had not been held in years.[77]

That rulers paid respect to the Imperial Shrines was certainly nothing new. An illustrious example is Ashikaga Yoshimitsu's pil-

---

[76] For a translation, see Tsunoda et al., *Sources*, 1: 319–20; text in *Dai Nihon komonjo: Iewake*, 11, 1: document 503, p. 480; see also Fujiki, "Tōitsu," pp. 37–38, and Miki, "Taikō-kenchi," p. 87, 91, 101. Notice that Tsunoda translates *tameshi aru bekarazu* as "In our country such an experiment *has never been made*" rather than "this *should not be attempted*."

[77] Miki, "Taikō-kenchi," p. 91.

grimage to Ise immediately following his lavish entertainment of the emperor in 1408. During the heyday of the Ashikaga bakufu, such shogunal visits occurred often: over a fifty-year period (1394–1443), spanning the reigns of the fourth through the eighth Ashikaga shoguns, there were thirty-three shogunal pilgrimages to Ise. During the civil wars, however, such high patronage had disappeared. The elaborate rituals of rebuilding the Inner Shrine (the Imperial Shrine dedicated to Amaterasu) and Outer Shrine (dedicated to the Food Goddess) at twenty-year intervals were not held, and had been replaced by smaller renewal rites of temporary shrines. The ritual for the Outer Shrine was not performed after 1434 for 129 years, until 1563, when the ten-year effort of a wandering priest made it possible again through the contributions he had collected. The Inner Shrine, rebuilt thirty-one years late in 1462, was ritually renewed only 123 years later in 1585. Although Oda Nobunaga had made a minor contribution in 1582, it was Hideyoshi's substantial support that made the 1585 renewal possible. The Tokugawa bakufu continued the tradition and faithfully pledged every twenty years the considerable amount of 30,000 koku for the ritual.[78]

Shinto was relevant in another way to the structure of power in the late Muromachi period. Shinto metaphors were often used to express authority relationships. Mōri Motonari (1497–1571), for example, was spoken of as more venerable than *kami* or *hotoke* (Buddhas). In the Mōri domain, the lord had to be served as an *ujigami* (clan god) (1610). In Uesugi Kagekatsu's domain, the peasants were enjoined to "look upon their lord as the sun and moon and venerate the stewards (*jitō*) and intendants (*daikan*) as the local ujigami" (1589). This is reminiscent of the language Hideyoshi used in his letters to Coelho and the governor-general of the Philippines, which should thus not be dismissed as only the irresponsible rhetoric of a megalomaniac. Such religious language was the medium through which power and authority were signified. Hideyoshi also seems to have followed up on Nobunaga's wishes in that he donated fifty koku to manage the Sōken chapel (with the same name as Nobunaga's Azuchi temple) in Kyoto's Daitokuji in honour of Nobunaga.[79] Moreover, Hideyoshi ultimately chose to give his authority a religious base. In his will, he requested that a shrine dedicated to himself be built next to

[78] Sakurai, *Ise jingū*, p. 199, 201.
[79] Fujii Sadafumi, "Kinseishi," pp. 175–79.

the Hōkōji, where he had erected the Great Buddha. His divine title is revealing: "Toyokuni daimyōjin" (also read "Hōkoku daimyōjin") was not only written with the characters alluding to his name (Toyo/Hō) and the country (kuni/koku), but, as stated in his will, was also an abbreviation of a name for Japan in the *Kojiki* (*TOYOashihara no nakatsuKUNI*, "The Central *Land* of the *Plentiful Reed Plains*"): the land was Toyotomi's land, the Land of the Gods, and he was its divine protector.

The warriors had won the contest against the peasants and the commoners. Japan would not be a *hōbōryō*, a Buddhist domain under the rule of Shinran or Nichiren's descendants, but a *shinkoku*, a divine land protected by a *daimyōjin* (great august deity). Kōgi (public authority) had become sacralized in a pilgrimage center. Hideyoshi's shrine, his mausoleum, the Great Buddha he built, and the hill where the "eares and noses of Coreans" (Richard Cocks) were buried attracted large and devout crowds. Branch shrines in honor of Hideyoshi as Toyokuni daimyōjin sprang up in various domains.[80] Ieyasu's challenge was to expropriate the Toyotomi line and appropriate the kōgi structure for himself, which entailed a confrontation among the increasingly charged symbols of authority.

IEYASU, THE DIVINE RULER

It took little time for Ieyasu to wrest the fiduciary authority over Hideyori from the regency council Hideyoshi established on his deathbed. In early 1599, he entered Fushimi castle, Hideyoshi's base since 1594, and appointed a caretaker: a signal that it was he who would be in charge of Hideyori, who resided in Osaka. Ieyasu acted very cautiously to maintain a front of legality. Even after the battle of Sekigahara, he displayed his powers in an apparently even-handed manner when disposing of domains (acquired through confiscation or territorial reduction) that comprised more than one-third of the country. Although Ieyasu had strategic objectives in mind when he transferred powerful fiefs, eighty percent of the confiscated territory and seventeen percent of the increases went to Toyotomi supporters. Two years later he could

[80] See Cooper, *They Came*, pp. 336–39 for descriptions by foreigners who visited the site in the early years of the seventeenth century; Toyoda, "Eiyū to densetsu," p. 21; Kondō Konomu, "Toyokuni daimyōjin," p. 359.

also invoke *raison d'état* when he ordered contributions from all daimyo for repairs of Fushimi, his Kansai headquarters.[81]

Ieyasu's problem with Hideyori was similar to the one Nobunaga and Hideyoshi confronted with the court. Hideyori provided Ieyasu with a legitimate authority that was, however, temporary and beyond his control. Ieyasu had to find another base. On 1603/2/12, when he received the titles of Minister of the Right and Shogun, he acquired kōgi in his own right. He could now exact corvée contributions for his own projects in Edo, where his castle was being built, and other places. Yet the court had not given all away: at each promotion of Ieyasu, including the final one, Hideyori also climbed the ranks, a few rungs behind. In 1602, when Ieyasu received junior first rank, Hideyori was granted senior second rank, and in 1603, at age ten, he became Minister of the Center.[82]

Kyoto had to be watched very carefully. Of the twenty-nine months that Ieyasu was shogun, he spent only eight in Edo; the rest of the time he resided in Fushimi and Nijō-jō, supporting the court financially through daimyo levies but also humiliating the court by arrogantly laying down petty rules of proper behavior for the courtiers. His first court rules were issued on 1603/9. In 1605/8 he issued new ones, although it seems unclear for whom they were meant. They certainly were contemptuous: "no pissing but in the pissoir" read one of them.[83] On 1605/4/16 Ieyasu abdicated in favor of his son Hidetada, a decision that no one was in a position to oppose, given the impressive military parade of over 100,000 men that Hidetada had led through the capital less than two months earlier. Hideyori's permission had apparently been requested for this transfer of power, a request that was pure formality, for his denial was ignored. This abdication secured the succession and freed Ieyasu from the court's grip, which he completely dissolved a year later (1606/4/28) by forbidding the court to grant any court rank without his own recommendation. Ieyasu could now block any attempt by Hideyori to increase his symbolic capital through court promotions. For the next four and a half years Ieyasu did not come near Kyoto, busy as he was building yet another castle, for his retirement, in Sunpu.[84] From now on, in his relations with the

[81] Takagi, "Edo bakufu," pp. 120, 122–28.
[82] *Ibid.*, pp. 129–31; Asao, "Bakuhansei," p. 211.
[83] Takagi, "Edo bakufu," p. 137.
[84] Asao, "Bakuhansei," p. 212.

court, Ieyasu had only to keep that source of prestige neutral through further legislation (rules issued in 1613 and 1615) and marriage. In 1608 he conceived the plan to make his grand-daughter Kazuko, born the previous year, an imperial consort, which she became in 1620.[85]

Meanwhile, Ieyasu was exploring other avenues to gain acceptance for his regime, in international diplomacy. China and Korea had loomed large in the fantasies of Nobunaga and Hideyoshi. They played an equally large place in Ieyasu's politics, not as territories of conquest, but as impressive adjuncts to the ritual display of his authority.

Ieyasu reestablished relations with Korea. Although he had to pay a price for this in the rather humiliating terms he had to accept, the return he received on this investment was worth it: an impressive visit by a large embassadorial cortège in 1607, and the promise that similar missions, underwritten by the Tokugawa treasury (and much more elaborate than Korea's tribute missions to China), would be repeated after each shogunal succession. These cortèges passed through Kyoto without being received in audience by the emperor and were entertained by the shogun in Edo. In 1617, the court members were invited to attend Hidetada's reception of the Koreans in Fushimi—but so were all the daimyo, who were reconfirmed in their fiefs on that splendid occasion. Many no doubt interpreted the Koreans' presence, as did Hayashi Razan, as an expression of a tributary allegiance to the shogun. Ieyasu also had it in mind to use the Koreans to seek legitimacy from the Ming emperors, even though this raised subtle questions about Japan's autonomy. With the gradual invasion in the 1620s and 1630s of Korea by the Manchu and the weakening of the Ming, however, the bakufu shifted more and more to an autonomous stance toward Korea, and abandoned altogether any hope for an increase in prestige from an association with China.[86]

In spite of his diplomatic successes, by 1614 Ieyasu finally had to face the fact that he could no longer ignore the existence of Toyotomi Hideyori, who had recently come of age. One last time brute force had to be used if he wanted to remove forever the specter of a Toyotomi comeback. Although the purpose and effect of the Osaka campaigns were obvious enough, the extermination of

[85] Ono, "Bakufu to tennō," pp. 328–31.

[86] McCune, "Exchange of Envoys between Korea and Japan," in Harrison, *Japan*, p. 84; Toby, "*Sakoku*," pp. 330, 336, 339–40, 348–57.

the Toyotomi could not be admitted openly. Ieyasu had on several occasions sworn loyalty oaths to Hideyoshi's last will. The two families were even related through marriage. Ieyasu himself had taken Hideyoshi's younger sister as his wife, and Hidetada was married to an adopted daughter of Hideyoshi, while Hideyori had married one of Hidetada's daughters. Ieyasu was in great need of some distorting rhetoric. For this he turned to Hayashi Razan, who was willing to provide him, on the level of general principles, with the proper justification through an abstract discussion of *raison d'état* overruling ethical concerns. On the tactical level, others provided Ieyasu with an unscrupulously concocted case of *lèse majesté* as an excuse for war against Hideyori.[87]

It is perhaps time to clarify the nature of Ieyasu's authority. Unification did not mean the elimination of daimyo power but effective control over it—pacification. The question Nobunaga, Hideyoshi, and Ieyasu faced was how far they could go in subjecting all daimyo to their own control. As feudal lords, they expanded the size of their vassal bands and armies, the number of their allies, the territory they ruled directly, and their power to allocate fiefs. At no point in the careers of the three "unifiers" was their authority as feudal overlords tested, that is, their authority as guarantors to all other lords of their rights over their fiefs. In 1611–1612 Ieyasu had succeeded, in two stages, in extracting a three-point loyalty oath from all the daimyo, possibly with an eye on the coming confrontation with Hideyori.[88] Before and during the Osaka campaigns, however, his scholar-secretaries were working on legislation for the whole warrior class and the court (and temples and shrines). Within two months of the fall of Osaka, he and Hidetada solemnly issued in Fushimi the *Regulations for the Military Houses* (*Buke shohatto*) and the *Regulations for the Court*.[89]

Ieyasu also held certification powers over fiefs, which he exercised, although rarely, through his vermilion-seal letters. The first time this confirmation seal was used for all daimyo was by Hidetada in 1617, on the solemn occasion of the reception for the Korean embassy in Fushimi castle. Only then were the western daimyo (mainly *tozama* or outside lords), who had been sym-

---

[87] See Hori, *Razan*, pp. 159–64, 182–99; Sadler, *Maker*, pp. 273–74.

[88] Sansom, *A History of Japan, 1615–1867*, p. 6.

[89] For the Japanese texts of the *Regulations for the Military Houses* and the *Regulations for Retainers*, see NST 27: 454–67. For an English translation, see John Carey Hall, "Japanese Feudal Laws. III."

pathetic to Hideyori and had always been dealt with more directly by Ieyasu than Hidetada, brought into a legal feudal relationship with the shogun. Legal control, however, did not mean effective control. The latter was achieved only in 1632, one year before the death of Hidetada, who had abdicated in favor of his son Iemitsu in 1623. In that year a shogunal envoy with a retinue of over 10,000 men set foot for the first time in the predominantly tozama territory of Kyūshū. That same year, bakufu emissaries were dispatched all over Japan not only to check on all daimyo but also to look into the conditions of the common people.[90] Furthermore, Iemitsu issued rules for his liege vassals (*hatamoto, gokenin*; bannermen, housemen): the *Regulations for Retainers* (*Shoshi hatto*) as separate from the *Regulations for the Military Houses*. The outer lords, the liege vassals, and the people had come into shogunal reach under what closely resembled a kingly authority.

Within this political space, there was no longer a place for the court. After the death of Hidetada, Iemitsu displayed for one last time the kingly power of the new order on the central stage of the older order—an occasion that had the character of a national rite of passage. In 1634 he paraded through Kyoto the biggest army ever assembled in Japanese history (307,000 men; the combined armies at Sekigahara totaled only 110,000 men); this was the last shogunal visit to Kyoto for some two hundred thirty years. At the same time, he confirmed all the daimyo as lords in their fiefs. The next year, Iemitsu issued a revised set of *Regulations for the Military Houses*, widening their scope, prohibiting private marriages to all categories of warriors, and introducing the *sankin kōtai* or alternate attendance, which in 1642 was expanded to include all fudai or vassal daimyo. He did this without even requesting loyalty oaths from the daimyo. In 1636, another Korean embassy came to Edo, and also paid its respects at Ieyasu's mausoleum in Nikkō.[91] The new order passed the test of rebellion when, in 1637–1638, a "national" army of 125,000 men could promptly be dispatched to subdue the rebels in Shimabara.

Since Nobunaga's building of Azuchi castle, new and visible seats of power away from the imperial court had become important symbolic expressions of a new authority. Nobunaga and Hideyoshi had planned to rearrange all other powers—the daimyo, the emperor, and even religious establishments—as satellites around

---

[90] Asao, "Shogun seiji," pp. 4–6, 10–13.
[91] *Ibid.*, pp. 13–14, 19.

a new center and express this subordination either through geographic relocation around it or though periodic pilgrimages to it. As long as Kyoto was important as a source of legitimacy, they themselves and the first Tokugawa shoguns were exposed to a display of dependence by their trips to Kyoto. Iemitsu finally broke this bond by making the bakufu the sole autonomous center of authority in Japan. The daimyo were not the only ones to demonstrate regularly, through their attendance duties, the centrality of the shogun. The Dutch trade mission also traveled yearly from Nagaski to Edo, starting in 1633, and the court even participated in this ritual by sending a yearly delegation on a pilgrimage to the founder's tomb in Nikkō from 1645 on. There were always great numbers of people on the move in Tokugawa Japan, especially if one takes into account the hundreds of thousands of commoners that in certain years trekked to the Ise shrines. Movement had great symbolic significance, and the bakufu made it speak of its own political hegemony.

The last phase of Tokugawa history pertinent to the present study concerns Ietsuna's rule (1651–1680). This period is dominated politically by the shogunal regent—Ietsuna was ten when Iemitsu died in 1651—Hoshina Masayuki, who remained influential until around 1665, well beyond Ietsuna's coming of age in 1659. Masayuki officially resigned his advisory role in 1669, and died three years later.[92]

The Ietsuna decades were marked by political infighting among certain warrior classes. This attempt by various groups to secure permanent claims on bakufu offices led to new ideological emphases. Whereas the first two shoguns had relied heavily on fudai warrior houses, with which they had cemented bonds on the battlefield, Iemitsu, who had brought all daimyo under effective control, granted a larger place to the tozama than had either Ieyasu or Hidetada. He also relied more on direct bakufu retainers.[93] The result was growing alienation and distress among the fudai. Under Ietsuna they maneuvered to alleviate their anxiety about their position in the bakufu structure. A decree of 1659/6 constituted an important victory in this struggle. It stipulated that entry into the guard system (*iriban*) would not be determined by ability or service performance but by position, rank, and family, and that offices would not lapse after one generation,

[92] Totman, *Politics*, p. 211.
[93] *Ibid.*, pp. 58, 101, 140, 149, 283 n30; Bolitho, *Treasures*, p. 162.

but be inherited; deathbed adoptions to secure the continuation of the house had already been allowed since 1651. The *ie* (house) thus gained ideological prominence as a fundamental political unit. The *Regulations for Military Houses* of 1663 make reference to this new reality by stipulating that unfilial behavior be punished. This constituted an extension of an emphasis that was already present in the *Regulations for Retainers* of 1635, which mentioned loyalty and filial piety (*chūkō*) in its first rule (these regulations were first issued in 1632 and were absorbed into the *Regulations for the Military Houses* after 1683). The *Regulations for Retainers* of 1663 also say that *kagyō* ("house employment") should be uninterrupted.[94]

This new trend of tying family to office to preserve fudai interests was resisted by a group of powerful daimyo that had been closely linked to Iemitsu and that developed a different philosophy. The most important among these were Hoshina Masayuki from Aizu (Iemitsu's brother and Ietsuna's regent), Tokugawa Mitsukuni from the collateral house of Mito (Iemitsu's cousin), and Ikeda Mitsumasa from Okayama (son of an adopted daughter of Hidetada and married to a niece of Iemitsu). All three held advisory privileges to the shogun and were actively interested in ideology. They sponsored various theories of benevolent government (*jinsei*) and the kingly way (*ōdō*), formulated in Confucian and Shinto concepts. As we will see in more detail later, Hoshina added Yoshida Shinto to Neo-Confucianism as a doctrine with political potential; Ikeda switched from Wang Yang-ming to a more orthodox Neo-Confucianism; and Mitsukuni initiated loyalist historiography in Mito. They all conducted Buddhist purges in their domains in favor of Shinto. Closer than other daimyo to Iemitsu's absolute power, they stressed total loyalty to the bakufu and pacification of the people—Shimabara may have been on their minds—entrusted to them by the shogun through benevolent government; it was an ideology in tune with Iemitsu's kingly power. Moralists, convinced of the value of ethical self-cultivation, they saw themselves as embodiments of *jinsei*, and gained reputations as exemplary rulers, *meikun*. In their own eyes, it was their selfless intentions, pure dedication, and moral fiber, not the fact that they were born sons of daimyo, that qualified them to look after the welfare of the people.[95]

Iemitsu's rule, it is generally agreed, brought the bakufu to its

[94] Asao, "Shogun seiji," pp. 35–36, 39–40; Bolitho, *Treasures*, pp. 166–68.
[95] Asao, "Shogun seiji," pp. 37–39.

apogee of power. He legislated on offices, stabilized the administrative apparatus, introduced the *sakoku* ("closing of the country")
policy, and ruled Japan like a king. This new kingly authority was
the result of a conscious transformation wrought by Iemitsu in the
years immediately following Hidetada's death in 1632.

Until that moment, his position had been overshadowed by that
of the ex-shogun, just as Hidetada's had been for the eleven years
of Ieyasu's retirement. After the deaths of their predecessors,
Hidetada and Iemitsu had to prove their authority against the
cliques that had formed around the ex-shoguns. Both used the
court and the Korean embassies for that purpose, Hidetada in 1617
and Iemitsu in 1634 and 1636. Moreover, Iemitsu, born in 1604,
could not rely on the victories of Sekigahara and Osaka that were
the work of Ieyasu and Hidetada. He made up for this lack of
military achievement by enhancing the symbolic expressions of his
now nationwide authority. The *mise-en-scène* he constructed for this
enactment of his authority was the sacralization of Ieyasu as the
"divine founder" of the Tokugawa dynasty.

In 1634, immediately after his return to Edo from Kyoto,
Iemitsu ordered the rebuilding of Ieyasu's shrine in Nikkō into the
sumptuous mausoleum that it remains today. The work was completed just in time for a pilgrimage by the Korean delegation in
1636. In 1645 the shrine was upgraded by imperial decree from a
sha to a *miya* (*gū*), possibly having in mind the yearly imperial
pilgrimages that began two years later.

This construction in Nikkō was an important project. It cost the
Tokugawa house over 500,000 ryō, which amounted to about one-
seventh the treasury left by Hidetada;[96] it also enhanced the
already divine status of Ieyasu. Iemitsu may have been personally
obsessed by his grandfather, as reports of his visions and dreams
seem to indicate, but the result was that he converted his political
mandate into a sacred one, linking his rule to that of an ancestral
divine lord. It is from this time on that Ieyasu came to be referred
to officially as *shinkun*, divine ruler.[97] Shogunal rule became sacralized as an incarnation of the Way of Heaven.

The Nikkō mausoleum, however, was no more than a baroque
overstatement of the character Oda Nobunaga and Toyotomi

[96] Totman, *Politics*, pp. 77, 82.
[97] Miyata, "Tōshō daigongen," p. 71. For recent discussions of Ieyasu's deification, see
also Fujii Sadafumi, "Kinseishi," pp. 183–85; Kitajima, "Ieyasu no shinkakuka;"
Tamamuro, "Sūden." For a partial treatment in English, see Sadler, *Maker*, pp. 324–31.

Gate to Ieyasu's Mausoleum in Nikkō

Hideyoshi, before Iemitsu, had tried to give to their new authority. Ieyasu himself seems to have learned from Hideyoshi, and possibly even from Nobunaga, how to manipulate symbols of authority. Not only was he at Azuchi around the time Nobunaga launched his cult, but he had had to eradicate the Toyokuni daimyōjin cult, which had spread very quickly. Months after the erection of Hideyoshi's Toyokuni shrine in Kyoto, Katō Kiyomasa, the famous general of the Korean campaigns, had built a Toyokuni shrine in his domain in Higo; other tozama soon followed. The seventh memorial service to Hideyoshi at the Toyokuni shrine in 1604 was a particularly grand and popular event, to judge from paintings of the time.[98] In 1613 Hideyori built a shrine in Osaka castle. Immediately after the Osaka campaign, however, the Kyoto and Osaka shrines were razed on Ieyasu's orders, although tozama lords seemed to have continued the cult for a much longer time.[99]

[98] There exist a folding screen in six panels in Tokyo (Tokugawa reimeikai collection) entitled *Hōkokusai zubyōbu*, and one in Kyoto in the Hōkokujinja, painted by a Kanō artist who was commissioned by Hideyori. For a description of the festival and the paintings, see Malm, "Music Cultures," pp. 181–85.

[99] Kondō Konomu, "Toyokuni daimyōjin," pp. 359–71.

Ieyasu was eventually to establish his own cult. In his testament, he requested that he first be buried on Kunō mountain in Sunpu and also, it seems (we will come back to this point later), that his remains then be transferred on the first anniversary of his death to Nikkō, where a hall (*dō*) be built in his honor. Some bickering took place among the powerful priests of Ieyasu's entourage as to a proper title and the religious affiliation to be connected with this cult. Bonshun, who had presided over the Toyotomi cult in the Yoshida Shinto tradition, supported by the Zen monk Sūden, argued for *daimyōjin*. The association of this title with the Toyotomi house, which had perished in the second generation, however, was too ominous, and Tenkai, a Tendai monk of the Sannō tradition (a Buddhist-Shinto syncretic tradition) received Hidetada's support for *gongen*. The full title finally read *Tōshō daigongen* or "Great Incarnation (Avatar) Shining over the East," an overdetermined symbol that contained references to Japan, to benevolent rule nurturing the people like the light of the sun/Amaterasu, and to a Shinto reincarnation of the Buddha Nyorai. What was important was the sacredness of the idiom, not the particular tradition in which it was phrased, at least as far as Hidetada and Iemitsu were concerned. Nor was religious affiliation a serious matter to Ieyasu, although it was for his clerical scribes, who each saw a political opportunity to associate their clerical establishment with Tokugawa power.[100]

From the *Sunpuki* (Sunpu Record) it is known that in his private conversations with monks Ieyasu dealt most with the Pure Land sect to which his house belonged (12 out of the 25 recorded instances), but of the no fewer than 112 recorded official expositions of doctrine before him, by far the greatest number (51) were Tendai lectures.[101] Gozan monks were mostly used as scribes, and the New Pure Land sect and Nichiren sect, associated as they had been with Ikkō and Hokke disturbances, were never represented. On several occasions in 1613/3 and 4, Ieyasu listened to Bonshun's lectures on the *Nihongi* (including a discussion of the Ō-ana-muchi deity who enshrined his own spirit after having pacified the land, a mythological exemplar of central importance to the political teachings of Yoshida Shinto),[102] and was to be initiated on 6/6 into a particular Yoshida teaching on *Shinkun Shinto*. The

[100] Tamamuro, "Sūden," p. 58; Miyata, "Tōshō daigongen," p. 70.

[101] Kōmoto, "Ieyasu to Bukkyō," pp. 51, 53 n1.

[102] On these lectures, see Hori, *Razan*, p. 170; on Ō-ana-muchi, see below p. 231, and Ooms, *Bureaucrat*, pp. 45, 46n, 173.

Tendai monk Tenkai intervened, however, and Ieyasu was instead (according to Tenkai) initiated into the Tendai teachings on 1614/5/21.[103] The *shinkun* tradition resurfaced under Iemitsu, however, when Ieyasu was referred to by that title—a title written with the two characters for deity and lord, *kami* and *kimi* (a phrase that evokes Hideyoshi's argument that in Japan *kami* and *kimi* were the same).

Two further points need to be made about political cults of the period under study. First, the cult at Nikkō was openly a political cult for the warrior class. Gongen, in contrast to Nobunaga's sacred image or Toyokuni daimyōjin, held no promises of earthly health or wealth or otherworldly blessings. Ieyasu qualified as a deity purely for his political achievements. *Fuda* (talismans) were distributed at the mausoleum only to the daimyo and bannermen, who were the only ones allowed access to the premises for worship. The housemen, who also, in contrast to the above two categories, did not have the privilege of shogunal audiences, could merely look on from the outside and were in this respect no different from the commoners. (After Matsudaira Sadanobu restored the mausoleum with daimyo support in the 1790s, access was widened to the housemen.) In the second half of the Tokugawa period commoners— probably local people who did not travel far distances—seem to have shown some interest, since over 30,000 visitors were reported yearly; this was still a small number compared to the hundreds of thousands, even over one million, who visited Ise in certain years.[104] Ieyasu shrines were also found in all provinces, but it is likely that he was venerated there more as one local protective deity among others than in his capacity as protector of the whole country.[105]

Second, during the period from Nobunaga to Iemitsu a new image of personal authority was being constructed. Analytically, this construction required three components: the conscious effort by the leaders themselves at self-deification, the availability of doctrines making such sacralization possible, and the acceptance by an audience of the results of such symbolic transactions. *Daimyōjin, gongen, shinkun, meikun* (great august deity, avatar, divine lord, model lord) all express sacrality, although over time the numinous seems to become more and more concentrated in the

[103] Fujii Sadafumi, "Kinseishi," p. 185; Kōmoto, "Ieyasu to Bukkyō," p. 52.
[104] Akimoto, "Nikkō Tōshōgū" pp. 3, 4, 6, 9, 13, 14.
[105] Miyata, "Tōshō daigongen," pp. 72–73.

purely political, which by then, however, had become "the virtuous." Military power, the naked instrument of domination, was
transubstantiated through association with the sacred into political authority of a religious character.

The religious traditions appropriated for this operation were
various: Buddhist, doctrinal Shinto, and folk beliefs. Nobunaga
chose a popular Shinto deity, Bonsan. Hideyoshi relied on Yoshida
formulations for his *shinkoku* ideology in his correspondence abroad
(continued by Ieyasu) and for his own cult. Ieyasu was swayed
by Tendai teachings (as was Katō Kiyomasa, who also made
provisions to be remembered as a *daigongen* after his death, which
occurred in 1611), but also became a *shinkun*. The *meikun* title of
the ideologue-lords of Aizu, Mito, and Okayama shows a Neo-
Confucian influence, which did not imply a lessening of religious
aspects. These exemplary rulers were considered to be living embodiments of ethico-political virtues. Like Nobunaga, Hoshina
Masayuki arranged while still alive for his veneration as a living
kami; all his successors would also be venerated as kami.

Although the doctrinal medium through which political power
found religious expression varied, Yoshida Shinto teachings were
particularly strong in the promotion of kami status during life or
after death. In domains where these teachings prevailed, such as
Aizu (or Sōma from the mid-Tokugawa period), many lords were
venerated as gods. Yamazaki Ansai, Masayuki's tutor, also paid
ritual respect to his own spirit while still alive, as did Matsudaira
Sadanobu, the bakufu leader of the late eighteenth century.[106]
Sacredness was the borrowed idiom within which Tokugawa authority was legitimized; a legitimation that entailed a distortion
and veiling of the real nature of domination—a fraud that was
exposed in the eighteenth century by Andō Shōeki, who called it
not domination but exploitation[107] Nobunaga and Hideyoshi
directed this language at warriors and commoners alike because
the commoners then constituted a political force. Ieyasu's cult was
addressed to the warriors, but only those that were politically
relevant: the daimyo and bannermen.

Once this language was created, however, and validated
through its acceptance as a proper discourse on authority, nothing
stood in the way of its reappropriation by other groups. This is

[106] *Ibid.*, p. 74; Ooms, *Bureaucrat*, pp. 43–47.
[107] According to Andō Shōeki, all thought systems were schemes to "rob the world"
(Maruyama, *Studies*, pp. 253–56).

what happened in the latter half of the Tokugawa period, when peasants and other commoners turned their fallen heroes into *gimin* (martyrs to duty) and *daimyōjin*, embodiments of virtue and divine assistance.[108] Throughout the whole period, rulers and commoners alike resorted to the sacred to add a surplus value to the political.

[108] For the language and justifications used by the peasants in the 1780s, see Walthall, "Ethics of Protest."

Three. Trajectory of a Discourse: Systemic Sacralization and Genesis Amnesia

To expand the principle of oneself is to fill it with Heaven and Earth; to reduce Heaven and Earth's principle is to hide Heaven and Earth in one's mind.... One can never go wrong by comparing things to oneself.—
Tokugawa Ieyasu[1]

Nobunaga, Hideyoshi, and Ieyasu were self-made men. Through their cunning strategies they refashioned history. As Jürgen Habermas argues, however, "strategic action" (of which military conquest is but the purest example) as action always motivated by self-serving intentions, can never lay claim to truthfulness if it is left recognizable as such.[2] The results of such action will not be accepted by others beyond the immediate threat of coercion. In order to have themselves accepted, these rulers had to resort to a different mode of action that could validate such a claim. Only then could they become legitimate rulers and their power be accepted on a basis other than brute force. "Symbolic action," through which they sacralized their position, achieved this goal. This symbolic action was inherently ideological because it bore on power and authority in a public way.

Ideology, however, does not truthfully and objectively represent or reflect the reality it speaks of. This reality, in our case, was the extraordinary position of domination these men occupied. To use Roland Barthes's terminology, their ideological experiments were not attempts at "representing" that position as one that rested on the threat of coercion but, rather, were efforts at "signifying" that reality in ways that transformed it into something else.[3] These warlords, one could say, wanted to obfuscate certain aspects of the

---

[1] *Tōshōgū goikun* ("Ieyasu's Testament"). In NKB 8: 256–57. This seems to be a paraphrase of Chang Tsai's "By enlarging the mind, one can enter into all the things in the world.... The sage ... regards everything in the world to be his own self". I owe this reference to Irene Bloom's lucid paper, "On the Matter of the Mind: The Metaphysical Basis of the Expanded Self."

[2] For the definition of strategic action as a type of action different from communicative action that aims at understanding, see Habermas, *Communication*, pp. 40–41, 209. The paragraphs that follow rely heavily on that work.

[3] For the difference between representation and signification, see Barthes, *Mythologies*, p. 137.

history they themselves had made; distort their role as strategists bent on promoting their own interests; justify themselves as other than successful warlords. Victory was not their sole business, as it had been for the daimyo of the mid-sixteenth century. They had to have their victory accepted, and therefore their intentions had to be put beyond question. Their aim was to create a false consciousness of their position in society.

By mythologizing themselves, they diluted the contingent historical dimension of their persons, drew attention away from their violent pasts, and transformed themselves into sacred custodians of a stable society. In this way they silenced possible questions concerning their character and self-serving intentions: a process of mystification through mythification.

Iemitsu found himself in a different position. As the successor to a legacy of achievements not of his own making, he faced two major tasks. First, since he inherited his predecessors' military power and an authority structure (which he further consolidated and perfected), he had to find acceptance for his *received* position at the top. His personal motives were thus less of a problem. Although his truthfulness had still to be validated, the dissonance he had to harmonize was not as great as that of his predecessors. Second, he had to justify a system of domination that by now had spread over the whole country and claimed to regulate the lives of all the members of a highly stratified society. His main task was thus to persuade them all that the system he presided over was less a system of domination than a just social order. Rightness, correctness, properness was the claim he most had to validate.

Iemitsu accomplished his first task by casting himself as the successor to a founder whose sacred character authorized his own position. The political order of domination, however, remained what it was and did not disappear simply because Ieyasu had become a god. Not only the ruler but the particular society that he presided over had to be signified in a way that precluded questions about the historical, contingent, and hence contestable and reversible character of the whole power structure. The consciousness of people (especially of possible challengers), their social knowledge, had to be united and bound to the one, present political order. This required a discourse that emphasized a synchronic consciousness and deemphasized a diachronic consciousness of the human and political genesis of the new system of domination.[4]

---

[4] Habermas, *Communication*, p. 113.

Social genesis amnesia in the public sphere was the necessary result of such discourse.[5]

The level of justification required for this task was broader than the one a personal mythologizing discourse could provide. Myths may possess a constitutive signifying power, but their efficacy is largely limited to establishing the legitimacy of rulers. They can hardly provide legitimacy for a complex political order already in place. But under Iemitsu, the general social and political order had to be justified and clarified—illuminated, but so as to leave the realities of power and domination in the dark. The political order had to be the focus of such discourse to the extent that discussions of social stability could allow for the *possibility* of rulers transgressing against the order—without, however, there being any serious danger that this could threaten their position, since any particular ruler could always claim that he supported and maintained that order.[6]

According to Jürgen Habermas, such wider justification necessarily draws upon cosmologically grounded ethical philosophies and religions that provide rationalized world views in the form of dogmatic knowledge. In other words, narrative explanations through exemplars (the mythological mode of discourse) are displaced, although not necessarily completely, by deductive explanations through arguments (a reasoned discourse): philosophical arguments that establish ultimate grounds; unifying principles that explain the world, both natural and human, as a whole.

A new discourse of this kind often depreciates previous legitimations; or, at least, certain past *kinds* of reasons become less convincing for a significant number of people who are now persuaded by new kinds of reasons, or act as if they were. For instance, such discourse, like the mythological one, rests upon ultimate and authorizing "beginnings," but it transforms the originating, generative actions of myth into "beginnings of argumentation beyond which one cannot go."[7] Thus, Habermas continues, rulers and their order are considered worthy of recognition as long as political domination is rendered plausible as a "legacy of an order that is posited absolutely." Iemitsu's symbolic negotiations achieved precisely this by signifying the order of his regime as an embodiment of tendō, the Way of Heaven.

[5] Genesis amnesia is a term coined by Bourdieu. See his *Outline*, p. 79; Bourdieu and Passeron, *Reproduction*, p. 9.

[6] Habermas, *Communication*, pp. 179, 183, 230–31.

[7] *Ibid.*, pp. 104, 111, 184–185, 178.

IEYASU'S TESTAMENT

Tokugawa Ieyasu's Testament (*Tōshōgū goikun*: Venerable rules left by the Tōshō Shrine—The Great Avatar Shining over the East) is the text that spells out this tendō philosophy.[8] This document was published during Iemitsu's reign, although it may have been composed before then, and belongs to a genre that produced in printed form oral traditions of *otogishū* tales, narrations by teacher-raconteurs of experiences, anecdotes, sayings, and common wisdom. These storytellers entertained daimyo around the camp-fires during their campaigns of long ago, or their young heirs in more recent peaceful times.[9] The *Testament* indiscriminately uses Confucian, Shinto, and Buddhist terminology (Confucian terms had been appropriated by Shinto theologians much earlier) with the sole purpose of sanctifying the political order. It signifies that order as a body (the same metaphor as in our "body politic") transfigured into a sacred organism.

The central concepts of the text are related to tendō: *tenbatsu* (punishment by Heaven), *tenmei* (Heaven's Mandate), *tendō no ri* (the principle of Heaven's Way), and *tenchi no dōri* (the principle of Heaven and Earth). Other important ones are: *budō* (the Way of the Warrior), *chūshin* (loyalty/trust), *jihi* (benevolence), and *shōjiki* (straightforwardness). The arguments are both practical and theological: practical, because constant reference is made to historical and experiental examples, especially to ruling houses that collapsed (when they did not follow tendō); theological, not only because the discourse draws in sacred content, but because it formally rests on unexamined metaphors. As Jacques Derrida puts it, "a theologian is someone who rests satisfied with metaphors."[10]

"When as ruler of the realm, one enjoys trust and support, tendō accepts his authority over the realm; if one looses the realm, one's house will completely perish" (258). Unjust regimes will be punished by Heaven (276, 284). The very survival of the Tokugawa house over three generations (in contrast to the Oda and Toyotomi) was thus a sign of Heavenly protection. The ruler's position was conditional, but the Tokugawa had passed the test. In the *Testament*, "Ieyasu" says that he had been entrusted with the administration of the realm by tendō, but that if he were to slide

[8] References that follow in the text are to page numbers of NKB 8.
[9] On this genre, see Kuwata, *Daimyō to otogishū*.
[10] Derrida, "Mythologie blanche," p. 319 (my translation).

into bad rule, this mandate would be taken away by Heaven and given to others; and that the same applied to rulers of provinces and houses. Hence, to rule the realm is an act of obedience to tendō. Loyalty, therefore, is not due to Ieyasu as a ruler of his own house but as to one who himself is loyal to tendō. Obedience to Ieyasu equals submission to *tenmei*, Heaven's mandate (285, 297, 329–30). Oda Nobunaga had identified himself with kōgi and tenka, Toyotomi Hideyoshi with shinkoku. Ieyasu (and Iemitsu through him) stood for tendō.

Heaven, not the emperor, was the source of Ieyasu's authority. Nowhere is there any mention of a delegation of authority from the emperor to the shogun. The emperor simply had attached to his house special occupations (*kagyō*), which were mainly ritualistic (306). Since ancient times, however, the shogun's task had been to purify the realm of evil through the Way of the Warrior. Clear reference is also made to the kingly status of the Ashikaga shogun Yoshimitsu. Rather than follow past tradition that had been critical of the title of King with which the Ming emperor addressed Yoshimitsu, the text offers an approving explanation that a king is a man who rules the realm and that it was standard practice to be elevated to high rank if one came to rule the realm (*ibid.*). Beyond these statements, one looks in vain for any discussion, even one favorable to the shogun, of a relationship between emperor and shogun that would define their spheres of authority. This striking silence, as we shall see later, had a clear political purpose.

The quality of the government of the realm is further determined by the quality of all classes of the warrior elite, including the bannermen. That is an unchanging feature of the Way of Heaven (*tendō no tsune*). One has thus to maintain one's house—even if the present incumbent happens to lack skill or intelligence. If his ancestors were loyal to the realm, one should maintain the house through observing the house laws (284, 277). Those who put their lord last will receive punishment from Heaven (295); those who disobey the laws passed down to them are unfilial (285: the only mention of unfiliality).

Loyalty/trust toward superiors, a quality of the mind-heart (*kokoro*) (302), is the cardinal virtue required of retainers (286 ff., 294–95, 301 ff., 309). Samurai led by selfish desires turn their back to tendō and are its great enemies (294). Toward the people a universal benevolence or generosity of heart (*jihi*) is required (256, 273). Jihi is a Buddhist term; *jinsei*, the (Confucian) benevolent government that refers more directly to policies is not mentioned. Hoshina Masayuki, it is worth noting, also complained that "when he discussed matters with people in the government, and he explained *jin* (humaneness), his words fell on deaf ears, as they did not when he explained jihi." [11] Thus in Hoshina Masayuki's experience of the late 1650s or possibly later (he read his first Neo-Confucian work in 1652), Neo-Confucianism was an idiom that was not yet generally understood.

Through a discussion of jihi, the common people are introduced into the political discourse as objects that ought not to be exploited. Jihi, it is stated, is fundamental to man. Without it one does not qualify as a human being, as is shown by the example of Toyotomi Hidetsugu (294). It is the wellspring of straightforwardness (*shōjiki*) and wisdom (256). People are the spiritual kernel (*rei*) of all things: different as they may be, they are all born the same as tendō's children, and Heaven will hate and destroy those who hurt Heaven's children. To alienate or harm them is an offence against tendō. Those who are useful to the people, however, will be rewarded by Heaven (255, 293–94). Rulers have therefore to love the people as parents love their children; their love will be returned by the people (286).

Heaven's Way is upheld by the Way of the Warrior, which is the instrument for killing evil (286, 306). Military rule watches over the country and holds chaos back (255–56, 261, 282, 296–97, 308).

The *Testament* thus shows that the use of military force by the Tokugawa warrior rulers was a means of establishing a good society. Empirical, historical arguments are used to demonstrate this truth (abuse causes houses to collapse), but these arguments are not considered persuasive by themselves. They receive their force from "theological" grounds or reasons (ten, tendō) and thus cannot be singled out as proof of a gradual progress of secular, rational thought; they are ultimately theological, in the double sense of doctrinal (pertaining to a doctrine of the sacred) and uncritically metaphorical.

Benevolence together with straightforwardness and wisdom are divine virtues (*shintoku*). They are at the root of all things. They are the principles (*ri*) that underlie the three symbols of Japan (not of the emperor's authority, let it be noted): wisdom is the principle of

[11] *Hanitsu reishin gengyōroku*, p. 278; quoted in Watanabe, "Tokugawa zenki Jugakushi," p. 46.

the mirror; benevolence, the principle of the sword; straightforwardness, the principle of the jewel. These three Shinto symbols had originally been used exclusively to signify imperial authority in a mythological narrative of authorizing beginnings. Here they ground principles of government that are fundamental and therefore require no further justification. As will be shown later, this was not the first time that this conceptual transposition had taken place. The *Testament* appropriated symbolisms that had been available for some time. It is important to point out, however, that they are ordered hierarchically here: benevolence, the hallmark of a peaceful and just government, is the fundamental virtue, and the other two divine virtues flow from it (256, 309). Benevolence is the principle of the sword, of military government. Military power is fundamental and indispensable for a right society, but its character as an instrument of domination is not recognized as such because benevolence is its principle.

These three virtues also give their practitioners divine status. According to an oracle by Sumiyoshi daimyōjin, mortals acquire divine substance, power, and penetration (*shintai, shinryoku,* and *shintsū,* three central concepts of Yuiitsu Shinto, here misappropriated)[12] by practicing wisdom, benevolence, and straightforwardness (256). The exercise of power by warriors becomes a practice of virtue by divine men. Moreover, a *military* Minister of the Center has his divine exemplar in Sumiyoshi daimyōjin (307–308)—a symbol whose significance will be clarified later in this chapter.

On four different occasions in the text (257, 274, 297, 325), it is admitted explicitly that one must resort to metaphors when one faces the crucial task of signifying the polity as a whole. But it is also asserted that there is one privileged metaphor that never produces false knowledge and that therefore ought to be applied when discussing the government of the realm and the nation (*tenkakokka*). That metaphor is the body. The nation and any other political units such as provinces/domains (297) or (warrior) houses (325) are each best thought of as a "body" politic. Ieyasu himself allegedly made the following pronouncement:

To expand the principle of oneself is to fill it with *tenchi* (Heaven and Earth); to reduce tenchi's principle is to hide tenchi in one's mind, and it is the conditions of one's mind that determine the length of one's life, the

---

[12] Instead of *shintai*, the Yuiitsu Shinto concept as expounded in the *Myōbōyōshū* (Outline of Yuiitsu teachings) is *shinpen*, divine transformations. See NNS 14: 150–52, 156, 162.

well-being of one's body. . . . The same holds true for ruling the realm and the nation. . . . One can never go wrong by comparing things to oneself, reducing the realm (tenka) to oneself, or expanding oneself to tenka. That is the way one should govern. One should understand tenka as the shogun's body, the Way of the Warrior as his mind, and his vassals as his five senses. (256–57).

The five senses, although they each may not be aware of the others' roles, report to the mind, which then makes judgments and issues orders that make the body move (257). The mind functions as the lord of the body (325). The same holds for provinces or domains, where the senses are the samurai and the people (297), and for the warrior houses, where the lord is the mind, the domain's people the body, the elders the senses, and the samurai the hands and feet (325). (Elsewhere [254–55] not the human body but the bodies of birds or hawks are used as metaphors.)

In the above passages, one detects an awareness of the artificial, disputable nature of metaphoric language; further justification is thus provided by the assertion that the metaphor of the human body is a fundamental instrument of correct knowledge and that it is linked with a cosmology of Heaven. Thus Heaven is simultaneously the absolute guarantor of the correctness of the Tokugawa order and of the correctness of an (admittedly subjective) knowledge that asserts the correctness of that society. Both social reality—the object of knowledge—and a particular way of knowing are grounded in an absolute way; it is an operation that erases its own human tracks.

At this point, the question of the persuasiveness of the views set forth in the *Testament* has to be addressed at least briefly. Did the author and his readers believe the argument? Unfortunately, the author is unknown. He may have been a schoolman in Tokugawa service, possibly Hayashi Razan, whose identity was kept secret because these were all supposed to have been Ieyasu's words (which is highly unlikely). This at least is certain: the printing and distribution of a testament purported to be Ieyasu's could not have been done without the bakufu's consent.

Belief, as Rodney Needham has brilliantly shown, is a descriptive category that should be handled very carefully, because it refers to an unverifiable inner state and is a notion with a complex Western history. People do not necessarily believe what their culture trains them to say. This does not mean that the ideas lacked persuasive effect. The metaphor of the body is a very powerful one. The human body is the "one specific kind of natural resemblance among men that all human beings recognize and which permits effective comparison ... the one thing in nature that is internally experienced."[13]

Although language about the body is culturally conditioned, within any particular culture the body may serve as a powerful symbol because internal experience (unreflectingly organized by particular categories whose singularity goes unnoticed) immediately verifies as absolute truth what is asserted in a language using the human body as a metaphor. In this way, the *Testament* grounded its statements in a symbolic language that was already accepted *a priori* as self-evident, in an unquestionable discourse on nature. There is no clearer indication that one is dealing with a full-fledged ideology than when historical phenomena, society, and the knowledge of them are presented in a mode of "naturalness" that hides their own genesis.

Within this anthropo-logical discourse, however, a clear distinction is made between the body and the mind. A preeminent position is granted to the mind as the seat of power over the body. It thus provides a ready metaphor for signifying authority relations in a stable polity; but it is also the source of good and evil. As such, it is the locus in man where authority has to anchor itself. Kokoro, the mind, the seat of ratiocination, can also develop into a threat to the system of domination if it rejects the authority with which the system intends to perpetuate itself.

Although Neo-Confucianism offered a theory of the mind, some scholars have pointed out that the particular emphasis the mind received in Japan is better explained through Shinto (which, it should be added, had appropriated Neo-Confucian notions even before the early seventeenth century).[14] An evaluation of the relative contributions made by Shinto and Neo-Confucianism to the construction of early Tokugawa ideology inevitably raises the question of Neo-Confucian orthodoxy. If, as I have argued up to now, Shinto thought was an essential part of early Tokugawa political discourse—a view that I will stress even more later on—then where does the standard assumption of a Tokugawa Neo-Confucian orthodoxy come from?

[13] Needham, *Belief*, pp. 5, 44, 137–39.
[14] Imanaka, *Seikagaku*, pp. 247–52.

NEO-CONFUCIAN ORTHODOXY AND THE HAYASHI HOUSE

There are two sides to the question of orthodoxy. For a very long time it has been assumed that early Tokugawa political thought was simply a transplant of a monolithic body of thought from (Sung) China, that it was thus identical to early Neo-Confucianism. This view overlooked, however, developments in Neo-Confucianism between the Sung and the late Ming periods. (Maruyama Masao's work shares this erroneous understanding.) Abe Yoshio has corrected this view by demonstrating that variety and pluralism characterized Japanese Neo-Confucianism from the beginning: scholars chose from among a number of Ming Chinese and Korean interpretations. This revision has recently been incorporated into the writings of a group of American scholars associated with Wm. Theodore de Bary. In concluding that early Tokugawa Neo-Confucianism was not monolithic, these scholars, working from the vast Chinese perspective, quite naturally also tend to emphasize continuities along lines found in the Chinese and Korean experience.[15]

The accuracy of this analysis in its general lines and as it pertains to Neo-Confucianism is beyond dispute. Since the writing of history, however, is a matter of perspective, it is also understandable that this analysis cannot give due weight to the question of early Tokugawa ideology, that is, to the conversion of thought constructs into a servicable ideology. Moreover, since most research on early Tokugawa thought (de Bary, Maruyama) has concentrated on Neo-Confucianism, the impression has been created that political thought at that period comprised only Neo-Confucianism.

This research, since it did not focus sufficiently on the process by which an ideology is put into place, has also tended to assume too readily that Neo-Confucianism occuped in Japan a position although not precisely identical but nevertheless closely analogous to the one it held in China as an officially sponsored "state" ideology. This assumption ignores the fact that in Japan, as elsewhere—including China—orthodoxies are always established through political struggles: a discourse on power that achieves the status of orthodoxy is itself a successful exercise in power.

The analysis that follows indicates that Hayashi Razan was primarily responsible for making all later generations believe that

---

[15] Abe Yoshio, *Chōsen*; de Bary and Bloom, *Principle*, pp. 15–33, 27–30, 130–39, 143, 146, 156, 174.

political thought in early Tokugawa Japan was Neo-Confucian, and that the bakufu was its active sponsor. In order to understand how this projection of orthodoxy served Hayashi interests, it is necessary to review briefly Razan's career and examine the position he sought to secure within the bakufu.[16]

At age fourteen Razan, the son of a rōnin family, left Kenninji, a Zen temple in Kyoto that he had joined two years earlier and where he otherwise would soon have been ordained. In 1605, at age twenty-two, he entered Ieyasu's service, not as a Confucian scholar or Buddhist priest but as an exceptionally learned young man who impressed his interviewers with his broad knowledge of Chinese scholarship; a knowledge which he had picked up from a number of teachers and from any book that he could get his hands on.

At Kenninji, Razan studied under scholars who belonged to the Kiyohara tradition, since Heian times one of the few houses that studied Confucianism. In more recent times, this house used a mixture of traditional Confucian and Neo-Confucian texts. Through one of his former teachers he made ambitious but fruitless attempts to become a disciple of Kiyohara Hidekata, one of the most famous official court scholars. Razan, no doubt, believed that Hidekata, whose functions brought him in contact with Ieyasu, Toyotomi Hideyori, the kanpaku, and the emperor, could provide him with the right connections to start his career.[17] Razan failed, however, and instead sought introductions to Fujiwara Seika, who accepted him as his disciple in 1604.

Razan was employed by the bakufu from 1605 until his death in 1657—fifty-two years—during which he outlived the first three shoguns as well as his great rivals in the bakufu bureaucracy, the monks Sūden and Tenkai. When Tenkai died at age one hundred seven in 1643, Razan replaced him as policy advisor. Razan's career was not that of a Confucian scholar. Rather he used his career to establish himself as one, notwithstanding the fact that in 1607 Ieyasu ordered him to shave his head and adopt a monk's name (Dōshun).

During the Ieyasu and Hidetada years, Razan must have been a frustrated functionary, an ambitious clerk/librarian whose talents were rarely called upon for lecturing, and whose future as either a

[16] Most of the data on Razan's career come from the standard modern biography (Hori, *Razan*) unless indicated otherwise.

[17] Wajima, "Kinsei shoki," pp. 92–94.

scholar or a bureaucrat was not very bright. In 1610–1611 he was allowed to draft some official documents related to foreign trade and also the three-point loyalty oath Ieyasu exacted from the daimyo, but from then on until Iemitsu's succession, his duties seem to have been insignificant.[18] In 1611 he complained to Seika that he felt like a fraud (*kyōgen*). He was not allowed to teach, he wrote, what Seika had prepared him for (the Chinese classics), but instead received assignments on works such as the *Azuma kagami* (a history of the Kamakura bakufu); and yet he could not change his situation because he had to support his parents and felt obliged to his friends.[19] Razan had other reasons to complain. His duties required frequent trips between Sunpu, Edo, and Kyoto, where he had to leave his wife and family, without seeing them for up to two and a half years. Only in 1634—he was fifty-one then—did he bring them to Edo.[20]

In 1614, Razan requested Ieyasu's support to open a school in Kyoto, where he intended to put up Seika as a teacher,[21] but this plan to enhance his scholarly position failed. Ieyasu, busy with preparations for his Osaka campaign, had no time to pay attention to Razan's wishes. Moreover, Ieyasu seems to have lacked a basic interest in matters of great concern to Razan. Ieyasu certainly did not take either to Razan's virulent anti-Buddhism or to his love of Neo-Confucianism. Among the many books that were printed under Ieyasu's patronage—printing presses had just been introduced to Japan—there were a number of works on Buddhism, military science, history, or traditional Confucianism (only two), but not a single one on Neo-Confucianism.[22]

Under Iemitsu, Razan's position improved, although in 1623 he was still listed simply as a *ohanashishū* (another term for *otogishū*, moralizing raconteurs), a post with thirteen incumbents and a status similar to that of pages, attendants, doctors, and monks.[23] He was gradually entrusted with more important assignments, such as drafting the new edition of the *Regulations for Military Houses* of 1635, compiling genealogies of all warrior and noble familes, and dealing with the Korean embassies. But he was also charged with odd assignments such as the writing of a treatise on tobacco

[18] Hori, *Razan*, pp. 139–40, 152–55.
[19] RB 1: 27; quoted in Minamoto, "Seika to Razan," p. 4.
[20] Hori, *Razan*, pp. 263, 285.
[21] *Ibid.*, pp. 201–202.
[22] *Ibid.*, p. 252.
[23] *Ibid.*, pp. 223, 255–56. See also Wajima, "Hoshina seiken," p. 84.

smoking. This essay was commissioned by the lord of Mito in 1650 who, however, sought neither the service nor the advice of the Hayashi house when seven years later he started his monumental work on the history of Japan. Razan was often part of Iemitsu's entourage at the latter's falconry outings, and he was in Nikkō on all important shogunal visits (eleven between 1617 and 1653). These included the years of 1634, when construction of Ieyasu's mausoleum started, and 1636, when the grand inauguration took place, which Razan celebrated in several essays.[24]

In 1630, one of Razan's dreams came true. Iemitsu granted him, probably as a gesture of gratitude for twenty-five years of service to the bakufu, a plot of land on which to build a school. This grant, however, did not signify bakufu sponsorship of Neo-Confucianism as its official ideology. The bakufu did not even finance the school's Confucian temple (built in 1632), which was a gift from the lord of Owari, who had a similar temple in his own domain in Nagoya. The following year the first Confucian ceremony took place (without a bakufu delegation). To Razan's great delight, however, Iemitsu paid the school a visit later in the year (although it does not seem to have been of great importance to Iemitsu). Iemitsu stopped by at the school on his return from a visit to a more impressive place where he had invested considerably more funds: the Kan'eiji, built in 1624 by Razan's rival, Tenkai. Razan received only four acres (5,340 tsubo) of land and 200 gold coins (ryō) for a school that serviced some twenty to thirty students. Tenkai, to house thirty-six monks, was given building materials and 50,000 ryō for his temple.[25] Ietsuna never visited the Hayashi College.

It is clear that the Hayashi College, located in the vicinity of the shogunal palace grounds, was of no importance whatsoever to the bakufu. Yet when scholars discuss Tokugawa ideology, they always mention Neo-Confucianism and the Hayashi College as proof of the bakufu's concern with these matters. They overlook the frequent shogunal visits to the remote mountain place of Nikkō, the astonishing outlay of funds for the building of Ieyasu's mausoleum there, and the building of Kan'eiji, the center of the Ieyasu cult in Edo. It seems that scholars have seen what Hayshi Razan wanted them to see and ignored what he wanted them to ignore.

[24] *Ibid.*, pp. 283, 290, 345.
[25] *Ibid.*, pp. 275–82. For the number of students that studied at the Hayashi College, see Ooms, *Bureaucrat*, p. 127.

In 1644, Razan was empowered to decide on a change of era names, a function that until then had been the prerogative of traditional Confucian court scholars such as the Kiyohara's; he also started work that year on a compilation of Japanese history. His first task as a Neo-Confucian scholar to the bakufu came only in 1656, one year before his death, when he lectured on the *Great Learning* to the fifteen-year-old Ietsuna.[26]

The trajectory of Razan's career indicates that Neo-Confucianism was never perceived by the early Tokugawa shoguns as a tradition deserving specific support. Neo-Confucianism, in the first half century of Tokugawa rule, cannot in any responsible way be spoken of as an officially espoused "state ideology" or orthodoxy, no matter how one qualifies the term.[27] Razan, often portrayed as the bakufu's ideologue, functioned more as the sacristan than as the theologian of the system; the latter role, as we shall see, was played by someone else: Tenkai. Consisting mainly of private notes or occasional compositions, Razan's writings never reached a wide audience during his own lifetime. The bulk of his writings was not printed until after his death, when Razan's two sons published his complete works.[28] To conclude from this, however, that Neo-Confucian teachings were not being studied or taught would be erroneous. They were—but not with bakufu support.

Indeed, toward the end of Razan's life, and in the years following his death, the Hayashi house had to deal with serious competitors in the field of Chinese learning. By that time other scholars, like Kumazawa Banzan and Yamaga Sokō, had not only made names for themselves; they also were better paid than Razan: his stipend had climbed from 300 hyō in 1611 to 917 koku in 1651, whereas Banzan and Sokō received stipends of 3,000 and 1,000

---

[26] Wajima, "Hoshina seiken," p. 87.

[27] De Bary, in de Bary and Bloom, *Principle* (pp. 15–22), differentiates between a mandarin and a bakufu orthodoxy. In the latter, the state played a lesser role than in its Chinese counterpart. My interpretation would go even further in that direction. In my view, de Bary ascribes in his *Orthodoxy* too great a role to Ieyasu in the realm of education (p. 51); too much initiative to the bakufu ("sponsorship," "sanction," "choice": pp. 190, 193, 205) in relation to a "Neo-Confucian ideology"; and too much credit to Razan as the founder of a "bakufu orthodoxy" (p. 204).

[28] Most of Razan's writings on Neo-Confucianism, except for the *Shunkanshō* (Selections called "Modeled after Spring") and the *Santokushō* (Selections on the Three Virtues), written and published in the late 1620s, were personal study notes, published for the first time in 1662, five years after his death, in *Razan sensei bunshū* (Prose writings of Master Razan).

koku, respectively.[29] Moreover, just before Iemitsu died, he seems to have been on the verge of inviting Banzan and Sokō into the bakufu. In 1658, Yamazaki Ansai, who had opened a private Neo-Confucian school in Kyoto three years earlier, started to divide his time between Kyoto and Edo, where he lectured to daimyo. In 1665, Hoshina Masayuki, Ietsuna's regent, hired Ansai, and rumors spread that he would ask Ansai to open his own school in Edo.[30]

Masayuki was keenly interested in learning, but he did not turn to the Hayashi College for his intellectual needs. He had discovered Neo-Confucianism by reading the *Elementary Learning*, and further increased his knowledge through a medical doctor in bakufu service. Although it was probably Masayuki who in 1656 asked Razan to lecture to Ietsuna, three years earlier he had ordered the composition of a Neo-Confucian compendium for the benefit of Ietsuna, at which time he had again called upon a doctor, not upon Razan. Moreover, in the 1660s, Masayuki spent as much time and energy on Shinto as on Neo-Confucianism; his involvement with these two traditions will be documented in detail in the chapters on Yamazaki Ansai. For now, it is sufficient to remember that his championship of Neo-Confucianism in the early 1660s was radical, rigorous, and ultimately rejected by the bakufu bureaucrats. His personal involvement in the punishment of Yamaga Sokō for his critique of Neo-Confucianism and Banzan's earlier harassment by the Great Councillor Sakai Tadakiyo in the mid-1650s do not seem to have reflected the administration's commitment to Neo-Confucianism: in 1675, the bakufu lifted Sokō's exile in Akō, and from 1679 until his death in 1685, Sokō could lecture at home on his *Seikyō yōroku* (Synopsis of the teachings of the Sages), the work that at the time of its publication fifteen years earlier had been the cause for his exile from Edo.[31]

Under Masayuki, the Hayashi family continued to receive scholarly commissions, the largest of which was the resumption of work on a history of Japan, a task that was completed in 1670. But even here the Hayashi house faced competitors. Tokugawa

[29] Hori, *Razan*, p. 378; for the social and economic aspects of the careers of early Tokugawa schoolmen, see Abe Yoshio, "Edo jidai jusha." Stipends (and wealth) were most often calculated in bushels of rice: 1 koku = 2.5 hyō = 5.12 U.S. bushels.
[30] Wajima, "Hoshina seiken," pp. 85–86, 92.
[31] Wajima, "Kanbun igaku," pp. 139, 143–47.

Mutsukuni from Mito had started his monumental historiographical enterprise in 1657, and Ansai had plans for a similar project.

It is within this context that the Hayashi family, whose hopes for a more genuinely scholarly role had been raised by Razan's lecture to the shogun in 1656, sought to secure a firmer hold on the Neo-Confucian field that was opening up under Masayuki. The publication of Razan's collected writings in 1662 by his two sons was meant to draw Masayuki's attention to the family's achievements and to argue a special relationship between Hayashi, Neo-Confucianism, and the bakufu. The two biographies (written in 1659) attached to this edition do not simply chronicle Razan's career,[32] but fabricate for Tokugawa Neo-Confucianism a beginning that was meant to bestow unassailable authority in this field to the Hayashi house.

In these biographies, the Hayashi sons dramatize public lectures Razan gave in Kyoto in 1600 and 1603. In the first one, Razan lectured alone on Neo-Confucian texts, an event that "in the same year that the great divine lord Tōshō [Ieyasu] established his military authority over the country, established in our country the authority of Neo-Confucianism [*dōgaku*: Teachings of the Way]."[33] The lecture of 1603 allegedly led to a suit by Kiyohara Hidekata that was settled by the divine lord in Razan's favor. As Wajima Yoshio has demonstrated, however, a conflict between the most famous Confucian scholar of the times (whose favor Razan had sought) and the young Razan—let alone a suit settled by Ieyasu—is incongruous and lacks both historical evidence and legal grounds. The story, however, pits Kiyohara as the representative of traditional Confucianism against Razan, whose Neo-Confucianism received support from the divine lord even before his employment in 1605.

A similar role of founder had already been ascribed to Fujiwara Seika in the latter's biography, which Razan had published together with Seika's works in 1620. Here it is said that Seika punctuated the Classics by himself in Neo-Confucian fashion, and although the help of a Korean scholar is suggested, this infor-

---

[32] *Razan shishū*, vol. 2, "Furoku" (Appendix), pp. 1–55. For the distortion of facts concerning the alleged settlement by Ieyasu of a suit between Kiyohara Hidekata and Razan, and its political significance, see Wajima, "Kinsei shoki," pp. 96–102, or *id.*, "Razan no kōsho." For a translation of the *Tokugawa jikki* passage concerning this incident, see Maruyama, *Studies*, pp. 14–15 n24.

[33] *Razan shishū*, vol. 2, "Furoku," pp. 3–4, 36.

mation follows a quotation by Seika saying that sages never have teachers.[34] Seika is also portrayed as more radically anti-Buddhist than he actually was.[35] Moreover, Razan gives the impression that he succeeded to Seika's scholarship, although they very soon seem to have become estranged, and Seika had designated a relative of his, Matsunaga Shōsan, as his successor.[36] Minimized or simply glossed over are both Seika and Razan's indebtedness to their earlier teachers before they left the monastery. These teachers were of the Kiyohara Confucian and Shinto tradition, and profoundly marked the intellectual orientations of Seika and Razan, as Imanaka Kanshi has demonstrated.[37]

In the 1650s and 1660s, three powerful daimyo close to the bakufu (Hoshina Masayuki, Tokugawa Mitsukuni, and Ikeda Mitsumasa) perceived a need to instill certain ethico-political values in their samurai through some form of public teaching. Their concerns created a market for an as yet ill-defined commodity, ideology. They certainly did not see the problem in the way it is often presented by historians, as simply a matter of "borrowing" a ready-made doctrine (Neo-Confucianism).[38] Since the shape of that commodity was unclear (samurai had never systematically been subjected to teachings nor had anyone ever seen a need for such undertaking) that commodity itself had to be constructed, and they were in the market for any scholar who could perform such a task.

In this open market, the Hayashi family sought a competitive advantage as best as it could. It was in 1651–1652 that Razan wrote his virulent attack on Christianity (and not immediately after the Shimabara Rebellion of 1637–1638, which one could have expected). In this attack he linked Kumazawa Banzan, who had just been considered by Iemitsu for an eventual bakufu post, to the rōnin plot of Yui Shōsetsu of that year, and branded his teachings as crypto-Christianity. He also castigated scholars who produced military works (Yamaga Sokō). Both these attacks are

[34] Seika's biography by Razan can be found in RB 2: 18–24; a more readable, annotated version is available in SGT 13: 43–54; see esp. p. 45.

[35] Imanaka, *Seikagaku*, pp. 24, 86–88, 95.

[36] Minamoto, "Seika to Razan," p. 4; Hori, *Razan*, p. 100. Hori's date (1621) for the official transmission of Seika's teachings to Shōsan must be mistaken, however, since Seika died in 1619.

[37] Imanaka, *Seikagaku*, especially pp. 1, 169, 271–292, 303.

[38] I discuss the "borrowing" metaphor in my "Neo-Confucianism."

best understood as political maneuvers by Razan against threatening competitors.[39]

It was thus in the 1650s and 1660s that "orthodoxy" became important. The issue, however, was created not by the bakufu but by the Hayashi scholars, who saw their opportunity to become purveyors of official teachings—a position they had long coveted—threatened by others. Their aim and motivation was not to promote correct knowledge, but to secure the power to produce official knowledge.

Ultimately, the Hayashi house had great responsibility for creating the emblematic links between Ieyasu, the bakufu, Seika, Neo-Confucianism, and Razan. The Hayashi helped establish the fiction of a Neo-Confucian, bakufu-supported orthodoxy, which not only informed the text of Matsudaira Sadanobu's Ban on Heterodoxy in 1790,[40] but still dominates much of today's scholarship. They, and not the bakufu leadership, were eager to have Neo-Confucianism clearly marked as a separate tradition under their own aegis.

One is led to conclude that the issue of orthodoxy or official ideology was limited to the middle decades of the seventeenth century (1650–1670), and that since then (at least until the time of Matsudaira Sadanobu), although there was an expanding demand for teachings and learning, there was none for orthodoxy. Neither was the issue historically linked to ideological or political beginnings in the opening years of the Tokugawa bakufu. In creating the issue, only a small number of people appealed to "orthodoxy," and for personal reasons. The Hayashi scholars sought political advantage for their house. Hoshina Masayuki was seriously interested in Neo-Confucianism, but not to the point of excluding Shinto. (And the two Sakai Great Elders—*tairō*—also exploited it in their harassment of Banzan from the Ikeda house.)

AN EVER-EXPANDABLE DISCOURSE WITH AN EMPTY CENTER

The use of orthodoxy as political leverage did not mean, even for these few men, exclusive reliance on Neo-Confucianism. Although

[39] Hori, *Razan*, pp. 397–99. George Elison interprets these texts as proof that Razan was blinded by his own fanatical rhetoric (*Deus Destroyed*, p. 235). Elison's too ready reliance on psychologizing interpretations prevents him from uncovering the political dimensions of the actions taken by the historical figures he discusses.

[40] The text of Sadanobu's Ban on Heterodoxy starts with a reference to the establishment of an official doctrine by Ieyasu and to the Hayashi scholars as upholders of that doctrine since the beginning (see Ooms, *Bureaucrat*, p. 133; Tsunoda et al., *Sources*, 1: 493).

most learned men of the time had reservations of various degrees of intensity about Buddhism, many did appropriate Shinto teachings into their political thinking, as did the supporters of orthodoxy. Masayuki's commitment to Neo-Confucianism was matched only by his enthusiasm for Shinto, and the Great Elder Sakai Tadakatsu even commissioned—from Razan!—a Shinto political treatise, the *Shintō denju* (Shinto initiation). Razan again tried to politically exploit this situation by presenting this treatise as an exclusive, secret teaching of the Hayashi house and as superior to all other Shinto teachings (Sd, 19, 57; RB 2: 419).[41]

Shinto had been amalgamated with Confucianism and Neo-Confucianism since the Muromachi period, especially in the Kiyohara and Yoshida schools. Although Shinto theologians such as Bonshun and Yoshikawa Koretaru (the teacher of Masayuki and Ansai) continued this tradition throughout the seventeenth century, many Neo-Confucian scholars also included Shinto interpretations in their writings. Some of them, it is true, were uninterested in Shinto (Seika, Kinoshita Jun'an); others put Shinto on an equal footing with Neo-Confucianism as Japan's indigenous version of the Way, parallel to the Chinese version (Banzan, Sokō); still others found in Shinto a religious tradition that was missing in Neo-Confucianism (Tōju). It is striking, however, that scholars close to power during the Iemitsu and Masayuki years (Sokō and Banzan as opposed to Itō Jinsai) all had an interest in Shinto, and that it is the two scholars most directly associated with the center of power (Razan and Ansai) who wrote their own versions of Shinto political theory with the intention of creating their own schools. Yet Razan and Ansai also claimed a pure understanding of Neo-Confucianism.[42] It was thus mainly Neo-Confucian scholars proud of their Chinese scholarship who created Confucian Shinto teachings for the rulers, not Shinto theologians who felt the need to update their teachings with new Chinese concepts (although Yoshikawa Koretaru, as we shall see, belongs to the latter category).

Razan's involvement with Shinto teachings—unlike Ansai, who created Suika Shinto—did not lead to a flourishing new Shinto school. The *Shintō denju* was presented to Sakai Tadakatsu and also

[41] In the following pages title abbreviations will be used for texts, followed by page numbers. References to the *Shinto denju* (Sd) are to NST 39; RB refers to *Razan sensei bunshū*.
[42] Ansai started his school in 1655 with purist claims. By the 1640s, Razan had come to a clear grasp of Neo-Confucianism, as Ishida Ichirō has shown: "Zenki bakuhan taisei no ideorogii," pp. 422–24.

kept in the Hayashi family, but it did not continue as a full-fledged teaching and seems to have disappeared altogether from the writings of the Hayashi house after Hayashi Hōkō (1644–1732).[43] In *Razan sensei bunshū* (Collected works), one finds a number of treatises on Shinto subjects, but many of these were private notes or occasional pieces that came to be widely known only posthumously. In addition, there exists another, as yet unpublished, manuscript that expounds Razan's particular Shinto: the "Shintō hiden setchū zokkai" (Sh) or "Plain explanation of secret Shinto eclecticism." [44]

Shinto notions, however, were a routine part of Tokugawa political discourse. We find them in the private writings of Razan, and much more publicly in a number of anonymous works that circulated widely, first in manuscript form and later (by the 1650s) in printed editions: the *Kana shōri* (Ks) (Nature and principle discussed in kana script), the *Shingaku gorinsho* (Sg) (Treatise on the Five Relationships in Mind Learning), and the *Honsaroku* (Hr) (The Honsa—*Hon*da, lord of *Sa*do—record).[45]

The first two texts are almost identical and obviously related. The *Honsaroku* presents arguments similar to those in *Ieyasu's Testament* (they were published around the same time). All these works offer critiques of Buddhism and center their arguments, like *Ieyasu's Testament*, on the Way of Heaven, the mind, and a micromacrocosmic philosophy of correspondences. These arguments are interspersed with Shinto data. The views they present are very similar to those Razan expresses in his two main Shinto texts and in two smaller works that constitute Razan's systematic exposition of Neo-Confucian teachings, the *Shunkanshō* (Sk) (Selections called "Modeled after spring") and the *Santokushō* (St) (Selections of the Three Virtues), both written and published in the late 1620s.[46]

It is not my intention to discuss either the obvious or the obscure ways in which these writings differ. Rather, I shall focus on the common political discourse that is represented through these var-

[43] Kobayashi Yasumori, "Razan to Shintō," pp. 261–62.

[44] Manuscript in the Cabinet Library of National Archives. No pagination; page references in the text are my own.

[45] Page references in the text are to NST 28. Tokugawa scholars and printers have attributed these works to various authors (Seika, Banzan). The *Shingaku gorinsho* seems to be the oldest (possibly written before 1620) and the source for the *Kana shōri*. Modern scholars have ascribed these works, or at least the above two, to others. Imanaka Kanshi argues for a Razan authorship in his *Seikagaku* (pp. 38, 155–56, 187, 191). Hori Isao rejects Imanaka's hypothesis (*Razan*, p. 374). Ishige Tadashi has argued first for Fabian, and more recently for Bonshun; see his "'Shingaku gorinsho' no seiritsu," NST 28: 500.

[46] Page references in the text are to NST 28.

ious appropriations of doctrinal traditions. (Koretaru and Ansai's teachings will be examined later, since they came to form an important Shinto school.) One should keep in mind, however, that in Razan's case his two Neo-Confucian introductory texts had an audience from the 1630s on, whereas his two purely Shinto treatises never circulated widely. The other anonymous works (including *Ieyasu's Testament*) were already in circulation for some time before their publication in the 1650s. They elaborate on the theories that are only briefly mentioned in *Ieyasu's Testament*.

The discussion that follows draws a composite picture of various elements taken from half a dozen works. One may object to this treatment because it would seem to distort the integrity of the originals. Such a collage is useful and justified, however, for it shows how heterogeneous elements were juxtaposed, a procedure that allowed meaning to travel from one element to another. Most of these works were themselves collages, put together with elements from various traditions and from each other. No rigid lines separated Shinto from Neo-Confucianism or the various texts from each other. Furthermore, they were not scrutinized then, as they should not be now, for doctrinal purity, influences, or the particular thought of the author (who was often not known). Rather they offered a variety of arguments that expressed in multiple ways an ideology whose principle points were widely accepted as a plausible discourse on man, society, and the cosmos. These views were teachable and dogmatizable in a variety of ways: in narrative mythological form or in an abstract conceptual format, allowing for a broad spectrum of assenting (or "believing") attitudes. Such assent, one may argue, is always grounded more in a direct reading of social and political reality than in a world view or ideology. Yet, such a reading is never "direct," but is rather informed by that world view or ideology (whose claims to validity rest ultimately on the social and political reality that ideology in turn legitimizes).

Political rule in these texts is the victim of overjustification. Tendō philosophy linked political rule to the beginnings of creation and interlocked it with the cosmic order. The regime became the subject of an argument that was not just a mythological tale of sacred beginnings. Such tales or narrative expositions were still present, but they became linked to, or even overpowered by, arguments from principles—in fact so many that today one cannot escape the impression of a discursive "overkill." To us, the intellectual effort seems out of proportion to its avowed end.

This disregard for the economics of rational discourse, as Dan Sperber has argued, is precisely the hallmark of symbolic discourse, which "only retains from experience a minimum of fragments to establish a maximum of hypotheses, without caring to put them to the test." The meaning of these symbols is not the problem: "what they mean is almost always banal." [47] What deserves our closer attention, then, is the actual construction of this meaning.

The epistemic horizons within which this construction took place differ from the ones we inhabit today. Scholars have in various ways described the contrast between that past world and our own. That world was (as in the West) marked by symbolic thinking and uncritical reliance on metaphors rather than by a dichotomizing and differentiating rational logic. Today, however, we have a strong tendency to "put in quarantine anything we consider as time-off for reason." [48]

The people that produced and read texts in that tradition were, to use Carolly Erickson's phrase, "aware of more possibilities, because they were less inclined to dismiss any of them as unimaginable." Erickson, a scholar of medieval Europe, cautions one when approaching "medieval" views with the following words:

Only by an effort of the imagination can we who perceive a controlled, atomistic and one-dimensional world step into the chaotic, holistic and multidimensional reality of the middle ages ... strictly speaking, no one in the middle ages sought to discover truth, but merely to illuminate the obscurer parts of a web of verities whose general outlines were already clear. Here the educated and the illiterate were on common ground. Both looked at experience from the viewpoint of someone putting together a jigsaw puzzle in which each piece bore clues to its place in the whole. Both allowed the shape of what had already been formed to determine the usefulness of the odd pieces.

What demands our understanding is the congruency of a world view that is put together through uncontrolled analogous association, "a growth of thought by agglomeration." [49]

World views are always conscious elaborations that ultimately rest upon, and are given an epistemic direction and dynamism by, preconceptual perceptions and arrangements of reality in terms of one basic metaphor or another. [50] The world view under consider-

---

[47] Sperber, *Rethinking Symbolism*, pp. 4–6.

[48] Durand, *Structures*, p. 15.

[49] Erickson, *Medieval Vision*, pp. 32, 218–19, 137. Rodney Needham speaks of an associative logic governed by proportional analogies (*Reconnaissances*, ch. 2).

[50] See White, *Metahistory*, pp. x–xi, 30–33, and also his *Tropics of Discourse*, pp. 2–4, 72.

ation is informed by a synecdoche: the integrating metaphor of microcosmic-macrocosmic correspondences. This cosmic metaphor has a long and universal history and is by no means original to the Tokugawa period or even to "traditional" societies such as premodern China and Japan.[51] It does not help one's understanding to view such a system as "one of the most perfect examples, perhaps the most elaborate model ever produced by the human mind of pedantry in extravagance, of method in madness."[52] Rather, man lives, as Michael Polanyi suggests, "in the meanings he is able to discern. He extends himself into that which he finds coherent and is at home there." Metaphorical thinking is not erroneous thinking: all metaphysics is poetry of the mind, a thought poem, "ein Gedankengedicht."[53]

A basic metaphor, however, is more than the static structure scholars may detect in a completed edifice of thought. A root metaphor is the mental operator that produces the structure, which is always in the process of being built or transformed. Such genesis, Piaget writes, "is simply transition from one structure to another ... but this transition always leads from a 'weaker' to a 'stronger' structure. It is a 'transformative' transition. Structure is simply a system of transformations, but its roots are operational." The "gulliverization" of the micro-macrocosm does not stop half way; it has a momentum of its own.[54]

Whether or not all the texts under consideration were produced by the same author, and whether that author was Razan, someone else, or several others, is therefore irrelevant, if, with Jean Piaget, one keeps in mind that "an epistemic subject, that cognitive nucleus which is common to all subjects at the same level ... cannot be the *a priori* underpinning of a finished posterior structure; rather it is a center of activity." Cosmologies are not necessarily expressions of the thought of an individual and linked to institutions. They are institutions of their own.[55]

The microcosmic-macrocosmic metaphoric operator underlies and unifies the various arguments, conceptualizations, and doctrinal appropriations through which the tendō world view is con-

[51] For a history of the microcosm-macrocosm metaphor, see Conger, *Theories of Macrocosms and Microcosms*; of interest is also Temkin, "Metaphors of Human Biology."

[52] Berthelot, *La pensée de l'Asie et l'astrologie*, p. 120.

[53] Polanyi and Prosch, *Meaning*, p. 66; Biese, *Die Philosophie des Metaphorischen*, pp. 109, 115.

[54] Piaget, *Structuralism*, p. 141; Durand, *Structures*, p. 158.

[55] Piaget, *Structuralism*, pp. 139, 142; Douglas, *Purity and Danger*, p. 89.

structed. This epistemic operation was briefly revealed in *Ieyasu's Testament*. Razan elaborates on its principles:

the ancients saw the past through the present, Heaven and Earth through the body, yin and yang through the ether (*ki*), the mind through gods; there is no need to seek far away for other things: one can see all things through man's body; the ancients took Heaven and Earth and made it an exemplar or metaphor (*tatoe*) of the mind ... one has to take Heaven and Earth and apply it to man; if, however, one considers Heaven and Earth only as yin and yang and does not apply it to the body, then one does not know the deep meaning of the scriptures.[56]

One last remark. The heterogeneous conceptual and mytholo-gical material that was used to construct the early Tokugawa discourse on society that is summarized below requires expla-nation, but such glosses will be held to a minimum here. Yamazaki Ansai arranged most of these ideologemes and mythemes more systematically into a well-structured ideology. In the two chapters devoted to his thought, the reader will find more extensive com-ments on the various items and their antecedents in Shinto and Neo-Confucianism that are only briefly mentioned here.

Central to the discourse under review is a manipulation of symbolizing correspondences between nature and man, expressing a "mutual imbrication of everything with everything else at every moment."[57] All the evolutive, cosmogonic concepts marshaled here shed their generative aspects for structural synchronicities that cut across the physical and ethical realms to meet in man.

Cosmology, Gods, Man. "Man's head is round because Heaven is round; the top cowlick on his head corresponds to the Polestar; his eyes to the sun and moon; his Five Viscera and groups of five fingers and toes to the Five Evolutive Phases [five elements]" (St, 175). The physical formation of the embryo is a process that reduplicates

---

[56] Sh, 7, 54. It is noteworthy that Claude Lévi-Strauss assumes the validity of a similar microcosmic-macrocosmic paradigm: "As the mind too is a thing, the functioning of this thing teaches us (something) about the nature of things: even pure reflection comes down to being basically an *internalization of the cosmos*." (*La pensée sauvage*, Paris: Plon, 1962, p. 328). He also writes that "myths signify the mind that develops them by making use of the world of which the mind is itself a part. This makes possible the simultaneous production of myths by the mind, and by the myths, of *an image of the world which is already engraved in the structure of the mind*" (*Le cru et le cuit*, Paris: Plon, 1964, p. 346; translations are mine; emphases added). Compare also with Ieyasu's pronouncement pp. 69–70.

[57] The phrase is Jean Soustelle's, quoted in Durand, *Structures*, p. 28. The full reference is: Soustelle, *La pensée cosmologique des anciens Mexicains* (Représentations du Temps et de l'Espace; Paris: Hermann, 1940), p. 9.

the cosmic production of the Five Evolutive Phases (Sd, 26, 47). Fire resides in man as his body temperature, Water as spittle and sweat, Earth as his flesh, and so on (Sd, 14, 33–34, 39–40). The ethical world is based on the Five Constant Virtues and the Five Relationships; to organize one's behavior in accordance with them is to become one with tendō (Ks, 243).

Ki, energy, is the primal dynamism from which sprang yin and yang, then the Five Evolutive Phases, and finally man (but in man, it is the mind that controls *ki*) (St, 161–62). This original *ki* is variously referred to as *ikki* (the one *ki*), *shinki* (the divine *ki*), *genki* (the original *ki*), and also as the origin of movements and shapes (Sh, 6–7). *Ikki* is the primeval chaos (*konton*) of the *Nihongi* from which sprang the yin and yang deities Izanami and Izanagi. In turn, they gave birth to the five gods of the Five Evolutive Phases that produced man (Sd, 15–16). The gods manipulate the Five Evolutive Phases like marionettes (Sd, 34, 39–40). In this *ikki* or *konton*, the principles of gods/spirits (*shinrei*) originated spontaneously—a process that is like the origination of thoughts in the mind. A recapturing of the pre-thought mind is thus a return to the *konton* before creation (Sd 25–26). The deity of Kunitokotachi is none other than *genki*, original *ki* (Sd, 33) or the ultimateless, *mukyoku* (RB, 2: 419). He is the first of the Heavenly Gods, the creator, while Amaterasu is the first of the Earth Gods (Sd, 55). Kunitokotachi opened, created Heaven and Earth through the fission of his body (Sh, 9); it is through him that man's basic mind can penetrate everything (Sd, 13, 26).

Nature's principles and the original principle of man's mind are the same (St, 180). Man is the noblest living thing in Heaven and Earth, and in his mind rest the principles that govern all things (St, 175; Sk, 116): his *ki* is the energy of Heaven and Earth, his mind is the mind of Heaven and Earth (RB 1: 268), and Heaven and man are thus one (Ks, 242, RB 1: 266; 2: 405); Heaven is in man and surrounds him, like water and fish (RB 2: 379). The creation is nothing but the mind that produces all things (Sk, 116). Principles and mind are one (St, 175, 180; Sh, 43). There is thus no principle besides mind (St, 153); no gods besides mind (Sd, 19, 57).

Gods are shapeless but have a spirit, which is principle and is moved by *ki* (Sd, 28). The gods are the basis of Heaven and Earth (Sd, 44). Gods are the spirit of the mind (Sd, 46); mind is god (Sd, 36), or mind is the divine in man (St, 168–69). The mind is the dwelling place of the gods (Sd, 12); the sacred place where the gods dwell; even the *himorogi* (heavenly divine fence, shrine) of the *Nihongi* is nothing other than the mind (Sd, 29) and the pure brightness of the mind nothing other than divine light (Sd, 19, 22).

The recurring metaphor that expresses the divine in-dwelling in man and the mind's rule over the body is the house: as a lord rules over his house, so does the mind rule over the body, and just as man lives in a house, so do gods dwell in the mind. The mind is the dwelling place of the gods (Sd, 12; St, 161–62, 180–81; Ks, 240; RB 1: 188, 281; 2: 204, 360, 386, 400, 404, 409, 416). Or schematically:

> lord:house : : mind:body : : gods:mind

This proportional equation is rooted in late medieval Shinto theology and in Neo-Confucian writings.[58]

The intimate link between man and the gods is expressed in one other way. Man's existence is divided into a past, present, and future. His past is his existence before birth when he is at one with the gods. His present begins at birth, and his future refers to the time after death when he returns to the gods. This sequence parallels natural time in its succession of day and night. Night is the time of quietness when the gods hide, and daylight stands for movement and appearance, the world of man. In his mind, however, man can unify the three worlds of night-day-night or past-present-future. This leads to the conclusion that man's mind is not pure quietness but a combination of movement and quiescence (Sd, 55–56).

Mind, the Ethical Agenda. To maintain a pure mind is thus man's ethical assignment. One's body will be pure only if one's mind is (Sd, 44). The mind is produced through a fission of Heaven (Ks, 240). Just as Heaven's mind is invisible yet all-penetrating, man's mind is invisible and penetrating (Hr, 277; St, 153). And man's mind first of all penetrates his whole body (Ks, 240).

The mind thus dominates *ki*, the dynamic and material element (St, 161–62), but this control entails a continuous struggle. Evil enters into man through the five senses (Sd, 17) and thus destroys

---

[58] The mind as the dwelling place of the gods is argued in the *Shinto taii* (Great essence of Shinto) and in other Shinto writings; references to the mind as ruler over the body are to be found in Kiyohara writings and in Chu Hsi's. See explanatory notes to the texts in NST 28: 388 (*hito no kokoro wa*), and NST 39: 12 (*kokoro wa*). Some of these texts will be discussed further in the chapters on Ansai.

the mind's primal vacuity (*mu*) (Sd, 46).[59] This does not mean, however, that the mind is quintessentially at rest. It pertains to the nature of things that rest and movement are mutually exclusive, but in the realm of the sacred, movement and nonmovement, rest and its absence are one (RB 2: 386–87). The mind of Heaven and Earth is poised between rest and movement (RB 2: 416). Movement and rest are inseparable in the mind. It pertains to the mind's nature not to remain quiescent, but to respond actively to stimuli. Likewise, the state of the primeval chaos was not absolute rest without movement, but an undifferentiatedness that was the basic dynamism (*ki*) out of which rest and movement sprang (Sd, 56).

The mind of *tenri*, Heavenly Principle, also has a specific moral character: *jin*, humaneness. This is the mind of Heaven and Earth that produces all things (RB 2: 387). In man, humaneness becomes *jihi*, compassion, generous benevolence (Sk, 117; Ks, 242)—the quality on which *Ieyasu's Testament* insists so much. Benevolence defines man's nature and has an enemy, *yoku* or desires (*ibid.*). This dichotomy within man is expressed in various ways. Man's mind (*jinshin*) is originally the same as tendō's mind (*dōshin*) (Hr, 296; Ks, 251; RB 2: 384), but this mind of desires (*yokushin*) can be corrected through *reigi*, rites and obligations. *Tenri*, the Principle of Heaven, is public (*kō*) and must overcome the private character (*shi*) of man's heart (Sk, 124)—a struggle that is often portrayed as the combat between two men within oneself (St, 168–69).

Heaven, the Way, the Realm. The Way of Heaven, tendō, is usually described as the natural, vital order of all existing things. Sometimes, however, tendō is personified as the lord of Heaven and Earth who, penetrating everything, regulates the seasons (Ks, 240) and metes out rewards and punishments. For example, if one lives in accordance with the Five Constant Virtues and the Five Relationships, one will be blessed through one's offspring (Ks, 243; Hr, 296–97). Compassion (*jihi*) is rewarded in the same way (Ks,

---

[59] The origin of evil seems to have been a problem that vexed Razan throughout his life. Given the pure substance (*ri*) that defines man's nature (*sei*) it is hard to accept that *ri* could produce evil, because then nature would also have to be evil; if, however, evil originates somewhere else, then that something does not share a nature and escapes *ri*, which is also impossible. It seems, he concludes in the middle of his career, that this problem has been left unanswered by the sages (RB 2: 390 and 397). He raises the same problem in 1648 (*ibid.*, 484) and seems to have leaned toward denying the unredeemable quality of *kishitsu*, man's second, individuating nature (*ibid.*, 407).

244; Hr, 283). One may also be rewarded after death by a return to one's original state: to tendō's homeland or original nature (*honchi*) (Ks, 250–51; Hr, 296–97) or to Kunitokotachi (Sd, 35–36). Through obeying the gods, one fulfills tendō (Sd, 12).

The punishment of Heaven is inescapable. If one is not punished in one's person or children, then one's grandchildren will be subjected to Heaven's wrath (Ks, 245). One does not offend Heaven only through one's rejection of the ethical virtues and relationships in general. Any kind of selfishness (Ks, 247) or any action that causes suffering to the people is a heavenly offence (Ks, 245). History bears witness to this law. The house of Minamoto Yoritomo (the Kamakura bakufu) was punished for such trespasses (Ks, 246), as were many other ruling houses (Ks, 252–53; Hr, 290): Nobunaga and Hideyoshi's rule did not last longer than one generation (Hr, 293). Correct knowledge on which to base proper government existed in Japan at one point, but has been lost, as is evident is recent times through the many instances of houses that collapse in one or two generations (Hr, 277). Moreover (in contrast to a personal tendō, and as one may be surprised to find in a Shinto text), one does not necessarily have to believe that it is the gods who distribute rewards and punishments: in a depersonalized, "karmic" order, man's ethical actions trigger their own consequences (Sd, 45).

Heaven determines who shall rule. Rulers are supposed to display parental attitudes toward their subjects. They therefore represent tendō (Ks, 245)—an idea that was already present a century earlier in Kiyohara Nobukata's writings.[60] They receive their charge, just as the Son of Heaven is mandated by tendō, to rule over the realm (Hr, 285). Rulers are caretakers of the things that belong to tendō—a concept that is akin to the Buddhist doctrines of the sixteenth-century Ikkō sect. Rulers, therefore, cannot just take things from the people and store them, for this would amount to stealing from Heaven and Earth. After they have taken care of the people, however, they may indulge in some luxury (Hr, 290).

To observe tendō's rules in the public realm means to respect the warrior laws (Hr, 289). This is especially true in times of turmoil, when military might (*bu*) is the only source of order. Such times are followed by *bun*, rule through "letters," when tendō's directives are followed spontaneously and without effort. Even then, however, a

---

[60] See *tendō* note, NST 28: 245.

benevolent government that displays compassion has to be very firm (Hr, 298). Yet, the need for military might and firmness should not obscure the fact that rule over realm and nation stems from the mind (Hr, 277).

Hierarchy. The order that military might upholds, alone or behind jihi and bun, is a hierarchical social order where the upper and the lower, the exalted and the vulgar, keep their place, just as in nature, where Heaven is above and Earth is below. The Sage Kings who received Heaven (Sk, 131) originally defined this hierarchical stability as the fundamental principle of Heaven and Earth (RB 2: 402), the will of Heaven (*tenmei*) (Sk, 129). This order is objectified through rites or regulations (*rei*) (Sk, 179).

A number of virtues, such as loyalty and filial piety, are said to contribute to the maintenance of this proper hierarchy. Sometimes the aspect of reciprocal duty inherent in these virtues is emphasized (Ks, 242–43; Sh, 258). In other texts, the unilateral character of absolute obedience is stressed (Sk, 119; Hr, 295). In still other passages, these virtues are explained as being based on jin, humaneness (Sk, 119). One virtue, however, clearly stands out as the mental attitude par excellence for maintaining the order spelled out in the rites: *kei*, reverence (Sk, 132).

Kei is the lord of one's mind, the quality that makes of the mind the dwelling ground of the gods (RB 1: 188, 310–11; 2: 360, 404, 409, 416). Reverence means restraint, discretion, deference, prudence, and self-control (*tsutsushimu*) (RB 2: 204). It is the source of all things, governing rites great and small (such as weddings and daily etiquette) (RB 1: 188), and plays a central role in the regulation of man's inner psyche and outward comportment. One can distinguish several aspects of the mind such as an essential nature (principles: the Five Virtues) and an emotional quality (functions: the Seven Emotions). The mind's activity can further be analyzed as having a movement (*ki*), a starting point (*i*, the will), a direction (*shi*, intentions), thoughts (*nenryo*, defined as an overflow of will) and a locus, the body. Kei, however, dominates the entire life of the mind because it regulates all this activity and disciplines the body (RB 1: 310).

Buddhism, Shinto, Neo-Confucianism. In some texts, Buddhism is the object of strong criticism, both ideological and philosophical. The *Honsaroku*, for example, argues that Buddhism is a doctrine that was used in the past as an instrument of political order. The concepts of paradise and hell were merely conjured up for this purpose. Through them, the people were misled and made to believe in things that do not exist. Rulers were venerated as gods and Buddhas, but Buddhist rule always turned into an exploitation of the people (Hr, 293–94). One particular criticism concerns the failure of Buddhism to develop a consistent theory of the mind: in the beginning Buddhists held to the existence of the mind, then they taught that the mind was emptiness, and still later they maintained that the mind neither existed nor did not exist. These mutually contradictory positions are attributed respectively to Pure Land, Zen, and Tendai Buddhism (Ks, 249–50).

What really counts is a pure mind (RB 2: 360). The gods do not accept offerings unless they come from a pure heart, but with a pure heart there is no need for prayers and offerings (Hr, 294; Sh, 19, 45). Neither this teaching nor Confucianism is foreign to Japan; Buddhism is the alien teaching (RB 2: 360). Amaterasu's rules that stressed shōjiki (straightforwardness) and jihi (benevolence)—it will be recalled that this pair also shows up in *Ieyasu's Testament*— were observed by Emperor Jinmu, the first of the Japanese emperors, who ruled in an idyllic past over an ideal society (Ks, 246; Hr, 294). A counter example of a ruler who did not observe these principles is again Minamoto Yoritomo, the founder of the Kamakura bakufu (Ks, 246). Just government in Japan was lost, therefore, with the advent of Buddhism (Hr, 279; RB 2: 360), but an oracle by Yamato-hime directed attention to this state of affairs and ordered the country to be purified from Buddhism's nefarious influence and to return to the gods (Sd, 37).

The assumption of this historical vision is that Shinto and Confucianism are not only compatible but the same. This is, indeed, asserted by proclaiming that their minds are identical (Ks, 249). The rules that Emperor Jinmu kept were none other than those of the Sage Kings Yao and Shun (Sd, 37). Emperor Jinmu is probably even a descendant from the house of Chou (RB 1: 281). What Amaterasu asks one to believe is that to follow the Way is tenri, the Principle of Heaven (Hr, 281). Ruling over the people is thus an act of divine veneration because the gods reside in the people (Sd, 14). To rule the country is to exercise divine power; a lost tradition that goes back to Amaterasu (Sd, 19).

Shinto existed before Japan had a written language, at a time when there were no letters, only divine words. This language is truthful because it takes Heaven and Earth as its text and adduces the sun and moon as proofs. It is a natural language (like the cries of a newborn) (Sd, 39) that is not man-made and was only later transcribed with the help of Chinese characters (Sd, 38). Even the composition of the *Nihongi* reflects this natural origin, because the work consists of thirty chapters, the same number as there are days in a month. The two opening chapters treat the age of the gods, symbolizing Heaven and Earth. The remaining twenty-eight chapters each chronicle the reign of an emperor, reflecting the twenty-eight constellations (RB 2: 418–19). The *ri* or principle that is expressed in Shinto, and without which nothing exists, is a natural truth (Sd, 38). Shinto is thus the same as Confucianism, for it rests on the same *ri*; only its practice (*waza*) is different. Shinto is *ōdō*, the Way of the Kings (Sd, 12–13, 19, 21, 57; Sh, 28–31; RB 2: 360).

The three treasures (mirror, sword, and jewel) express this truth of the Kingly Way. In nature, they stand for the sun, the moon, and the stars, respectively. In the mind, they manifest wisdom, humaneness, and courage: the mental tools that are indispensable for proper government (Sd, 12–13) and the virtues that are the dwelling place of the gods (RB 2: 419). Treasures outside, inside they are political virtues (Sh, 22–23). These treasures may be man-made, but they express the Way that is made by Heaven (RB 1: 281).

THIS synopsis of tendō philosophy may have left the reader dizzy. But if it appears as a patchwork of concepts without a center or as a maze of linkages lacking rigorous logic, it is because the texts themselves display such characteristics. They are the textual equivalents of *emakimono*, picture scrolls where the scenes or units can be arbitrarily marked off from each other and where the only order is sequential. They are works that are the result of *bricolage*—to use Levi-Strauss's celebrated term[61]—where the odd shapes of the parts determine the unpredictable contours of the whole.

It is tempting either to dismiss such work as a crazy quilt or to cut some statements from it and rearrange them in another sequence, turning them into advances or breakthroughs in the development of Tokugawa rationalism, that is, as instances of a demythologization of religious doctrine or an internalization and spirituali-

---

[61] *The Savage Mind*, Ch. 1, esp. pp. 16–35.

zation of values (Buddhism misleads and exploits the people; the divine descent of the emperor is denied; offerings are said to be useless). Such an interpretation, however, misconstrues the thrust of such statements.

Razan's theory of the Chinese ancestry of the imperial house, for instance, was not intended to desacralize a myth but to link Japan genealogically (physically) with the Way. Nor is it Razan's own peculiar theory. Rather, this interpretation was well known; it had already been mentioned much earlier in the works of Kitabatake Chikafusa (1293–1354) and Ichijō Kanera (1402–1481). Although, as Hori Isao argues, Razan may have held this view as a private opinion that he did not reveal in his public writings, it did not constitute a sacrilege.[62] In this respect, once secular interpretations were available they did not automatically displace sacred ones. For instance, in his historical sketch of culinary practices, written many years after his theory of imperial descent from China, Razan argues that whereas in China man's history developed from a barbaric primitivism through the cultural creations of the Sages, in Japan the history of food and culture had divine origins.[63] Sacred traditions were eminently malleable, and the manipulations that occur in these texts were at the time unobjectionable.

The symbolic transactions and manipulations of these texts provide justifications that, in Mary Douglas's words, "turn the furniture of the universe into an armory of control." This is not an innocent or misdirected enterprise, as Douglas suggests elsewhere when she writes that "the symbolic mode insidiously seduces the intellect to its own estate ... as if the symbolic mode had overwhelmed the freedom of mind to grapple with reality."[64] The intellect here produces nothing but symbolic thought, and in doing so is fully in its own estate; it grapples with reality and has a clear political purpose.

The bewildering aspect of this thought, to us at least, lies in its mode of operating and the way it posits the unity of the self. Parallels are built between the biological reproduction of man, the creation of the universe, the generation of thoughts, and the construction of the social order. It is the refusal to recognize separate realms of reality that respond to different laws of formation that offends us. This refusal, however, has a point to make. These

[62] Hori, *Razan*, pp. 362, 367, 368.
[63] *Hōtei shoroku* (Cook book), pp. 212–13.
[64] Douglas, *Natural Symbols*, pp. 136, 183.

parallels all point to the political order that is therefore presented as an instance of the cosmic coherence of things. In this mental construct, through "gulliverization" and "gigantization," *tenchi* (Heaven and Earth) becomes an intimate substance, and man coterminous with the universe. There are no limits to this extension and reduction of figures. Not analysis but identification of similitudes is the explanatory procedure—an operation that produces more harmonics as the score gets longer.[65]

This procedure decenters man, even if he is the *analogum princeps*. He finds his self in the projected unity of the world and the cosmos. *This discourse refuses to recognize man as a source of initiative other than for action confirming that general order.* The rulers, in this scheme of things, may be divine, but they no longer have a monopoly on the sacred, as singular daimyōjin like Nobunaga or Hideyoshi had. All men share in the same sacrality because they are part of an order that ought not to be upset lest one commit a sacrilege.

When these texts were written, the strategic cunning of the sixteenth century was a far memory but also an ever-present fear (witness the Shimabara Rebellion of 1637–1638). Politics and personal power are thus banned from a discourse that talks not about an order that has to be achieved by daimyōjin, but an order that exists and has to be maintained: the existing order with a very human and contingent history that is better forgotten. History is therefore dangerous and has to be obliterated and replaced by a nature that is sacred. The pullulation of images and parallels leaves no room for contingent events: they are reduced to synchronic instances that partake of the mythical and eternal. Man as maker of his own destiny, and history as a record of this struggle for power, are the silences that form the empty center of this discourse.

The metaphoric character of this discourse, it should be noted in passing, has its parallels in the West in elusive thinkers such as Paracelsus. Temkin Owsei's characterization of the thought of Paracelsus is perfectly applicable to the present case. "The picture," he writes, "may have something compelling, but it remains a picture. There is no necessity for its choice . . . the movements (of his thought) seem to lack necessity . . . an approach that may yield personal conviction, yet does not allow objective certainty."[66]

The author of *Ieyasu's Testament*, as we have seen, is aware of different epistemological approaches. So is Razan. There are two

[65] Durand, *Structures*, pp. 319, 477–78; *id.*, *Nouvel esprit*, pp. 114, 170.
[66] Temkin, "The Elusiveness of Paracelsus," pp. 210, 217.

passages in which he mentions the problem, each time in relation to metaphysical speculation. One can go about discussing the origin of things in two ways, he writes to Seika. One is to look at their transformation from the standpoint of creation in terms of *ki*, the other by analogizing from human things and injecting human behavior into mythical tales of origin. Both make sense, he writes (RB 1: 20–21). Elsewhere, after debunking the story of Sugawara Michizane's spirit punishing his Fujiwara persecutors through lightning and other natural disasters, Razan notes that as far as discussing natural phenomena (the traces of creation) is concerned, if one does not approach it through *ri*, one will wind up with fairy tales that elucidate nothing (RB 1: 297).

Razan thus recognizes two modes of thinking. In the mythological mode, explanations are transferences of human psychology onto natural phenomena. In rational discourse, concepts are adduced that are free from anthropomorphic connotations. Sometimes he extolls the latter over the former, but his rejection of mythology is not pursued as a fundamental intellectual *parti pris*. In his Shinto writings he mixes the two approaches and its two modes, narration and argumentation. The reason is that these two modes are ultimately informed, in Razan's writings and in the other texts analyzed above, by the same synecdoche: man's psyche, his physical nature, society, and the cosmos are interlocked and enclosed within each other as divine loci of the gods or as expansions or contractions of Heaven or Mind.

This philosophy of Heaven and Mind marked political discourse during the first three-quarters of a century of Tokugawa rule: it was espoused in what may be the bakufu's only explicitly ideological piece we have (*Ieyasu's Testament*), it informed the private and official views of Hayashi Razan, and was expressed in a number of anonymous texts that circulated widely at the time. This is the political discourse that functioned in early Tokugawa Japan as a legitimating ideology.

PRE-TOKUGAWA ROOTS AND THE *WARONGO*

To identify this discourse simply as a transplant of ("rational") Neo-Confucian thought from the continent would be incorrect, even if one allows, after Abe Yoshio and Wm. Theodore de Bary, for variations within "orthodox" parameters. It is true that Seika, Razan, and Ansai rummaged freely within the Neo-Confucian field and sorted out interpretations for themselves through private study or through discussions with each other. This coming to terms with Neo-Confucianism, however, was not indispensable to the formation of the tendō world view and its philosophy of mind. New Neo-Confucian contributions to the development of that discourse were not essential. They were mere embroideries that further embellished but did not alter or steer a discourse that had taken shape over several centuries prior to 1600. By the middle of the seventeenth century, however, a new class of intellectuals had emerged who fully deployed the political and ideological potential of this discourse. Again, a "purer" Neo-Confucianism from the continent was not a necessary stimulus for this deployment.

This mature discourse consisted of a kind of talk—distorting talk—about the military system of domination that during Iemitsu's regime had come to include the whole country. Through this discourse, the new authority structure that was undoubtedly *respected* because of the sheer military power that stood behind it, was also *accepted* as the only way that a just society could be maintained.

During the pre-Tokugawa phase of its career, this discourse was very restricted. It provided a theory of the mind to a very limited group of religious thinkers, and insofar as its formulations included Neo-Confucian terminology, a Neo-Confucian input certainly cannot be denied. The two traditions that appropriated elements from Neo-Confucianism were Zen and Shinto, but especially the latter.

Zen Buddhism's preoccupation with the mind is well known. During the Kamakura and Muromachi periods, the monks used Neo-Confucianism, or to be more precise, "Chinese Learning," as their philosophical handmaiden to write about the mind. Japanese scholars have pointed out the Neo-Confucian elements in that tradition of scholarship, and have discerned a gradual awareness of Neo-Confucianism as a separate and independent tradition that may have made possible in the seventeenth century genuine Neo-Confucian studies.[67] The Zen Neo-Confucian tradition, however,

[67] See Wajima, *Chūsei*, and Haga, *Chūsei Zenrin*. Another little explored avenue through which Neo-Confucianism emerged in Japan was medicine. In early Tokugawa Japan, many medical doctors lectured occasionally on Neo-Confucianism, and several noted scholars started their careers in medicine or were sons of physicians. Sugimoto Masayoshi reports that Yüan medicine, which was based on Neo-Confucian principles, was fully assimilated as a whole system a half century before Razan started his career, and that a reaction (the Ancient Practice School) set in against the Neo-Confucian dogmatism of the Yüan tradition a decade before Yamaga Sokō and Itō Jinsai advocated a return to Ancient Learning (Sugimoto, *Science in Japan*, pp. 215, 251, 282).

is of no concern here because, during the centuries under question, it never built linkages to a political philosophy of any sort. (As we shall see later, however, such linkages were built by Suzuki Shōsan in the period between 1630 and 1650.)

Shinto presents a different case. Shinto writers used an eclectic vocabulary to articulate more and more clearly a metaphysical and ethical teaching about the mind that from the beginning had political dimensions. It is this tradition that gave substance to the political ideology as we identified it in the mid-seventeenth century. A discussion of these teachings will thus provide a necessary perspective on early Tokugawa political thought.

Ieyasu's Testament partakes of that tradition through its interpretation of the three imperial regalia as divine virtues, its stress on shōjiki and jihi, and through two references to an oracle made by Sumiyoshi daimyōjin, which frame the entire text (pp. 256 and 307–308).

In Osaka there is a famous Sumiyoshi shrine where three gods and empress Jingū are worshiped.[68] According to the *Nihongi*, these gods ordered empress Jingū to conquer the Korean kingdom of Silla (199 A.D. ?). The order was first given through the empress to Emperor Chūai, who was about to attack the Kumaso clan in Japan. The order entailed a promise that the Kumaso would surrender after the conquest of Silla. The emperor disobeyed the oracle and died. Empress Jingū, then pregnant with her successor, the future emperor Ōjin, set out on the Korean expedition, accompanied by the three gods, and after her victorious return subdued her enemies at home.[69] The oracle also had said that the child in empress Jingū's womb would inherit the fruits of this military expedition. Later emperor Ōjin became deified as Hachiman, the war god.

The sequence of domestic turmoil, foreign conquest, death of the ruler, and succession to domestic rule in itself provided a divine template of the position of the Tokugawa. But there is more. Direct reference is made in the *Testament* to Sumiyoshi daimyōjin as the divine shogun. No such portrayal of either the gods or of the empress is found in the *Nihongi*. This reference inserts the *Testament* in a popular Shinto tradition. Both the popular and the elite sacred traditions that are appropriated here belong to Yoshida Shinto, a theological system that was fully worked out during the

[68] *Nihonshoki* (Nihon koten bungaku taikei, vol. 67) 1: 615–16 n21.
[69] See *Nihongi*, translated by W. G. Aston, pp. 221–22, 233 ff.

Muromachi period and was gradually popularized in Shinto lore. The *Warongo* is the text that exemplifies this tradition.

The *Warongo* (Japanese Analects) was published in 1669 by someone whom later scholarship has identified as Sawada Gennai, a layman from Ōmi who does not seem to have had any formal training as a Shinto scholar. The work consists of ten fascicles or chapters that together form a collection of 882 sayings and aphorisms by deities (108 oracles in the opening chapter), emperors and princes (chapter 2), courtiers (chapters 3 and 4), warriors (5 and 6), illustrious women (7), and Buddhist monks (8–10).[70] It is an eclectic work, but it presents predominantly Yoshida beliefs. The author gathered its content from a great variety of sources, learned and popular, and presents that learning in a simplified, formulaic, often aphoristic manner.

In this work we find a direct mention of Sumiyoshi daimyōjin as a (divine) shogun. The Sumiyoshi daimyōjin oracle, the tenth in the first chapter, is given as follows: "I pacify all evil men and thus, for Heaven's pleasure, I punish the wicked. In the past I was the great shogun and Hiyoshi [Sannō daigongen] was the vice-shogun. After I had pacified the plotters to establish an ever lasting peace, Hiyoshi became shogun and I vice-shogun. Hiyoshi had reached a perfect appreciation of the *ichijō* law and therefore surpassed me in divine power."[71]

This *ichijō* law is further clarified in the same chapter, in Hiyoshi Sannō daigongen's oracle (the sixth one). This oracle states how Hiyoshi (or Hie, whose main shrine was located on Mount Hiei) watched over the Tendai Sannō doctrine that protected the nation. This doctrine explains with some "ethymographical" sophistry the *ichijō* law. The two characters that compose the name of Sannō each consist of three parallel strokes, vertical in the first, horizontal in the second, that are linked with a single perpendicular stroke (山王).[72] In both characters, the three strokes each

[70] The *Warongo* text can be found in Katsube, *Warongo*. I have not used the free (and rather twisted) translation of some *Warongo* sections by Kato Genchi, "The Warongo."

[71] Katsube, *Warongo*, p. 9. The comparison with the Hiyoshi deity may have been added by the author to glorify his native place of Omi, where the Hiyoshi shrine was located (on Mount Hiei). Later we will see how Hiyoshi legends were associated with Hideyoshi.

[72] A similar "ethymographical" interpretation is to be found in Hayashi Razan's *Shintō denju* (NST 39: 21): "the character *ō* (王), king, is to be understood as follows. Its three horizontal strokes signify Heaven, Earth, and Man. The vertical stroke penetrates Heaven, Earth, and Man; this is Shinto. In *ōdō*, the Kingly Way, the first man is the ruler of *tenka*, the realm, and hence is called *ō*, king." Razan then goes on to explain other political terms that are similarly composed: *shu*, (主) lord, is composed of the character for king with a dot on

time symbolize the three realms of emptiness, phenomenality, and the mixture of both: three realms of reality that are but one, as the stroke that links them indicates. This oneness of the universe is the one mind. The one thought and the three thousand thoughts are similarly related. The deity's name, his body, and the law are not three separate entities; they are one, called *ichijō*, and will protect the whole country.[73] Tendai doctrine was thus also a teaching that did not accept the autonomous character of different kinds of reality: they were all subsumed under a monistic unity.

Most of the oracles in the *Warongo* stress purity of heart and uprightness of mind, ethical concepts that one first finds mentioned in imperial edicts of the Nara period (eighth century), where the emperor's subjects were expected to have a pure and bright heart. During the Heian period, shōjiki (straightforwardness) was introduced in Shinto writings as the reverential quality one ought to have toward the emperor as a manifest deity. The attitude that ought to accompany the performance of ceremonies was also described as a reverential, pure, and submissive spirit. In late medieval Shinto writings, this disposition came to be considered the basic requirement for the human heart-and-mind.[74] This teaching was popularized through the "Oracles of the Three Shrines," one of which is already present in Mujū Ichien's collection of tales, the *Shasekishū* of 1283, where it is ascribed to Shōtoku Taishi. A second one is to be found in another collection of tales, the *Jikkinshō* of 1311.[75]

The first two of these three oracles state that the kami dwell in the heads of the correct and upright. (Later "the heads" become "the minds-hearts," possibly under the influence of Chinese texts.) Although it is possible that the "Oracles of the Three Shrines" were later formalized by Yoshida Kanetomo, they seem to have been well known toward the end of the Kamakura period, and became part of popular religious wisdom (see, for instance, the alphabetic

---

top, which signifies fire, symbolizing that he receives the sun, Amaterasu, whose descendants have ruled Japan, which is therefore called the Land of the Rising Sun, Nihon. *Tama* (玉), treasure or jewel, is written with a dot on the side: "what penetrates Heaven, Earth, Man also penetrates *tama*." *Kō* (皇), emperor, is written with the character for king under the character for white, which again symbolizes a king under the sun goddess.

[73] Katsube, *Warongo*, p. 8.

[74] Umezawa, "Heian shoki no 'shōjikishin,'" pp. 275, 279–80, 293.

[75] Muraoka, *Studies in Shinto Thought*, pp. 32–34.

booklet, the *Unpo irohashū* of 1548) and of theological elaborations by Kitabatake Chikafusa (1293–1354) and Yoshida Kanetomo (1435–1511).[76] They are also the opening oracles (one, two, and four) of the *Warongo*, whose author seems to have relied on their formulation in the *Unpo irohashū*.

These three oracles were uttered by Amaterasu, Hachiman, and the Kasuga daimyōjin,[77] and proclaim, respectively, that straightforwardness (shōjiki), although it may not produce immediate gain, will bring Amaterasu's blessings; that Hachiman will accept offerings only from men with a "pure heart" even if it costs him hellish sufferings to refuse those offered by defiled hearts; and that the deity of Kasuga will approach only compassionate (jihi) men, whether they are ritually pure or not. (In 1784 these oracles were debunked by Ise Sadatake as concoctions of the Yoshida house.[78] The *Warongo*, it should be noted, constituted a basic text for Ishida Baigan [1685–1744] and his popularized mind teachings. The work was even quoted in local gazetteers.)[79]

Although the *Warongo* culls its material from popular works such as the *Unpo irohashū*, the *Shasekishū*, Yoshida writings such as the *Myōbōyōshū* and the *Shintō taii*, of particular interest is its use of Ise Shinto (the *Gobusho*).[80] The five works that compose the *Gobusho* were probably drafted in the last decades of the twelfth century by priests of the Outer Shrine in Ise to argue for equal status with the Inner Shrine. These writings stressed inner purity and shōjiki qualities that gradually emerged as cardinal virtues. Moreover, these books came to be referred to as the *Gobusho*, as a corpus of doctrinal teachings, only in the mid-seventeenth century.[81] One can thus safely say that we are confronted in the mid-seventeenth century with a fully elaborated discourse whose first utterings can be detected in the early Kamakura period.

The *Warongo*, for instance, includes a long oracle by Yamato-hime that goes back to the *Yamato-hime no mikoto seiki* (Record of the life of the deity Princess Yamato, one of the five works of the

---

[76] *Ibid.*, p. 36; Kato, *Warongo*, p. 17.

[77] Katsube, *Warongo*, pp. 6–7, 301; Kato's translation of the three oracles is not very precise (Kato, "Warongo," pp. 17, 20, 24); Muraoka (*Studies*, p. 35) is more trustworthy.

[78] See Ise Sadakata, *Sansha takusen-kō.*

[79] Katsube, *Warongo*, pp. 269, 339–41.

[80] *Ibid.*, pp. 301, 316.

[81] Kubota, *Shintōshi*, p. 483; Kawano, *Shintō kenkyūshū*, p. 58; Hammitzsch, *Yamato-hime*, p. 3.

Gobusho), but the *Warongo* oracle also incorporates post-*Gobusho* theological elaborations.[82] The Yamato-hime oracle in the *Warongo* provides a good illustration of the late appropriation of this theological tradition and deserves a full translation. It echoes the basic harmonics of the monistic tendō and mind philosophy, although it does so with the staccato rhythm and in the elliptical mode typical of the oracular style.

The deities of the Inner and Outer Shrine in Ise have no beginning and no end. They are the great original kami; spirits before the birth of one thought. Expel the breath/life of the Buddhist Law and worship our gods again.

The inner truth of the kami is like a mirror. It reflects everything without adding anything of its own. That is why Heaven produced the Mirror. It does not dwell but in a mind emptied of all things (*kokoro ni manbutsu o okazu shite kokū no naki ni totomarazu*).

If all men do not purify their minds, the wild kami will dwell in their spontaneous thoughts. Therefore our Shinto concentrates on the singleness of one thought.

Worship the gods with no mind and no thought. Without fail, what you think will be what your mind is. The Earth receives assistance from Heaven without putting its mind to it (*tsuchi wa ame no tasuke o ukuru ni kokoro nashi*).

The so-called *honchi* (original nature) or Buddha is all living things (*shūjō*); the original nature of all living things is one spirit (*ichirei*) and the original nature of one spirit is the kami.

Making the beginning the beginning and entering into the beginning of beginnings, making basic what is basic, and trusting in the basic mind (*moto no kokoro*), you will experience the breath/life of the kami of Heaven.

Rather than offering our gods a hundred favors or hanging before them for one thousand days the sacred rope to thus venerate them, purify yourself (*ichiza*) and offer a simple cloth offering. Even when you are in an impure place, if you invoke the gods, then that place becomes pure. Respect Heaven, serve the Earth, worship and venerate the gods, venerate your parents and make practice (*shiwaza*) your teaaher.[83]

Purity of mind as no-thought mind, further equated with a basic cosmic state, is presented here as the core of the Shinto tradition. We have already encountered this emphasis in the Tokugawa texts

---

[82] Kato, "Warongo," pp. 90–92; for a German translation of the work, see Hammitzch, *Yamato-hime.*

[83] Katsube, *Warongo*, pp. 161–62; for a paraphrased translation of the oracle, see Kato, "Warongo," pp. 87–88.

analysed thus far, and we will find it again later in the works of
Fujiwara Seika, Suzuki Shōsan, and Yamazaki Ansai.

Before returning to the *Warongo*, I shall briefly continue with the
Gobusho (where the above oracle originated). The first and oldest of
the five works of the *Gobusho* (the abbreviated title of which is
Hōkihongi, The basic record of the treasures) records an oracle of
the twenty-sixth year of the reign of Emperor Suinin (3 B.C. ?) in
five points:

1. Man is the kami matter [*mitamamono*, written with the character
kami] and has to conduct himself in purity; the mind is the residing place
of the kami, and one should not injure the mind-kami.

2. For the kami to come down, you need first of all prayers; to receive
blessings, you need straightforwardness, and if thus you gain the Great
Way, the realm will prosper in peace.

3. Therefore, when kami and men [or kami-men] preserve the [un-
differentiated precreation] beginning chaos (*konton*), if they hide the
breath of the Buddhist Law, venerate the kami and pray to the imperial
court, all between the seas will be in peace.

4. For worshiping the kami, purity and honest trust are important.

5. In the Age of the Kami, man's mind was always holy, but toward
the end of the Age of the Earth Kami, man's mind turned bad, disobeyed
the will of the kami, sunk into the flowing and changing world, and
welcomed Buddha's Law instead of the kami. That is why the oracles of
the Great Kami [Amaterasu] stopped, and men had to find the right path
on their own.[84]

This is a key text to which some of the writings analyzed earlier
refer; it is a text that is also important for Razan and Ansai.

It should first be noted that in a later Yoshida textbook, the first
point of this oracle was further explained in a way that we have
already encountered (see p. 88). There it is said that the need to
purify the mind stems from its defilement by six roots: the five
senses and the body.[85] Furthermore, the opening line of Razan's
Shintō denju ("the people are the residing place of the kami") is
clearly a transposition of the oracle's first point. Finally, the second
point of the oracle is the text from which Yamazaki Ansai took the
name for his own Suika Shinto (*sui* is the character for "coming
down" and *ka* the one for "blessing").

Another oracle by Yamato-hime in the twenty-third year of the

[84] Translation based on Kubota's translation and paraphrase; see Kubota, *Shintōshi*, pp.
479–80.
[85] Kawano, *Shintō kenkyūshū*, pp. 92–93.

reign of Emperor Yūryaku (478 A.D. ?) states that Amaterasu shines upon all, but especially upon the heads of the upright: that the mind-kami is the basis of Heaven and Earth, the body a mutation of the Five Evolutive Phases, and that the Earth originated from the mind and the will from a believing heart—all formulations we encountered in the early Tokugawa texts.[86]

Ichijō Kanera, in his *Commentaries on the Nihongi* (*Nihongi sanso*) which he composed in the 1470s, wrote as follows:

The Three Regalia are the center of the sacred scriptures, the center of *ōbō*, the Kingly Way; *ōbō* is the single principle [*dōri*] of the two teachings of Confucianism and Buddhism. This one principle is the one mind. There is no law outside the mind, no mind outside the law. The mind *is* kami; the law *is* the Way. They are three in one and one in three. Therefore, the Three Regalia signify one mind-heart. That there are three different kinds of regalia under Heaven [in the realm] is because they correspond to the lights in Heaven. The mirror is the sun because of its shape and brilliance; the moon is the jewel because the essence of the moon is Water and jewels originate in Water; and the sword is the stars because the essence of the stars is Metal. The three lights are Heaven; the one to whom the Three Regalia are transmitted is the Son of Heaven. In Confucianism, the three treasures are the Three Virtues (wisdom, humaneness, courage), in Buddhism they are the Three Causes (the Body of the Law, of Observance and of Adaptation).[87]

Most Shinto teachings such as these were for a long time jealously guarded as secret family traditions by the houses that produced them. (It is said that the *Gobusho* could not be read by priests under the age of sixty.) However, the monistic world view they developed found its way in less restricted circles (such as Kitabatake's works), and by the sixteenth century had spread further, until it was popularized in the works of the mid-seventeenth century that we have already analyzed.

A quick sketch of the transmission of these teachings will illustrate this development and show how, toward the end of the sixteenth century, it resulted in a considerable crossover between Shinto and Confucian scholarly houses. Ichijō Kanera (1402–1481) was a courtly scholar who studied the Yoshida interpretations of the *Nihongi*, especially its first two chapters of "the Age of the Gods" as they had been transmitted to his father in 1397,

[86] Kubota, *Shintōshi*, p. 487.
[87] Muraoka, *Nihon shisōshi gaisetsu*, p. 574.

and he worked out his own equivalences between Shinto, Buddhism, and Confucianism. Yoshida Kanetomo (1435–1511) built a new synthesis from the teachings of Ichijō and the Yoshida teachings, and institutionalized Yoshida Shinto (also called Yuiitsu Shinto) throughout the country. His third son, Kiyohara Nobukata (1475–1550) was adopted by the Kiyohara house, one of the traditional scholarly families that provided Confucian (and occasionally a sprinkling of Neo-Confucian) teachings to the imperial and shogunal courts and some shugo houses.[88] One of his son was adopted back into the Yoshida house, and his grandson eventually adopted Fujiwara Seika. Another of Nobukata's sons continued the Kiyohara tradition, his grandson being Kiyohara Hidekata, whom Hayashi Razan first sought as a teacher after having studied under a scholar of the Kiyohara tradition, and with whom he was later allegedly involved in a legal suit. As Imanaka Kanshi has demonstrated, the Kiyohara-Yoshida traditions exercised a profound influence on Razan's thought, especially his Shinto theories.[89]

Three final citations from the *Warongo* will suffice to illustrate how political thought in the mid-seventeenth century, even at the level of popular lore, was governed by the monistic mind philosophy. An oracle by Ube daimyōjin teaches that because the mind of every man is an abode of the gods, the mind becomes kami when it is pure and Buddha when its jihi is profound. Metaphysical pronouncements are attributed not only to gods but also to warriors. For example, to Minamoto Yoshisato is ascribed the following wisdom: "What is called *ri*, principle, is Heaven. People who transgress against ri transgress against Heaven. All those who transgress against Heaven, be they elevated or low, will perish." Toyotomi Hideyoshi summed up his views by declaring: "Tenka, the realm, is not tenka: I am tenka. Kami and Buddha are not kami and Buddha: I am kami and Buddha. Men are not men: I am mankind [lit.: men]. The creation is not the creation [lit.: all things of the world]: I am creation. Japan is not my country, China is not my country: China, India, Japan are all my body. Therefore, if the people of China or Japan are grieved it is as if I am afflicted in my whole body."[90]

[88] Wajima, *Chūsei*, pp. 159, 162–70, 189, 205–10.
[89] Imanaka, *Seikagaku*, pp. 1, 70, 22–23, 193, 271–92.
[90] Katsube, *Warongo*, pp. 23, 154, 153.

GENESIS AMNESIA

Public discourse on society in the mid-seventeenth century was dressed in garments from a rich intellectual wardrobe. Its producers freely appropriated the partial and private products the various traditions (Shinto, Buddhism, and Confucianism) had generated in the limited, circumscribed settings of the scholarly houses of past centuries, adding to these the latest formulations from the continent. This discourse was predominantly a religious one that left little room for straightforward functional discussions unadorned with ethical and religious justifications, as one finds earlier in the *Tako House Code*. Social reality and political truths were dressed in a religious fashion. First the rulers sanctified themselves, then a new breed of schoolmen (mostly defrocked monks) spun a religious discourse over the whole society, glossing over the political divisions in society and effecting a misrecognition of power and domination as virtue.

By highlighting only the organic unity of social and political reality, this monistic discourse left unattended class divisions, partial and conflicting interests, and the arbitrary character of the new power structure. In this way, it considerably reduced, if it did not totally eliminate, the existential status of these realities, because it did not objectify them as items of knowledge. Political reality was made unrecognizable under a blanket of metaphysical truths. The view of man as a self-motivated actor, a view the warlords certainly held ("victory is our business") was buried under a theory of man centered around the empty mind.

The echoes of recent power struggles were still resonating in the private memories of men, yet they found no expression is this new discourse except as illustrations of the evil human desires can bring about. The past had been severed from the present. A social metaphysics and ethics had bracketed history as a closed past quintessentially different from the present regime of virtue. The present was neither indebted nor genealogically linked to the violence of the preceding decades. It is as if in its public knowledge early Tokugawa society made a concerted effort to forget its own genesis.

This "genesis amnesia" was, in part at least, the goal of the rulers themselves, although it was furthered by a new class of intellectuals. The mythologizing strategies of the rulers were undeniably intended to produce such an effect. Even Ieyasu's decision in 1566 to change his family name from Matsudaira to

Tokugawa ("river of virtue") betrayed such an intention. This does not mean, however, that the past was effectively erased from private memories, as the following incident demonstrates.

In 1634 Iemitsu transformed his two-month-long progress to Kyoto into the most dazzling display of Tokugawa political and economic power ever seen. He paraded over 300,000 warriors (equal to the size of Kyoto's population) through the capital. In addition he bestowed a gift of 5,000 kan of silver upon the city, which was distributed among all the households (134 momme, the equivalent of 3 koku of rice, per household; before setting out on his journey for Kyoto, he had distributed 20,000 kan to the people of Edo). Yet, on this most blinding of occasions, some Kyotoites, sixty-eight years after Ieyasu had changed his family name to Tokugawa, scornfully referred to Iemitsu as the third Matsudaira shogun (*Matsudaira sandaime no shogunsama*).[91]

All these official symbolic manipulations could obviously not prevent some individuals from privately demystifying the present by refusing to forget the past. Tokugawa power could prevent them, however, from doing so in public. Thus, documents and writings related to the rise of the Tokugawa house were declared secret and could not be circulated.[92] It is also significant that private histories presenting the recent past as epic power struggles were printed only after they were rewritten by Confucian scholars who framed history as a natural process in which victory went to the virtuous and defeat to the evil. Nevertheless, the Tokugawa were not much interested in producing a history, even one that flattered them. The Hayashi scholars who in the 1660s and 1670s wrote a history that had been commissioned by the bakufu had to fight a lack of enthusiasm among the bakufu to see the project through to the end. Moreover, they were well aware of the existence of certain issues that could not be discussed openly. These taboo subjects were those that had a direct bearing on the legitimacy of the public authority the Tokugawa house had arrogated for itself—the legitimacy of the imperial line and bakufu-court relations.

The obliteration of certain aspects of the past was thus con-

---

[91] Asao, *Sakoku*, p. 184.

[92] Ozawa Eiichi, *Kinsei shigaku*, p. 215. The *Mikawa monogatari* (Tale of Mikawa), for instance, contains many details about the Tokugawa's rise to power. Yet it was never meant to leave the Ōkubo house, a vassal house, where it was written (*ibid.*, p. 58). Toward the end of the seventeenth century, however, many manuscript copies of the text were circulating, although the work was never printed during the Tokugawa period.

sciously pursued by the new rulers. In this effort they were assisted by a number of new intellectuals who filled the remaining space of what could be said with a religio-ethical discourse that by its very nature was synchronic. Although these scholars were not told by the bakufu to produce an ideology, they in fact provided the new ruling class with a discourse that served its interests perfectly because it hid them from public objectification. The discourse that was thus constructed was a ruling discourse in the double sense of that term: it provided significations that helped the rulers to rule, and it became the predominant discourse in seventeenth-century Japan.

Four. Disseminators of Ruling Ideas: Monks, Laws, Bestsellers

The ideas of the ruling class are in every epoch the ruling ideas, i.e. the class which is the ruling *material* force of society, is at the same time its ruling *intellectual* force.—*Karl Marx*[1]

Past discussions of early Tokugawa ideology have always been bound by a functionalist concept of ideology that is far too narrow and circumscribed. The bakufu was assumed to have been the conscious initiator of this ideology that was identified with Neo-Confucianism. With this interpretation, traditional historiography—sometimes unwittingly—subscribed to a crude Marxist view of ideology (crude because it grossly oversimplifies Karl Marx's views). A complex historical process was forced into a formula that assumed two clear identities: a purposeful producer and a ready-made product.

The previous chapters have modified that picture. The highest bakufu leadership did not commission an ideology, and was rather indifferent to Neo-Confucianism. Thus the "purposeful producer" of the usual formula has to be qualified or dropped altogether, in relation to the bakufu. We also know that the product was not Neo-Confucianism pure and simple. Yet there was a product; by the mid-seventeenth century we are confronted with a sprawling socio-political discourse that was supportive of the new system of domination—a discourse that looked very much like a made-to-order ideology.

We have not yet investigated the full expanse of this discourse, and have only begun to look at the relations between the producers of this discourse and the new ruling class. This chapter takes the investigation further in these two directions.

Concerning the second question (the relations of ideological production), it should first be pointed out that Marx does not speak of intentions or purposes on the part of the ruling class. On the contrary, he holds that, although ideology serves the ruling class, this is not a simple matter that is obvious to anyone, *especially*

---

[1] Karl Marx and Frederick Engels, *The German Ideology, Part One*, edited by C. J. Arthur (New York: International Publishers, 1976), p. 64 (original emphasis).

to its own members. Marx merely says that the ruling class also exhibits the characteristics of a ruling intellectual force. The relations of production between the ruling class and ruling ideas are by no means simple and direct; they are mediated in sometimes complex and multiple ways. (Gramsci and even Engels have also stressed this point.)

We do not pretend here to unravel in their totality such mediations, but only to illustrate how ideas that served the rulers were formulated in various quarters and disseminated from several points in different directions. The doctrinal picture, already diversified in the previous chapters, will be further differentiated in some surprising ways.

First, we will consider a source that might be expected to be purely Neo-Confucian, namely, the writings of Fujiwara Seika (the "founder" of Tokugawa Neo-Confucianism); they reveal an undeniable Buddhist slant. In addition, Seika kept himself at a considerable distance from the bakufu. I shall argue, however, that these qualifications of his teachings and his career do not nullify Seika's political significance. His ideological contributions, although not as direct as one might think, are nevertheless real.

Second, although Buddhism itself is usually dismissed as irrelevant to the ideological creativity of this period, we shall see that Suzuki Shōsan's activity belies such a judgment. He mined Zen Buddhism to construct a powerful ethic that was perfectly tailored to the bakufu's political needs. Moreover, Shōsan claimed that his teachings were more timely and appropriate than what the Confucians were proposing.

That there was some truth to this claim becomes clear when one juxtaposes Shōsan's ethics with the Tokugawa agricultural laws that were issued during the time that Shōsan was preaching. This legislation was the first in Japan to define in very specific ways what was expected of the peasants. Detailed prescriptions tightly structured peasant life. They defined the boundaries and structure of the local community and the nature and timing of work to be performed within it. Shōsan's teachings aimed at nothing less than making these structures function as effectively as possible by creating dynamic subjects whose minds and efforts were totally geared to perform their assigned tasks.

Finally, the reader may have the impression that where others have seen nothing but Neo-Confucianism, I have found only its absence. As far as the bakufu is concerned, this is by and large

correct. It should be recalled, however, that Neo-Confucianism
was knocking at its doors through scholars like Yamaga Sokō and
Kumazawa Banzan and the ambitions (and school) of Hayashi
Razan. We can illustrate this trend further by examining a popular
tale, the *Kiyomizu monogatari* (Tale of Kiyomizu). This work, published in 1638 and again in 1645, presents a self-conscious and
aggressive defense of Neo-Confucianism. Moreover, it was a
"bestseller" that sold between two and three thousand copies
within a five-year span. Its "popularity" testifies to the strength
Neo-Confucian discourse was gathering, even while the bakufu
remained indifferent.

The disparate material brought together in this chapter draws
attention, therefore, to means of ideological dissemination that
have heretofore been ignored (Buddhist writings, agricultural legislation, popular works). It further argues that certain well-known
ideological linkages (between Seika, the bakufu, and Neo-
Confucianism) need to be redefined.

FUJIWARA SEIKA: LOFTY SPIRITUALITY

Fujiwara Seika, as we already know, was given by Razan an
emblematic significance through his overlapping roles of occasional advisor to Ieyasu, mentor to Razan himself, and founder of a
Neo-Confucianism that was clearly distinct from Buddhist and
old-Confucian textual interpretations.[2] This picture of Seika,
which served the political aims of the Hayashi house well, requires
reexamination.

Seika was a familiar figure to Ieyasu and other powerful daimyo
both before and after 1600, but his relationship to the new warrior
power was ambiguous. Seika, born in Harima province west of
Himeji, had moved to Kyoto, where he became an important
member of the old elite whose cultural stock the daimyo drew
upon. He was a scion of the Reizei noble family that specialized in
court poetry. The prestigious Yoshida Shinto house had adopted
him. In the Buddhist hierarchy he held the office of Chief Seat
(*shuso*) at the Rinzai Sōkoku temple, a second-rank Gozan
temple—an office that ranked just below that of abbot. As *shuso*
Seika participated in 1591 at a poetry party sponsored by the new
kanpaku Toyotomi Hidetsugu, then Hideyoshi's designated heir.
Two years later he served in Nagoya, Kyūshū, at Hideyoshi's

[2] See above, pp. 78–79.

military base for his Korean campaign, as *otogishū*—a post he had obtained through family connections—to another adopted son of Hideyoshi, (Toyotomi) Kobayakawa Hideaki (1582–1602). There he met Ieyasu for the first time. This meeting led to an invitation to Edo for a lecture on the *Chen-kuan cheng-yao* (Jp *Jōgan seiyō*, The essentials of government of the Chen-kuan [627–649] period).[3] Seika's oldest and closest tie to warrior society, however, goes back much earlier, to around 1580, when he was twenty. Through his uncle he then befriended the daimyo Akamatsu Hiromichi (1562–1600), who was Seika's age and like him from the province of Harima. Hiromichi's enthusiasm for things Chinese and Korean crossed the line into exoticism, for it extended beyond an interest in learning into matters of dress, food, and even mourning rituals.[4]

These connections gave Seika ample opportunities to feed his growing appetite for Chinese culture. In 1590 he was able to meet the envoys from Korea, with whom he communicated in writing. In 1593 he managed an audience with the Ming ambassadors. Three years later, Seika even made an attempt to sail to China, a trip that failed because of a storm. Around this time, probably in 1598, he left the Buddhist order to pursue his new interests full time. From the fall of that year until the spring of 1600, he had the unique opportunity of working closely with the Korean scholar Kang Hang, a war prisoner entrusted to the custody of his friend Akamatsu Hiromichi. Together they edited and punctuated the classics according to Neo-Confucian principles.[5] It was from this intense immersion in Chinese learning with a Neo-Confucian scholar, within the sinified setting of his patron's mansion at Fushimi, that Seika emerged to appear before Ieyasu in the fall of 1600 dressed in the garb of a Confucian literatus. For Seika, who no longer held a high clerical post, this dress was the only way he could express, on such a formal occasion, his identity as a man of learning whom Ieyasu might want to hire.

Seika's disaffection with Buddhism must have been a long process. Unlike Razan, who spent only two years in training

[3] Razan, *Seika sensei gyōjō*, NST 28: 189; Imanaka, *Seikagaku*, pp. 24–27, 107–108. The *Chen-kuang cheng-yao* was not a Neo-Confucian work, as David A. Dilworth seems to suggest (de Bary and Bloom, *Principle*, p. 477). Emperors and shoguns had heard lectures on it on many occasions in the past, for instance in 1317, 1359, 1401, 1503 (see Wajima, *Chūsei*, pp. 74, 99, 171, 184).

[4] Imanaka, *Seikagaku*, pp. 28–32.

[5] Abe Yoshio, *Chōsen*, pp. 42–77.

(1595–1597), Seika was an accomplished monk. He was in the monastery for about thirty years (from 1568, age seven, until around 1598, age thirty-seven). For quite a number of years he held the second highest office (*shuso*) in a Gozan monastery, which made him eligible to become abbot. Chief Seat office holders functioned as the principal monks and mediation leaders in the monastery hall. They were usually experienced monks who had spent ten or more years under monastic discipline and were thus capable of guiding others in all aspects of the monastic life.[6] These thirty years of monastic experience profoundly affected Seika's approach to "Chinese Learning."

Within this new field, Seika was able to pursue his old ideals and continue in a direction that he had maintained in spite of his break with Buddhism. The spiritualistic and compassionate outlook Seika maintained was at odds with the charged world of power that whirled about him. The distance Seika kept from this world was informed by his idealism and reinforced by a disdain for the warrior class that he shared with the old Kyoto elite. This world-weariness and class prejudice were further rooted in two tragic encounters with the violence of warrior power. At age seventeen, his father and elder brother were killed in a military conflict that also destroyed the family estate. In 1600 (on 10/28), less than a month after Seika's audience with Ieyasu, his longtime friend, patron, and intellectual companion Akamatsu Hiromichi committed suicide on Ieyasu's order for his role in the battle of Sekigahara. In Seika's eyes, Hiromichi was "without sin" (*tsuminaku*).[7]

Occasionally Seika expressed contempt for upstart warlords: he spoke of Hideyoshi as "only an ordinary man from a small province."[8] He showed his disdain in other ways, as well. He did not enter Ieyasu's service in 1600, and twelve years later refused to participate in a political discussion on loyalty and power because it would have provided Ieyasu a justification for eliminating Toyotomi Hideyori.[9] Equally significant is that after 1600 Seika

[6] Collcutt, *Five Mountains*, pp. 229, 238.

[7] SGT 13: 132.

[8] Kinugasa, "Hōken shisō no kakuritsu," p. 273.

[9] Hori, *Razan*, pp. 159–64. Tetsuo Najita, (*Japan*, Prentice Hall, 1974, pp. 18–19) is incorrect on two points concerning this discussion. First, the discussion took place with Razan and not with Seika (who, it is said, refused to get drawn into such discussion). Second, a more plausible and immediate context for these discussions in 1612 is not the issue of general principles of governance, but how to reconcile Ieyasu's obligation of loyalty to Hideyori with his decision to get rid of him—an issue of "regicide" that Ieyasu had to confront before his Osaka campaigns. This explains Seika's refusal to respond.

led a rather simple life that was not without hardship and a degree of isolation. In 1615, he retired as a semi-recluse to a cottage in the hills north of Kyoto where, supported by some friends and disciples, he engaged in cultural pursuits.[10]

In his first and very formal letter to Razan, dated 1604/3/12, explaining the reasons for his isolation, Seika expresses his disillusionment with a world filled with unprincipled but thriving compromisers:

The world is in decline and customs are loose. Things are not discussed publicly, yet one hears a clattering of tongues: elevated men speak in lofty abstractions, lower ones plunge into profit seeking. [All around one finds] laxity, flattery, and compromises with the world: in social intercourse, people [following their drives] seek what feels warm, shun what is cold. Truth in the morning [turns into] falsehood at night. In extreme cases, if people like something, they pursue it uncompromisingly and do not even notice the blood from the stabs [they give each other] in the back.[11]

In his *Suntetsu roku* (A record of pithy sayings), written in 1606, Seika inveighs against fake virtuous men *kyōgen*) whom people seem to praise and strive to emulate: they are men who "rely on their wits or talents or on their gifts for sophistry. They all have hidden designs. . . . Small people are mistakenly being taken for wise men." [12] According to Razan, Seika told him when they first met in the fall of 1604 how he regretted "not having been born in China or in some past age in Japan rather than in this age that did not suit him; but then, Seika surmised, Confucius was not born in Yao and Shun's time but during the Spring and Autumn Period, a time of military upheaval; and Mencius was no contemporary of Kings Wen and Wu but lived during the Warring States period. If one strives after the Way, he concluded, the time in which one is born does not matter." [13]

Seika's general approach to the recorded wisdom of China was conditioned by this principled stance toward the world of power that was being forged around him, and by a fundamental predilection for matters spiritual and ethical. Chinese learning therefore provided Seika with a vast body of knowledge with which to satisfy his ecumenical intellectual inclinations, which were not hemmed

[10] Imanaka, *Seikagaku*, pp. 93–95.
[11] NST 28: 96; SGT 13: 83.
[12] NST 28: 27, 33. *Kyōgen* (Ch *hsiang-yüan*) are referred to in the *Analects* 17: 13, and *Mencius* 7B: 37: 8–13. In 1611, Razan admits to Seika that he himself felt like a *kyōgen* (see p. 74).
[13] *Ibid.*, p. 198.

in by scholastic or doctrinal partitions. In his correspondence, for instance, he constantly argues with Razan who, from the very first time he sought contact with Seika, showed a high concern for such partitions. Like a new student eager to impress his teacher with his knowledge, Razan expounded the irreconcilable differences between Buddhism and Neo-Confucianism, and between pre-Sung Confucianism and Neo-Confucianism. He further emphasized the need to separate clearly Chu Hsi orthodoxy from the idealistic school of Lu Hsiang-shan and Wang Yang-ming, which, according to Razan, Seika favored too much.[14]

Rather than stress the differences within the overall tradition, Seika held that one should focus on the sameness underlying the differences. What all scholars in the Confucian tradition shared Seika argued, was first, praise for the sage kings Yao and Shun and condemnation of the evil kings Chieh and Chou; second, veneration of Confucius and Mencius and rejection of Taoism and Buddhism; and third, the belief that Heaven's principles are what constitute the public realm as against the private realm of human desires.[15] There is an explanation, Seika continues, for the differences that

do not offer as stark a contrast as day and night, and are not limited to the texts you [Razan] cite. Various interpretations are rooted in something close to the temperaments of the philosophers in question. These are then formulated in a number of key terms that provide one with different entries [into the same teachings of the Sages]. Such are, for instance, the terms "reverence" (*kei*; Ch *ching*) for the Ch'eng brothers, Chu His's "probing of principle" (*kyūri*; Ch *ch'iung-li*), Lu Hsiang-shan's "natural enlightenment" (*ikan*; Ch *i-chien*), and Wang Yang-ming's "innate knowledge of goodness" (*ryōchi*; Ch *liang-chih*).[16]

Seika teaches his eager student a lesson by telling him that there are many more differences than he, Razan, may know of, but that they are ultimately irrelevant. According to Seika, one ought not to just read books all day long but immerse oneself in the teachings, experience them, marinate, so to speak, one's mind and body in them (Seika uses the image of wet penetration and fattened meat). That is what scholars do: "they learn by straightening their mind and experiencing [the truth] personally in themselves; with a mind stilled and fully at ease they will be suddenly and totally suffused

[14] SGT 13: 85–86, 99, 108, 123.
[15] *ibid.*, pp. 86, 99.
[16] SGT 13: 90; see for an almost identical statement, NST 28: 204.

[by the realization of the truth]; then their eyes and ears will no longer know either sameness or difference, for they will have acquired a knowledge that will last." [17]

For Seika the assimilation of the teachings of the Sages was a religious, holistic experience of truth. Seika urged Razan to approach the classics with such an attitude: "the classics and one's mind should interpenetrate one another." Even a closing epistolary formula "to take care of your health in this winter cold" turns into an occasion for telling Razan "your body is not a private thing; one, you received it from your parents and two, it is the place where the Way resides." [18]

The great importance of inner experience for Seika made him an enthusiast for certain Chinese scholars who also stressed the spiritual and experiential side of Neo-Confucianism. [19] Having discovered the *Dialogues with Yen-p'ing* (*Yen-p'ing ta-wen*, one of Chu Hsi's last works; Yen-p'ing is Li T'ung, Chu Hsi's teacher), Seika urged Razan to expose himself totally to inner enlightenment and attain *sharaku* (*Ch sa-lo*) or "untrammeled spontaneity," which would "not only give happiness to you, but to me also, and to all people, the whole country, nay the whole world." Seika acknowledged that the inner harmony of a subconscious state of mind that one reached through quiet sitting (*seiza mihatsu no chū*), Li T'ung's prescribed method, was dangerously close to Buddhist enlightenment, and that one therefore had to heed the warnings of Confucian scholars, but he wondered nevertheless "whether *sharaku* was not to be found if one persisted in the practice of [Ch'eng Hao's] 'sincerity and reverence.' " *Sharaku* is also present, Seika writes, in Wang Yang-ming's poems. [20]

Li T'ung, Ch'eng Hao, Wang Yang-ming, "untrammeled spontaneity," "personal experience," "harmony of the subconscious mind," "quiet sitting": Seika clearly identified himself with what is usually referred to as the idealistic interpreters of the Neo-Confucian "Mind-and-Heart Learning." [21] To these should be

[17] SGT 13: 86, 91.

[18] NST 28: 199; SGT 13: 122.

[19] De Bary and Bloom, *Principle*, pp. 131–32.

[20] SGT 13: 98, 110. On *sharaku* in Seika's thought and in later popular Tokugawa culture, see Abe Yoshio, " 'Sharaku' dangi."

[21] To refer to these interpreters as a school would be incorrect insofar as there was no institution of learning, persisting over time, where these scholars studied or taught. Yet, as de Bary demonstrates (*Orthodoxy*; see also de Bary and Bloom, *Principle*, pp. 16–17), even the teachings of Wang Yang-ming, who claimed to be orthodox although his claims never received official sanction, are a direct outgrowth of this Learning of the Mind-and-Heart.

added the Korean scholar Yi T'oegye and especially Lin Chao'en
(1517–1598), a Ming contemporary of Seika whom Judith A.
Berling judges to have "developed more than any thinker to date
the religious dimensions of Neo-Confucianism."[22]

Chao-en's teachings were dear to Seika, Razan writes. Seika
even adopted for himself a name that referred to Chao-en's teachings on "stilling in the back," a meditative method to achieve the
sagelike harmony and stillness of mind.[23] Chao-en epitomizes the
late Ming ecumenical approach to tradition. He founded a cult
that systematically combined Taoism, Buddhism, and Neo-
Confucianism into a synthesis informed by Neo-Confucian categories of mind and mind-cultivation that had been most developed
in the idealistic School of the Mind, including Wang Yang-ming.
For Chao-en (as for Seika) the individual thinkers were less important in their differences than in the practical guidance they
provided for realizing the ideal of sagehood in oneself. Chao-en
also maintained that the Buddhist Teachings are to be found in the
world, not separate from it, but only if one is in the world as if not of
the world: an inner-worldly ethical goal that must have greatly
attracted Seika, since it rejected the Buddhist monastic requirements without giving up the ideal of enlightenment.[24]

Seika's thought on civic ethics is preserved in two short works,
the *Suntetsu roku*, written in 1606, and the *Daigaku yōryaku* (Epitome
of the *Great Learning*) written in 1619 not long before he died.[25]
Seika produced both works on invitation from daimyo. The
former, consisting of comments on thirty-two sayings gleaned from
the classics, was composed for Asano Yoshinaga, daimyo of a
376,000-koku domain in Wakayama, where Seika spent his win-
ters after 1606. The latter, very heavily indebted to Chao-en's *Ssu-
shu paio-che cheng-i* (Correct interpretation of the Four Books by
topic), was based on lectures he gave in 1619/5 to Hosokawa
Tadatoshi (soon to be daimyo of the Kokura domain in Kyūshū
and later daimyo of Kumamoto, 540,000 koku) and Yoshinaga's

---

[22] Abe Yoshio, *Chōsen*, pp. 104–105; de Bary and Bloom, *Principle*, p. 132; Berling, *Lin Chao-en*, p. 236.

[23] Razan, *Seika sensei gyōjō*, NST 28: 195–96. This name was written with the characters for *kitaniku yamabito* (North-flesh mountain hermit), and refers to Chao-en's *Hsin-sheng chih-chih* (Direct pointing to the mind as sage), written in 1564, where it is explained that the character for back (of "stilling in the back") is composed of the characters for north and flesh. See Berling, *Lin Chao-en*, pp. 116, 146.

[24] Mano, "Rin Chōon," pp. 25, 28, 30; Berling, *Lin Chao-en*, ch. 5.

[25] NST 28: 10–39 and 42–78. Page references in the text are to this edition.

younger brother Asano Nagashige, a retainer of Tokugawa Hidetada.[26] These two friends were in Kyoto on the occasion of the shogunal progress to the capital, and Nagashige seems to have brought Tadatoshi along when he went to visit Seika.[27]

In *Suntetsu roku*, Seika spells out general Confucian ideas. He starts out concretely with discussions on topics such as the gradation to be applied in punishments, the need to accompany knowledge with action, and the need to instruct the four classes of people lest they revert to animalism (10–12). Seika defines man as a hierarchical being (*hito to wa ... kurai aru mono nari*), from which follow warnings against faction-building for private purposes (12). Seika draws a clear distinction between the gentleman who observes the principles of the Way (*dōri*) and produces peace and harmony because he is motivated by the public-spiritedness of duty (*giri no ōyake*), and the small man who turns his back on principles and congregates with people out of self-interest because he is driven by a private desire for profit (26). Government thus means, as the root of the Chinese character with which it is written indicates, to correct people—an operation that starts with oneself and expands outward (29). There is no difference between the principles governing oneself and the world beyond oneself, between inner and outer. Rites are not simply rules of etiquette: they are norms of Heavenly Principle (32).

Seika gradually leads his reader, Lord Asano, up to the kernel of Neo-Confucian teachings by saving for the end comments on a text from the *Doctrine of the Mean* and another one from the *Great Learning*.[28] They posit the central importance of character cultivation for the ruler, and urge, for the production of wealth, activity in the producers and frugality in the consumers.

In his later work on the key Neo-Confucian text of the *Great Learning*, Seika follows Chao-en's lead very closely. He pushes the inner-directedness of this text even further than had Chu Hsi's commentaries. The *Great Learning*, Seika begins, abolishes the distinction between oneself and others because a) "illuminating illustrious virtue" consists of b) "nurturing the people"; and between inner and outer because c) "resting in the highest excellence"

[26] Kanaya, "Seika no Jugaku shisō," NST 28: 456.

[27] Razan, *Seika sensei gyōjō*, NST 28: 195–96.

[28] Pp. 32–38. For the texts, see *The Doctrine of the Mean*, 20: 12, and *The Great Learning*, Commentary, 10: 19.

consists of a and b (51–52). Seika stresses that these three categories are not a matter of progressive functional learning, but express essences. Illustrious virtue is not achieved; it is inborn in the form of the Five Relationships (45, 47, 55); these secure the order of the realm and hence are also called "order/submission virtues" (*juntoku*) (46). The "resting" of the mind refers to a mind ruled by reverence; "supreme excellence" refers to the penetrating non-manifest state of total excellence, the sudden and total penetration of harmony. This state, c, is the source of all action, the essence from which the functions of a and b will follow (51–52).

Peace and stillness of mind have to be such that they can maintain themselves in any active, worldly setting: at the court, in military affairs, or in the mountains—Loyola's ideal of being *contemplativus in actione*. This mental freedom consists of the absence of all differentiating thought. The "things" in the phrase "investigation of things" refer to things of desire; hence the whole phrase stands for the acquisition of the correct, innate knowledge of the mind (43, 54). This knowledge is present from the beginning and cannot be tapped or activated from the outside: anything outer is a speck of defilement producing thoughts that are not born by themselves, naturally, from the harmonious, still, undifferentiated void of the highest excellence. Hence the traditional "things" of the "investigation of things" have to be avoided: they are the dust that clouds the mind's mirror and have to be "removed" (not "investigated") (55). The prethought state of mind is thus pure excellence (57). One has to watch the purity of one's mind not every day or every hour but every split second (60–61). This is best achieved by "abiding in reverence," which means "always abiding in quiet, enlightened stillness" (*seisei*, the character with which Seika's name is written), which is the prime virtue of the minister toward his lord (62). Rulers should rest in humaneness (jin) that will emanate over the whole country; otherwise the result will be military and moral chaos (56–57, 67, 70). Profit and profit-seeking are the beginning of chaos (47, 67, 71), the opposite of duty, and therefore constitute the wrong drive for government—although to seek profit not for oneself but for the realm is not reprehensible (76). On a more practical level, the people need teachings and nurturing, but if the teachings are not obeyed one should resort to punishments (*kei*) and military force (*hei*): the occupations of the four classes of people should be useful (42) and there should be no idle people (*yūmin*) outside the four classes; moreover, the diligence of the peasants should result in a long-term improvement of the fields (75).

Seika's Neo-Confucianism was clearly not simply Chu Hsi thought. He relied very heavily on the particular way in which the Teachings of the Mind-and-Heart and Chao-en had further elaborated the tradition in a spiritualistic direction—a tendency that Seika pushed even further. Moreover, within his idealism Seika had room for military coercive power if the teachings should prove to be ineffective.

Besides the two texts discussed above, there exists another intriguing statement by Seika on the relationship between Confucianism and Shinto. The occasion was an epitaph Asano Yoshinaga commissioned in 1606 for the dedication of a new shrine to Sugawara Michizane. In this formal document, Seika writes:

Today's shrines to the gods are the Confucian shrines of other days [past]; today, domain rule (*kokusei*) is the government of the realm (*tenka no seiji*) of other days [past]. The Way of the Teachings of the Gods is the Way of the Former Sages. The teachings one wants are the Teachings of the Former Sages. Fortunately, in the past the gods have submitted to that Way and have continued to do so until today, but while these teachings were held in the dark [in the past], today they have become manifest. In this, the gods have proven themselves to be [truly] gods.... Sincere reverence for the gods in reality comes from the Teachings of the Sages.[29]

Seika's "political thought" is a very ethereal construct. It is not that Seika deals with cosmological questions like the *ri-ki* problem. Rather he upholds a lofty spiritual ideal that is essentially monastic and ascetic, although the world and not the monastery is where this ideal is to be realized. This worldly setting notwithstanding, Seika is more preoccupied with the personal attainment of sagehood than with the political reality of early seventeenth-century Japan. The understanding is, of course, that once this ideal is realized, the country will be well governed. Beyond this, Seika seems largely uninterested in the workings of society. Whether one has to ascribe this spiritual proclivity to his long Zen training, to his reading of Wang Yang-ming, or to his enthusiasm for Lin Chao-en's writings is ultimately irrelevant. It is clear that his vision of man was heavily slanted toward the School of the Mind—so much so that some scholars even hold Seika's influence upon Razan responsible for

[29] SGT 13: 63 and 64.

the latter's confusion until the mid-1620s concerning the distinction between Wang Yang-ming's and Chu Hsi's teachings about the relationship of *ri* and *ki* (principle and ether).[30] The few times that Seika concretely touches upon problems of governance, his advice to the daimyo holds nothing new. Other than a general admonition to nurture the people, he urges the application of punishment and military force if they do not obey; he also supports productive employment for all classes. Moreover, it is noteworthy that, if the occasion demanded, Seika could point out Shinto's political potential for instilling, along the same lines as Confucianism, civic values conducive to the maintenance of a hierarchical society.

Seika's contribution to a bakufu ideology in the strict sense of the word was thus very limited. His withdrawal from society, both socially and intellectually, started from around the time Ieyasu came to power. Nevertheless, his lofty but sincere spirituality, his ambivalence toward the world of power, and his small production of "ideological" works notwithstanding, it is not difficult to perceive that Seika played an important function in giving a spiritual orientation to the construction of an early Tokugawa discourse on society.

No longer a prelate, and neither a courtier nor a member of the new ruling class, Seika occupied a marginal place in society that became typical of later Confucian teachers. Yet he was held in high esteem for his learning and his spiritual achievements. Later in his career, Seika's circle of friends, students, and acquaintances included people from various walks of life. There are literateurs such as Matsunaga Teitoku and Shōsan, father and son; patrons of the arts (Suminokura Soan, who helped finance Ieyasu's Osaka campaigns and a construction project at Edo castle, had an atelier-salon-cum-library in Kyoto and was close to the artist Hon'ami Kōetsu, whose works he published); and doctors (the several doctors in bakufu employ including Ieyasu's physician, and Hori Kyōan, a Confucian scholar-doctor who later served in Owari). There were also Confucian *érudits*: Nawa Katsusho, who later did work for the bakufu and the lord of Kii; Miyake Kisai, who had connections at the court and also spent some time in the domains of Tsu and Fukuoka. From the warrior class there were ex-daimyo (Kinoshita Chōshōshi), daimyo (Katō Kiyomasa—a hero of the

---

[30] Ishida, "Zenki bakuhan taisei no ideorogii," NST 28: 422–24.

Korean campaigns—Asano Yoshinaga, and Hosokawa Tadatoshi), and retainers (Asano Nagashige and Naoe Kanetsugu, who wrote a manual for peasants).[31]

Insofar as elite members of the new ruling class sought Seika out and enhanced their public image by associating with him; and insofar as Seika's advice to these new power holders, whose problems were political, addressed solipsistic spiritual questions that had as their sole social dimension an assumed emanation of exemplary virtue, Seika showed a way to obfuscate the reality of political domination by means of an ethico-metaphysical discourse. Seika's career itself pointed to a rich source for such constructs: Neo-Confucianism. Unwittingly perhaps, the recluse played an important political role. The publication of his *Daigaku yōryaku* in 1630 is a further indication of the timeliness of such discourse.

SUZUKI SHŌSAN: DEFENDING THE TOKUGAWA BY SWORD AND WORD

Although one can detect strong Buddhist overtones in Seika's thought, it can be argued that they were no different from those to be found in the Teachings of the Mind-and-Heart within the Neo-Confucian tradition. Suzuki Shōsan presents a totally different case. He was a Buddhist monk who consciously constructed a Buddhist ethic that he maintained was more effective than Confucian teachings.

Students of Suzuki Shōsan often characterize his thought as "feudal" and supportive of the bakufu system. Shōsan's originality, they say, consisted in the new ethics he formulated to meet the demands of the new political regime. Discussions of Tokugawa political thought never even mention his name, however. The reason for this lacuna is simple: Tokugawa thought has always been identified with Neo-Confucian teachings propagated by a new brand of secular intellectuals in bakufu or daimyo employ, who belonged to one school or another of Chinese learning. Suzuki Shōsan remained outside a territory thus defined. He was a Buddhist monk, and his audience consisted exclusively of commoners and lower samurai. His intellectual genealogy is, however, far from clear. As we shall see, even his precise affiliation with a

---

[31] *Fujiwara Seika shū* 1: 14–22. Naoe's manual will be discussed later in this chapter.

Buddhist sect is still in dispute. Moreover, not all scholars agree that Shōsan's thought is best typified as "feudal." Some admire the "modern" character of his teachings.[32]

To start with the last point, Shōsan propagated for men and women of all walks of life an ethic that was tied to the particular conditions of their occupations in society, and assured them salvation outside the framework of any Buddhist institution. This inner-wordly asceticism could not avoid comparison to the "calling" of the Protestant Ethic, and hence interpretation as "modern."[33] The Weberian framework, however, rests on an evolutionary scheme for the development (rationalization) of religious thought. From today's perspective, Shōsan's formulations certainly seem remarkably "rational": they deny the need for ritual or institutional links to attain salvation, and stress instead the importance of inner-motivated performance of one's quotidian work, thus transformed into religious activity. Whether this constitutes a lasting "breakthrough" is debatable, however, since Shōsan's teachings were not institutionalized in a movement or school. Moreover, if one approaches Shōsan not in an evolutionary or comparative perspective, but examines his teachings in their contemporary setting, their political thrust is unambiguous: they enjoined commoners in a most urgent way—namely, a religious one—to take their assigned place in the new social and political arrangements of early seventeenth-century Japan.

Shōsan's career provides an interesting insight into the unexpected ways supporters of the bakufu put their intellectual and persuasive skills to work in order to secure stability for the Tokugawa power structure. Shōsan was a samurai who in middle age turned from the sword to the word to help consolidate the new warrior power. In this respect, the course of his life is analogous to the process of ideological formation, if one conceives of ideology as a continuation of warfare but with other means.[34] Ideas, as Oda Nobunaga had come to understand in his wars against the Ikkō-

[32] The modernist view was first expressed by Nakamura Hajime in 1949 in his *Kinsei Nihon no hihanteki seishin* (The critical spirit in early modern Japan) (pp. 1–243); in English, see his "Suzuki Shōsan, 1579–1655." The feudal interpretation has been supported by, among others, Ienaga Saburō and Kashiwahara Yūsen. For a complete bibliography, see notes 5–7, pp. 2–3, of Aomori, "Shōsan."

[33] However, Shōsan escaped Robert Bellah's attention and is not mentioned in his *Tokugawa Religion*.

[34] Michel Foucault speaks of power as a continuation of war with other means: *Power/Knowledge*, p. 90.

ikki, are both a means of warfare and a field of battle. To keep the interests of the peasants subordinated to the interests of the new rulers, the effort to make the "ideas of the ruling class the ruling ideas" had to be successful.

Shōsan's life (1579–1655) coincided almost exactly with Razan's: four years older than Razan, he died two years earlier. He was born into a samurai family that lived on the land in the Asuke fief of Ieyasu's domain.[35] When the fief was abolished, Shōsan was the first member of his family to join the band of Ieyasu's immediate retainers. He served as guard (*kinban*) in Sunpu, became a member of the elite Great Guard (*ōban*) in Edo after Ieyasu's death, and in 1619 performed guard duty at Osaka castle. One year later he (and his son) quite suddenly took tonsure and returned to the old family fief which had meanwhile been restored. He remained there almost uninterruptedly for the next twenty-eight years, but spent his last seven years again exclusively in Edo.

The Asuke domain was a political anomaly in those days. The entrenched power of samurai-on-the-land was still great there. It was a place where the separation between peasants and samurai had not yet been enforced. There Shōsan served in the clan temples of the Suzuki and other related families. In the 1630s the bakufu increased its efforts to reduce the independent power of local fief holders in its own territories. Shōsan became involved in that policy. Gradually he revived his ties with the bakufu through his younger brother Shigenari (1587–1653), who had become a bakufu district intendant (*daikan*). Shōsan was put in charge of the Onshinji temple, which was restored by Shigenari in 1632. The temple was an important symbol of bakufu presence in the domain. It had been built by Iemitsu with funds left by Hidetada, and housed memorial tablets of Tōshōgū (Ieyasu) and Taitokuin (Hidetada). Aomori Tōru seems to suggest that in Asuke, daikan efforts to increase control over local samurai were pursued partly through the revitalization of temples (run by Shōsan), even though the bakufu had issued a general prohibition against temple building.[36] There is no doubt, however, that a similar strategy was followed in Amakusa after the Shimabara rebellion of 1637–1638.

Shigenari, who had distinguished himself in quelling the rebellion, was entrusted with the military control of the Amakusa district and became its first intendant when the region became

---

[35] For the data on Shōsan's life, I have relied on Aomori, "Shōsan," pp. 3–18.

[36] *Ibid.*, pp. 7, 12.

bakufu territory in 1641. His task was to restore agricultural tax production in the area, devastated by famine and war, and to secure a lasting "pacification." He achieved these goals through an *ōjōya* village structure to control local headmen, compulsory population transfers from other parts of Kyūshū, and a temple policy for which he enrolled the services of his brother Shōsan for a period of three years (1641–1644).

Shōsan used 300 koku provided by the bakufu to build a network of thirty-two temple-chapels that were incorporated into the network of the domain temples.[37] The center of this network was a Pure Land temple where memorial tablets to Ieyasu and Hidetada were enshrined. (The Tokugawa family was affiliated with the Pure Land Sect.) The other temples were all Sōtō Zen, the sect with which the Suzuki family was affiliated. In all thirty-two temples a copy of Shōsan's *Ha Kirishitan* (Christians countered) was deposited.[38] These temples also seem to have been centers where the population was subjected to *fumie* tests.[39] Shōsan's assignment to root out Christianity was an ideological one, but as we shall see, his polemical refutation of Christianity was only a small part of the way in which he served the bakufu. In 1653 Shigenari clashed with his superiors over their refusal to alleviate the tax burden of the peasants, and he committed suicide, for which he was deified in a Suzuki shrine in Amakusa that honored him (as it later honored Shōsan and Shigetatsu as well). Shigenari's place as intendant was taken by Shigetatsu, Shōsan's son whom Shigenari had adopted. (Shigetatsu also was a monk: he had taken Buddhist orders in 1620 together with his father Shōsan.)

In 1648 Shōsan left Asuke, where he had returned four years earlier, to take up residence in Edo with another brother (Shige-yuki), a bannerman. There, during his remaining seven years, he lectured and preached to other bannerman families such as the Kumagai and Morikawa. Shōsan thus spent his whole life on Tokugawa territory in service of the warrior class, mostly at the point where warrior rule touched the lives of the people: as an active samurai in three major campaigns against Tokugawa enemies (at Sekigahara and twice in Osaka) and on guard duty; as a

---

[37] The number of these temples has recently been questioned by a local historian. See Wakaki, "Shōsan no shisō to kyōka," especially pp. 144–45.

[38] For a translation of the *Ha Kirishitan*, see Elison, *Deus Destroyed*, pp. 377–88.

[39] *Fumie* (trampling pictures) were Catholic icons which Japanese suspected of being Christians were forced to trample—a test that would prove whether they were Christian believers or not. Kurachi, "Shōsan no shisō," p. 32.

Buddhist monk contributing to policies that, through the strategic use of temple networks, helped establish bakufu control in remaining pockets of resistance (landed samurai families and rebellious peasants); and finally as "chaplain" to bannerman families.

Shōsan's position and his teachings were unlike those of the early, better-known Neo-Confucian teachers of his day such as Seika, Razan, Kumazawa Banzan, or Yamaga Sōko. These scholars circulated among the elite of the warrior class and addressed themselves to problems such as Neo-Confucian cosmology, general ethical problems (with or without a social dimension), broad administrative policies, or the problems of class structure. Shōsan was active at a social and intellectual level, where the system of domination touched the lives of the people. From his position of authority (which derived from his status as a Buddhist priest and his bafuku association), he dealt with immediate, practical questions that were generated at a juncture where warrior power intersected with the everyday life of the commoners; and he was expected to harmonize the demands of both. Almost all of Shōsan's written work (which includes two compilations by disciples) directly addresses these kinds of problems.[40]

Besides the *Ha Kirishitan* (written in Amakusa and printed in 1662), four works are immediately relevant to the present study. The *Mōanjō* (A safe staff for the blind) was written in 1619, one year before Shōsan's conversion, when he was still on duty in Osaka. His aim was to counter the anti-Buddhist argument of a Confucian scholar he knew. It was printed in 1651 and reprinted in 1653 and again in 1664. The *Banmin tokuyō* (Right action for all) is a book that today refers to a composite work printed in 1661 and consists of two works Shōsan had issued separately in 1652: *Shūgyō no nengan* (Desire for ascetic practice), and *Banmin tokuyō*, which was intended as a commentary on the former. This commentary in turn has two parts: "Sanbō no tokuyō" (Right action based on the Three Treasures), written in Edo in 1650; and "Shimin nichiyō" (Daily guidance for the four classes), written in 1631 for the Kanō family of Wakayama.[41] (Of the separate "nichiyō" for each class, the "bushi nichiyō" for the warriors is older than the other three.) The remaining two works are compilations of sayings by Shōsan,

---

[40] The only exceptions are two tales Shōsan wrote and an exposition of Sōtō doctrine for novices. I shall discuss the latter later in this chapter.

[41] The *Zenshū* gives the wrong date for this work (p. 334). Instead of Genna 8 (1622), the date should be Kan'ei 8 (1631).

brief conversations with visitors, or anecdotes about him. They are the *Roankyō* (Donkey saddle bridge) and the *Hogoshū* (Collection of useless things). The former appeared in printed form in 1660 and again in 1669; the latter in 1671. This quick survey shows that a demand for Shōsan's thought developed in the 1650s and 1660s: his first works were published soon after he developed an audience among the bannermen in Edo.[42]

It was Shōsan's lifelong conviction that the Buddhist tradition could mediate a new social ethic and was better suited for this task than Confucianism.[43] Shōsan had Zen Buddhism in mind insofar as it grasped the essence of the Buddhist approach to life, but even Zen Buddhism had to be reformulated to fit the times. In his appropriation of teachings and ascetic methods, Shōsan was fiercely independent. He upheld only one requirement for religious practice: that it not interfere with worldly practice. Officially, he was a Sōtō Zen monk, but the practice he prescribed most was *nenbutsu* (invocation of Amida Buddha). Pure Land Buddhism could thus also claim him, just as Rinzai and even Shingon sometimes have.[44] For Shōsan, however, established Buddhism in its contemporary form was of no use whatever. "Nowadays," he writes, "many monks study Buddhism from a young age, covet a name for themselves as learned men, have a temple post on their mind ... they are nothing but peddlers of Buddhism" (*buppōshōnin*) (Z 287). "Buddhism (like Taoism and Confucianism) is all about intellectual discrimination (*funbetsu*) and the interpretation of texts" (Z 156, W 99). As we shall see, to use one's intellect to make judgments is for Shōsan the source of all evil, and very specifically of political subversion.

Thus, according to Shōsan, all Buddhist theologies are to be rejected. They are nothing but lies, as the following exchange indicates: "A monk said: 'Abbot Ikkyū asked if a liar goes to hell what one has to make of Sākyamuni, who made up things that never were. Why does the Buddha tell falsehoods too?' The Master replied: 'It is precisely because Sākyamuni and Amida told lies that

---

[42] References to Shōsan's works, in the text and notes, will not identify the individual works but give the page number in *Suzuki Shōsan dōnin zenshū*, hereafter cited as Z. Whenever an English translation of a passage is available in Royall Tyler's *Selected Writings of Suzuki Shōsan*, this will be cited as W. Of the works relevant to this study, Tyler has provided a translation of the whole *Mōanjō* and *Banmin tokuyō* and roughly two thirds of the *Roankyō*.

[43] Shōsan's *Moanjō* was motivated by such criticism of Confucianism. See also Z 188 (W 131), 203.

[44] Tyler, "Reply to Winston L. King," p. 2.

they are Buddhas. If they told the truth they would be ordinary men." (Z 208, W 133). Some people, according to Shōsan, had "the disease of Buddhism" (Z 181, W 123). Anything that smelled of intellectual Buddhism (*rikutsubuppō*) had to be abandoned for practice (Z 152, W 93). Even practice that aimed at enlightenment was dangerous (Z 158). Enlightenment was useless because the essence of Buddhism consisted of putting one's mind to use right now: practice is to use your mind forcefully for action (Z 162, W 105–106). That is all Shōsan pretends to know: "I know nothing about Buddhism" (Z 238, W 147). He did not even have anything good to say about his own Buddhism (Z 154, W 96).

Shōsan's radical anti-intellectualism clearly fits the Zen mold. Royall Tyler, however, has argued perceptively that Shōsan is best understood as a *gyōja* (wandering ascetic), a religious figure marginal to the religious establishment.[45] Indeed, in Shōsan one finds an active obsession with the flesh and death; strenuous efforts to overcome both by "practicing death"; special psychic powers, including the gift of healing; and an independence from institutions expressed in a wandering, hermetic existence. (He lived as a mountain gyōja for a long time and almost died of his ascetic regime.) Shōsan, however, was a gyōja with a social and political consciousness who aimed his teachings at the whole society, hoping that one day they would receive official bakufu sanction.

Buddhism, Shōsan states with great confidence, has been adulterated for the last three hundred years, and the government ought to reestablish its truth, that is, its usefulness for the whole world (Z 159, W 101–102). In principle, Buddhism is not foreign to the world's teachings (*sehō*), Shōsan argues. Buddha's teachings and the world's are more than simply mutually supportive, as the traditional image of the two wheels supporting the carriage of society makes one believe. Once you enter the world fully, there is nowhere left to go. Buddha's teachings and the world's teachings do nothing else but establish the right principles, are nothing but the practice of duty and the acting out of uprightness: they are one.[46] The annihilation of passions is what the world teaches (Z 226, W 140). Shōsan was emphatic on this point: the world's teachings *are* the Buddha's teachings; through them one attains Buddhahood (Z 61, W 54).

[45] *Ibid.*, pp. 2–5.

[46] Z 64, W 59. The view that the world is a fullness that one cannot (and should not try to) escape is presented as a saying by Buddha and is dear to Shōsan. See also Z 61 (W 54), 203, 233, 293, 328.

Shōsan knew that this was a bold statement, and he indeed thought that he was the first to advocate using the teachings of the world in everything (Z 251, W 166). Although Rankei Dōryū (Lan-ch'i: 1213–1278), one of the founders of the Kamakura Rinzai establishment (Kenchōji, Zenkōji) is said also to have supported the principle of nondifference between the teachings of the world (*seken no hō*) and those of monastic Buddhism (*shusseken no hō*),[47] Shōsan clearly pushed this identification much further. Kamakura Buddhism maintained, at least theoretically, an overall separation between *buppō* (the laws of Buddha) and *ōbō* (the laws of man), even if the original claim of superiority by the former became somewhat diluted in the *ōbōihon* formula of Rennyo (*ōbōihon* held secular authority as fundamental and obedience to it as a duty). Shōsan, however, enthusiastically subscribed to the bakufu's social order and its laws. Since it was in that world that man had to achieve spiritual fulfillment, there was no sacred realm separate from the world: "The teachings of the world are the teachings of the Sages" (Z 203).

Sometimes Shōsan suggests that Buddhism could improve the world still further, but this is said in a context that praises contemporary society: "Up to the time of Taikō [Hideyoshi] as many as 3,000 people a year were condemned to death for fighting and murder. Under the present rule, government is correct and the world is clean so that death penalties for murder number [only] 1,000. When you consider the problem in this light, you see that if people, however ignorant and obdurate they may be, were governed by Buddhism, death sentences would certainly drop to five or six hundred" (Z 188, W 129).

Life, Shōsan teaches, is structured by obligations one contracts for being a recipient of a generosity (*on*) that flows from four sources: Heaven and Earth, one's teachers, the lord of the land (*kokuō*), one's parents (Z 52, W 37). This view entails a decentered definition of personality: not only is there no autonomous center within the self, but man is constituted by several centers outside of himself. His life task is thus to repay this *on* by abolishing the distinction between self and others (Z 63, W 57; Z 289). One owes indebtedness to the lord because he provides peace in the country and right government. Here Shōsan identifies the Tokugawa regime with the dispensation of sagely government (*seiōseiji*) (Z 291). In other words, according to Shōsan, the bakufu provided

---

[47] Kawai, *Chūsei buke shakai*, pp. 114–15.

the ideal social environment within which to achieve one's spiritual destiny.

The values Shōsan stresses are all extension of an ideal samurai ethic of courageous, active service. His aim is to extend to the whole society an ethic tailored to the battlefield. The basic premise is that one does not belong to oneself: "it is wrong to feel that . . . your body is yours. Know well that it is to your lord's generosity that you owe your own life, and serve him by giving your body to him. . . . Your body is your lord's" (Z 50, W 32). One's body is only valuable if purified through service; otherwise it is wrong to attach great importance to it for it's own sake: "One's body," Shōsan loved to repeat, "is nothing but a bag of phlegm, tears, urine, and excrement." [48] "There is a self, but it is not a self; it is distinct from the four elements, [yes,] but it belongs with them, accompanies them, and avails itself [only temporarily] of them" (Z 51, W 34). Man has several life-constituting points of gravity and they all lie outside himself.

This samurai ideal is true not only for warriors. All members of society are interlocked in intricate dependencies: there is the *on* of the peasants, tradesmen, cloth makers, and merchants; the *on* of mutual interdependence of all occupations (Z 53, W 38; Z 291). The activity of all four classes fills the needs of the world, and that is precisely why all occupations are Buddhist practice: there cannot be any activity outside Buddhist practice (Z 70, W 69). The essence of ascetic practice is to rid oneself of oneself (Z 50, W 33; Z 152).

This fundamental characterization of man's place in society is further defined both in functional terms and through religious categories. Functionally this means that "for ascetic practice, nothing surpasses service (*hōkō*). Be a monk and you'll on the contrary create hell. Service is ascetic practice" (Z 239, W 147–48). This was Shōsan's advice to a warrior who requested the tonsure from him. "And," he continued, "rather than eat off temple offerings it is better to eat by offering this body to your lord by serving him. . . . Ascetic practice especially requires a strong mind—so you are better off a warrior than a monk." One should serve with a mind as taut as a well-strung steel string on a steel bow (Z 314).

The service one ought to perform is defined by one's family occupation (*kashoku*). That family occupation should not be thrown away to seek the Teachings, he admonished the warrior.

---

[48] Z 163 (W 106), 228, 297. See also in *Ha Kirishitan* (Z 136; Elison, *Deus Destroyed*, pp. 386–87).

Not to exert oneself in one's kashoku leads to perversion of the mind
(Z 295) because kashoku provides an entrance way into Buddhism.
To be a public officer or official (*yakunin*) one needs a firm mind
(Z 285). If one simply exerts oneself in one's kashoku, no matter
where, one will naturally have something to eat. If one forgets one's
kashoku, however, and looks for a living outside one's status (*hibun
ni*), then one does not fulfill Heaven's will (Z 260-61).

Shōsan's view is identical to the one Ogyū Sorai formulated
some sixty years later: everybody functions as an officer for all the
world.[49] That whole which one thus serves, however, is more than
the sum of all its members. Through pursuing one's occupation,
one becomes an officer not simply of society but of the Way of
Heaven:

One day some doctor came with some questions, for he was concerned
about ascetic practice. The Master said: "There is no need for a special
concern; one has simply to teach how to be a doctor. Foremost, there is the
order from Heaven to save the sick. Be firm in your mind that you are
Heaven's official (*yakunin*), then hurl your body and mind to the world
and don't think of what you will charge for medicine or anything else, but
entrusting yourself to Heaven, singlemindedly dispense your medical
skills." (Z 264)

Everybody, by contributing to the whole from his station in life, is
an official of Heaven: "to receive life as a peasant is to be an official
entrusted by Heaven with the nourishment of the world. Without
the least thought for your body, entrust it singlemindedly to
Heaven and thus work in the fields in true service to tendō" (Z 69,
W 67–68). Peasant labor is not toil; it is service to Heaven. "If you
entrust everything to Heaven, keep upright and do not dwell on
your selfish desires, you will receive Heaven's blessing and both this
life and the next will be fine" (Z 168, W 111). Identical advice is
given to merchants: they also should give their life to tendō, study
uprightness, and thus secure Heaven's blessings because they function as officers entrusted by Heaven with ensuring the free flow [of
goods] throughout the land (Z 71, W 71–72).

The world Shōsan is envisioning in his teachings resembles a
well-ordered corporation or army where everyone in his own
station—which one ought to know, observe, and not trespass (Z
55, W 42)—forgets himself, abolishes the distinction between his
self and others, and thus abandons himself to the execution of his

[49] Maruyama, *Studies*, pp. 91–92.

duty. A very modern vision indeed: one whose oppressive nature Foucault has analyzed under the rubric "discipline." [50]

Such self-sacrifice required rewards. Tendō's blessings were the promise, but also Buddhahood. Since work undertaken in this spirit is a perfect tool to empty the mind and "salvation depends upon the quality of one's mind, and not upon [religious] works (*waza*)" (Z 69, 141; W 67, 81), work is the ideal medium within which to achieve salvation. "Any occupation (*jigyō*) whatsoever is Buddhist practice. It is on the basis of men's actual work that Buddhahood is to be attained. There cannot be any activity that falls outside Buddhist practice because everything one does is for the good of the whole world" (Z 70, W 69). "Peasant work *is* Buddhist practice and not a shameful occupation (*sengyō*) (Z 68, W 66) . . . when you put yourself into each sweep of the sickle and labour without other thought, the fields are the Pure Land" (Z 69, W 68).

This ethic that demands practical exertion is further buttressed by a determinism that is meant to absorb and neutralize any suffering that may result from faithful performance. A witness to the misery of the peasants (even before his experience in Amakusa), Shōsan described in vivid detail the exhaustion and anguish they suffer, which, according to him, call for empathy and understanding (Z 53, W 38). Poverty, however, is not to be disliked, since it is decided by karma (Z 71, 168–69; W 70, 111–12): "poverty and wealth are determined by one's karma of the past and do not come from one's striving in this world; tendō does not deceive in the least" (Z 301).

Shōsan's call for compassion is nonpolitical. He does not appeal to administrators for leniency. He limits himself to asking that one "put oneself in their [the peasants'] place." Without any further comment or protest, he includes within the unalterable fate of the peasants the sufferings that result from their inability to pay their debts or taxes: "Imagine the agony when your crop will not pay your taxes and debts, of having to sell your wife and your daughters, of having to part from them in this life and of having to move to a far-off province" (Z 53, W 38). We will encounter these same words elsewhere, but outside a context that calls for compassion. They appear in a document for district intendants in the Yonezawa domain (written by Seika's disciple Naoe Kanetsugu, a domain elder) where the peasants are exhorted to work hard lest such punishments be their fate.

---

[50] Foucault, *Discipline and Punish*, especially Part Three.

If the bakufu had commissioned an ideology tailored to its political needs, it would have been hard to improve on Shōsan's teachings. As it turned out, bakufu initiative was not necessary. Certainly, Shōsan spent a good part of his life serving bakufu district intendants and bannermen (and so must have numerous other Buddhist monks). It was Shōsan himself who enthusiastically undertook the task of producing a fitting ideology, convinced as he was that Buddhism, his Buddhism, could be useful for the law: "it is a treasure that can be used for the *shohatto*" (Z 303). He speaks repeatedly of his conviction that the Buddha's teachings depend upon kings, ministers, and powerful followers (Z 159, W 101; Z 231–33).

The authorities (*kōgi*) ought to restore Buddhism to its right principles, or as the truth (*shōri*) (Z 61, 141, 159, 257; W 53, 79, 101, 172; Z 268), by which Shōsan means its practical, political usefulness. He intends to present his view to the authorities (Z 161, W 105; Z 189, 328), although Heaven has not let him do it yet (Z 140, 275; W 79, 189). He regrets that the government, while having regulated sword connoisseurship, calligraphy, and all the arts by providing standards to distinguish the genuine from the fake, had neglected to do the same for Buddhism, leaving it without standards or supervision (Z 275, W 123). Shōsan was ready to settle the truth of his Buddhism once and for all in a public debate before the authorities. If he were to lose, they could cut off his head (Z 159, W 102). Without Buddhism, as he conceived it, the world could not be freely put to use (Z 225, W 140).

This last statement is important. For Shōsan it meant first that a Buddhism practiced in the world effected a radical detachment from things. In addition, this detachment or indifference allowed a freer, better, and fuller use of the world. Since Shōsan was so concerned with implementation of public policy, another meaning is certainly also implied. Shōsan seems to have some vague notion of political economy. With his Buddhism, Shōsan maintains, the government could tap the resources of the world and society much more efficiently. His Buddhism would mobilize to the highest degree possible the minds and energies of all to perform selflessly within the established order, because his teachings instilled a military discipline that would mobilize the whole country and make everybody "useful." There would be no waste. Shōsan, indeed, preceded the above remark on putting the world to use by a comment on his earlier work, the *Shimin nichiyō* (Daily guidance for the four classes). He started this work by responding when someone asked him for something useful on martial courage, and followed this piece up by writing the other three chapters (for the peasants, artisans, and merchants); but, he said, "the attitude is the same for all, only the work is different (*shidan tomo ni mochisama hitotsu nari, gyō kawaritaru bakari nari*)" (Z 225, W 139). The *Roankyō* gives us some insight as to who was being reached by this samurai ethic. Among his audience one finds groups of several dozen peasants (Z 168), young samurai (181, 187), old women (185, 258), a recluse (238), bannermen (238, 257), a ship captain (244), a doctor (264), women (255), and even a *shoshidai* (Kyoto deputy, 246).

This ethic required that one approach life as if one were dead, that one practice freely while alive the inevitable detachment that death imposes upon all (Z 154, 161, 164; W 95, 104, 107; Z 200). The only knowledge Shōsan seems to value is the knowledge of birth and death. His first work opens with a discussion of this knowledge (Z 49–50, W 31–34). This knowledge, however, is far from an intellectual understanding. Rather, it is a total realization that generates an energy: "to understanding (*kenkai*) I prefer the arousal of death energy (*shiki*) . . . which is the beginning of leaving birth and death" (Z 149, W 90–91).

This emptying of oneself occurs most notably in utter dedication to one's work. But as simple practical exercises, Shōsan also prescribes the recitation of *nenbutsu*: learn dying with the nenbutsu (Z 141, W 80); throw out all intellectual understanding and delusions you have in your chest, erase *dōri* [basic principles] with Namu-Amida-Butsu-Namu-Amida-Butsu, erase yourself and be one with emptiness (Z 155, W 97); through the accumulated merit of nenbutsu, everything will vanish by itself (Z 158, W 100). Peasants should recite nenbutsu in time with the strokes of the hoe (Z 69, W 68).

This appropriation of nenbutsu to achieve the same goal as the one Zen meditation aims for, it should be noted, was not Shōsan's innovation. The combination of Zen and Pure Land beliefs and practices was common in China throughout the Sung and Ming.[51] For Shōsan, it did not matter how one achieved the state of no-mind and no-thought (*munen mushin*); Nō chanting or dancing could achieve the same result (Z 160, W 103)—although the pathetic little voice with which one sings ditties (*kouta*) would not do (Z 253, W 167). "Be earth, become earth," Shōsan urges his

[51] Berling, *Lin Chao-en*, pp. 34–35, 58, 59, 94, 202.

listeners.[52] The samurai who stands on guard duty is practicing *zazen* (Zen meditation) (Z 181, W 123).

To cultivate the mind is thus to destroy it (Z 59, W 50)—to achieve a selfless mind (*muga no kokoro*) (Z 63, W 57; Z 290–91). The Sages also had no self (Z 52, W 36). It would be a mistake, however, to read into this ideal a quietism removed from involvement in the world. Indeed, all Shōsan had to offer was advice on how to act. Like Seika, he held that all action stems from no-mind and no-thought. Shōsan asked once, concerning the subject of all virtues, what it was that showed up in action, what its substance was. A layman replied "emancipation or worldlessness (*shutsuri*)." "Emancipation is emancipation all right," Shōsan replied, "but it would have been better if you had said that no-mind and no-thought is the substance. It is from there that everything comes into action. When you are in a state of no-mind and no-thought you are in tune with everything" (Z 160, W 103). This state is our original mind (Z 53, W 39), the Buddha nature that is in all sentient beings (Z 54, 58; W 40, 48; Z 294), the Amida Buddha that is in us (Z 59, W 50).

The mind is all-important because it is there that we find not only Buddha but also hell and demons, starving ghosts, beasts, and Heaven (Z 58, W 48; Z 294). It all depends on whether the mind is overcome by things or whether it conquers them (Z 66, W 62). The One Mind is the treasure to use in all endeavors (Z 63, W 57).

Shōsan attributed great powers to the mind. The properly cultivated mind would not only sharpen diligence and improve efficiency, its energy (*ki*: sometimes written with the character for cosmic dynamism as in *ri-ki*; more often, however with the character for machine, loom)[53] could be transferred (Z 177, W 119; Z

---

[52] Z 141, 143, 144, 155, 256; W 80, 84, 96, 169. Tyler explains that this expression may be partially based on a poem by Ikkyū ("None of us know we are born, none of us have a home; when we go back we'll be earth as we were before") (W 258 n17). This may be correct. For Shōsan, however, the expression has a stronger practical meaning than "memento homo quia pulvis es et in pulverem reverteris." Be earth, now, while alive, is a variation on his theme of practicing death in life. Another possible source for this expression, closer to a concern with self-cultivation, as was Shōsan's, may be the Chinese phrase *hsin t'u yeh*, "mind is Earth," which means that mind is central (Berling, *Lin Chao-en*, p. 22). Lin Chao-en's fourth stage of mind-cultivation is called "Resting it in the Earth," which Berling explains as "another way of resting it in the Center, the base of moral equilibrium . . . to move inward, to reverse the centrifugal and dissipating forces and return to the stable core and source of Being, deep within" (*ibid.*, p. 168).

[53] The "machine" *ki* refers to the inner workings of the mind (*kiten*) or to the inexpressable inner workings of enlightment (*kiyō*). Also, as Berling points out, sometimes it refers to the motive power and secret force of the universe (*chen-chi*) that can increase like yin and yang or

157) and put to use for healing purposes.[54] "Everyone comes to ask for a good word, or just to get a look at Shōsan (*Shōsan kenbutsu ni*)," he once said, "but if you really want to meet me, there is only one thing to be concerned with: if you don't get my energy, you can meet me a thousand times a day and it will do you no good" (Z 173, W 117).

Shōsan's spiritual advice was meant to work in everyday life and generate an energy that never slackened, like the energy the warrior acquires through zazen. This energy carries him through battle where, among the chaos and the "*batabata* of gunfire he puts his meditation into action" (Z 171, W 115). It is, therefore, the mind that counts, not the works. This, Shōsan maintains, constitutes the difference between his teachings and the popular Mind Learning: "Shingaku addresses itself to works (*gyō*) so it can be practiced just like that, whereas my teachings are ascetic practice (*shugyō*) that addresses the mind" (Z 171, W 114). He knows, however, that he is very demanding, and he is therefore lenient toward Shingaku. He defends the movement against criticism (*ibid.*) and also answers to a detractor of Kumazawa Banzan (Z 154). It is interesting to note that Shōsan argues that Banzan "must have some good points and be a man of great virtue because he became the teacher of a domain even before he reached the age of forty": for Shōsan, public acknowledgment of one's teachings by the authorities is proof of one's usefulness and virtue.

Often intellectual historians, when dealing with a particular thinker, are compelled to turn to the question of his originality, the implication being that what is not original is of less interest. For Suzuki Shōsan, one could easily argue that the central thrust of his teachings could already be found in China—a hypothesis that has

---

like the *ki* of *ri-ki* (*ibid.*, pp. 172, 183). For a discussion by Wakabayaski Kyōsai of the "machine" *ki* as the mental state of being about to act, see NST 31: 494–95. For Yamazaki Ansai on the same subject, see SGT 12: 173.

[54] Z 250, W 165. Shōsan tells how he cured a man possessed by the ghost of his bitter mistress in an exorcism service. In deep concentration he recited sutras in front of a comb stolen from her. He performed this service at the moment when in the morning she would be looking for the comb. This he did for several days until the man was cured. Shōsan said that he had had healing powers since he was young, and that otherwise he would not have held the service. The key word is *kiten*, literally "transfer of energy," meaning also the working of the mind. Tyler's translation here is too free: *tomurau* (to placate a spirit) he renders as "guidance" and *kiten* as "sharp attention." Elsewhere Shōsan also relates how "stealing thoughts" cured a crazy monk and a man's constricted throat (Z 235, W 142–43), and how, when he officiates for the dead, he concentrates his mind to the utmost and actually changes places with them (Z 158, W 100).

been forwarded about the whole variety of early Tokugawa Neo-Confucianism.[55] Whether direct influences can be identified is not clear, and ultimately of limited importance, but one can find striking parallels to Shōsan in Ming China, especially in the careers, idealism, and political views of Li Chih (1527–1602) and Lin Chao-en (1517–1598).

With Li Chih, Shōsan shares a career as a rather unusual monk. Both were strong and unconventional individuals. They both advocated as equally valuable the practice of Zen meditation and nenbutsu recitation. Li Chih was very skeptical about accepted traditional judgments of right and wrong, and avowed an ambition to achieve peace and order.[56] Shōsan shared the same purpose and, as we shall see, also asks the question about the possibility of differentiating between good and evil: "what shall we judge to be good and what bad? We truly must realize that all things are one" (Z 56, W 45). He despised traditional moralists, both preachers and mountain ascetics (Z 150, W 91). Shōsan's prescription for the whole society was a firm military discipline. His admiration and longing for powerful shogunal rule is undeniable.[57] Li Chih, also an idealist who held moralists in great contempt, ended by advocating the need for a strong military rule.[58] Li Chih, however, did not work out a practical method for self-cultivation that could guide the people. This task was performed by his contemporary, Lin Chao-en.

Lin Chao-en propounded an inner-wordly monastic ideal: "while in the world withdraw from it." It was based on teachings by the sixth Zen patriarch Hui-neng (638–713): "One learns the Buddha's teachings in the world, without separating oneself from the world. To seek Buddhahood in separation from the world is like looking for the unicorn ['for horns on a rabbit'].''[59] Hui-neng (who also had reconciled Zen with Pure Land teachings and practice) was obviously Lin Chao-en's hero.[60] He is also one of the few Buddhist authorities Shōsan refers to in his exhortation to

---

[55] De Bary and Bloom, *Principle*, pp. 28–30, 156, 167, 174; for a qualification of this hypothesis, see p. 32.

[56] On Li Chih's life and thought, see de Bary, "Individualism and Humanitarianism," pp. 188–225.

[57] Besides the evidence already presented, it should be pointed out that Shōsan specifically hoped that during his own lifetime Ietsuna would reestablish Buddhism as the official religion (Z 257, W 172).

[58] De Bary, "Individualism and Humanitarianism," pp. 205, 208, 209.

[59] Mano, "Rin Chōon," p. 30.

[60] Berling, *Lin Chao-en*, p. 202.

novice monks (the only one he mentions twice), *Fumoto kusa wake*
(Separating the grass at the foothill) (Z 77, 87). Lin Chao-en also
advocated mind concentration for all social classes: "Peasants must
have the mind within to be peasants. Artisans and merchants must
have the mind within to be artisans and merchants." To refine the
body is "to refine it with the Three Bonds, the Five Constant
Relationships, and the callings of scholar, peasant, artisan, and
merchant." [61] Lin urges that not clinging to the body be practiced
with a pure and single-minded effort: "not only at the court, but
even in the midst of the three armies . . . not only in the midst of the
three armies, but even while going into the midst of barbarians and
confronting danger." For beginners he prescribes recitative exercises as though one were standing in attendance, without daring to
relax even for a moment. [62]

Shōsan never developed a graded meditation technique like Lin
Chao-en's Nine Stages. His advice was simple and direct, and he
insisted again and again that he had nothing special to offer: his
listeners had only to cultivate a proper mind in their occupations.
His teachings, however, were vigorous, powerful, even stunning at
times. It is hard to distinguish between his advice to monks and his
advice to warriors or to commoners.

To novice monks, as for commoners, he stressed the importance
of *on* (Z 75, 77, 85) and the necessity of applying oneself to one's
occupation (*kashoku*) (Z 85). The virtues monks ought to cultivate
are applicable to the arts and to human relationships (Z 82). All
past devices and techniques for mind control are disparaged; the
emphasis is instead on the maintenance of a lasting inner disposition that should accompany one when visiting a temple (Z 75)
or when making the rounds on a mendicant tour (then one should
strengthen the mind, grit one's teeth and fix one's gaze, applying
the mind acquired in zazen) (Z 78). There is no doubt: Shōsan
speaks to his monks as he does to warriors, and not the other way
around. The most important thing is to have a spirit that exudes
courage and fierceness (Z 76, 83) because the essence of Buddhist
practice is to guard oneself (Z 139, W 76; Z 84). Shōsan uses here
powerful metaphors such as "gritting one's teeth" or "staring with
a fixed gaze or warrior's glare" (Z 159, W 100; Z84). This prompt
and keen self-censuring alertness has to be maintained twenty-four
hours a day without slackening even for an instant (Z 83–84). One

[61] *Ibid.*, 108 and 165 (I substituted "peasants" for "farmers"). See also pp. 82–83.
[62] *Ibid.*, pp. 155–56, 131. Satō Naokota uses the same image; see below, p. 279.

has to look upon oneself as one looks upon the hated house of an enemy (*ibid.*). In this context, Shōsan developed elaborate military metaphors:

When, within the castle of the truth of the Teachings, hated enemies of oneself arise, ready to conquer the country, where will such enemies come from? Know it clearly that they come from the single thought of "self" [or "body"]. From this thought spring the Three Evils and the Four Inclinations; they split into the 84,000 desires which all become the hated enemies of oneself. [To defeat this army] one appoints a shogun (firmness of powerful faith), advances first the soldiers (throwing away one's body), appoints samurai as chiefs (valorous and fierce spirit), uses the sword of illusion and evanescence, faces the source of oneself and applies sharp and prompt censure to oneself twenty-four hours a day. But it all too often happens that the sensual self [body] becomes the fortified quarters of the desires. Then the mind becomes an unenlightened master [producing] bad karma and destroys the self. Such a mind is our enemy. This body is a bag of desires. (Z 83)

To extinguish such a mind is one's assignment for life, and those who succeed are clearly distinguishable from the others: vulgar men have minds that are alive; men of the Way have minds that are extinguished (Z 85).

A strenuous tone and militant spirit pervade Shōsan's teachings. The calls for staying alert, for fierce courage in the struggle against the "self" by energetically throwing oneself into one's work never slacken. In his teachings one perceives the deployment of prescriptions initially developed in the military camp to the rest of the social territory through the medium of Zen. Shōsan seems to admit as much when he states that his teachings are more fit for warriors than for monks (Z 144, 168, 244; W 84, 111, 157).

The main obstacle to the necessary functional ("useful") integration of Tokugawa society was autonomy or secession, whereby one pitted oneself or one's group or class against the larger whole. Yet, separateness or "apartheid" (*sabetsu*) was a cardinal feature of Tokugawa society and had been imposed by coercive force: the system served foremost the interests of a new, clearly defined warrior class, set apart from the remainder of society. The ruling class, therefore, faced the political quandary of strictly maintaining such separateness in order to stay in power while minimizing the potential of secession or withdrawal it entailed. As we have seen, even the idealistic Seika understood the need for coercive force, as did Shōsan (if only through his Amakusa experience). Shōsan,

however, even more than Seika, set out to provide spiritual ammu-
nition to maintain the people in that precarious balance between
separateness and secession. This is an important question that
directly touches upon Shōsan's political views. On a few occasions
Shōsan expressed these unambiguously.

In the following text, Shōsan gives his opinion on the rōnin plot
of 1651 against the bakufu, led by Yui Shōsetsu (1605–1651) and
Marubashi Chūya (?–1651). The context within which he discusses their abortive attempt and swift punishment is important
and requires full citation:

One day a practitioner of Shingaku came and asked about the essence of
the Teachings. The Master replied: "Buddha's teachings do not rule the
body through judgmental distinctions (*funbetsu*). Unless one does not
think of what will be left [after death], makes no judgments about the
future, and goes beyond the emptying of the one thought of the present
moment, one will not use [the mind, body, or self] in purity. The ancients
therefore, when they recommended foremost to value time, meant that by
guarding one's mind actively, shaking off thoughts of good and evil, one
should separate oneself from oneself. Moreover, to correct the mind, it is
good to observe the principles of karma. For instance, although people
hate me, not to hate them back. Why would people hate me without
reason? I should wonder whether it is not because of karma, and ponder
what kind of karma it could be. That is the way I should criticize myself.
Keeping the order of karma that governs everything, one should not act
on judgment (*funbetsu no shioki subekarazu*). Moreover to act on judgment
is useless. Last year, two bad fellows Chūya and Shōsetsu [both names
written with the wrong characters for *ya* and *shō*] were killed instantly
after they attempted a plot. They had swallowed whole the notion that if
one makes good judgments, things will turn out all right. Be that as it
may, Heaven forgave them! In all things, nothing happens in accordance
with judgment. Everything happens according to the order of Heaven. If
you observe this well, your mind will be greatly purified. (Z 175–176)

In this passage Shōsan reveals the linkage between his teachings
and politics. The "essence of the Teachings" his visitor inquires
about point to a political stance so important that it rules over life
and death. In this text, Shōsan contrasts two series of oppositions:

judgmental distinctions	shaking off thoughts of right and wrong
taking time seriously	concentrating on the present moment only
reacting in time, in accordance with such judgments on society	emptying one's mind, self-criticism

basing judgments on perceived reasons	reading situations according to karma
calculating that things could change according to reason	things happen according to Heaven
evaluation: uselessness	assumption: usefulness
result: death	result: purity

The left column is the value-perception-action cluster of political initiative culminating in death. In contrast, on the right, the religious practice of guarding the mind to instill political acquiescence is presented as useful and pure: a summation of the ideology that unifies all Shōsan's teachings.

Shōsan extolls energetic, courageous, and fierce action that transcends the fear of death, but only when it serves the bakufu. He unconditionally condemns such action when it is directed against the bakufu. Moreover, in the above case, the punishment of the plotters is assumed to be part of Heaven's order. Such an assumption is clearly spelled out elsewhere in Shōsan's defense of the death penalty. Some Buddhists objected that continuation of capital punishment might make it difficult for Buddhism to bring peace to the world. Against them Shōsan argues that to execute or kill those whom one must execute or kill is not a crime but an act of great compassion. Moreover, such action is socially beneficial because the sight of crucified criminals warns the people against evil. In certain respects it is even more valuable than Heaven's punishment.

Shōsan seems to suggest first that Heaven's punishment is often not understood as such, and hence does not have the right effect but only causes suffering; "For instance, there are many who are struck by Heaven's punishment and come to spend their life as lepers or outcasts. Yet they aren't in the slightest weary of their state and enjoy their evil minds" (Z 169, W 112–13). The result is that incarnation after incarnation they do not change their karma. (That is why in the passage on the rōnin plot, Shōsan urges reflection on karma; otherwise karma will not have the desired social effect.) Second, in an execution all these shortcomings of Heaven's punishment are corrected: "the criminal comes to a quick end, repents, and cuts off his evil mind at the root." In other words, there is no ambiguity about why he is meeting his fate: his fate is clearly a punishment. Moreover, it is effective because it cuts his bad karma, and compared to the prolonged accumulated suffering of Heaven's punishment, capital punishment is less painful, which is why it is an expression of compassion. The sword, as we have seen in other texts, is again praised as an instrument of compassion, and the bakufu as a more efficient and even a more compassionate dispenser of justice than Heaven.

Efficiency and predetermination are two central values in Shōsan's ethical system. In a different context, these lead him to argue against another form of death: *junshi* or the custom among retainers of following their lords voluntarily in death. The point Shōsan makes is that services for the dead have an effect on their karma. To hope for a free ride (without services) to Heaven on the tail of one's lord (who would be carried by such services) is clever nonsense. "Whoever is with his lord in this very life, if wise, will be useful to his lord; and if a fool, will be resented by his lord" (Z 211, W 135). The quality of one's performance in one's status will decide one's fate in the hereafter: "A lord is a lord, an inferior is an inferior, a parent is a parent, a child is a child, and each will be taken to places either good or bad according to their karmic order." A junshi death will not set a man free from his own karma; only useful performance will.

The division within society is thus preordained by karma and Heaven. In order to preserve peace, however, that social cleavage cannot be perceived as such. More precisely, the political truth of this social division must not be objectified as such but transformed through symbolic significations as a religious truth. Man should not apply his judgment to such a sanctified edifice.

Such views are perfectly in line with a Zen apprehension of reality, which precludes the formulation of explicit (political) judgments. Because Shōsan, however, served the bakufu, such a refusal to engage the mind in political questions turns into an acquiescence to the given political situation. It is his attempt to promote such view that makes Shōsan a political and ideological activist. It is in this light that one should consider Shōsan's war on discriminating judgment and his emphasis on reducing in one's mind (but not in social reality) the distinction between oneself and others (Z 287). The only thing we have to fear is our mind, he says (Z 295). In Buddha's mind there is no discrimination (*sabetsu*), only great compassion (Z 297). One therefore has to leave the mind that discriminates between all things, and dwell in the One Mind; this very mind is to be used in all endeavors whatsoever (Z 63, W 57). Although all things are distinct from one another, the original mind is one (Z 53, W 39). This one, empty, rather than the discriminating mind is the tool given to man to meet the preordained diversity of the world: "Although the blessings of Heaven and Earth do not change, there are differences between one thing and another. . . . [But] we must realize that all things are truly one" (Z 56, W 45). Shōsan's self-discipline blinds one to the *political* importance of social apartheid. It asks one to recognize falsely a system of domination (which the world *also* is) as something totally else. This self-discipline, however, goes far beyond reorienting perception. It generates action. It does not leave the individual to himself but addresses him, urges him to make himself productive and useful for that system.

LEGISLATION

Although a general acquaintance with Tokugawa (and present-day Japanese) society leads one to believe that Shōsan formulated an ethic that became or was already pervasively operative during his own time, there is no way to verify empirically what Shōsan's role was apart from such a formulation. He held up norms but had no way to enforce them. The bakufu, however, did have the power of enforcement. It is therefore important to examine what the bakufu proclaimed, through its laws and regulations, it would enforce.

Tokugawa laws, like legislation everywhere, were issued by those who held a monopoly on the use of coercive force. The greater the compliance with the laws, the less obtrusive coercive power has to be and the less it runs the risk of being challenged. Any transition from a regime of force to a system of rule thus triggers legislative growth. Moreover, the more total the legislation becomes, regulating ever greater areas of life and society, the more the decrees will include justifications for their comprehensive character. Any extensive legislation thus contains two ideological dimensions: an overt one, consisting of arguments why decrees have to be obeyed; and a covert one, embedded in the norms expressed in the decrees—norms that entail definitions of what an individual's place in society is and even what an individual is, what public behavior is, what a community is. Legislation is thus another means whereby ideology shapes society.

A quick survey of Tokugawa legislation reveals that for the period under study, the Iemitsu years saw a great increase in bakufu agricultural laws.[63] Ieyasu issued only one seven-point

[63] *Kinsei nōsei shiryōshū* 1: 1–40.

directive; Hidetada issued thirteen directives, and Iemitsu thirty-eight. Most of the Iemitsu legislation occured between 1642 and 1649. The "Keian Laws" of Keian 2 (1649) are the first comprehensive attempt at a detailed regulation of agriculture, and constitute a composite reissue of the ordinances promulgated after 1642.

The laws prior to 1642 rarely refer to agricultural production itself, but deal with many disparate issues. One finds, among others, currency exchange regulations, warnings against leaving the roads without reason, prohibitions against traffic in human beings, prohibitions against Christianity, punishments for hiding fields from surveyors, and regulations concerning the length of time for indentured service.[64] Among these issues, those that touched the everyday lives of the peasants most were prohibitions against tobacco smoking and tobacco production (because such production reduced the number of fields available for rice cultivation and taxation). The first one was issued in 1612.[65] Other laws regulated clothing (prescribing cotton), the first one being issued in 1628.

Perhaps there is no way to verify empirically the extent to which these laws and the more comprehensive ones of the 1640s were actually enforced. What is certain, however, is that these laws created ideals and norms that, for the first time in Japanese history, tried to structure peasant life. And normative ideals are real too: at the very least they impinged upon peasant consciousness. It would be wrong to assume that a peasant society that is subjected to such a set of norms is no different from one that is not.

At five different times between 1642/5 and 1643/8, detailed legislation directly affecting the peasants appeared. This legislation was the bakufu's response to its first serious economic crisis. Bad weather, the cause of crop failures (which together with abusive government had brought about the Shimabara rebellion of 1637), did not let up: the years 1640 and 1642 brought even greater famines throughout the country. In 1642, therefore, inspectors were busy checking on the bannermen in shogunal territory. The intendants of the six provinces under the Musashi intendant of finance (*kanjōkata*) were called together. With the information thus

---

[64] On these various topics, see the following pages *ibid.*: currency exchange, p. 4; leaving the roads, p. 5; traffic in people, pp. 9, 13; Christianity, pp. 6 (1612), 7 (1616), and 17–19 (1638–1639); hidden fields, p. 15; indenture, pp. 6, 13.

[65] *Ibid.*, p. 8.

gathered, the council of elders formulated a plan to strengthen the rule of the daimyo and bannermen and to promote agricultural production.[66] Bakufu leaders had come to understand that more than sumptuary laws were needed to redress the situation— agricultural production itself had to be strictly regulated. The new laws reveal what this meant for the peasants.

On the one hand, peasants were not to be pressed unnecessarily. Peasants who had paid their taxes fully but had moved to another village to protest illegal actions by their lords were not to be harassed. Rules for the land surveys were standardized with the aim not of squeezing more out of the peasants, but of supporting the smaller peasants.[67] Finally, the regulation of water to the fields had to be fair and harmonious.[68]

On the other hand, specific attention was paid to productivity. This had to be achieved in two ways: by preventing waste, which entailed self-discipline in all matters of consumption, and by maximizing the labor available through cooperation within the village. The former aspect entailed sumptuary laws, but of a far more comprehensive scope than in the past. Not only clothing and food were legislated, but luxuries such as tobacco smoking and the use of carts for fetching brides were prohibited, expenditures for festivals curtailed, and the size of dwellings regulated in accordance with one's status.[69]

Peasants were divided into two categories: those of "good status" (landowners, neighborhood chiefs) and those of "bad status" (including bachelors, among others). The former were allowed profits after taxes (for example, from interest on loans to peasants who did not have enough to pay their taxes). The latter had to apply themselves to agriculture very assiduously, avoid unnecessary expenses (except for tools and clothes), and, if they had to sell their produce to pay their taxes, sell it at maximum prices.[70] Moreover, the village as a whole had to help bachelors and others in need of assistance to produce sufficiently to pay taxes. The bakufu was thus, through its legislation, giving a very specific structure to local communities: it defined what "the whole" meant for the peasants and what its internal social divisions were. It also made sure that

[66] Sasaki, *Daimyō to hyakushō*, p. 233.
[67] *Ibid.*, pp. 234, 237, 238.
[68] *Kinsei nōsei shiryōshū*, p. 26.
[69] *Ibid.*, pp. 22, 26, 29, 31–32, 37.
[70] Sasaki, *Daimyō to hyakushō*, pp. 239–40.

everybody contributed his maximum share to the whole. The intendants had to see to it that in each village everybody worked diligently. What this work consisted of was spelled out in minute detail. Weeds had to be pulled. The front yard had to be kept clean, and only certain kinds of plants could be cultivated there. The kind of work to be done in the morning, at noon, and at night was clearly differentiated. It was forbidden to plant tobacco in the main dry fields, cotton in the wet fields, and oil-producing plants in either kind of fields.[71] One wonders, looking at this this legislation, where the much heralded self-determination of the Tokugawa village is to be found.

Although the villages governed and policed themselves, they also constituted production units whose tasks were clearly regimented. Sasaki Junnosuke, from whose work some of the above information is drawn, has concluded that before the legislation of the 1640s the emphasis indeed lay on increasing the number of fields, whereas after that date the overriding concern was increased productivity.[72] This was something new. To underscore the historicity of this notion, it will help to look briefly into its development in the Tokugawa period.

The notion of productivity was first used as a measure of wealth, and later came to be applied to new territory, acquiring in the end even a religious meaning. Accurate measurement not of the products but of the *productive potential* of the land informed Hideyoshi's national *kokudaka* survey. The size of each field was measured with rods and ropes and recorded in village ledgers that also stipulated yield. Thus all landowning peasants not only knew precisely what taxes to pay but also became acquainted with the concepts of land valuation, productivity, and measurability—something Russian peasants were not aware of even in the early twentieth century.[73]

This notion of measurability is thoroughly historical. It was present in a limited fashion for a few decades during the eighth century, when the Nara government allocated tax land to families, but appears to have become a fundamental concept only in the 1540s, when one encounters it in the *Tako House Code* as a central principle of government. Indeed, so central was this principle of calculation (*sanyō*) said to be that it applied to spiritual matters, as

---

[71] *Kinsei nōsei shiryōshū*, pp. 23, 25, 26, 32, 35, 37.

[72] Sasaki, *Daimyō to hyakushō*, p. 261.

[73] George Yaney, *The Urge to Mobilize: Agrarian Reform in Russia, 1861–1930* (Champaign: University of Illinois Press, 1982), p. 178.

well. This development is strikingly parallel to what happened in the West. Although the Domesday Book (1085–1086) was the first national cadastral survey known in the West, the principle of the measurability of all things seems to have been clearly formulated for the first time much later, by Sir William Petty, the supervisor of the Down Survey of Irish estates (1655–1656). He divised ways to calculate "the value of people" (1665, *Verbum Sapienti*, ch. 2) through his *Political Arithmetick* (1670s). This led Jean François Melon, a French pre-physiocrat, to write in 1736 that everything can be subjected to calculation, even purely moral questions (*Essai politique sur le commerce*, ch. 24). In Japan, this same principle, first enunciated in the 1540s, was developed systematically by Kaiho Seiryō (1755–1817).

The Keian legislation of the 1640s went one step beyond Hideyoshi's measurement of the productive potential of the land and aimed at *increasing* its productivity. This governmental effort was given ideological underpinning by Shōsan's this-worldly ethic that tried to eliminate psychological and behavioral barriers that hampered "usefulness" and productivity. In Shōsan's teachings, political submission and economic productivity went hand in hand. In the first half of the eighteenth century, Ishida Baigan became instrumental in coopting merchant productivity for the polity by redefining the place of the merchants in the social system as indispensable and the profits they made as honorable. (This is Robert N. Bellah's famous thesis in his *Tokugawa Religion*.) At the same time, the practice of criminal justice was modified to accommodate the value of productivity.

Throughout the whole Tokugawa period, criminal punishment was cruel, public, and exemplary.[74] The public character of executions was more than a visible sign of bakufu authority. Commoners were to learn discipline (*migoroshi*) and respect for the social order through the vicarious experience of the effects crime had on the bodies of the criminals: decapitation, crucifixion, or bodily mutilation. *Sarashi* or exposure was a predominant form of punishment in the Tokugawa period: *hikimawari sarashi* (parading the criminal through the streets), *shitai sarashi* (exposing the corpse), and so on. In the eighteenth century new variations were instituted. Under Yoshimune, bodily mutilations such as cutting off ears or noses could be replaced by tattooing, leaving the body

[74] For the data on the Tokugawa criminal code, I relied on Ishii, *Edo jidai manpitsu* 4: 189–202.

intact and fully functional. Moreover, penal servitude was introduced. The Kumamoto domain seems to have been the first to
introduce in 1755 a full-fledged system of prison terms under which
the prisoners performed labor, were taught skills, and received
wages which they could save. After their terms were over, they
could thus reenter society, rehabilitated as productive members.
Thus another wasteful sector of society had been reclaimed for
usefulness and productivity. Matsudaira Sadanobu implemented
a variation of that system for the bakufu. In 1790, he founded
Japan's first penal colony (*ninsoku yoseba*, "meeting place for laborers") on Ishikawa Island. The camp was first populated with
skilled laborers who were then joined by convicts as their
apprentices.

One's first impulse may very well be to credit growing humanitarian concerns with these developments. Upon reflection, however, such explanation is not entirely satisfactory. Humanitarian
voices can be found, no doubt, throughout all history. As far as
Japan is concerned, respect for life has always been central to
Buddhist doctrine. We saw, for instance, how some Buddhists were
arguing in the 1640s against the death penalty (defended by
Shōsan). One should thus not invoke as a specific cause for developments at one particular time (the eighteenth century) an
element that had been present for centuries. A more plausible
conjecture would be that what one reads today as a humanitarian
breakthrough is not an explanation but a (partial) description of a
phenomenon that is not explained by describing it in one particular way. If one nevertheless characterizes it as a breakthrough,
then its occurence at that specific time has to be explained. In this
case, it would seem that a new space was created within the mid-
Tokugawa penal system through a further application of the
concept of man as a productive human being. One could also
say that the requirements of productivity were the ideological
notions behind which coercive power could hide, even in an area—
criminal   punishment—where   its   exercise   would   be   least
challenged.

In the early nineteenth century, new theological interpretations
further validated productivity as a religious activity in the area of
agriculture. The contrast between these Shinto formulations and
Suzuki Shōsan's teachings of nearly two centuries earlier is striking. The ethic Shōsan had prescribed for the peasants of the mid-
seventeenth century was severe, stark, and almost totally stripped

of ultramundane justifications. He had reduced the meaning of work almost to work itself. His message was that, if one needed religious meaning in life, it ought to be found in work. As long as productive performance went unhampered, Shōsan showed little concern for the religious significance one chose to construct around it. In the early nineteenth century, however, new Shinto teachings (exemplified in Hirata Atsutane's writings) redefined agricultural productivity as participation in the creative work of the kami.[75] Popular Shinto thus caught up with a work ethic Shōsan had preached nearly two hundred years earlier. Mythology was mobilized to reinforce a definition of man as a producer for society.

Let us return for a moment to Shōsan, this time in regard to Tokugawa legislation. The peasants and other commoners Shōsan reached through his lectures and writings should have had no doubts as to what was meant when he urged them to exert themselves within the boundaries of their status. The *shohatto* (laws) for which Buddhism could be put to use were not limited to the *Buke shohatto* (Laws for the warrior houses). The social and work discipline he sought to instill was meticulously spelled out in the legislation of 1642 and 1643 that, when reissued in 1649, was presented as official legislation (*kōgi shohatto*) for the districts and villages of all the provinces. It is also interesting to note that the legislation of 1649 was the first to contain elements of a sacral discourse. The *nanushi* (landowners) and neighborhood heads were to be regarded as one's real parents; filial piety was stressed, and reference made to the blessings of Buddhas and gods.[76] Shōsan was obviously very much in tune with the bakufu's problems of governance when he mobilized spiritual resources to bring about a higher level of productivity or "usefulness" among the people. His focus, later in life, on the class of the bannermen was also timely.

Starting in 1642, the bakufu strengthened the role of the bannermen.[77] They were ordered back to their territories that year to take care of the people and fight the effects of the famines. Also, their number was increased by letting second and third sons qualify for bannerman status. Sasaki Junnosuke interprets the enforcement in 1642 of the alternate attendance for vassal daimyo as a move not to bring them to Edo for one out of every two years but to get them

---

[75] Harootunian, "Consciousness of Archaic Form," p. 98. For a representative Shinto text, see Miyaoi Yasuo, *Kokueki honron* (NST 51: 291–309).

[76] *Kinsei nōsei shiryōshū*, pp. 35, 39, 40.

[77] The information that follows comes from Sasaki, *Daimyō to hyakushō*, pp. 241–42.

out of Edo (where they had tended to reside permanently to secure posts in the bakufu administration) and thus have them partially replaced by bannermen. For the first time, *kashoku* (family occupation), one of Shōsan's pet themes, acquired importance in the new order—by 1663, it had found its way into the Laws for Bakufu Retainers (*Shoshi hatto*). The last article of that code urges the hatamoto to "exert themselves diligently in their *kagyō* (family occupation)."[78]

For those exposed to Shōsan's teachings, the truth about life in the new feudal order was defined in a spiritual and ascetic way. Even the first comprehensive Tokugawa laws for the common people, while imposing a highly regimented ascetic discipline, showed a touch of spirituality. Considerably before either the Tokugawa agricultural legislation or Shōsan's teachings, a document directed to the peasants balanced spirituality and asceticism more evenly, and provides further evidence of a pervasive presence in this period of a politico-religious discourse of which Shōsan may have been but the most eloquent and dynamic formulator and promoter. The document in question is the *Naoe Kanetsugu shiki nōkaisho* (Agricultural admonition booklet for the four seasons by Naoe Kanetsugu).[79] When he composed his admonitions for use by his intendants, Naoe Kanetsugu (1560–1619) was an elder in charge of a 60,000-koku fief within the 300,000-koku Uesugi domain of Yonezawa. He was close to bakufu elders, and appears in a list of Fujiwara Seika's disciples. This booklet draws a composite picture of the ideal peasant. It spells out in minute detail what kind of work the peasants should be engaged in during each month of the year. Moreover, it lectures the peasants on the attitude they should maintain toward their work and the authorities.

The *Nōkaisho* opens with the statement that one should regard the lord of the domain as the sun and the moon, the intendant's representatives (the tax collectors) as one's protective gods (*ujigami*), the village headmen as one's real parents. More concretely, the tax collectors should never be troubled even if they show up early in the eighth month; whether the peasants are doing well or whether they are starving, they should never slight tax collectors. Selling things is allowed if the purpose is to pay one's

---

[78] NST 27: 467.
[79] The text of the Naoe document can be found in *Dai Nihon shiryō*, vol. 12, fasc. 32, pp. 84–91. (Kanetsugu is listed as a disciple of Seika in *Fujiwara Seika shū* 1: 22.)

taxes. If the peasants work diligently, no one will suffer famine, there will be no poverty, and they will fulfill the intentions of the gods and Buddhas, flourish in this life and be reborn in paradise.

Meeting their tax quotas is regarded as the peasants' best guarantee of security for this life and the next. This argument is presented in a way very similar to Shōsan's discussion, mentioned earlier, of the hardships that will be the peasants' if they fail in this respect: "If your taxes are not paid by the twelfth month, one's treasured wife may be taken as security for taxes to the tax collector's or the intendant's place and made to work, and [there] a servant may take her as his wife. To avoid this, pay the taxes by the eleventh month. One will thus avoid going against Heaven and being despised by one's fellow peasants." [80] Cruel enforcement of the laws is part of the Heaven-ordained order of things. Naoe's admonitions, Shōsan's teachings, and the Tokugawa ordinances are all efforts at articulating for the commoners a vision of society that caught all under its net of discipline. By ridding himself of any self-serving ambitions, all a man's energies could be channeled to fill productively the corner of the net that held him down.

The Tokugawa period, including its first decades, is often characterized as marked by rationalism and a progressive rationalization under the impetus of Neo-Confucianism. It is evident that such a picture seriously distorts Tokugawa reality. There are a number of phenomena that are often said to typify rational progress: political authority, civil obedience, political discourse, the work ethic. Yet these phenomena are all wrapped in symbolizing strategies that sacralized them in new ways. In other words, the dichotomy between rationality and arationality is inappropriate for understanding early Tokugawa Japan.

KIYOMIZU MONOGATARI: A POLEMIC DEFENSE OF NEO-CONFUCIANISM

At the "popular" level, where Shōsan operated and where the laws touched the lives of the people, we have not yet met any significant contributions that might be labeled "Neo-Confucian." Seika's Neo-Confucianism was very inner-directed, solipsistic, and by and large disengaged from society. Moreover, he moved in circles far removed from the circumstances of peasant existence.

[80] *Dai Nihon shiryō*, vol. 12, fasc. 32, p. 90.

Razan's writings, much less oriented to self-cultivation, were the product of a bureaucratic servant, albeit a very learned one. Was Neo-Confucianism totally absent from the construction of political ethical views for the commoners?

After a close examination of the *Kiyomizu monogatari* (The tale of Kiyomizu), one is forced to answer with a qualified no. Strictly speaking, it is hard to determine what could constitute a Neo-Confucian tenor or content (as opposed to a merely Confucian one) in any popular work. Neo-Confucianism distinguishes itself from Confucianism chiefly by an elaborate cosmology that does not easily lend itself to popular treatment. Do some of Chikamatsu's plays illustrate Confucian values or Neo-Confucian ones? (Do Graham Greene's novels explore Thomistic questions of theology or general Catholic ones?) Be that as it may, the *Kiyomizu monogatari* was a popular work of the "kanazōshi" genre of early Tokugawa Japan. It was a didactic book in the form of a tale, actually a discussion between an inquiring pilgrim and a wise old man, from a Confucian and anti-Buddhist standpoint. It was polemical in tone and in 1643, five years after it was printed, an anonymous reposte in defense of Buddhism appeared: the *Gion monogatari* (The tale of Gion)—Gion and Kiyomizu are two places in Kyoto associated with popular temples. The latter was a refutation, paragraph by paragraph, of the most important sections of the *Kiyomizu monogatari*. The publication dates of the *Kiyomizu monogatari* (1638 and reprinted in 1645, two years after its rebuttal appeared, which seems only to have added to its popularity) are of interest because this was the time when most of the other works we have discussed also found a market. *Gion* in its first page testifies to *Kiyomizu*'s popularity: in five years the work reputedly sold two to three thousand copies "in Kyoto and the countryside." [81]

Kiyomizu monogatari was written by a certain Asayama Irin'an (1589–1664) who had started his career as a monk at one of the Gozan temples in Kyoto. In 1609 he acquired a first-hand knowledge of Neo-Confucianism from a Korean visitor. This contact had the same effect upon Irin'an's career as it had upon Fujiwara Seika's: he left the monastery. As a Confucian teacher he first served Hosokawa Tadaoki (1563–1645) from the Kokura domain (399,000 koku), then tutored the second shogun's third son

---

[81] The texts of the *Kiyomizu monogatari* and the *Gion monogatari* can be found in *Kanazōshi-hen*, pp. 7–48 and 51–116, respectively. The reference in *Gion* to *Kiyomizu*'s popularity can be found on p. 51.

Tadanaga (1606–1633), Iemitsu's brother, and finally returned to serve the Hosokawa again. (By this time Tadaoki had retired in favor of his son Tadatoshi, for whom Seika had written his *Daigaku yōryaku*.) In 1653, Irin'an lectured on the *Doctrine of the Mean* to emperor Gokōmyō.

It is not known what prompted Irin'an's writing of this tale, besides a general concern for the welfare of society. Given the circles in which he moved, however, such a concern may have been stimulated by two events that shook samurai society. One was the Shimabara rebellion, which was quelled six months before the *Kiyomizu monogatari* appeared. The uprising occured in a region bordering on the Kumamoto domain (540,000 koku), which since 1632 was ruled by the Hosokawa. Moreover, tradition has it that it was the Hosokawa army that caught and killed the rebellion's legendary leader Amakusa Shirō. The other event was the suicide of Tokugawa Tadanaga (Irin'an's student), who in 1633 killed himself after a year of house arrest for high treason.[82]

Judging from the content of the work, the primary audience of the work was the ruling class, since it often touches upon practical questions of government: the rōnin problem (29, 45), the degree of power that should be entrusted to elders (*karō*) (27–28), *seppuku* (41–42), the example of the Chinese Chi Tzu who chose not to revolt against the tyrannical Chou, the last Shang king (45–46), and the place of the ruler under Heaven (48).[83] Its popularity, however, may indicate that it reached beyond the warrior class. It is at least certain that some Buddhists perceived it as a threat that could not go unchallenged.

Kiyomizu monogatari is of interest for several reasons. It presents an interpretation of society's needs that the author hopes to meet by self-consciously turning to Confucianism. Although the thrust of his solutions is actually quite similar to Shōsan's Buddhist formulae, unlike Shōsan, Irin'an felt it necessary to address the problem of the foreign nature of Confucianism, its universal pretentions not-withstanding. He had thus to argue the appropriateness of what that tradition had to offer for Japan and defend its "usefulness."

[82] Tadanaga's arrest was probably the result of a political coup by his brother Iemitsu, with whom he did not get along. Hidetada, their father, had favored Tadanaga with many lands to groom him for an eventual shogunal succession should Iemitsu die childless. For Iemitsu, Tadanaga was thus a threat that he eliminated a few months after Hidetada's death. Hidetada died on 1632/1/24; Tadanaga was put under house arrest and his lands confiscated on 1632/10/12.

[83] Page references in the text are to the *Kiyomizu monogatari* in *Kanazōshi-hen*.

This he does mainly by attacking Buddhism, the established tradition that for so long had posed as the purveyor of ethics in Japan.
There is another point, however, in which Irin'an differs from
Shōsan. Although close to the highest authorities, he never seems to
have expressed the ambition of having his solutions officially
backed or implemented by them.

Irin'an opens his tale with an elegant statement of purpose:

> For those who are fond of good prose, there are books such as the *Three
> Histories* [*The Book of History*, *The Han Dynasty History*, and the *Later Han
> Dynasty History*] or the *Poetry Anthology* [from the later Liang Dynasty of the
> Five Dynasties]. For those wanting to entertain themselves with *waka*
> verse sequences, there are works like the *Tale of Genji*. For interesting
> quotations there exist many compilations, published in our own country,
> of all schools, masters, and Buddhist sutras. Those, [however,] who wish
> to know the Way should study the *Four Books* and the *Five Classics*. This
> tale has [knowledge of the Way as its] only aim. In anything else, this tale
> cannot measure up to the books of old. (11)

In classical *dōgaku* (Way-learning") fashion, Irin'an claims
seriousness: *gakumon* or learning is different from the reading of *sōshi*
(books) (12). For some people, the knowledge they acquire is a
marketable commodity, for others it is merely an ornament. Very
few study to benefit their mind. Others study for years without any
sign of improvement because their initial intention was wrong
(18). The purpose of learning is to improve behavior by enabling
one to distinguish between the principles of the Way (*dōri*) and
what runs counter to it (*muri*). This teaching precedes the existence
of letters and books: in antiquity the Way of Heaven was the
teacher (12).

The content of this natural knowledge consists of yin and yang
and the Five Evolutive Phases which are, however, immediately
linked to political hierarchy: Heaven and the ruler are yang who
send their blessings down; the Earth and the vassals (*shinka*) are
yin who are recipients and foster all. The lord therefore fixes the
laws and orders everything. Within this order, children serve their
parents and women obey men; behavior as natural for them as it is
for fire to burn or for water to be wet. Its opposite is *muri* (12).

Man has thus his own specific (*hito no hitotaru*) nature and way,
like everything else in nature (hawks catch birds, not mice; cats
catch mice). Man's way can be summed up in six characters: *hon-
matsu/zen-go* and *sō-ō*. *Honmatsu* and *zengo* express two corresponding
hierarchical oppositions, namely,

basis-source-origin:end-posterity: :prior-preceding:later-following: :
superior:inferior

Parents are the origin of children and therefore have precedence
over them in everything. This is filiality. The reverse is unfilial
behavior. The same holds for lords and retainers, and so on. *Sōō*
means adaptation. There is adaptation to years (age?: *nen sōō*), to
rank (*kurai sōō*), to status (*mi no ue sōō*), and to the times (*toki no sōō*).
Good action that does not adapt itself to the proper frame is in
reality not good action (16–17). Behavior is morally correct and
natural only if it conforms generally to the hierarchical social
structure and particularly to its minute and precise status
stipulations.

The pilgrim of the tale wonders at one point whether, if these
teachings are heeded by the rulers and others, everything will
become as it was during the time of the Chinese Sages (*morokoshi no
hijiri no miyo*). To this, the wise old man replies that it will take
time—that for a tree to bear fruit, the seeds have first to be planted,
and time for growth is needed (14). But, he adds, the minds of the
Japanese are easier to correct than those of the Chinese, although
some are hopelessly incorrigible and impermeable to any reason.
These are the Christians, the Ikkō believers, and the Nichiren
followers (15). Here we find the pockets of ideological resistance in
Japan explicitly identified.

When the old man mentions the word *kunshi* (nobleman, man of
virtue), the author sets the stage for a long disquisition on the ideal
man. The pilgrim inquires whether by true gentlemen are meant
kenjin, wise men who are misanthropes and, deep in the mountains,
lead rustic lives and a simple existence ("enter the brushwood gate
and grow moss"). That, according to the old man,

is a grave misunderstanding. First of all, there are the sages (*seijin*) who by
birth have no evil or defects. Wise men (*kenjin*) are by birth slightly
inferior to them, but through learning become good like the sages. They
are the great wise men. Rulers of the realm, great warriors, and all the
princes [or kings: *ō*] are *kenjin*. Among ministers/vassals (*shinka*) their
number is also great. There are also recluses that study learning; and
there are wise men that retire to the mountains but visit the world. Other
wise men hide in town. The place where they are varies and changes
according to the moment. Wise men are not men who isolate themselves.
They are mostly nearby, within reach . . . whether you are in the center of
the realm, or in town or at the court or retired in the mountains, that is not
what makes you a kenjin. . . . Retirement (*inkyo*), [the old man clarifies

further,] can take different forms. Hermits have an aversion for people, are bored with things, believe that whatever one does is of no use, hide deep in the mountains, and would not return to the world even if someone were to offer them the whole realm. The Confucian hermit, however, knows not to separate himself from the world. Therefore, when he dislikes being in the middle of the dirt [of this world] he hides for a while in the mountains, but when a man appears who could honestly be put to use for the world, then he will reenter the world and save the people of the realm. (19–20).

The old man further specifies the other types of "retirement" in the city or even in the service of a lord, to drive the point home that the Way can be pursued in any setting.

Usefulness is also a theme in this text. Hence the warnings against idlers (*yūmin*). The four classes of people are the treasures of the country; all others are idlers, although they are also found among the four classes. The cause of idleness is selfishness (22–23). Courage is also needed, but there are two kinds of courage:

small courage is the hot-blooded kind and is *muri ni* [a play on words, since it can mean "unreasonable" but also, as defined earlier, "counter to *dōri* "]; great courage is tied to duty (*jingi*) and is strong *dōri ni*. Small courage is the energized action of one man. Great courage is the action of a man who, in one show of indignation, can make the whole realm tremble with fear.... Courage is nothing other than the strength acquired after firming up one's mind.... Both kinds of courage can be useful. A man of great courage can be made shogun; a man with hot-blooded courage can be used when things have to be smashed by force. (27)

The advice advanced here parallels Shōsan's emphasis on fierce courage and usefulness, and dovetails with Seika's reliance on both teachings and military might. Although moral courage is valued highly, coercive force is not completely rejected. They even merge at the point where military power is concentrated, namely, in the shogun.

If the world is a place that ought to be filled with usefulness and practicality, one may anticipate that there is little or no room for Buddhism. This is indeed what Inin'an argues. Whether the future life is near or far or good, one has to live in *this* world, he writes. If everyone became a monk, the fields would be emptied of people. Who would then cultivate the five grains (32)? Moreover, if you only believe in Buddhism, they say, this world will be quiet and peaceful, but all the problems and disasters would still be left untouched (33). One has to try a sword out [and throw it away if it does not cut]. Buddhism also speaks about miraculous events, but "they are nothing but things we happen to be unaccustomed to. Things we are accustomed to seeing, we do not think of as miraculous. Isn't it miraculous to see birds fly in the sky? Yet, we do not think so because since a young age we have been accustomed to seeing birds fly in the sky" (34).

Now, in order to follow the Way, one has to pay careful attention to one's thought, to the one thought of every moment. One mistake here can turn one into a bad human being. Each thought has to conform to Heaven and one has to check oneself morning and evening on this point (36–37). People with little wisdom can be helped by rites (*rei*):

they have to ask everything of people who know *rei* well. But *rei* are not the Chinese rites, nor are they the Japanese rites. When I speak of *rei*, I mean knowledge of the basic intention of etiquette. If you want to listen carefully only to the basic intention then you do as in the past if there are good things that correspond to past customs, and you act in accordance with present customs if they are good. For each thing you have to act with a knowledge of its basic intention: that will then be *rei* even if there is a slight difference from etiquette. (37)

The present world is the world we have to live in; a world that is held together by the Three Bonds and the Five Constants:

If the way of the Three Bonds and the Five Constants is destroyed, then it does not matter whether good things await us in the future world. Before we get that far, we must not fall into sin. As long as the Three Bonds and the Five Constants are fixed, then, whether the future world is near or far, there is no danger—and no need for prayer either. I have not yet heard of anybody coming back [from the dead] saying that he had taken the wrong road. Know that the Way is easy. First of all, without the way of lord and subject, this world could not last a single day. "Lord and subject" means to fix rank, the way of high and low. (31)

Stable political hierarchy is the pillar of order. This, however, is not limited to the social class structure. Hierarchy also applies to ordinary human interaction within the guidelines set by etiquette. One's very bodily behavior becomes a mnemonic device that reminds one of hierarchy. Once lodged in the body, hierarchical structure is beyond the reach of criticism because then it has become nature. The text continues: "Without hierarchical rank, even casual encounters will develop into shoving and pushing, violent quarrels, and running someone through. People should want to congregate. The way of man is established through the separation of high and low. [This hierarchy as fixed in] the way of parents and children separates man from the beasts." (And men who are filial to their parents are loyal to their lords—23.) What is suggested here, in this most commonplace of Confucian wisdom, is that (as Seika declared), man is a hierarchical being from birth. His very body, from the time he is a child, speaks of hierarchy so that further socialization in that direction through etiquette or rites is not unnatural. To the contrary, without it, man would not be man. His bodily behavior has to be a visible and natural, unconscious and therefore unquestionable, reminder of that onto-logical truth.

The tale ends in a grand tendō finale in the form of an exchange between men practicing target archery in a wood near Gion. Says one archer: "Everybody speaks about the order of tendō, but this man tendō, where does he live? In the sky? In the mountains? In a man-made house? Who is this tendō?" To this, one of the men replies:

You should not conceive of tendō as something that was fixed by some person. What in the world is called this Way and that Way, each and everyone of them should be seen as tendō. And it is difficult to determine how many there are. First of all, children should establish their parents as tendō. When [however] they leave the parental home for service of the lord, then he is tendō. Women call men tendō. There is where tendō has its residence. To turn one's back to this is to turn one's back to tendō. People who do not know this say that tendō is in the sky, listens to what we say and grants happiness.... Tendō is not a man who decides everything alone. Tendō simply refers to *dōri* (principles of the Way).... Heavenly punishment is the most frightful thing that exists. It is hard to escape reward or punishment for good or evil even the size of the tip of a hair, but this does not mean that Heaven has a mind like that of a man. Evil invites punishment just as water, although without mind, finds its way to a place no bigger than the eye of a needle.... Neither does Heaven, as if it had a mind, give presents like men do in return for favors. Good is rewarded automatically by Heaven, like fire that cannot but warm things that are near it. (47)

In other texts, such as the *Honsaroku*, tendō is presented in an almost anthropomorphic way (which is why scholars have sus-pected Christian influences on that text).[84] Here it stands for a

---

[84] For a discussion of possible Christian influences on the *Honsaroku*, see Ishige, "'Shingaku gorinsho.'" This theory is very old and goes back to Muro Kyūsō, Arai Hakuseki, and Kinoshita Jun'an.

sacred but immanent, ineluctable moral imperative. Irin'an seems to want to claim tendō back from the purely religious realm to increase its social function. Shōsan engages in a similar argument in his anti-Christian polemic when he accuses the Christians of having "fraudulently stolen [misappropriated] the worship of tendō."[85] Irin'an may have aimed his tendō doctrine in the same direction. Not only must he have known of the strong Christian element present in the Shimabara rebellion, but the former wife of his first lord Tadaoki (and mother of Tadatoshi) was the famous Christian convert Hosokawa Gracia.

When Irin'an finally discusses the position of the ruler in the general scheme of things, he gives him the same place as the one assigned to him in *Ieyasu's Testament*: not at the very top, but one step below the top. *Ieyasu's Testament* unambiguously puts the shogun under tendō. Although Irin'an suggests a similar subservience to tendō, his argument has more of a practical quality (although it rests upon a text of the *Book of Changes*) when he states that once on top, there is only one way to go, namely, downward. He then suggests how that can be avoided. Irin'an explains graphically what he means by referring to the first hexagram (Ch'ien) of the *I ching*,

which one can call tendō's book. On the six unbroken lines, the lord's place is indicated by the second stroke from the top, the fifth from the bottom:☰. Why not the first stroke on the very top as some would argue? If the ruler of the realm and the nation thinks that he is the top in everything, that in terms of status, rank, honor, fame, there is no one above him, he should be told that this clearly is contrary to tendō, that he will do evil things. The place at the top has the negative commentary in the *I ching* of a "Dragon at the top will have cause to repent." The dragon at the top is a dragon that has climbed to heaven. Such a dragon had no higher place to go and therefore has to come down. If one goes too high, one will have cause to repent. (48)[86]

Irin'an could easily have expanded on the interpretation of the bottom four strokes as representing the four classes, but it is not our task to flesh out his social ontology. He discusses the proper place of the four classes (that is, the people) in other passages. Another silence, for which he does not make up elsewhere, is more striking. One might have expected in the above passage a reference to the

[85] Z 137 (Elison, *Deus Destroyed*, p. 388).
[86] See *The I Ching or the Book of Changes*, pp. 3, 375, 383.

place of the emperor, but he is not even mentioned. His absence here is as striking as it was in *Ieyasu's Testment*. The obvious conclusion to be drawn from this silence is that the emperor was irrelevant to an ideological representation of the system. How can one interpret this silence when, from our perspective, the shogunal office seems to have derived its legitimacy, structurally and legally, from the emperor?

BEFORE exploring this question in the next chapter, let us take stock of the argument so far. We can summarize the production of ideology at the level of written discourse in early Tokugawa Japan as follows. A number of constructs were produced through the manipulation of available traditions: eclectic combinations of mainly Confucian, Shinto, and folk traditions (analyzed in Chapters 2 and 3); exclusivistic, polemical (re-)articulations of one tradition against another (Shōsan's Buddhism against Confucianism; Irin'an's Confucianism against Buddhism); the universalization of samurai ideals (by Shōsan); and, for the first time, the creation of a comprehensive legislation for the peasants.

Furthermore, beneath this diversity of forms and formulations, there is a clear unity of purpose and a striking similarity among key arguments: the emptiness of mind, an inner-worldly asceticism, and an ontology positing the individual as a hierarchical being and the political stratification of rulers and ruled as a Heavenly order.

Finally, the "ruling class" was society's "ruling intellectual force" in a mediated way. The shogun, daimyo, or samurai were not the immediate initiators of ideological production (with the exception of bakufu legislation). On the contrary, the ruling class was not the producer but the main consumer of ideological products (as it was of material products). The daimyo and samurai constituted the audience for a new breed of teachers. These intellectuals, as time went by, sought to make themselves the interpreters of, and spokesmen for, the new order. To use Gramsci's terminology, they endeavored to become "organic" intellectuals who contributed to the reproduction of society through the dissemination of an ideology.[87] Later, they became more clearly identified with the class of *jusha* or Confucian scholars. The intellectuals we encountered, even the would-be Confucians, were at this point still partly what Gramsci calls "traditional" intellec-

[87] For Gramsci's discussion of "organic" and "traditional" intellectuals, see his *Selections from the Prison Notebooks*, pp. 6–22.

tuals, rooted in a tradition that was predominant in an earlier epoch, namely, Buddhism. They all were close to the world of Buddhism through their own past (all ex-monks), the quality of their persistent spiritual ideals (Seika), or as active preachers (Shōsan).

Their association with the bakufu in one form or another had a double effect. They gained prestige for themselves, which, without making them members of the ruling class, nevertheless made them uncommon commoners. They also endowed with prestige and authority the discourse they (together with scholars such as Yamaga Sokō and Kumazawa Banzan) were producing. What they said and wrote came to constitute the totality of the available discourse on society, which therefore acquired the character of a publicly sanctioned discourse. The Ikkō and Hokke world view, produced by and for the commoners in the sixteenth century, had been successfully displaced.

The result was that, even in the limited ways in which this new discourse finally, in the 1640s, included commoners as its object and audience (Shōsan), it did so not from the standpoint of intrinsic commoner interests. That part of the new knowledge about society which was addressed to the commoners was formulated *for* them—in no way was it formulated *by* them. When, in the second half of the Tokugawa period, commoners started to objectify their own perspective on society, they had to work within the language, framework, and substance of the "ruling ideas" as they had been established (as "natural" ideas) in the first half of the seventeenth century.

Five. Ideological Space: Recentering the Court, Ritual, and Religion

Shouldn't the place where the king of the country, the shogun who protects the realm resides, be called the capital?—*Miura Jōshin (1614)*[1]

Some Confucian scholars recently have come to use in their letters "Eastern Capital" (Tōkyō) rather than "Eastern Warrior [City]" (Tōbu). This is a most serious breach of the proper use of names (*meibun*) and a loss of established standards. He is a criminal who, for the shogunal house, turns his back on venerating the Son of Heaven.—*Asami Keisai (1706)*[2]

By 1600, the emperor had been the pinnacle of the Japanese polity since time immemorial; Kyoto had been the capital of the realm for eight hundred years; Ise its ritual point of gravity for about a millennium. The emperor, Kyoto, and Ise formed the center of Japan's ideological space.

The early Tokugawa shoguns tried nothing less than to rearrange this space around the shogun, Edo, and Nikkō—and to a large extent they succeeded. Although they were not the ones to initiate this deconstruction of the past to signify a new present—Nobunaga's Azuchi castle was the first expression of this quest for a new center—they nevertheless went much farther in this direction than Nobunaga or Hideyoshi. Their ambitious plan was a gigantic maneuver to signify in a visual, ritual way their unprecedented hegemonic power as the new and sole center of the realm. It is at the level of ritual signification, rather than through the vehicle of public teachings, that the bakufu took the initiative and that the policies of the first three shoguns show consistency and continuity. It is in this ritual domain that their principal efforts to find legitimacy took place. The linchpin in this strategy was the emperor, for he was the center of the center. It is thus with him that an analysis of this strategy should start.

What was the emperor's role in the legitimation of shogunal authority? Legitimacy may be defined as involving the formulation (and acceptance) of an argument about the grounding of authority and thus of power. Depending on who makes the argu-

---

[1] *Keichō kenmonshū* (Collection of observations on the Keichō era [1595–1614]), p. 497.
[2] *Satsuroku* (Miscellaneous notes). NST 31: 355.

ment and when, and who is supposed to accept it, one can readily distinguish two types of legitimacy: a founding or operative legitimacy and a retrocognitive one. The former operates when new powerholders seek to ground the coercive power they hold in something beyond it, thus transforming that power through new significations into authority. Retrocognitive legitimacy, constructed after the new authority is well in place, may be the product of nonpowerholders who may present arguments different from the original one. For instance, Ieyasu may very well have reached out for the shogunal title as a way to legitimate his new position, whereas later generations may argue, for their own reasons, that he became accepted as Japan's supreme ruler because he renewed Heaven's Mandate—an argument that would not have had great persuasive power the day after Sekigahara. Both constructs, it should be noted, are strategies motivated by political purposes.

On the surface of things, Tokugawa power seems to have been publicly sanctioned and legitimized in 1603, when emperor Goyōzei (r. 1586–1611) granted Ieyasu's request to receive the title of shogun. This appointment signified the delegation of authority to the Tokugawa to rule the country in the emperor's name: such is the "natural" interpretation one finds in both Tokugawa and modern discussions of the emperor-shogun relationship. This interpretation, however, narrows the question of legitimation to the very specific notion of delegation of powers.

The Meiji Restoration greatly contributed to this view. The Restoration has often been spoken of, both retrospectively by historians and prospectively by bakumatsu activists, as a return to the emperor of powers delegated to the shogun, presumably in 1603.[3] Yet this representation of the court-bakufu relationship as a "delegation of powers," which undeniably existed in the mid-nineteenth century, does not go back to 1603. In other words, the delegation theory is a retrocognitive legitimacy that developed at some point during the Tokugawa period and therefore raises questions about the nature of the founding legitimacy at the beginning of the period.

NEUTRALIZING IMPERIAL AUTHORITY AND PRESTIGE

The question is one of perspectives on the bakufu-court relationship. The views on this subject put forth by three classes of people

[3] For the development of a delegation theory as a political weapon during the bakumatsu period, see Ōkubo, "Bakumatsu seiji to seiken inin mondai," pp. 292–95.

are especially important: bakufu leaders, bakufu scholars, and scholars not directly attached to the bakufu. For the first half century of bakufu rule, however, the bakufu-court relationship is passed over in silence in the political discourse of all three categories of spokesmen. The first hint by a bakufu leader of a theory of delegation does not appear until Matsudaira Sadanobu. In 1788/10, as shogunal regent, Sadanobu wrote a fifteen-point instruction about the proper character of shogunal rule.[4] There he explains that the whole of Japan had been entrusted by the court to the shogun, whose function it was to serve the emperor and the court. As a fitting expression of the relationship, Sadanobu also proposed in another writing of the same year that it would be desirable to see the shogun again make a progress to the emperor in Kyoto, something that had not happened since 1634.[5] Clearly, for Sadanobu, this trusteeship had not been expressed for over 150 years. It is important to note that ritual is seen here as the proper medium within which to express that relationship.

The idea of the shogun as a representative (*gomyōdai*) of the emperor had already been expressed in the early eighteenth century by famous writers such as the astronomer Nishikawa Joken (in his widely read *Chōninbukuro*, Merchant bag, 1719) and the Confucian scholar Asami Keisai (in his *Satsuroku*, Miscellaneous notes, 1706).[6] Seventeenth-century writers, however, are either vague on the emperor-shogun relationship or phrase the problem with a pragmatic argument in favor of the shogun. Nakae Tōju was vague. When in the 1640s he discussed the hierarchy of his broadly conceived duty of filial piety, he mentioned as the recipients of such duty the Son of Heaven, the lords (daimyo), the great ministers (major vassals), the samurai, and the commoners.[7] Tōju's terminology is Chinese, and since China had neither a shogun nor a warrior class, Tōju had to make adjustments. Yet, it is curious that although Tōju adapts the Chinese hierarchy to Japan by pointing out that "lords" stand for daimyo, and "great ministers" for the major vassals, and by finding a place for the samurai in his scheme, nowhere does he explicitly mention the shogun (unless he was subsumed together with the emperor under "Son of Heaven").

---

[4] Shibusawa, *Rakuō-kō den*, p. 116. Several scholars have suggested that this text constitutes the first reference by a bakufu official to a delegation theory. See Kinugasa, "Bakuhanseige no tennō to bakufu," p. 83; Asao, "Bakuhansei to tennō," p. 191.

[5] Matsudaira, *Kanko-dori*, p. 7.

[6] NST 59: 138; NST 31: 355, 390.

[7] *Okina mondō*; NST 29: 27–30.

Yamaga Sokō, on the other hand, argued that in the present the shogun was the ruler because the emperors in the past had failed in their duties; the shogun therefore ruled *in lieu of* the court.[8]

The legal historian Ishii Ryōsuke pointed out some thirty years ago that the representation of the emperor-shogun relationship as one of delegation occurred only late in the Tokugawa period. By 1603, the emperor had in fact long lost all political authority and could not, therefore, have delegated it.[9] When emperor Goyōzei gave in to Ieyasu's request for the shogunal title, he merely acknowledged that Ieyasu was the most formidable military power in the land. Neither then nor previously did the shogunal office entail administrative and political jurisdiction over the whole realm. The ideas of trusteeship, representation, and proxy rule were later theoretical attempts to make sense of the coexistence of two hierarchical pinnacles, an emperor and a shogun.

The shogunal title certainly helped Ieyasu make official his position at the top of a new hierarchy of domination, but this was only one element in a grand legitimizing effort. Deploying other strategies, as we will see, the Tokugawa leadership skillfully used the emperor and ultimately robbed him of his prestige-granting authority. The shogunal appointment was thus not the culmination and closure of Ieyasu's legitimizing effort, even in the eyes of bakufu-hired scholars. The bakufu, through a number of devices, came over time to pose as a national government, and in the process came to outshine the court, drawing all attention to itself as the sole center of political authority.

Hayashi Gahō, Razan's son and successor, ends his short national history (the *Nihon ōdai ichiran* or Overview of Japanese reigns, 1652) with a portrayal of Ieyasu as the new recipient of the mandate in 1600, suggesting that the imperial line had lost it under the inept rule of emperor Godaigo (r. 1319–1338) more than 270 years earlier.[10] The longer *Honchō tsugan* (General mirror of Japan), compiled by Razan and Gahō between 1644 and 1670, on the other hand, ends in 1614, just before the Osaka campaigns in which Ieyasu eliminated the Toyotomi family—in hindsight the last threat to his power. In an appendix, moreover, Sekigahara is

---

[8] Bitō, "Sonnō-jōi shisō," p. 60.

[9] Ishii, *Tennō*, p. 153; id., *Edo manpitsu* 1: 167–68.

[10] For the historiographical information that follows I am partly indebted to Nakai, "Domestication," and to her forthcoming *Arai Hakuseki*. *Nihon ōdai ichiran* (1664) 7: 60b–61a; 6: 10a–b.

celebrated as the completion of the founding work and the beginning of enlightened rule. For Ogyū Sorai, also, Tokugawa national rule started with the disappearance of the Toyotomi (*Seidan* or Political discourses, 1725–1727). Arai Hakuseki sees Sekigahara as the time when Heaven's Mandate was renewed (*Hankanpu* or Account of the feudal domains, 1702), and he ends his survey of Japanese history (*Tokushi yoron* or Views on history, 1712) with Ieyasu subduing the whole realm through divine martial virtue. The *Dainihonshi* (Great history of Japan), compiled in the Mito domain between 1657 and 1720, also suggests that Ieyasu received the Mandate.[11]

These scholars were all advisors to the Tokugawa or (as in the case of Mito) closely related to the bakufu. In their justifications for the hegemonous character of Tokugawa rule, they either gloss over the role of the emperor—as was also done in *Ieyasu's Testament*—or argue that the court had lost its mandate to the warrior houses. Thus their common view was that Ieyasu simply received or "renewed" the Mandate. In relying on the Confucian idea of the change of the Mandate of Heaven, these scholars were not only saying that Ieyasu's government was now seen as a just government, but that it rested on the successful application of military force to stabilize the country. Yet Japan was not China. The Tokugawa situation was anomalous in that the emperor, although arguably having lost the Mandate, was still on the throne. This created a very delicate political situation. As Kate Nakai has pointed out, the Hayashi and Mito scholars maintained a deliberate ambiguity concerning the bakufu-court relationship.[12] Hayashi Gahō, for example, was very well aware that he had to proceed cautiously on controversial issues: he made a distinction, already established by Razan, between his personal views and his public writings. Certain things, he admits in his diary, call for discretion in the way they are presented.[13]

In a private conversation of 1664 with Tokugawa Mitsukuni from Mito, Gahō discussed the thorny question of the *Nanboku* period (1332–1392), when Japan had a northern and a southern imperial court.[14] Emperor Godaigo from the southern court had

[11] *Honchō tsugan* 15: 5709; *id.*, "Furoku" 2: 751; NST 36: 306–307; *Arai Hakuseki zenshū* 1: 1 (of "hanrei," introductory remarks); NST 35: 418; *Dainihonshi sansō*, NST 48: 164–65, 173.

[12] Nakai, "Domestication" and *Arai Hakuseki*.

[13] See the diary Gahō kept during the process of compiling the *Honchō tsugan: Kokushikan nichiroku* (vols. 16–17 of *Honchō tsugan*) 1: 41, 18.

[14] *Ibid.*, 1: 40–41. for a lucid exposition of this thorny question, see Nakai, "Domestication," and *Arai Hakuseki*. See also Kurihara, "Mitsukuni," pp. 562–66.

been deposed by a treacherous vassal in 1331, and the southern line ultimately disappeared. Emperor Goyōzei, who had made Ieyasu shogun, was a descendant of the northern line, which had been set up as a puppet court by Ashikaga Takauji in 1336. As Hakuseki argued later, the legitimate imperial house had disappeared in the fourteenth century. On the other hand, Ieyasu claimed descent from Nitta Yoshisada, a loyal defender of the southern court which, if construed as a justification for Ieyasu's succession to the shogunal post, would still not resolve satisfactorily Ieyasu's relationship to the existing imperial house.

This indicates that, at least for bakufu historians in the mid-seventeenth century, there were serious problems with grounding shogunal authority in an imperial decree. The absence of any discussion of the court-bakufu relationship during the first half of the century shows that similar problems had also existed during the founding period. It is probable that these problems were more complex than Watanable Hiroshi's suggestion that the Japanese at that time were unable to differentiate between authority and power.[15] Watanabe's explanation does not solve the problem of the court; as the sole prestige-granting agency in the realm, the court held a kind of authority that had to be used and neutralized by the Tokugawa. In 1600 or in 1615, Ieyasu could not simply have claimed, as later historians could, that he had received or renewed the Heavenly Mandate.

A carefully balanced political strategy of simultaneously using and domesticating the center of prestige at the imperial court runs through the careers of all the great powerholders from Oda Nobunaga until Tokugawa Iemitsu. We have already documented the policies of Nobunaga and Hideyoshi in this regard. It should be recalled that Nobunaga requested the abdication of Emperor Ōgimachi, and intended to replace him with his own candidate, Prince Sanehito. Hideyoshi helped Goyōzei to the throne, lavishly entertained the court at his Jūraku mansion, and became kanpaku. Hideyoshi used this office (in a novel way) to issue nationwide directives to all daimyo. His successor to the kanpaku office, Toyotomi Hidetsugu, ordered a national cadaster survey and a population count. These orders were executed by all daimyo in their respective domains, but the results were registered by district and province, the old imperial administrative units. Nobunaga had escaped the framework of court rank and office, but Hideyoshi

---

[15] Watanabe, "Tokugawa zenki Jugakushi," p. 25.

clearly showed how it could be put to use to transform his limited authority as feudal lord into a national authority. These surveys, it should be noted, were also conducted in the context of the national war effort in Korea. Earlier, daimyo had sometimes relied on the old administrative provincial framework when they came to rule over a whole province; they then issued their laws as *kokuhō* or provincial laws.[16] Nevertheless, court rank and court office could only be issued by the emperor, who thus held some largely symbolic but nevertheless real authority.

Ieyasu also exploited this source of authority as early as 1566, when he changed his name from Matsudaira to Tokugawa and started on the court rank ladder by receiving junior lower fifth rank, the lowest rung in the upper echelon of the ten-layered system. As Nobunaga had already understood, however, although court rank increased one's prestige and may have been very desirable for a young and rather obscure warlord, it was also a domesticating device to absorb military power into the traditional framework. Moreover, it was a path that was open to competitors. When in 1602 Ieyasu received junior first court rank, Toyotomi Hideyori, although only nine years old at the time, received senior second rank. Ieyasu's acquisition of the shogunal title therefore meant that he had outdistanced Hideyori for good (although Hideyori also became Naidaijin when Ieyasu became shogun): there could be only one shogun in the realm. That shogun was, however, appointed by the court.

The domesticating function of court ranks and offices rested on the assumption that they were so desirable that once offered, they would be eagerly and gratefully accepted. In other words, they were unilateral gifts that could be neither refused nor reciprocated in kind. The inescapability and irreversability of a situation in which the court had the initiative automatically signified the subordinate position of the recipient. Oda Nobunaga was the first to have seen through this strategy and reversed it: with his refusal of new titles and return of the ones he already held, the initiative became his. The court was left with no further recourse in a position that signified the irreducible secondary nature of imperial authority vis-à-vis Nobunaga's. Hideyoshi redeployed Nobunaga's strategy when he retired from the kanpaku office. And Ieyasu also, after increasing his symbolic capital through the ac-

---

[16] Miki, "Sengoku-kinsei shoki ni okeru kokka to tennō," pp. 19–22, 28.

ceptance of court rank, title, and office, increased it even further by severing himself and, step by step, the whole warrior authority structure from the court.

First Ieyasu escaped imperial authority by turning the shogunal office over to his son Hidetada in 1605 and becoming retired shogun (*ōgosho*), a title and position without court office. Then, on 1604/4/25, he ruled that henceforward recommendations for court ranks and offices for the warriors could be initiated only by the bakufu. Ieyasu used the rank system to turn the daimyo into semi-public servants—their titles of "*kami*" (lord) of such and such *province* had the same purpose—yet at the same time, he took the initiative away from the court.[17] In article seven of the *Rules for the Court*, issued in 1615, Ieyasu decreed that ranks and offices for warriors would be separate from ranks for the courtiers (so that two incumbents could eventually hold the same office and the service function to the court would attach to courtiers only). After 1620, moreover, warrior ranks were no longer listed in the court's official rank annals (*Kugyō bunin*) published annually.[18]

During the reigns of the first four shoguns, there was still a need for misrepresenting the legal relationship between the court and the bakufu. A certain formality made it appear as if the court had the last word in granting court rank to warriors. The court was usually petitioned by the bakufu to grant a certain rank to a warrior and only then was the appointment made. From Tsunayoshi's rule on, however, even the pretense of imperial permission was eliminated. The bakufu proceeded directly with the appointment and then informed the court.[19] Before that occurred, however, Iemitsu turned a refusal of a court office into a public demonstration of the bakufu's independence from the court.

The occasion provided one of the grandest settings of the whole Tokugawa period for the display of bakufu power: the last shogunal progress to Kyoto in 1634. More than 300,000 troops and all the daimyo were in Kyoto for the two-month-long visit by Iemitsu. On 7/15 the ex-emperor Gomizunoo announced privately to

---

[17] Miyazawa, "Tennō no ideorogiiteki kiban," pp. 205–206; Ishii, *Edo manpitsu* 1: 173.

[18] Ishii, *Tennō*, pp. 159, 161.

[19] *Ibid.*, pp. 159–61. In the early eighteenth century, both Arai Hakuseki and Ogyū Sorai argued for the creation of a separate system of merit rank exclusively for the warriors in order to completely sever the last tie between the warrior houses and the court provided by the court rank system. For Hakuseki, see *Arai Hakuseki zenshū* 6: 465–74; for Sorai, *Seidan*, in NST 36: 348. I owe this information to Kate Nakai, who analyzes these arguments in her *Arai Hakuseki*.

Iemitsu his wish to grant him the title of Dajōdaijin (Prime Minister), but Iemitsu refused. Two days later Gomizunoo renewed his proposal, but Iemitsu again declined the honor, invoking his young age ("not yet forty"—he was thirty then) as the reason. A similar incident had happened in 1626, when on 8/18 Hidetada was made dajōdaijin. He also first declined, but accepted the appointment a month later, on 9/12. Whereas the argument over the acceptance of a court office in 1626 was a private affair between Hidetada and the emperor, in 1634 Iemitsu decided, after his final refusal (and after consulting with the Three Houses), to make his stance toward the court public. On 7/19 he announced to all gathered daimyo that he had refused the title of dajōdaijin "for state reasons." [20] The court had publicly and shamefully been put in its proper and rather insignificant place in the new order. Shogunal largesse toward the emperor on i.7/3 in the form of tripling the emperor's lands from three to ten thousand koku further drove the point home: the emperor was enconomically dependent on the shogun. The emperor owed *on* and gratitude toward the shogun, and not the other way around.

Why did the Tokugawa rulers not simply eliminate the emperor? The answer, with the benefit of historical hindsight, is that they felt that a simple and final solution would have deprived their power of legitimacy. For all practical and symbolic purposes, however, they did away with the emperor over the long run. The neutralization (one could call it the de-symbolization) of the court was a prolonged operation. It is not that a more drastic formula was never contemplated; there is, in fact, some evidence that it was. Although the evidence is "soft" it does make political sense.

This evidence consists of an alleged conversation between Ieyasu and two advisors, Tenkai and Tōdō Takatora.[21] Takatora was a trusted daimyo who had made a great career under Ieyasu; having started with a 5,000-koku fief in the 1580s, by 1615 he ruled over a 323,900-koku domain. This conversation is supposed to have taken place immediately after Ieyasu's victory over the Toyotomi (Osaka castle fell on 1615/5/8). Ieyasu was then at the height of his power. The very change of the era name to Genna (Basic Peace) expressed the historical awareness that a momentous point had been reached. Barely three months later, Ieyasu issued comprehen-

[20] Fukaya, "Kokka to tennō," pp. 263–64.
[21] This conversation is to be found in *Tsushi-shi* 1: 119–120. See also Fukaya, "Bakuhansei to tennō," p. 4.

sive national legislation for the warrior houses (7/7), the court and nobility (7/17), and the religious establishment (7/24). Around that time Tenkai allegedly suggested to Ieyasu that the emperor and the whole court be moved to Ise, where they would function in a purely religious role as Shinto priests. Thus, Tenkai argued, the shogun could have the same power as the Son of Heaven. Takatora, however, objected that the daimyo and the people would not accept anyone as being on the same level as the emperor, and that this would result in new warfare for the whole country. Ieyasu, it is said, followed Takatora's advice. Apocryphical as the report of this strategy session may be, it accurately reflects the thrust of Ieyasu's court politics, the ritual strategies Tenkai was to develop in the years to come, and Iemitsu's ultimate achievements in his policies vis-à-vis the court.

Japanese historians have recently identified another way in which the bakufu succeeded in expanding its influence at the cost of the court. Tamamuro Fumio has shown that Ieyasu's temple legislation was aimed not only at preventing the reemergence of populist movements like the Ikkō and Nichiren sects but also, and perhaps mainly, at breaking the traditional ties that bound the imperial court to the great Buddhist establishments.[22] The Kamakura and Muromachi shoguns never touched the links between the court and traditional Buddhism. They simply became patrons of a new brand of Buddhism (Zen) that had no previous ties with the court. Ieyasu could have continued the past bakufu policy of sponsoring Zen Buddhism, but he did not do so. He sought to control and regulate the whole institutional world of Japanese Buddhism. As Tamamuro suggests, Ieyasu's institutional legislation of Buddhism yielded, among other things, a weakening of imperial centrality.

This legislation developed gradually, sect by sect and sometimes region by region; its pace and tempo were adapted to particular situations, to the strengths or weaknesses of each sect. Ieyasu's measures against the Shingon sect illustrate this policy well.

First, in 1601, Ieyasu used an internal dispute to split the holdings of Mount Kōya among two categories of monks, the *gakuryo* or learned monks and the *kōjin* or wandering ascetics. Between 1609 and 1613, he issued laws for the Shingon sect in the Kanto area (where the sect had less powerful temples and where Ieyasu's

---

[22]Tamamuro, *Shūkyō tōsei*, p. 19. See also Fukaya, "Kokka to tennō," p. 236.

authority was strongest), regulating in great detail the life and training of the monks, and also establishing a clear hierarchy between main and branch temples. Finally, in 1615/7, after securing control over the Kanto Shingon, Ieyasu extended his legislation for the sect nationwide.[23]

The power of the Tendai sect had already been broken when Oda Nobunaga put the torch to Mount Hiei in 1571. The Tendai temples in the Kanto area were brought under control between 1608 and 1614. Legislation for the Pure Land sect was issued all at once in 1615. The following year, a general prohibition was issued, barring the building of new temples. On 1613/6/18, the Rinzai sect was forbidden to receive the appointment of abbots from the imperial court without prior approval from the bakufu.[24] This decree was invoked in 1627, when the bakufu nullified the imperial appointments of two abbots for Daitokuji and Myōshinji in Kyoto. Takuan, a famous former abbot from Daitokuji, and two other monks protested the bakufu's interference. He was banished to the northeast in 1629. The bakufu, however, displayed its power again three years later by pardoning Takuan and inviting him to build the Tōkaiji in Shinagawa (Edo) in 1638.[25] In this way, Takuan was honored by the bakufu while remaining under close supervision. He was even "permitted" to lecture at the imperial court.

Traditionally, the larger temples (especially Tendai temples) had occasionally been asked by the court to perform special services on behalf of the imperial family or the nation. Such requests now came from the bakufu. Fukaya Katsumi has documented numerous instances in which the bakufu ordered prayers and services for peace, for a long-lasting warrior regime, or for the health of an ailing shogun. Even the court was sometimes ordered to conduct special prayers or *kagura* performances, as were the Izumo and Ise Shrines.[26] Whereas in the past the religious establishment had served the court, by Iemitsu's time all major temples, shrines, and even the court itself stood ready to respond to calls from the bakufu. The Tokugawa house had invaded another space that had traditionally been the court's.

Ieyasu and Iemitsu went even further in their use of religion to signify their regimes as parallel and equivalent to the imperial

[23] Tamamuro, *Shūkyō tōsei*, pp. 23–24.
[24] *Ibid.*, pp. 36, 41, 44, 224.
[25] Fukaya, "Kokka to tennō," pp. 260–62.
[26] *Ibid.*, pp. 245–46, 267.

order of the past. They did everything short of physically eliminating the emperor and occupying his throne to project the same sublime awe that the emperor once evoked. They diverted the religious respect that surrounded emperor and court (ordered in 1615 to occupy themselves with scholarship—scholarship was as unpolitical as a Shinto priesthood in Ise, one supposes) and appropriated it to add the most powerful dimension available to their authority.[27] Oda Nobunaga and Toyotomi Hideyoshi had also reached for this ultimate legitimizing strategy by their self-deification. The Tokugawa similarly strove to sanctify their rule, but used the imperial model. This did not happen "naturally" in the sense that all concentrations of power embody a religious intensity, as is sometimes argued.[28] With Ieyasu and Iemitsu there was calculation and manipulation; a master plan that was given structure and consistency by none other than Tenkai—the monk behind the proposed Ise solution to the problem of the imperial court.

TENKAI: RITUALIST-IDEOLOGUE

Tenkai (1536–1643) was a Tendai monk who entered Ieyasu's service in Sunpu in 1608 at the age of seventy-two.[29] From the beginning, he was far more influential than Razan, who had been hired three years earlier, and contributed more than Razan ever did to "legitimize" Tokugawa rule. If anyone deserves to be called a bakufu ideologue, it is he. The medium he used, however, was ritual. The Ieyasu cult was his creation. The inauguration of the Nikkō shrine in 1636 was for the then one-hundred-year-old Tenkai the highpoint of his career, and for the bakufu the apogee of a long effort for legitimation.

Of all the Buddhist sects in Japan, Tendai had since Heian times forged the closest ties with the imperial court. Through Tenkai, Tendai Buddhism became the bakufu's institutional religion (although the Tokugawa house remained attached to the Pure Land sect, not all shoguns were buried in Edo's Zōjōji; some have their grave in Kan'eiji and Iemitsu is buried in Nikkō).

[27] The first rule of the *Regulations for the Emperor and the Court* stressed the study of literature as a proper occupation for the emperor and the nobility. See Hall, "Japanese Feudal Laws. III" p. 276.

[28] For example, Edward Shils, *Center and Periphery: Essays in Macrosociology* (Chicago: University of Chicago Press, 1975), pp. 138, 151.

[29] *Jigen Daishi* 1: 288.

In 1613, Tenkai was put in charge of the Kita'in temple in Kawagoe, about 45 km northwest of Edo. Renamed the Eastern Hieizan Kita'in, it was hoped that this temple would be for Edo what Mount Hiei had been for Kyoto. (This was also the center from which the Tendai sect in the Kanto area was controlled.) In 1613 Tenkai further received from Ieyasu the Rinnōji temple in Nikkō, to which the Tōshōgū shrine for Ieyasu would later be attached.[30]

Tenkai was one of three "clerics" close to Ieyasu. The other two were Sūden (1569–1633) and Bonshun (1553–1632). Sūden, also hired in 1608, when Ieyasu started his temple legislation in earnest, was the abbot of the Nanzenji Zen center in Kyoto. He also played a role in the conflict that resulted in Takuan's banishment. Bonshun was a Yoshida Shinto theologian who had presided over Hideyoshi's Hōkoku shrine ritual. We have seen how these three clerics clashed over the proper posthumous title for Ieyasu immediately after the latter's funeral (conducted according to Yoshida ritual) at Kunōzan in Sunpu, with Sūden and Bonshun losing to Tenkai. The stakes for these men were high, because the victor was eventually to preside over the religious tradition that would serve the bakufu.

This struggle for the bakufu's soul had started during Ieyasu's lifetime. It will be remembered that Bonshun introduced Yoshida Shinto teachings to Ieyasu, but at the last minute seems to have been prevented by Tenkai from formally completing Ieyasu's initiation. Tenkai, on the other hand, claimed to have converted Ieyasu to Tendai, which Asao Naohiro argues is a fabrication.[31] Whatever the case, Tenkai writes that when, in 1616, he taught Ieyasu about *Sannō ichijitsu* (Tendai-Shinto teachings he allegedly received from the emperor), Ieyasu expressed his desire to be reburied one year after his death in Nikkō, like Fujiwara Kamatari (614–669), the founder of the Fujiwara family, who in 670 was reburied in Tōnomine.[32] Ieyasu's oral last will to Sūden and Honda Masazumi, however, does not seem to have contained any reference to a reburial, only to the building of a shrine in Nikkō on the first anniversary of his death.[33] Nevertheless, Tenkai succeeded in bringing Ieyasu's remains to Nikkō on the first memorial anniversary.

[30] Tamamuro, *Shūkyō tōsei*, p. 34; *Jigen Daishi* 1: 291.
[31] For Tenkai's claim, see *ibid.* 1: 378. Asao Naohiro makes this point in *Sakoku*, p. 273.
[32] *Jigen Daishi* 1: 46, 60, 81, 82, 380, 382.
[33] Asao, *Sakoku*, p. 272.

In 1624 Tenkai scored another victory. Although the Pure Land Zōjōji temple in Edo was the Tokugawa family temple, "Hidetada decided that year," writes Tenkai, "since his father had converted to Tendai, to build a family temple northeast of Edo castle that would protect the shogunal palace as Mount Hiei protected the imperial palace."[34] The next year the Kan'eiji, also called Eastern Mount Hiei, was built in Edo at the cost of 50,000 ryō, to which twenty-four daimyo contributed. At the same time, Tōdō Takatora (who had allegedly dissuaded Ieyasu from following Tenkai's Ise scheme) opened a branch shrine for Ieyasu within the precincts of Kan'eiji.[35]

Tenkai's next opportunity came when Iemitsu, probably prompted by a sincere admiration for his grandfather and no doubt encouraged by Tenkai, decided to expand the Nikkō shrine into an impressive commemorative mausoleum. It should be noted that Iemitsu decided not to honor his father Hidetada in a religious way; the two were said not to have gotten along well. Iemitsu may have had secret hopes for his own deification, however, since he kept in his amulet bag a slip of paper on which was written "the second *gongen*."[36] Whatever the entangled motivations behind Iemitsu's project (financed exclusively by the bakufu at the cost of 500,000 ryō), Tenkai gave it ideological shape and transformed Ieyasu from the protective guardian of the eight Kanto provinces into a deity that shone from the east over the whole of Japan and the world.[37] For this purpose he transformed the *Sannō* teachings into the *Sannō ichijitsu* (The Sannō One Truth) doctrine.

When Tenkai marshaled Sannō teachings and the *gongen* title for the celebration of Ieyasu's memory, he appropriated for the bakufu both a venerable Buddhist tradition long in the service of the court and a pattern of popular belief that recently had informed a novel kind of hero worship. Sannō Shinto is the particular brand of Shinto that had been worked out by the Tendai sect, and has traditionally been ascribed to Tendai's Japanese founder, Saichō (767–822). The *honji-suijaku* theory (whereby Japanese kami are considered avatars or *suijaku* of particular Buddhas or bodhisattvas who are their original substance or *honji*) with re-

---

[34] *Jigen Daishi* 1: 384.

[35] Fukaya, "Kokka to tennō," pp. 225, 238.

[36] Tsuji Tatsuya, *Kyōhō kaikaku no kenkyū*, p. 114.

[37] Asao, *Sakoku*, p. 273. The Ieyasu cult thus transcended the limited meaning that some scholars ascribe to it as an ancestor cult (Fukaya, "Kokka to tennō," p. 239) or as a cult for the Tokugawa clan aimed at incorporating the fudai daimyo (Miyazawa, "Tennō no ideorogiiteki kiban," pp. 197–98).

lation to Sannō had developed during the early Kamakura period but was ascribed to Saichō—just as Tenkai also presented as Saichō's own teachings his reformulation of the tradition into *Sannō ichijitsu*.[38] The original shrine (Hie) on Mount Hiei where Saichō founded Tendai, was dedicated to an agricultural god, Ōyamakui. The Tendai temples gave this god a new function, name, and identity. The god became their protective deity whose portable shrine (*mikoshi*) was occasionally brought down from the mountain during Heian times, when the monks had disputes to settle with the authorities in Kyoto. The Enryakuji, Tendai's main temple on Mount Hiei, also referred to the Hie shrine as Sannō gongen, the Sannō avatar.[39] The Sannō Hie deity was thus redefined as the *suijaku* of Shaka, the kami of the highest truth. In the late Kamakura period, the Hie god was further identified as Amaterasu.

During the late Kamakura-early Muromachi period, Yoshida Shinto had reversed the relationship between original Buddhas and reincarnated kami. This is what Tenkai did for the Sannō cult: he reversed the superior-inferior or prior-later relationship involved in the *honji-suijaku* theory, and made Amaterasu the *honji*. Ieyasu thus became the reincarnation of a national deity, Amaterasu, the ancestral goddess of the imperial house. His name Tōshō, Shining from/over the East, also alluded to this relationship: *shō* is the same character as the *terasu* of Amaterasu. At the end of the eighteenth century, Motoori Norinaga wrote: "The present age is one in which, at the discretion of the Great God (*ōmikami*) Amaterasu and under the trust of the imperial household, the successive [Tokugawa] shoguns, starting with Azumateru kamumioya no mikoto [Ieyasu], have conducted the affairs of state."[40] In assuming the proportional equation

[38] *Shintō jiten* (Umeda and Anzu eds.), p. 352; *Jigen Daishi* 1: 9, 81.

[39] Sannō was originally the name of an "exemplary" landlord venerated in a temple on Mt. T'ien-tai where the Chinese headquarters of Tendai Buddhism were located. The name, written with the characters for mountain and king (山王), has been interpreted as expressing the essence of Tendai doctrine: *santaiso-kuichi-isshinsankan* or "the three truths are one" (symbolized by the three vertical strokes of "mountain," linked by one horizontal stroke) and "one mind-three views" (the one vertical stroke of "king," linking the three horizontal strokes). The three truths or views entail a progressive Buddhist epistemological dialectic. First, things are negated because everything is empty by the law of karma. This first truth of emptiness (*kū*) however, is in turn negated by the nominalist truth that emptiness is only a temporary name (*ke*) and does not exist. Hence, emptiness must also be negated. This leads to the transcendance of all thought and language in the center (*chū*). To uphold these three aspects at once is the "one mind." For other interpretations, by Razan and the author of the *Warongo*, see above pp. 99–100.

[40] Matsumoto, *Motoori Norinaga*, pp. 138–39; also p. 224.

Amaterasu : Emperor : : Ieyasu : Tokugawa shogun

and in further approximating Amaterasu with Ieyasu by referring
to the latter as "Azumateru kamumioya no mikoto" (the High
Ancestral Deity, the God Azumateru—another reading for
Tōshō), Motoori was not involving himself in specious etymology.
He had perfectly understood the ideological message that Tenkai
had intended to communicate.

Tenkai went even further, however, than merely associating
Ieyasu with the supreme national deity. In a fabricated conversation between Saichō and Sannō gongen, the deity reveals himself
as the universal god of all gods, who precedes creation, yin and
yang, and is superior to all Buddhas—a revelation duly accompanied by earthquakes, a heavenly shower of flowers, and the
appearance of a pearl tower in the sky: "I am the mysterious god
(*meishin*) of Japan," Gongen says, "I do not fathom yin and yang,
neither do I make the creation. I reside in the nature of the law of
the mind; transformed I bring down the way of truth. The Great
Vow Buddha is inferior. My mind protects the country." What,
Saichō further inquires, is your original nature? Gongen replies:
"This whole world [expressed in the Buddhist term 'the Three
Worlds here (below)'] is mine and all the people are my children."
Tenkai's exegesis explains further that Japan, the land of the gods,
is the root and India and China the branches. All the gods that ever
appeared split off from Sannō's body; he is the fundamental god of
life for Heaven, Earth, and Man; there are no gods besides
Sannō.[41] This is the god with which Ieyasu was associated as its
Great Avatar.

Tenkai identified Ieyasu with a universalized Amaterasu-Sannō
by way of elaborate theological reconstructions. Others before him,
however, had effected similar equations that were less doctrinal but
no less sublime. Except for a few who have left their names, these
others were largely anonymous, "the people."

On 1581/2/29, Oda Nobunaga held an impressive military
parade for the whole court in Kyoto, on grounds cleared especially
for the occasion.[42] Jesuits who were present called it a "resplendent
and magnificent affair." Another witness has also left us his impressions: Ōta Gyūichi (1527–?) who had started his warrior career

[41] *Jigen Daishi* 1: 9, 11, 39. Tenkai formulated this new theology in the founding document
for the new Tōshō shrine, the *Tōshōdaigongen engi*.

[42] For a brief description of the parade, quotes of the two witnesses (the Jesuits and Ōta
Gyūichi), and bibliographical references, see Fujiki, "Oda Nobunaga," p. 179. For Ōta's
career, see Ozawa Eiichi, *Kinsei shigaku*, pp. 34–35.

with Nobunaga as a foot soldier at least thirty years earlier, and had kept a diary. From these notes Ōta compiled his *Shinchōkōki* (Public record of Nobunaga) in 1610—he was eighty-three then—which was an expansion of an earlier *Shinchōki* (Nobunaga record). These later reworkings of his notes (if indeed they were reworkings) notwithstanding Ōta's style is simple, straightforward, and unadorned. His impressions can be trusted as fairly immediate reflections of his own emotional reactions and those of people like him. The only interpretations he brings to the events he records are references to an ill-defined concept of Heaven('s Way) that included various elements of good luck, frightful retributions in the rise and fall of great men, and vague allusions to some ethical or proper social order. Ideologically, his work is flaccid and uninspired. That may be the reason why it was never printed and survived only in manuscript form, whereas another *Shinchōki* by Oze Hoan (1564–1640) was printed in 1622 (with a foreword by Razan, written in 1613). Oze had a clear purpose: to measure from a Confucian point of view how close his hero came to embodying the ideal Way of the Sages. Oze even criticizes Ōta for his "crude" reporting, which testifies to the absence (for Oze) of a conscious or serviceable political intent in Ōta.[43] Ōta thus seems trustworthy as a rapporteur of contemporary views when he describes the awe that struck everyone when Nobunaga made his entry on the parade grounds as "the uncanny feeling of a deity's presence: surely the appearance of the god of Sumiyoshi must be like this!"

It will be recalled that in *Ieyasu's Testament*, both at the beginning and the end, references are made to this god as a divine exemplar for the shogun. *Ieyasu's Testament*, however, is a semi-official document. Ōta's text, on the other hand (and also much later Sawada Gennai's *Warongo*), shows that as early as the 1580s, at the popular level, the theatrical display of concentrated warrior power spontaneously evoked an experience of awe, expressed in a terminology of the sacred. This suggests that at least by some of "the people" the supreme holders of warrior power in Japan were being sacralized and thus put beyond questioning—or, in other words, legitimized in a religious way.

Toyotomi Hideyoshi consciously exploited this legitimation device. The popular success of the posthumous cult to Hideyoshi as

---

[43] See Ozawa, *Kinsei shigaku* for the relationship between the *Shinchōki* and the *Shinchōkōki* (pp. 34, 42–43), Ōta's style and Oze's criticism of it (p. 38), and Ōta's use of *ten* and *tendō* in the *Shinchōkōki* (pp. 41–47). See also Matsuda, *Kinsei bungaku*, pp. 31, 42–43.

Hōkoku daimyōjin (stamped out by Ieyasu in 1615) testifies to the skillful manipulation of sacral elements from above.[44] But more intriguing is the patterning of the earliest Hideyoshi biography on a divine template—a scheme whose elements had also been provided by Hideyoshi during his lifetime. The model here is not Sumiyoshi daimyōjin or Hōkoku daimyōjin but the one Tenkai appropriated for Ieyasu: Hie or Hiyoshi Sannō.

As Matsuda Osamu has pointed out, this identification of Hideyoshi with Sannō gongen consists of several elements. First, although there exist three different birth dates for Hideyoshi, he himself seems to have stressed 1/1 of 1536, the year of the monkey, a date that most historians reject as inaccurate. The monkey is the sacred animal of Hie Sannō, and New Year's day of the year of the monkey as Hideyoshi's birthday suggests his birth as a reincarnation of the god.[45] Second, Hideyoshi's nickname was Kosaru or simply Saru, monkey. Third, Hideyoshi himself, in an official diplomatic document of 1593, writes that he was conceived by sunrays.[46] One can imagine that this tale was inspired by the *reading* (not the written characters) of the name Hideyoshi. Hideyoshi could mean "auspiciousness out of the sun," a reading that draws associations with Hie or Hiyoshi (written with the characters for sun and auspicious—this explains the association between Amaterasu and Mount Hiei). The most famous of all the *Taikōki* (Hideyoshi biographies), the one by Oze Hoan (with a preface written in 1625) reports that Hideyoshi's given name was Hiyoshimaru. Fourth, the Hie Sannō shrine, burned down in Nobunaga's attack on Mount Hiei in 1570, was rebuilt by Hideyoshi in 1591. Fifth, Matsuda Osamu has shown that the subtext for the *Taikō sujōki*, another Hideyoshi biography, is a popular legend called *Aigo no waka* (A protected youngster) which structurally patterns Hideyoshi's youth after the career of a young god who is none other than a reincarnation of Ōyamakui or Hie Sannō.[47]

Finally, Hideyoshi used the Nō theater as a medium for presenting himself as a god. Until 1593, Hideyoshi showed no interest in

[44] See above, pp. 50 and 58.
[45] Matsuda, *Kinsei bungaku*, ch. 3 (pp. 47–74), esp. pp. 49–50. For a discussion of the different sources concerning Hideyoshi's birthday, see Elison, "Hideyoshi," pp. 223–24, and nn. 1 and 5, pp. 329–31. The historically accepted birthdate is 1537/2/6. The third possibility (1536/6/15) is also associated with the sacred animal, the monkey.
[46] Matsuda, *Kinsei bungaku*, p. 50; Elison, "Hideyoshi," pp. 223, 224 and p. 331 n9.
[47] Matsuda, *Kinsei bungaku*, pp. 71, 51–60.

Nō whatever. Then he suddenly became more enthusiastic than any other daimyo about Nō drama. Most of the plays Hideyoshi acted out (sometimes, apparently, before the emperor) and the new ones he commissioned were staged celebrations of his military and political achievements. Sometimes he even took the role of a gongen. Nō drama, as Matsuda Osamu reminds us, was not theater as we conceive of it today—mere representation. God-plays retained a genuine religious aura. The actors, assuming divine characters, identified with the divine powers they acted out and drew emotional responses that one ought to describe as religious awe.[48] The Nō performance of a god-play, one could add, was in this respect no different from a *kagura* performance.

Hideyoshi's general goal of self-deification is not to be doubted, although the detail varies somewhat. Most elements connect him with the Sannō cult, but his posthumous cult did not. Neither was it Sannō that he acted out in his gongen role in the Nō play *Yoshino mōde*—or was scheduled to act out, because that particular performance may, in fact, have been canceled. On that particular occasion, Hideyoshi personified Zaō gongen, the deity of the Yoshino shrine. At the popular level, which most concerns us here, the identification of Hideyoshi with the Sannō deity, after the Hōkoku shrine was abolished, was the prevailing and maybe even the only one. The main evidence for this interpretation is the *Taikō sujōki*, which was composed at some uncertain date before 1676.[49]

This late date may suggest that the view of Hideyoshi as Sannō gongen was a post-Hideyoshi phenomenon motivated in part by Ieyasu's similar identification (rather than the other way around). Although the *Taikō sujōki* portrays Hideyoshi as Sannō gongen, it is unlikely that one should read an anti-Ieyasu motivation into this work or that it was inspired by the Nikkō cult. More likely, it was inspired by popular beliefs about Hideyoshi. The author, Tsuchiya Tomosada, was a bannerman, which makes him an unlikely candidate for writing literature that could offend the bakufu. A bannerman biographer, however, is hardly a commoner. What makes him a spokesman for popular beliefs? As Matsuda Osamu points out, the work is constructed as a number of tales Tomosada may

---

[48] *Ibid.*, pp. 61–62 and p. 301 n3; Elison, "Hideyoshi," pp. 243–44. On the transformative aspect of theater (and Nō), see Richard Schechner, "Performers and Spectators Transported and Transformed," *Kenyon Review*, New Series, 3 (1981), 4: 83–113.

[49] Ozawa, *Kinsei shigaku*, p. 499.

have heard from his grandmother and stepmother, who were from the same region that Hideyoshi came from. Another likely source for Tomosada seems to have been his father, Izusōkengyō En'ichi, who died in 1621 at the age of eighty, when Tomosada was already a young man. En'ichi was blind, and Matsuda surmises that this blindness may indicate that En'ichi was a wandering minstrel, or at least that he may have been a collector of tales.[50]

A sacred lore developed around Hideyoshi even during his own lifetime, as is evident from a pamphlet posted in 1591 in the streets of Kyoto: "The end of the world/ is nothing else but this:/ watching/ the monkey regent/ under the tree." The pamphlet was a satirical lampoon, as George Elison indicates.[51] The abomination referred to is that a commoner had become *kanpaku*, imperial regent. The pun on Kinoshita ("under the tree"), Hideyoshi's *alleged* original family name (for which there is no genealogical documentation) is clear, as is the reference to Saru, monkey, his nickname. The poem, however, also brings into play some of the elements (analyzed by Matsuda Osamu) that associate Hideyoshi with the legendary young deity of *Aigo no waka* (Ōyamakui, alias Sannō gongen): a being half-monkey half-human under a tree. The allusion in the text, meant for the "man in the street," to the names Kinoshita and Saru may well refer to popular and religious elements out of which Hideyoshi had constructed a sacred identity for himself.[52] Sannō gongen was thus a religious persona by which some commoners had for themselves aggrandized the stature and legitimized the position of Japan's supreme warrior-hero.

When Tenkai appropriated the daigongen title for Ieyasu, he was thus not only diverting imperial Buddhism, Tendai, to the Tokugawa house; he was also rechanneling religio-political popular constructs into the service of the bakufu. Tenkai's effort, however, was an artificial appropriation from above. Ieyasu never turned into the popular hero that Hideyoshi was (perhaps also because no one ever wrote a mythologically inspired biography for Ieyasu that could compete with the *Taikōki*).[53] Ieyasu succeeded in stamping out the daimyōjin cult of Hideyoshi, but the association of

[50] Matsuda, *Kinsei bungaku*, pp. 68–69.
[51] Elison, "Hideyoshi," p. 244.
[52] Matsuda, *Kinsei bungaku*, pp. 54–56. On Hideyoshi's assumed Kinoshita name, see Elison, "Hideyoshi," p. 224.
[53] Matsuda, *Kinsei bungaku*, p. 48.

Hideyoshi with the Sannō deity continued.[54] That Tenkai's theological framework for the Nikkō cult was a reappropriation may also indicated by a seemingly innocent incident: in 1637, one year after the inauguration of the Tōshōgū shrine in Nikkō, Prince Gyōnen of the imperial court went to Hideyoshi's grave and re-named the shrine of Hōkokuzan in front of the grave the Shin Hiejinja or the New Hie Shrine. The timing of this action by an imperial prince with high Tendai rank—he was to head the Tendai sect three years later—seems to indicate that Tenkai's new Sannō theology, centered around Ieyasu, did not go uncontested, and was understood by some for what it was, namely, a reappropri-ation of Tendai doctrine to legitimize the bakufu in a theological and ritualistic way.[55]

Under the exegetical direction of Tenkai, the daigongen of Nikkō had been transformed into a universal god whose authority would be acknowledged even beyond Japan's borders. This aspect of the Ieyasu cult was ritually expressed most regularly during the Iemitsu regime. The Korean embassies of 1636, 1643, and 1655 (the last one taking place four years after Iemitsu's death, under the regency of Hoshina Masayuki) all proceeded beyond Edo to pay their respect to Ieyasu in Nikkō. In 1644, a delegation from the Ryūkyū Islands also visited the shrine, and the Dutch made pre-sents for embellishing the shrine in 1636.[56] The Tokugawa, like the Chinese emperors, were receiving tribute from foreign nations. The pretension of universal rule was, in ritual form, visible to all.

The kingly rule of the Tokugawa, symbolically expressed most intensely during the Iemitsu-Ietsuna years, was also institutionally enforced then more than at any other time in the Tokugawa period. One usually thinks of the *junkenshi* or bakufu emissaries that were sent out to all domains as a permanent and regular feature of the Tokugawa political system. As Asao Naohiro has pointed out, however, they were sent out only eighteen times during the whole period: once during each of the rules of the fifth to the twelfth shoguns (1680–1853), but four times during the Ietsuna years and six times under Iemitsu (in 1635–1638 every year and in 1641 and

---

[54] See, for instance, the account of Hideyoshi's birth and the legend that his mother prayed for a child to Hiyoshi gongen in Takeuchi Kakusai, *Ehon Taikōki* (An illustrated *Taikōki*) (1797–1802) (Elison, "Hideyoshi," p. 223 and p. 329 n1).

[55] Matsuda (*Kinsei bungaku*, p. 71) reports the incident; the interpretation is mine.

[56] Asao, *Sakoku*, p. 274.

1650).[57] The crisis produced by the famines of the late 1630s and the need to gather accurate information for compiling the Keian legislation certainly contributed to the frequency with which Iemitsu checked up on local government, but the dispatch of emissaries from the center no doubt was also seen as an attribute of kingly government.

In Ise and Nikkō are to be found Japan's two most famous shrines (even today perceived as such: they are on every tourist's itinerary). They are located in rather remote places, at approximately the same distance from Kyoto and Tokyo, respectively. This parallelism is no accident of history. Nikkō was the place where the divine ancestor of the shogun was venerated, as was Ise for the imperial family. There is some indication that Nikkō was, in fact, ultimately to be signified as more important than Ise, as Japan's new ritual point of gravity. The upgrading of Nikkō on the Ise pattern was again the work of Tenkai. It should be recalled that he had also been responsible for the building of the Kan'eiji in Edo. This temple replaced the Kita'in in Kawagoe as a more dignified equivalent to Mount Hiei.

The plan to build a great shrine for Ieyasu was justified both in terms of motivation and timing with reference to the rebuilding of the Ise shrines. Tenkai writes that the construction of the Grand Ise Shrine was meant to organize and concentrate worship of Amaterasu, which had proliferated in over twenty-two different shrines. Similarly, he continued, Ieyasu had been worshiped in three different places.[58] Thus, like the Ise Shrines, rebuilt every twenty years, Tenkai argued that it was appropriate that in 1636, twenty years after the first shrine to Ieyasu was erected, it be replaced with another one.

The gradual displacement of Ise by Nikkō (and by implication of Kyoto by Edo and the court by the bakufu) took place in the mid 1640s. In 1645, the emperor granted the rank of *gū*, the highest shrine rank, to the Tōshō shrine, putting it on a par with the Ise Shrines. That year, the custom of dispatching yearly imperial messengers to Ise, interrupted since the turmoil after the Ōnin War, was reinstituted; but at the same time, imperial messengers were also sent to Nikkō—a custom that would continue uninter-

[57] *Ibid.*, p. 376.
[58] *Jigen Daishi* 1: 53. Tenkai may have been referring to the Three Houses, although by the 1630s more than twenty shrines to Ieyasu had already been built (Asao, *Sakoku*, p. 277).

rupted until 1867. The bakufu, however, did not reciprocate by sending its own messengers to Ise.[59] The court was further used in the Tōshō cult when two years later, in 1647, Emperor Gokōmyō's younger brother became Nikkō *monseki* (priest prince), assuming the joint abbotship of the two temples that serviced the two principle Tōshō shrines, the Rinnōji in Nikkō and the Kan'eiji in Edo. The emperor's brother thus became the supreme Tokugawa ritualist.

As the shogun overshadowed the emperor and Nikkō took preeminence over Ise (at least in the eyes of the bakufu), it became a question of whether Edo also had replaced Kyoto as the capital of the realm. Here the Tokugawa did not succeed completely, but they certainly raised doubts about the status of Kyoto as capital. When the first Westerners arrived in Japan in the mid-nineteenth century, they were confused about where the capital was and who the head of state was.[60] Some Japanese of the seventeenth century were no less confused. A work by Miura Jōshin (1565–1644), a disciple of Tenkai, related a discussion between two men, one guided by principles, the other a pragmatic realist. According to the first one, "Heaven does not have two suns, the earth does not have two kings. Therefore it does not make sense to give the name of capital to a city that has no palace or no court ritual. There is only one king in the realm and one capital." To this the pragmatist replied: "But shouldn't the place where the king of the country, the shogun who protects the realm, resides be called the capital?"[61]

[59] Asao, *Sakoku*, p. 276. It goes without saying that the bakufu continued to be interested in Ise. Every twenty years it allocated 30,000 koku for the ritual rebuilding of the shrines. The bakufu settled disputes between the shrines, donated lands (see e.g. Fukaya, "Kokka to tennō," pp. 230, 232) and occasionally sent messengers to the shrines to pray for the health of important Tokugawa family members (*ibid.*, pp. 228, 231, 232) or to report disasters like the Edo fire of 1632 (*ibid.*, p. 234). At the New Year, messengers were also dispatched both to Nikkō and to Ise to pray for blessings (*Kojiruien* 2: 44). Yet the decree of 1645, requiring the court to send yearly messengers to Nikkō on 4/16, the anniversary of Ieyasu's death, was not reciprocated by the bakufu with emissaries to Ise other than those just mentioned (for the text of the decree, see Ishii, ed., *Tokugawa Kinreikō* 1: 170). Moreover, Arai Hakuseki seems to imply that the yearly dispatch of imperial messengers to Ise, also instituted that year, was a concession by the bakufu to the court after the latter had been ordered to pay its respects yearly to Ieyasu's tomb (*Zenshū* 5: 694). The court thus seems to have protested the request. The bakufu made a concession without, however, altering the asymmetry of the situation.

[60] This confusion was based on the limited knowledge about Japan available in the West, especially in relation to the question of "dual sovereignty." See Jacques Bésineau, " 'Dual Sovereignty' under the Japanese Shogunate as interpreted by French Writers of the Eighteenth Century," *Monumenta Nipponica* 22 (1967), 3–4: 390–401.

[61] For Asami Keisai, about a century later, the practice by many of calling the shogunal city Tokyo—Eastern Capital—constituted lèse majesté. See notes 1 and 2 above.

For all practical purposes, and for many ritualistic ones (not including court ritual), the Tokugawa had, in the span of half a century, succeeded in eclipsing the court and making Edo the administrative as well as the symbolic center of Japan.[62]

The imperial court thus occupied a crucial position in the legitimizing strategies of the Tokugawa. The court's role, however, did not consist in delegating political authority to the new shogun or merely acknowledging Ieyasu as the supreme warrior of Japan. Rather, the emperor was slowly forced to render his status above any other warrior or religious power as a symbolic center and autonomous source of prestige, rank, and therefore order. The Tokugawa slowly usurped this role until the realm's ritual space had been refocused around a new center of authority. This achievement constituted visible proof that the Tokugawa were legitimate rulers. Ritual was thus the most important means by which the Tokugawa legitimized their regime.

Ritual is a particularly powerful legitimizing device. Legitimacy may, indeed, be a weak term to describe what ritual achieves. Legitimacy usually connotes intellectual assent or acceptance, which itself evokes the possibility of choice. The ritual and religious devices the Tokugawa manipulated exacted a religious awe, an experience of the sublime. (In this context it is perhaps appropriate to recall the *junshi* or suicides by several prominent daimyo, following their lord Iemitsu in his death.) In that strong sense, the new Tokugawa ritual space legitimized the new order of domination.

This ritual was meant, however, for the ruling class, not for the commoners. It was the daimyo who were invited to contribute to the construction of Kan'eiji, invited to Nikkō and offered court rank and office by the bakufu. The housemen were not even allowed within the precincts of the Nikkō mausoleum. The commoners were in varying degrees aware of the grandiose rituals that were staged, for instance, when the four-hundred-member Korean delegations proceeded from Osaka (bypassing Kyoto) to Edo and on to Nikkō. But they were not the primary target for this ritual legitimation..

Religious dispositions, even belief, were the returns the bakufu expected from its costly investments in symbolic capital. When in 1644, Ikeda Mitsumasa, brother-in-law of Iemitsu and daimyo from Okayama, requested from the bakufu permission to build a

[62] Even a group of *gagaku* (exclusive court music) performers was moved by Ieyasu from Kyoto to Edo (Malm, "Music Cultures," p. 164).

Tōshō shrine in his domain, the bakufu elder Sakai Tadakatsu replied that although he had no basic objections to such a proposal, if he were to grant it, "everybody would want to do the same thing and then many would erect a shrine without any real belief."[63] (The following year, however, Iemitsu granted Mitsumasa's request.)

STEMMING RELIGIOUS DIFFUSION; SUPPRESSING RELIGIOUS SEPARATISM

The relationship between the early bakufu and religion raises another question of bakufu ideology. Why did the bakufu perceive certain sects as threats and outlaw them?

The case of Christianity is well known and needs little elaboration. The exclusivistic character of its dogma (which too closely resembled that of the Ikkō sect), its identification with foreign powers, and the use of Christian symbols by the Shimabara rebels sealed Christianity's fate in Japan. Moreover, in the case of the Shimabara rebellion at least, the bakufu could draw attention away from the economic and administrative abuses the peasants had suffered by representing the uprising as a Christian-inspired political rebellion. One of the bakufu's strategies thus consisted of converting political realities into religious ones in order to have political reality either rejected (the Shimabara rebellion as a Christian uprising) or accepted (their own position as sacred rulers under tendō).

The early bakufu was apprehensive about mass gatherings, let alone mass movements. The fear of further military confrontations lingered for decades after the Osaka campaigns. The first article of the 1615 *Regulations for Military Houses* states that "in government one should not forget upheavals." Thirty-five years later, on 1650/5/6, the great elder Sakai Tadakatsu could still be critical of Ikeda Mitsumasa's famous Confucian domain school for the simple reason that "it was a place where crowds gathered."[64]

The *okagemairi* mass pilgrimages to the Ise Shrines are primarily a mid- and late Tokugawa phenomenon. There were seven such pilgrimages, six of them in the eighteenth and nineteenth centuries.

[63] Asao, *Sakoku*, p. 277.
[64] NST 27: 454; *Ikeda Mitsumasa nikki*, p. 157, quoted by Watanabe, "Tokugawa zenki Jugakushi," p. 15.

The second one, in 1705, is said to have brought 3,620,000 pilgrims to Ise in a period of fifty days.[65] The first, in 1650, is the least documented. It consisted mainly of Edo shopkeepers who made group pilgrimages to Ise, apparently prompted by an outbreak of smallpox.[66] There were, however, several outbursts of religious frenzy centered on the Ise Shrines before the first *okagemairi* of 1650. These movements, which caught the bakufu's attention, were called *Ise odori* or *(Ise) furyū odori*, Ise dances or Ise crazy dances. *Furyū* has connotations of extravagance and gaudiness in dress and deportment. The ideological significance of these sudden outbreaks of "mass hysteria" is not immediately clear, although some took place at politically critical moments. The bakufu's official interpretation was that they were "inauspicious," which may indicate that more was involved than fortuitous synchronicity between these outbursts and political developments.

In the spring and summer of 1614 (from the fourth through the ninth month), Ieyasu was constructing his *casus belli* against Toyotomi Hideyori and preparing for war. The order to attack Osaka was issued on 10/1. From 9/25 until 10/1, the court, the mansions of court nobles, and many Kyoto shrines were invaded by groups of frenzied Ise dancers.[67] These revelers spearheaded a movement that had started the previous month in Ise with an oracle that the Ise Shrines had flown off to Nokami mountain and had come back the twenty-eighth in the middle of a typhoon. The oracle also instructed the people to dance. The songs of these dancing groups referred to the Mongol invasions of the thirteenth century and to Hideyoshi's Korean campaigns. This mass concern with war and desire for peace spread throughout the whole country while the Osaka campaigns were being conducted. On 1615/3/25, Ise dancers appeared in Ieyasu's castle town of Sunpu. (Ieyasu had returned from the Osaka Winter campaign on 2/14 and left Sunpu again on 4/4, issuing the order for the spring campaign two days later.)[68] When the dancers reached Sunpu, Ieyasu outlawed the movement, although it is not known how effective this prohibition

[65] Fujitani, "*Okagemairi*," pp. 35–36, 39. Nishigaki Seiji (*Eejanaika*, pp. 205–207) reports on two additional smaller *okagemairi* that originated from Edo in 1638 and 1661.

[66] Nishigaki, *Eejanaika*, p. 207.

[67] For a detailed account of the *lèse majesté* case Ieyasu concocted against Hideyori, see Hori, *Razan*, pp. 173–99. A summary can be found in Sadler, *Maker*, pp. 272–76. Nishigaki, *Kamigami*, p. 58. On the 1614–1615 Ise odori, see pp. 52–67.

[68] For these dates, see *Tokushi biyō*, p. 363.

was. The movement seems to have spread as far as the northern provinces.[69]

In the spring of 1616, the *Tokugawa jikki* notes, all provinces were again affected by an outburst of Ise odori.[70] The rumor was that a sacred object had descended from heaven. This time the authorities remained silent. The *Tokugawa jikki*, however, speaks of the phenomenon (on a later occasion, in 1624/2) as ominous because it preceded Ieyasu's death "that summer" (just as the Ise odori was retrospectively seen as ominous because it preceded the end of the Toyotomi). Thus the official record suggests that the two were inexplicably related in a supernatural way but not linked intrinsically at a political level: Ise odori were followed by the death of important political figures. Ieyasu, however, fell sick that year on 1/21 during a hunting party away from home, returned to Sunpu the 25th, and died there on 4/17. The seriousness of his condition could not be kept secret, and news of it spread rapidly. The emperor was notified and agreed to bestow upon Ieyasu the court title of dajōdaijin. Rumors of Ieyasu's death had, however, been circulating months before he died. The Englishman Cocks heard the rumor as early as 1/24, and again on 3/31.[71] The second wave of Ise odori thus coincided with the widespread knowledge of Ieyasu's death. As Cocks relates, this news generated fears of renewed warfare.

The last of these large-scale Ise odori (in 1624/2; there were two more local ones in Nagoya in 1653 and Edo in 1678–1679) is more difficult to explain.[72] The bakufu, however, took the trouble of breaking it up, justifying its stance (in the *Tokugawa jiki* passage) by references to the ominous forebodings of the two previous odori outbreaks. This time again a rumor had spread that the two Ise Shrines had flown to another part of the country—a rumor that was duly investigated by the Kyoto deputy with the Yoshida and Watarai Shinto houses. Every day more and more people, young and old, abandoned the fields, organized themselves in groups, claimed carriers and horses from the way stations, and danced toward Ise. Laws were issued to disband the movement. Sacred

---

[69] Nishigaki, *Kamigami*, pp. 66–67; *Tokugawa jikki* 2: 9. The first occurence of group pilgrimages, caused by news that the Ise Shrines had flown away, appears to have occured in 1604. The event seems to be hardly documented (Fujitani, "*Okagemairi*," p. 26).

[70] Nishigaki, *Kamigami*, pp. 68–70; *Tokugawa jikki* 2: 318.

[71] Sadler, *Maker*, pp. 325–26.

[72] Nishigaki, *Kamigami*, pp. 70–71.

objects (*shintai*) were taken away from the pilgrims and discarded, and this brought the frenzy to a sudden halt.

When in 1635/7 Iemitsu was entertained with some dance performances, an Ise odori was part of the program. The songs that accompanied the dances were quite different from the earlier ones. They celebrated colors in nature, compassion in man, and the beauty of offering one's life to one's lord.[73] The Ise odori had been domesticated, transformed into a cultural, felicitous, unpolitical phenomenon.

The Ise odori fanned out *from* Ise (except the last one) as much as they drew people *to* Ise, unlike the later *okagemairi*, which were exclusively Ise-directed. They were diffuse expressions at a national level of people's fears and hopes, and seem to have been generated by momentous political events in the making. The *eejanaika* phenomena of two centuries later were no different. They straddled the fall of the bakufu (1867/8/4 to 1868/4) and displayed the same characteristics. Religious objects (*fuda* or talismans) traveled through the sky and descended to earth, which triggered nationwide "crazy" behavior and dancing.[74]

With regard to the relationship between the bakufu, religion, and ideology, these movements are instructive. The people perceived the momentous events in which they were caught or feared being caught to be of such magnitude that they turned to religious symbols to express their sentiments—as did the bakufu with the Tōshō cult. Only the symbolizing powers of the supernatural were felt, by rulers and subjects alike, to be commensurate to the task of signifying in an appropriate way the new society that was being produced. Moreover, the fear of more warfare and the hope for peace, expressed in such dramatic way on a national scale, attest perhaps to a willingness on the part of the people to accept the new order if it could prevent further chaos.

Besides the problems caused by Christianity and the Ise odori, the bakufu had to face other challenges from religion. Nichiren Buddhism had a tradition of militant exclusivism that tended to pit its believers uncompromisingly against the rest of society. Oda Nobunaga had to confront extreme expressions of such apartheid in the Ikkō and Hokke sects. That same world view, which claimed immunity from worldly powers, was no more welcome to the

[73] *Ibid.*, pp. 71–72.
[74] *Ibid.*, pp. 81–90.

bakufu than it had been to Nobunaga. The sect that challenged bakufu authority was the Fujufuse branch of Nichiren Buddhism. Ultimately it was outlawed and forced to go underground like Christianity.

This sect came into existence and successfully challenged Hideyoshi's authority in a religious matter in 1595. The affair had to do with a service to be held at the Hōkokuji (Tendai) temple where Hideyoshi had built Japan's largest Buddha.

In 1586 Hideyoshi had issued levies to twenty-one provinces to contribute to the building of the Kyoto Great Buddha, which was finished in 1588 and housed in a large structure in 1591. The complex was to be a national monument, as the Tōdaiji had been during the Nara period, only on an even grander scale. The statue was 19.20 m. high, 2 m. more than Nara's Great Buddha, and the *daibutsuden* (Hall of the Great Buddha) rose 66 m., fully one-third higher than its counterpart in Nara. Ceremonies at the Hōkokuji were also to be held on a national scale. On 1595/9/10, all ten Buddhist orders were asked to contribute one hundred monks each for a month-long service (*kuyō*) to offer prayers for Hideyoshi and his ancestors. (Religion was thus also used by Hideyoshi as a context within to pose as a national authority.) Within the Nichiren council of abbots, Nichiō (1565–1630) from Myōkakuji refused to comply. He argued that Nichiren had ordered his followers neither to receive (*fuju*) donations from nor provide (*fuse*) services to nonbelievers.[75]

In 1599, Ieyasu sponsored a similar service that involved a total of a thousand priests from all ten Buddhist orders, and again Nichiō refused to participate.[76] On 11/20, Ieyasu brought representatives of the two Nichiren factions together for a "public debate."[77] Nichiō clearly understood that this so-called debate was a travesty, like the debate at Azuchi organized by Oda Nobunaga. Nevertheless, debating against his *jufuse* opponents who did not refuse gifts from nonbelievers and who argued that secular law and Buddhist law were like the two supporting wheels of the carriage of society, Nichiō clearly asserted the preeminence and autonomy of Buddhism over political authority. Nichiō "lost" the debate and on 1600/5/30 was banished to Tsushima, where he stayed until he was pardoned on 1612/6/4. Nichiō's understanding

---

[75] Tamamuro, "Kakure daimoku," pp. 119–22.
[76] Tamamuro, *Shūkyō tōsei*, p. 64.
[77] Tamamuro, "Kakure daimoku," pp. 124–35.

of Buddhism's relationship to the authorities, it should be noted, was diametrically opposed to Suzuki Shōsan's. The latter also rejected the equivalence impled in the wheel metaphor, but he placed secular law over Buddhism.

During Nichiō's absence, the Nichiren temple on Mount Minobu became the leading center for Nichiren Buddhism. But after his return from exile, where his hardships had even further convinced him of his orthodoxy, as they had Nichiren, Nichiō started to rebuild his base in Kyoto (Myōkakuji) and Edo (Ikegamiji). He issued new rules in 1623, reasserting as strongly as ever Fujufuse's radical apartheid, warning against doctrinal corruption from Tendai teachings (which were also, like Nichiren's, based on the Lotus Sutra), and resisting pressures from the authorities to change his doctrine.[78] In 1629, Nichiō and Nichiju (1572–1631) from Ikegamiji challenged the Mount Minobu monks by accusing them of having participated in another one-thousand-priest service, and discouraging all Nichiren followers from visiting Mount Minobu because the temple had received lands from nonbelievers. Mount Minobu brought the matter before the bakufu, and another "debate" was arranged on 1630/2/21, pitting six representatives from each side against each other in front of an all-Tendai jury (except for Sūden; Razan was also present).

Several issues were involved in this confrontation. One point was the revival of the outlawed Fujufuse, which the Ikegami party argued had been approved both by Ieyasu's pardon of Nichiō and, in writing, by a document from Itakura, the Kyoto deputy—a document the Mount Minobu party claimed to be a forgery. Another point in dispute was whether land grants from the authorities constituted a mere gift or a *kuyō* ("service") act of devotion. The monks from Mount Minobu and the bakufu, which over the years had been bringing the Buddhist establishment within its orbit of control, argued for the religious interpretation. The political purpose of tying the main temples to the bakufu, and of having them render spiritual services to the shogun rather than to the emperor, was better camouflaged if those grants were represented not as generous gifts but as acts of religious devotion.[79] Finally, the bakufu exploited the rift within the Nichiren sect by

---

[78] *Ibid.*, pp. 142–49.
[79] On this dispute, see *ibid.*, pp. 156–64; on the *kuyō* interpretation by the bakufu of its land grants to temples, see also Fukaya, "Kokka to tennō," pp. 242–43.

clearly structuring it hierarchically into branch temples around the head temple on Mount Minobu, which was all too eager to cooperate with this effort.[80] One year later, the bakufu issued a nationwide decree ordering all Buddhist sects to submit lists of their head and branch temples.

On 1630/4/2, Fujufuse was outlawed again. Ieyasu's ban was reinforced, and the Itakura document was not recognized. Nichiō, who had died twenty days earlier, was nevertheless declared defrocked and sentenced to a second Tsushima exile. For the six loosers in the debate (including Nichiju, who died a year later), all Kanto and Kansai provinces were declared off limit. The sect survived, however, and quite vigorously—even to the point that in the late 1650s-early 1660s Mount Minobu felt it necessary to appeal repeatedly to the bakufu to suppress it. In 1663, on the occasion of the thirteenth memorial service for Iemitsu, Mount Minobu even accused Fujufuse of having refused to participate at Iemitsu's funeral thirteen years earlier! Two years later, the bakufu outlawed the sect again and began to suppress it in earnest. Not coincidentally, it was in the 1660s and 1670s that the bakufu started to enforce temple registration in all villages (*shūmon jinbetsu-chō*). In the past this policy had not been enforced nationally, and had been aimed only at Christians. Now, however, this measure was aimed at the bakufu's new religious critics or recalcitrants, the Fujufuse.[81] The bakufu thus succeeded in eliminating all pockets of ideological apartheid. For this operation, it had astutely enlisted the help of the Buddhist ruling class—the main Buddhist centers.

Three domains closely related to the bakufu (Mito, Okayama, and Aizu) appear on the surface to have deviated from a pro-Buddhist policy. In the 1660s the daimyo of these domains implemented strong anti-Buddhist policies. In fact, they achieved what the bakufu wanted. In Aizu, the population was ordered to register with Shinto shrines rather than with Buddhist temples. In Okayama, the same measure was taken, but in addition 847 bonzes were laicized. It appears, however, that many of the temples that were abolished there in 1667 were affiliated with Fujufuse. Mito's policies were the most thorough. Of a total of 2,088 temples, 1,098 or 52 percent were abolished. One temple was left to serve several villages, whereas every village had its Shinto shrine. (In 1667, Shinto priests were sent to Kyoto to study Yoshida Shinto; a measure that was in compliance with a bakufu order of two years

[80] Tamamuro, "Kakure daimoku," p. 166.
[81] Tamamuro, *Shūkyō tōsei*, pp. 81–84.

earlier that only a certificate from the Yoshida house would qualify
one to manage a shrine.) The losses to Buddhism in this domain
were most severe. Most of the temples that were eliminated, however, were small ones. Not a single protest from head temples in the
domain was registered.[82]

RELIGION and ritual were of paramount importance to the
shoguns for signifying their hegemony in a nonpolitical medium.
Through them, the Tokugawa transformed their coercive power
into sacred authority, established themselves at the center, and
thus gave order and hierarchy to the realm and legitimacy to
themselves.

The writings of the new schoolmen were also suffused with
traditional religious and metaphysical elements, as much as the
Tokugawa ritual creations were. The reader, however, may have
noticed a difference in consistency and articulation in the products
of the ritual mode of ideological expression and that of the discursive mode. The ritual constructs by the Tokugawa appear more
unified and coherent than the discourse of the schoolmen. The
respective natures of ritual and discourse do not fully account for
this difference; it can be explained by the fact that the construction
of ritual was initiated and planned by the Tokugawa. The discourse was not, but was left to develop (within certain limits) on its
own.

No single work or author we have studied so far appears to have
achieved a fully structured ideology, to have brought about what
one may call ideological closure. One might object that no ideology ever achieves such perfect closure, except in the writings of
historians who are fooled all too easily by the fallacy of misplaced
wholeness. Moreover, one could argue that the Tokugawa bakufu,
unlike modern governments, did not perceive itself as an educator
and hence did not coordinate official knowledge from above. In
addition, one may suppose that the "bricolage" method of discursive production may have had built-in limitations on the possible
construction of a holisitic ideology. With these problems in mind, I
shall turn in the following two chapters to an examination of
Yamazaki Ansai's formulation of Tokugawa ideological discourse.
He may be credited as the thinker who produced the coherently
structured discourse that was absent in the first half century of
Tokugawa rule.

[82] *Ibid.*, pp. 100–106, 110–12, 116, 118, 123, 131.

Six. Yamazaki Ansai: Repossessing the Way

The books written by the Sages are complete: they have left nothing unsaid.—*Yamazaki Ansai*[1]

The teachings of the Sages are complete. . . . That which the Sages did not express does not need expressing.—*Ogyū Sorai*[2]

From Oda Nobunaga through Tokugawa Iemitsu, Japan's supreme rulers turned to Shinto ritual to represent and thereby transform their power. Hideyoshi's daimyōjin cult was a Yoshida Shinto construct. Ichijitsu Shinto was created to provide the underpinnings for Ieyasu's Tōshō daigongen cult. By appropriating Shinto ritual, these rulers thus cast their legitimizing strategies in a mythologizing mode.

Discursive arguments, on the other hand, were formulated in the private and public writings of the learned. These men wrote of principles, virtues, and qualities pertaining to proper rule and ideal government. Most of these concepts were common currency in the Confucian tradition. Yet, as we have seen, *Ieyasu's Testament* and other anonymous compositions as well as some of Razan's writings were interlarded with Shinto elements. These references consisted mainly of occasional equations, made earlier by Yoshida theologians, between Confucian ideological elements or ideologemes (virtues or principles) and Shinto mythological elements or mythemes (names of deities, the three imperial regalia, and so on) from the *Nihongi*'s two opening chapters, called "The Age of the Gods" (*kamiyo no maki* or *jindai no maki, jindaikan*).[3] The overall argument, in Razan's succinct formula, identified Shinto as Ōdō: Shinto was a political way no different from ancient China's Kingly Way.

---

[1] "Yamazaki sensei goroku." Manuscript. No pagination (p. 18).

[2] *Bendō*, NST 36: 30.

[3] "Ideologeme" is a term coined by Fredric Jameson (in his *Political Unconscious*; see index), apparently after Lévi-Strauss's "mytheme." Just as phonemes form the smallest units of speech, mythemes refer to the minimal constituent units of mythological discourse, and ideologemes to those of political discourse. I do not restrict the concept of ideologemes to units of antagonistic class discourse. In my view, ethical and philosophical principles are ideologemes insofar as they inform political practice, which they do mainly by obfuscating power relations. Although mythemes undoubtedly also have political functions, they are not principles used in ethical or philosophical arguments but elements of mythological narratives.

Razan's forays into Shinto failed to take hold. A few decades after his death, his successors were making no further mention of any Hayashi Shinto teachings. Around the time that they were slipping into oblivion, however, Yamazaki Ansai was transforming Shinto into a powerful and lasting political doctrine. By way of Yoshikawa Koretaru's teachings, Ansai's elaborate Suika Shinto—Suika is Ansai's Shinto name—is rooted, like Razan's, in the Yoshida tradition, and strikes one today as even more far-fetched and arbitrary than Razan's. Yet Suika Shinto was the most dynamic force in the world of Shinto theology until the second half of the eighteenth century, when it had to make room for Motoori Norinaga. Even then, Suika Shinto did not leave the field to Norinaga's "pure" Shinto. Its tenets and ideological impact can be detected in Hirata Atsutane (1776–1843), Motoori's successor. It also played an important role in modern times. In the 1930s and 1940s, Suika Shinto was appropriated for the construction of an ultranationalist ideology.[4]

[4] Modern scholarship on Ansai and his schools reached its peak in the 1930s and 1940s within a general political and intellectual climate that interpreted Ansai as the first of a long line of imperial panegyrists and ideologues of the *yamatodamashii* or Japanese spirit. This scholarship brought about the publication of writings by Ansai and other members of his schools. In 1934, an eleven-fascicle collection of biographical and other data on members of his Kimon School was reissued. The work, originally put together in 1842 and added to in 1900, is called *Nihon dōgaku engen roku* (Fountainhead of the Learning of the Way in Japan). In 1936–1937, Yamazaki Ansai's complete works were published in five volumes: *Yamazaki Ansai zenshū*, 2 vols. (consecutive pagination); *Zoku Yamazaki Ansai zenshū*, 3 vols. (separate pagination for each volume); henceforward YAZ and ZYAZ. Two volumes of Suika Shinto teachings appeared in 1935 and 1937 (*Suika Shintō*; DNB 16 and 17). The complete works of Satō Naokata, one of Ansai's leading students in the Kimon School, were published in 1941 in a thousand-page volume (*Satō Naokata zenshū*; SNZ). Further, Yoshikawa Koretaru's teachings were published in 1939 as *Yoshikawa Shintō* (DNB 15). In 1937, the sayings and teachings of Wakabayashi Kyōsai (1679–1732), were printed. Kyōsai succeeded Asami Keisai, another of Ansai's famous disciples. The work appeared in twelve fascicles under the title "Notes on casual talks by Master Kyōsai": *Kyōsai sensei zatsuwa hikki* (KSZH). (The first of these fascicles has also appeared in NST 31.) Of all the above editions, only the DNB volumes are provided with some explanatory annotations. The YAZ and ZYAZ, as well as the Satō Naokata volume, are photostat reproductions; many works reproduced there are in handwritten form.

Two studies that are representative of the interpretive scholarship of this period are Kobayashi Kenzō, *Suika Shintō no kenkyū* (1940) and (*Zōho*) *Yamazaki Ansai to sono monryū* (1943). In the postwar period, two nearly book-length studies of Yamazaki Ansai and his schools are contained in the following works: for his Neo-Confucianism, see Abe Yoshio, *Chōsen* (1965); for his Shinto teachings, see Taira, *Kinsei* (1969). Modern annotated and critical editions of some writings by Yamazaki Ansai and his followers can be found in a number of larger collections (see note 11 below). Additional bibliographical information can be found in note 24 below. To my knowledge, the only extensive introduction to Ansai's thought in any Western language is Okada, "Practical Learning in the Chu Hsi School" (see also Tsunoda et al., *Sources*, 1: 354–62).

The mobilization of Shinto mythology for articulating political ideas was not Yamazaki Ansai's only achievement. He performed a similar feat with Neo-Confucianism. His Confucian followers, referred to as belonging to the Kimon school—*Ki* is the Chinese reading of *zaki* from Yamazaki, and *mon* means learning or school—rivaled Ogyū Sorai's disciples and outnumbered any other school during the eighteenth century. In the 1790s, they infiltrated the Bakufu College and formed the clique that initiated the Ban on Heterodoxy.[5] Theirs was also the first Neo-Confucian school to show new vitality during the Meiji period.[6]

In Yamazaki Ansai's writings we thus find in operation, more fully than in any previous texts, two modalities of discourse: mythological narrative and discursive argument. Not only did he extensively deploy each of these modes in parallel fashion, he also articulated them into each other. As we shall see, some of Ansai's disciples had serious problems with the latter. Nevertheless, for any student of Tokugawa ideology, a careful study of Ansai's triple achievement in the realms of Shinto teachings, Neo-Confucian learning, and their mutual harmonics imposes itself as an unavoidable but daunting task.

This task is further complicated by the tradition of scholarship on Ansai that forms the background for any such inquiry. Yamazaki Ansai, his teachings and followers, Shinto as well as Neo-Confucian, were in the past and remain to this day highly controversial. No other Shinto or Neo-Confucian doctrine has aroused a comparable range of feelings. No group of scholars and teachers has been credited and blamed for so much in the last three hundred years of Japanese history as those that trace their intellectual lineage to Ansai. To confound things further, Ansai himself has been heralded as the first scholar to have transmitted a pure and correct understanding of Chu Hsi's thought and at the same time to have accommodated it to Japanese dimensions, political and intellectual alike.[7]

---

[5] Ooms, *Bureaucrat*, pp. 133–39.

[6] Maruyama, "Ansaigaku," p. 604.

[7] For examples of praise and blame, see Maruyama, "Ansaigaku," p. 605; Bitō, *Hōken*, pp. 40, 67. Confucian scholars like Kaibara Ekken and Ogyū Sorai spurned the Ansai school's narrow-mindedness and moral rigorism; others were offended by its exclusivism. Motoori Norinaga rejected Ansai's Confucian interpretation of Shinto. Ansai's nationalist and loyalist teachings have been praised, and blamed, for the influence they had on—or more precisely, for their being so easily appropriated by—the Mito historical school, the scholars behind the Kansei Ban on Heterodoxy, Meiji patriots, and the supranationalists of this century. All scholars agree, however, that Ansai was the first Japanese to come fully to terms

Even a summary account of Suika Shinto and the Kimon school falls well beyond the scope of this study. Ansai is of immediate interest to us because with Seika, Razan, and Shōsan, he is one of the few schoolmen who was directly associated with the early Tokugawa bakufu. This association indicates at least that the bakufu leaders saw his teachings as politically beneficial, which also increased the prestige and official character of Ansai's school: he acquired his best students after his "bakufu service." To speak of Ansai simply as an official bakufu ideologue is, however, to overstate the case, as a closer look at Ansai's relationship with the bakufu will reveal.

IN THE FOOTSTEPS OF CHU HSI

Ansai's bakufu link consisted of part-time scholarly service (spring and summer of every year) to Hoshina Masayuki during the final seven years (1665–1672) of Masayuki's life. Masayuki, lord of Aizu, was Iemitsu's half-brother. He had functioned for the first decade after Iemitsu's death in 1651 as shogunal regent to the young Ietsuna, and remained an important bakufu advisor until 1669.

Like so many of his contemporaries, Masayuki had started with a schooling in Zen Buddhism (by Takuan) but switched to Neo-Confucianism (in 1652), which he learned from a bakufu doctor. Subsequently his interest in Shinto was aroused by Hattori Ankyū, a retainer who had introduced him to the *Nakatomi harai*, the Nakatomi purification ritual as described in a section of the tenth-century *Engishiki*. (Ankyū had started his studies under Razan.) Through Ankyū, Masayuki made the acquaintance of Yoshikawa Koretaru, the inheritor of the Yoshida Shinto doctrine. Their first meeting in 1661 must have been successful, because Masayuki ordered Ankyū to study with Koretaru (who lived in Kamakura), and he occasionally invited Koretaru to Edo to lecture on the "Age of the Gods" chapters of the *Nihongi*. It will be recalled that in 1665

---

with Chu Hsi's thought. This evaluation is found in every work on Ansai, starting with those of his earliest disciples, such as the critical Satō Naokata (SNZ, p. 11) down to the most recent essay (1980), written by Maruyama Masao, certainly not a sympathiser: "Ansaigaku," NST 31: 601, 663. As fairly representative of Japanese scholarship on the two themes of faithful transmission and the "naturalness' of Neo-Confucianism's adaptation to Japanese nationalistic thought, see Okada, "Practical Learning in the Chu Hsi School," especially pp. 247, 249, 257. See also Bitō, *Hōken*, pp. 41–42.

the bakufu required all Shinto priests to acquire a license from the Yoshida house. The Shinto world was thus brought under bakufu control through Yoshida Shinto. Clearly, Koretaru was instrumental in bringing this about. In 1666, Masayuki even created the new bakufu post of *shintokata* (Shinto intendant) under the Superintendant of Temples and Shrines for the study of Shinto texts and the administration of Shinto rituals. The post was tailor-made for Koretaru, who passed it on to his descendants. When Ansai entered Masayuki's service, the latter was thus being instructed by the highest authority of Yoshida Shinto, the branch of Shinto that for two centuries, institutionally and exegetically, had been the most prominent.[8]

Several measures taken by influential rulers during the 1660s testify to the growing prominence of ideological issues in this decade. In some quarters at least, a political doctrine in one form or another was perceived as conducive to more effective government. This awareness was by no means either universal or new. What was unprecedented was that three influential daimyo made a number of far-reaching policy decisions that were ideologically inspired: Tokugawa Mitsukuni from Mito, Ikeda Mitsumasa from Okayama, and Hoshina Masayuki from Aizu. They ruled large domains, ranging in size from 230,000 koku (Aizu) to well over 300,000 koku (Okayama and Mito), and were all related to the shogunal house. Although they expressed their interests in different ways, they shared a preoccupation with intellectual and ideological matters.

Ikeda Mitsumasa was one of the first daimyo to establish a domain school. In 1669, he converted a private school he had built in 1641 into an official domain school. For ten years (1647–1657) he employed the famous Kumazawa Banzan, one of the few, if not the only, Neo-Confucian scholar of the Tokugawa period to have profoundly influenced domain policies. In 1657, Tokugawa Mitsukuni embarked on his grand project to rewrite Japanese history. Masayuki, in 1654, implemented a system of emergency granaries that was inspired by Chu Hsi's writings. In the 1660s, moreover, these three daimyo conducted Buddhist purges in their domains and became active supporters of Shinto,. The political air was thick with ideological concerns. The Hayashi scholars breathed this air and, as we have seen, through the publication

[8] On the relationship of the Ansai-Masayuki-Koretaru trio, see Taira, *Yoshikawa*, pp. 24–39, 352–414; *id.*, *Kinsei*, pp. 14–38, 106–27. On the relationship of Koretaru to the Yoshida house, see *id.*, *Yoshikawa*, pp. 8–15, 40–50.

in 1662 of Razan's collected works, projected a new self-image as preservers of bakufu orthodoxy.

In the year 1665, when Ansai entered Masayuki's service, ideological preoccupations had changed since the first decades of the Tokugawa period, when all efforts went into sacralizing the ruling house. The bakufu was concerned with the suppression of those that were perceived as dissidents and with the propagation of some form of "right thinking." Thus in 1665, the bakufu, where Masayuki was still a powerful influence, again outlawed the Fujufuse sect and this time tried in earnest to suppress it. In that same year, Yamaga Sokō published his *Seikyō yōroku* (Compendium of the teachings of the Sages), which prompted his banishment from Edo by Masayuki. This was the year, too, that Masayuki converted a private academy into a domain school in Aizu. Mitsukuni also gave a new boost to his historiographical project when, that year, he hired the Ming refugee scholar Chu Shun-shui (1600–1682), who was then residing in Nagasaki.[9] Given this general political climate, how did Yamazaki Ansai come to enjoy the patronage of the prestigious bakufu leader Hoshina Masayuki?

By 1665, Yamazaki Ansai, who was then forty-seven years old, had made a name for himself as a self-proclaimed Neo-Confucian purist. Ten years earlier he had opened a private school in Kyoto, and for the last seven years had also been making yearly appearances in Edo. Ansai, the son of a rōnin-turned-acupuncturist, had (of course) started out as a monk. In his preteens he had been sent to Mount Hiei to serve as an acolyte, then returned home for several years in his early teens, and finally entered the Myōshinji temple of the Rinzai Zen sect in Kyoto. Because of his considerable talents, he was sent to the Gyūkōji temple in Tosa for further study. There he fell under the spell of Neo-Confucianism, and left the order at age twenty-eight. Ansai returned to Kyoto and there, supported by Nonaka Kenzan (1615–1663), an elder from the Tosa domain who had traveled the same spiritual journey, started studying and publishing Neo-Confucian materials.[10]

[9] On Chu Shun-shui, see Julia Ching, "The Practical Learning of Chu Shun-shui (1600–1682)," in de Bary and Bloom, *Principle*, pp. 189–229.

[10] For a brief biographical sketch of Ansai, see Taira, *Kinsei*, pp. 128–49; Ikeda, "Ansaijugaku." The best primary sources for biographical data on Ansai are his own short autobiography, *Yamazaki kafu* (Lineage) (YAZ 2: 651–54 and also 761–64), and a chronology of his life, partly based on the *kafu*, written sometime in the late Tokugawa period by a certain Yamada Omoihajime (?), the son of a disciple of Miyake Shōsai (with Satō Naokata and Asami Keisai, one of Ansai's three leading disciples): *Yamazaki Ansai nenpu* (in *Nihon jurin sōsho* 3.)

Ansai was a passionate man, quite the opposite from the ecumenical-minded Fujiwara Seika. He did not quietly tiptoe out of Buddhism; as the title of his maiden work, *Heresies Refuted* (*Hekii*; 1647), indicates, he rejected it loudly and clearly.[11] As one can surmise from the title, Ansai's work was more than a (by then fashionable) indictment of Buddhism's social evils, although Ansai argues that money spent on temples and monks would be better spent on building schools (241–43). Ansai's attack was an intellectual assault on Buddhism's errors, with arguments he had found in Neo-Confucian texts. The work is a fiery yet clearly reasoned public testimonial that its author had found the Truth and was compelled to prevent others from ending their days in error (247–48). This Truth that had overwhelmed Ansai and captured his soul was eternal and universal: the Way transcended all ages (217), was not man-made (191–92, 200) but Heaven-ordained— *tenri no shizen* (199)—and regulated the life of man and the universe. Yet the truth of this cosmic Way was very specific, and not different from Seika's definition of man as *homo hierarchicus*. In Ansai's words, "even the ants and bees have kings and vassals" (191). For man, this essentially hierarchizing Way was encapsulated in the Five Relationships (between parent and child, lord and minister, husband and wife, elder and junior, friend and friend). Ansai thus reduced the Way to a single ideologeme.

To maintain this stark simplicity of the Way, Ansai had to find a place for the voluminous teachings of various Sages and worthies, who, over the centuries, had steered discourse on the Way in many different directions. The Ming scholar Ts'ai Ch'ing (1453–1508) provided Ansai with the necessary distinctions (based on *Mencius* 5A: 4: 2) to solve this dilemma of unity versus diversity. Although

[11] Page references to *Hekii* are to NNS 17. All Ansai's writings (except for the classics he edited and the compendia he compiled) can be found in the YAZ and ZYAZ. This edition, however, is neither annotated nor provided with a critical apparatus. Whenever possible, therefore, I shall refer to more readily available, critical editions of his writings. They can be found in the following collections: for his Shinto writings, besides DNB 16 and 17, see NNS 14 and NST 39. For Ansai's Neo-Confucian writings, see NST 31; NNS 17; SGT 12. In order to simplify the references, as a rule notes will give the page numbers in the above general works without each time citing the title of the particular writing, which often consists of a preface or postscript to texts Ansai edited.

One other work, Ansai's *Yamato shōgaku* (Japanese Elementary Learning) can also be found in NKB 9: 25–95. Tajiri Yūichirō and Maeda Tsutomu started serializing in *Nihonshisōshi* (17: 1981) Ansai's notes on the *Hsia-hsüeh* (Elementary Learning) contained in YAZ 1: 91–101. The *Hekii* can be found in NNS 17: 185–250.

the explanations (*toku*) of the Sages may not be the same, Ts'ai Ch'ing argued, their meaning (*mune*) often is, and if their meanings differ, then what their message comes down to (*sono ki*) is the same. Hence, all appearances to the contrary, differences were naturally (*onozukara*) not allowed (217).

With his very first work, Ansai boldly put himself at the end of a long line of commentators on the Way. Like his predecessors, he made a paradoxical double claim that gave him a privileged position within the present state of the tradition while at the same time denying any originality. As a commentator he had, in Michel Foucault's words, to "say for the first time what has already been said, and repeat tirelessly what was, nevertheless, never said."[12]

After the publication of the *Heresies Refuted*, Ansai was to live another thirty-five years and write, compile, edit, and punctuate texts that cover well over two thousand dense pages in his collected works (published in 1935–1937; they do not include the classics he punctuated nor his anthologies of them). During all those years and through all those pages, Ansai posed as the servant of Truth, as a transmitter like Confucians, firmly believing that what he said was not novel, but only a reappearance of an already finalized Truth. To students who thought they had discovered something new, Ansai would ask where they had found such interesting things. When told that these were their own discoveries, Ansai smashed their conceit with an authoritative: "The books written by the Sages were complete: they have left nothing unsaid."[13]

Heresies Refuted was thus also calculated to advertise its author as one who had mastered the essentials of Neo-Confucianism. Ansai proceeded along two lines. One was a straightforward and lucid exposition of key Neo-Confucian terms such as the triple concept of Nature, the Way, and the Teachings; the virtue of reverence (*kei*; Ch *ching*); fundamental distinctions such as those between the *Elementary Learning* and the *Great Learning* and between the applications of the teachings in ordinary and exceptional circumstances (*kyō* and *ken*; Ch *ching* and *chüan*); and, of course, the Five Relationships. Concerning these relationships, he singled out a text, buried in the seventy-fourth chapter of *Chu Hsi's Collected Literary Works* (*Chu Tzu wen-chi*): "The Precepts of [Chu Hsi's]

---

[12] Foucault, *The Archeology of Knowledge*, p. 221.

[13] "Yamazaki sensei goroku," manuscript (p. 18). For Ansai's adoption of Confucius's slogan, "a transmitter and not a maker" (*Analects* 7: 1), see SGT 12: 174.

White Deer Grotto Academy" (*Po-lu-tung shu-yüan chieh-shih*; Jp *Hakurokudō shoin keiji*) (196–98).[14] Ansai gave power to this text by stressing that the precepts concerning the Five Relationships were not mere rules or prohibitions someone had made up. Rather, their normative power lay in the fact that they were lodged within one's body or self (*sono mi ni semuru ni hitsuzen o motte*) (198).

A second approach Ansai followed was to contrast Neo-Confucianism with Buddhism. For him, Buddhism's crucial fallacy lay in the thesis that nature (*sei*) was emptiness or nothingness (195). Consequently, Buddhism lacked a theory of mind-heart (234–35). Confucianism, on the other hand, held to a fullness of mind, programed as it was by the Five Relationships that were governed by the Five Virtues (humaneness, righteousness, propriety, wisdom, faithfulness).

Actually, the Buddhist theory of the mind's emptiness, rather than being a pronouncement about the metaphysical status of the mind as it functions in the world, was an ethical normative ideal to be achieved—like the Five Relationships—and could very well, in the hands of a Suzuki Shōsan, serve as the linchpin for a concrete ethics that differed little from Confucian ethics. Ansai's mind, however, had a strong literalist penchant that was not unrelated to his singular reliance on belief as the ultimate epistemological ground of knowledge. This urge to believe led him to reify his objects of knowledge. Ansai turned his points of belief into essences. In a lecture recorded by Yusa Bokusai (1658–1734), who joined Ansai's school in 1678, Ansai compares the Constant Virtues that constitute man's nature with the various ingredients that in Chinese medicine combine to form a drug.[15] He thus took, one can presume, the Zen statement about the emptiness of mind and nature as a quasi-physiological statement that was no match for the very elaborate and specific speculations on mind that formed

[14] This work (*Hakurokudō gakukishūchū*) can be found in ZYAZ 3: 1–5. In 1650, Ansai published these precepts with commentaries in a small single volume, which was reprinted over seventy times during the Tokugawa period. A translation of the text (without the commentaries Ansai collected but with most of Ansai's own introduction) is available in Tsunoda et al., *Sources*, 1: 355–57. For the introduction, see also SGT 12: 151–52.

[15] NST 31: 68–70. Yusa Bokusai, the son of a peasant, was a monk who after 1674 was employed in the Sendai domain. Between 1675 and 1679, he wandered in and out of Kyoto's academies, attending Itō Jinsai's lectures among others, until he finally entered Ansai's school in 1678/3. In 1693, he left the monastery and became a schoolman, propagating Ansai's Shinto and Neo-Confucian teachings in Sendai. On Bokusai's career and scholarship, see Taira, *Kinsei*, pp. 228–99.

the core of Neo-Confucian teachings.[16] In Ansai's view, Buddhism taught that the mind *was* empty and dead, Neo-Confucianism that it was full and active.

Ansai's predilection for a concrete metaphysics is shown in another detail that presages a central preoccupation of his scholarly life. The *Heresies Refuted* (189–90, 230–33), like virtually every Neo-Confucian tract, refers to the notion that the principles or regularities that program man's mind for ethical behavior are identical to those that move the universe. The four seasons in their regular succession are unavoidably mentioned in this context. Ansai, however, relying on a quotation from the Ming scholar Chan Ken-ch'ing, refers to the four hexagrams that symbolize the seasons (231). Although not out of the ordinary by itself, this nevertheless reveals in Ansai an unusual preoccupation with the concrete physico-metaphysical coordinates of Chinese learning. In his first lecture cycle of 1655–1656, he included, in addition to the works that were to remain the canon of his school, *Ch'eng Yi's Commentary on the Book of Changes (Chou I Ch'eng chu'an)*, an interpretation that read into the text a message on ethical norms. Later Ansai was to follow Chu Hsi, who had restored the *Book*'s original text, and view the work primarily, although not exclusively, as a divination manual.

Ansai's interest in the *Book of Changes* is an aspect of his scholarship that has often been overlooked. Yet, like Chu Hsi and all Sung scholars, he spent considerable time and energy studying this work. His short, four-page autobiography (*Yamazaki kafu*), replete with Shinto items (poems, visits to shrines, and so on), refers in only three places to Confucian works: to his reading of the *Elementary Learning* and some Chu Hsi poetry, to the content of his first lecture series, and to his publication of the *Kōhanzensho* (Complete writings on the *Hung fan* or *Great Norm*) in 1667.[17] He writes that in 1667, "two dozen years after he had started reading it," he finally understood the *Great Norm*. The *Great Norm* is a chapter from the *Book of History* and the first Chinese text to speak in numerical categories about the correlations between Heaven, Earth and Man, the Five Evolutive Phases (Wood, Fire, etc.), and the Supreme Standard (or the ruler's virtue, associated with the

---

[16] On the central place of the mind-and-heart learning in the Neo-Confucian scholarly tradition, see de Bary, *Orthodoxy*.

[17] YAZ 2: 651–54 (and also 761–64). The references are on pp. 652 and 653.

number five, which, as we shall see later, came to play an important role in Ansai's thought).[18]

During the Sung, the *Great Norm* was studied in relation to two
variant numerological reconstructions of the allegedly oldest diagrams that subsequently led to the *Book of Changes*: the *Lo shu*
(Lo writing) and the *Ho t'u* (River chart).[19] Chu Hsi discussed
these matters in the presence of a trusted associate, Ts'ai Yüan-
ting (1135–1198), a numerological expert whose son Ch'en
(1167–1230) published these views, with comments and geoman-
tic elaborations of his own, as the *Great Norm's Inner Section of the
Supreme Standard* (*Hung fan huang-chi nei-p'ien*). Ansai's *Kōhanzensho*,
about which he was so thrilled, consists of the *Great Norm*, the two
diagrams, Ch'en's work, and Ansai's own selection from the *Book of
Changes*.[20] Furthermore, during the last period of his life, after
Hoshina Masayuki's death in 1672, Ansai edited three works by
Chu Hsi on the *Book of Changes*: in 1675, the *Chou I pen-i* (Original
meaning of—) and in 1677, the *I hsüeh ch'i-meng* (Instructions to the
young on the learning of—) and the *Shu-eki engi* (Extended meaning of—by Chu Hsi). This last work does not exist as such in
Chinese; it is one of Ansai's famous collations from Chu Hsi's
writings. Here, after comparing the old text of the *Book of Changes*
with the prevalent one, Ansai gleaned all he could find on the
matter from the 100 fascicles of *Chu Hsi's Collected Literary Works* and
the 140 fascicles of *Chu Hsi's Classified Conversations* (*Chu Tzu yü-
lei*).[21] Chu Hsi's own careful critique of the *Book of Changes* had led
him to reject Ch'eng Yi's, replace it with his own reconstruction of
the older text and interpret the work as primarily a book of
divination. His reconstruction, however, was lost after his death,
when his text became mixed with Ch'eng Yi's text and interpretation.[22] Ansai's own research re-established Chu Hsi's version for
the first time since Sung times, and it was this version that was used
by the eighteenth-century Tokugawa authority on the *Book of
Changes*, Arai Hakuga (1714–1792).

As a commentator and faithful clarifier of his newly discovered

[18] For a translation of the essential parts of the *Hung fan*, see Wing-tsit Chan, *A Source Book
in Chinese Philosophy* (Princeton: Princeton University Press, 1963), pp. 8–12 and 249. For an
explanation, see Granet, *Pensée*, pp. 165–77.

[19] See Grant, *Pensée*, pp. 175–84.

[20] ZYAZ 2: 236–371.

[21] The *Shu-eki engi* can be found in ZYAZ 2: 186–235. For the preface, see SGT 12:
172–73.

[22] See Suzuki Yoshijirō, "Shushi to Eki," SGT 1: 213–32, especially pp. 213, 215, 224–25.

Truth, Ansai, in the *Heresies Refuted*, hid behind the authority not only of the Way but also of the commentator whose pronouncements were identical to the Way, namely, Chu Hsi. In order to take this step, which entailed a critique and often a rejection of scholarship after Chu Hsi (that is, Yüan and Ming), which constituted the bulk of Chinese learning at the time, Ansai relied on two authorities, Hsieh Ching-hsien (1393–1464) and the obscure Huang Chen. Their writings enabled Ansai to take Chu Hsi as the yardstick for all other commentaries, and at the same time to clarify Chu Hsi's own thought by textual comparisons of Chu Hsi's main commentaries with his *Literary works* and *Classified Conversations* (214–17). In this way Ansai was literally authorized: given legitimacy, turned into an author and made into an authority.

The task Ansai set for himself was enormous. The *Works* and *Conversations* together amount to well over eight thousand printed pages, filled with miscellaneous remarks, anecdotes, conversations, poems, notes, and commentaries. Again and again, Ansai went back to these inexhaustible sources to reach Chu Hsi in action. They are the most quoted sources in the five hundred fifty pages of *Notes* (the *Bunkai hitsuroku*) Ansai left behind.[23] Moreover, these *Notes* were Ansai's own "Literary Works" and "Classified Conversations," modeled and organized after Chu Hsi's. He used Chu Hsi's two posthumous works when he edited the *Reflections on Things at Hand* (*Chin-ssu lu*; Jp *Kinshiroku*), and he further teased from them some fifteen publications.[24]

In this thematization of Chu Hsi's work, as Abe Yoshio's exhaustive study has shown, Ansai closely followed the Korean scholar Yi T'oegye (1501–1570).[25] T'oegye's work is the second most quoted source in Ansai's *Notes*, and the two scholars had virtually the same lists of Sung and Ming scholars they accepted or—by far the longer list—rejected. They both ascribed to *kei* or

---

[23] YAZ 1: 91 to 2: 639 (consecutive pagination). See also Abe, *Chōsen*, p. 238.

[24] Further details on some of these works will follow in the rest of this chapter. For a summary description of each individual work of Ansai, see ZYAZ 3: 385–400. This introduction by Ikegami Kōjirō is based on the more extensive articles by Abe Yoshio, "Yamazaki Ansai no chosho." Furthermore, the Ōkura Institute for Spiritual Culture (Ōkura seishin bunka kenkyūjo, formerly Ōkurayama bunka-kagaku kenkyūjo) in Yokohama has a collection of 320 manuscripts of the Kimon school, the bulk of which came from Hiroshima, one of the Ansai school's strongholds during the Tokugawa period. For a bibliographical introduction to this collection, see Abe Ryūichi, "Kimon gakuha chosaku."

[25] Abe, *Chōsen*, pp. 232–73, 295–313. Several authors in de Bary and Bloom, *Principle*, rely on this important work of Abe (see index under Yi T'oegye).

reverence a central place among all the virtues, and gave great weight to *shūshin* (Ch *hsiu-shen*) or personal cultivation.[26] Several of the texts Ansai extracted from Chu Hsi's *Works* and *Conversations* had already been given a special place in T'oegye's writings.[27] T'oegye's influence on the Kimon school was so thorough that Satō Naokata, Ansai's most brilliant disciple, came to consider himself more closely linked to T'oegye than to Ansai.[28]

Following Chu Hsi's principles, Ansai also edited (in the 1660s and 1670s) the six books that became the canon of his school: the *Elementary Learning*, the *Reflections on Things at Hand*, and the *Four Books*; but his overriding obsession was with Chu Hsi himself. He even pain-stakingly completed several works that Chu Hsi had left unfinished or had simply planned to write.[29] The covers of his publications and the writing paper Ansai used were vermilion in honor of Chu Hsi (Chu is written with the character for "vermilion").[30] But the identification with Chu Hsi went even further. At age twenty-nine, Ansai adopted a new set of names, all of which referred to Chu Hsi. He took as his pen name a character similar to Chu Hsi's first name (the Japanese *Ka* 嘉, close to *Hsi* 熹); worked the character into his common name (Kaemon), adopted as a second pen name Moriyoshi, written with the characters for *keigi* (Ch *ching-li*), a reference to Chu Hsi's reverence-and-duty theory; and adopted "Ansai" as his studio name, which, although written

[26] Abe, *Chōsen*, pp. 232, 237–38, 255, 312, 365–66, 385.

[27] *Ibid.*, p. 301. They are the following works: 1) *Po-lu-tung shu-yüan chieh-shih* (Jp *Hakurokudōshoin keiji*, Precepts of the White Deer Grotto Academy); 2) *Jen-shuo* (Jp *Jinsetsu*, Treatise on humaneness); 3) *Ching-chai chen* (Jp *Keisaishin*, Exhortation for the Reverence studio). Ansai also mentions Yi T'oegye in his foreword to the *Kōhanzensho* (ZYAZ 2: 237). He also used a compendium of Chu Hsi's writings compiled by T'oegye; later Ansai's disciples annotated and printed it under the title *Shushisho setsuyō* (Compendium of explanations of Chu Hsi's writings).

[28] Satō Naokata's short spiritual testament (*Tōjibun*, Winter solstice writing), which he composed on the winter solstice of 1716, three years before his death, mentions not Ansai but T'oegye as the carrier of the Way whom Naokata enjoined his students to follow (SGT 12: 274). This document was read in his school on every winter solstice, down to the twentieth century. The winter solstice is important for its symbolic meaning. It is the day when the sun begins its yearly new cycle and thus refers to growing enlightenment. Ansai received both his formal initiation in Yoshida Shinto and his Shinto title of Suika on the day of a winter solstice (1671). (see p. 230. See also Chapter 7, note 12.

[29] The most important of these works are: 1) *Shūshisho* (Chou [Tun-yi]'s work; 1647); 2) *Kōkyōgaiden* (Unofficial classic of filial piety; 1656); 3) *Chūwashūsetsu* (Collected interpretations of "equilibrium" and "harmony" [of the *Doctrine of the Mean*]; 1672); 4) *Mōshi yōryaku* (*Mencius* compendium; between 1658 and 1672). Abe Yoshio, "Yamazaki Ansai no chosho," pp. 66, 71–73; for others, see *ibid.*, pp. 91–93.

[30] Ansai also wore a vermilion *haori* coat in the summer and a vermilion facial towel tuck in his belt (Sagara, *Jukyō undō no keifu*, p. 68).

with different characters, meant the same ("hidden abode") as Chu Hsi's studio name (*Hui-an*).[31] Ansai's identification with Chu Hsi is indistinguishable from his intense commitment to the Way. Just as Chu Hsi devoted his life to "repossessing the Way" (*tao-t'ung*; Jp *dōtō*),[32] Ansai, after he left the monastery, set as his life's goal the repossessing of Chu Hsi and through him, of the Way. Ansai was thus a Neo-Confucian not merely in the sense that he was a firm believer, a "slavish" follower of Chu Hsi, as has often been said. Neo-Confucian praxis included a critical stance toward tradition. The tradition that Ansai scrutinized included Chu Hsi himself.

Before returning one final time to the *Heresies Refuted*, it is best to clarify two characteristics of Ansai's scholarship that were admired by his followers and loathed by others: his reduction of the Neo-Confucian corpus to a handful of texts, and his fierce sense of orthodoxy.

Ansai's school is famous for limiting the study of Neo-Confucianism to the canon of the six works mentioned above. Although a few other texts Ansai edited were repeatedly lectured on in his school, as a rule his followers scorned literary and historical pursuits.[33] This makes Ansai unique in Japan. Theodore de Bary has pointed out that this reduction of the codex to the lowest common denominator had already occurred in China under the pressure of very specific historic circumstances.[34] In the Japanese setting, however, there were no political pressures for miniaturizing a vast tradition to such narrow orthodox dimensions. Many have speculated that it was Ansai's own psychology that made him cling with exclusivistic jealousy to the narrow core of the Chinese tradition. But the idiosyncracy of one man can not be the last word on this problem, for Ansai's restrictive choice became widely accepted and was institutionalized in one of the most vital Neo-Confucian schools in Japan. Tokugawa (and modern) Japan included many with Ansai's cast of mind.

The same holds true for Ansai's fierce orthodoxy. Ansai built a following that does not fit the tolerant, syncretistic, eclectic stereotype within which the Japanese are frequently cast (often by themselves). Ansai was single-minded, doctrinaire, and intolerant.

---

[31] See Ansai's autobiography (YAZ 2: 652), and Abe, *Chōsen*, p. 238.
[32] De Bary, *Orthodoxy*, pp. 1–9.
[33] See the recurring titles in NST 31.
[34] De Bary, *Orthodoxy*, pp. 56–57, 63–64, 71, 135.

His Shinto and Neo-Confucian followers found security in a rigid self-righteousness that projected an Other (a composite picture of father-slayers, lord-killers, arrogant scholars, and in general treasonous dissent) which became more real to the extent that more talk about "them" accumulated. Once again, de Bary points out that on the continent high seriousness also tended to develop a "paranoic style." In China there was at times, however, a genuine need to preserve orthodoxy against outside threats. Orthodox Neo-Confucians sometimes paid with their lives for their convictions. Moreover, through the institution of the imperial seminar or Classics Mat, scholars were deeply involved in policy debates.[35] They shared the responsibilities and risks that went with political power. In Japan, there were neither persecutions of Neo-Confucian scholars nor an institution like the Classics Mat.[36] Ansai's student Satō Naokata described the position of scholars in Japan quite correctly when he wrote around 1716:

Seven or eight out of ten Confucians who receive stipends from lords are vulgar Confucians (*zokuju*). Therefore they are of no use for matters concerning government ... they are less useful than doctors.... Even if they hold office, they are not consulted on administrative matters ... the only thing they do is read books and they are inferior to laymen as far as a "working knowledge" is concerned. In reality they are the idle class (*yūmin*) of the realm. One has to reflect on the need of scholarship if one looks at Chu Hsi's lectures for the emperor on the *Great Learning* which are contained in the *Ching-yen chiang-i* (Jp *Kei'en kōgi* or Lectures of the Classics Mat) and Chu Hsi's *Hsing-kung pien-tien tsou-cha* (Jp *Angūbenden no sōsatsu* or Memorials to the throne).[37]

No wonder that the stern and strident orthodoxy that marks Ansai learning often struck others at the time as ungrounded and

---

[35] *Ibid.*, pp. 1, 13–20, 29–32, 35–37.

[36] Kumazawa Banzan was criticized by Razan and subjected to public harassment. He resigned from his post in 1657 but never stopped writing. Yamaga Sokō was victimized by the Great Councillor Sakai Tadakiyo and banished from Edo by Hoshina Masayuki in 1666, but eight years later he was allowed to return. For the last six years of his life he could even lecture freely on his *Seikyō yōroku* (Essential record of the teachings of the Sages), the cause for his punishment. See Wajima, "Kanbun igaku," pp. 139, 143–47. The Ban on Heterodoxy of 1790, issued by Matsudaira Sadanobu, was limited to the Bakufu College and prescribed the content of learning for samurai wishing to be employed by the bakufu. See Ooms, *Bureaucrat*, pp. 133–50. On the general problem of orthodoxy and ideology, especially during the first century of the Tokugawa period, see also *id.*, "Neo-Confucianism."

[37] NST 31: 430–31.

hysterical. What was high-minded seriousness for those in the inner circle was perceived as narrow-mindedness by those outside.

It should be noted that every major tradition in Japan, as elsewhere in the world, has produced such exclusivistic fundamentalists. In Japan, admittedly, such movements, rather than remaining marginal, have a tendency to become significant, even part of the mainstream, and to veer in nationalistic directions. Such was the case with Nichiren's transformation of Buddhism in the thirteenth century and Uchimura Kanzō's Christianity in modern times. Ansai was the Nichiren for Japan's two other major traditions: Neo-Confucianism and Shinto.

From the very start of his scholarly career, Ansai's dogmatic convictions put him at odds with other Neo-Confucian scholars. He lambastes them in his *Heresies Refuted*, a pratice continued with great verve in his school.[38] Implicit in Ansai's castigation is the assumption that he possessed what they lacked: a religious faith manifested in practice. Those who merely engaged in textual critiques or composition of poetry Ansai called scholars not of the Way but "of the world," secular pedants (195):

They, like the Buddhists, do not know that there is nothing more to the Way than the Three Bonds [between ruler and minister, father and son, husband and wife] and the Five Constants. In attitude and temperament they are no different from those Shinran fellows. Applying themselves to books and justifying what they do through quotes from the broad learning of the Sages and Worthies, they compose poems for which they rely on the *Book of Odes* or the *Book of History*. (248).

The Shinran comparison is there. The analogy between Nichiren and himself is not far off.

In general, the secular or vulgar were all those who made a claim to knowledge of the Way yet did not share Ansai's intense views on practice. More specifically, however, he may have had in mind the Hayashi school since, through his publication of the *Heresies Refuted*, he was staking out his own territory. Four years later (in 1651), Ansai composed a short tract, aimed directly at Razan who, as a Neo-Confucian scholar-cleric, flouted all traditions, Japanese

[38] For a sampling of similar criticism by Ansai's leading disciples, see the following: for Satō Naokata—NST 31: 104, 430, 433, 436, and for a critique of Itō Jinsai, p. 439; for Asami Keisai—NST 31: 384 (and a critique of Itō Jinsai, pp. 356, 386–88) and SGT 12: 204; for Miyake Shōsai—SGT 12: 311.

and Chinese alike.[39] In his lectures he sometimes ridiculed inter-
pretations cherished by Hayashi Gahō,[40] who was not unaware of
Ansai's general low opinion of him nor of the specifics of Ansai's ire.
We hear from Gahō about this in 1666/10. His defense against
Ansai's attack was rather meek:

In recent years I have heard that I have been labeled a *zokuju* (vulgar
Confucian). [The accusation is] that I am reviving the Ch'eng brothers
and Chu Hsi with lofty talk about nature and principles and that I
brandish words of broad knowledge, both [allegedly] obstacles [to true
learning]. Well, he is who he is and I am who I am. If the Way is not the
same, then we don't [even have any common ground to] dispute with one
another. All I want to do is continue the family business (*kagyō*).[41]

Gahō then continues arguing that without grammatical and specific knowledge one cannot understand the classics or commentaries,
and he wonders "how that fellow could be opposed to that!"

Ansai's deepest scorn, however, was reserved for Gahō's father,
Razan. When Ansai heard of Razan's work on the *Honchō tsugan*, a
history of Japan in imitation of Ssu-ma Kuang's *General Mirror of
Government (T'ung-chien* Jp *Tsugan)*, he burst out:

Mr. Hayashi! What sort of a man is he! The whole world knows about his
unfiliality [having become a monk]. He has served under four shoguns
but has never expounded the Way of Yao and Shun before them. That is
what is known as lack of reverence.... Mr. Hayashi! What kind of
learning does he have! A so-called encyclopedic knowledge which he

---

[39] SGT 12: 136–37. Nakae Tōju had already written a similar tract, twenty years earlier
(NST 19: 13–15). Ansai and Tōju were mainly offended by Razan's clerical status and his
acceptance of high priestly rank. Yet this was not unusual in the early Tokugawa bakufu. As
during the Muromachi bakufu, nonsamurai purveyors of council and knowledge to the
shogun, such as Razan's colleagues Sūden and Tenkai, were Zen monks. Sugimoto
Masayoshi reports that since the late fourteenth century, priestly ranks were given to
practitioners of medicine (often but not always Buddhist priests) as recognition for their
excellence—a practice that continued until the nineteenth century. The court or bakufu
could recommend medical practitioners to these ranks, given by the court, if they wore robes
(Sugimoto, *Science in Japan*, p. 217). It should also be noted that in 1651, Razan's stipend was
increased to 917 koku (Hori, *Razan*, p. 378), although it is unlikely that Ansai was aware of
this.

[40] YAZ 2: 568. Here Ansai attacks Gahō's interpretation of Chu Hsi's twenty [*Chai-chü*]
kan-hsing poems (Jp *kankyōshi*, Poems [I was] moved to write [while dwelling in the studio])
from volume 4 of his *Literary Works*. In 1558, Ansai published these poems with a preface of
his own, written two years earlier (complete text: ZYAZ 3: 14–29; preface: SGT 12: 155–56;
see also Abe Yoshio, "Yamazaki Ansai no chosho," p. 88).

[41] Hayashi Gahō, *Seifūruido* (Western wind tears), quoted in Ozawa, *Kinsei shigaku*, p. 296.

trumpets about in his arrogance. His mind is dark and his knowledge blocked.[42]

In comparison to his father, Gahō seems to have received the kinder side of Ansai's indignation. Part of the reason for this may be that for Ansai, Razan was an evil he had not personally encountered: he died in 1657, one year before Ansai first came to Edo. Moreover, Ansai's patron Masayuki did not share Ansai's strong feelings against the Hayashi, and toward the end of his life seems even to have grown close to Gahō, who was then often seen at Masayuki's mansion. About a year before Masayuki died, between 1671/11 and 1672/2—Ansai was in Kyoto then—Gahō was even invited to preface all the works Masayuki had either commissioned with Ansai or co-authored with him; works that already contained introductions or postscripts by Ansai himself.[43]

A BLOCKED ALTERNATIVE: TO THE WAY THROUGH HISTORY

That Ansai deeply resented Razan's imitation of the historiographical enterprises of Confucius and Chu Hsi was not simply because he judged Razan unworthy of such an undertaking. Neither was it because Ansai scorned history, a trait later associated with his school. On the contrary, Ansai had historiographical ambitions of his own, as well he should have if Chu Hsi was his model—ambitions, as it turned out, that he was unable to fulfill. His pique at Razan on this point was, in all likelihood, provoked by the painful realization that Razan was doing what he had set as one of his own goals. Moreover, Ansai may have felt that Razan went about his historiographical undertaking in the wrong way: a genuine Neo-Confucian should take Chu Hsi as his model and not Ssu-ma Kuang. This is, at least, the conclusion one can draw if one considers the following circumstances.

During the decade following the publication of the *Heresies Refuted* (1647–1657), Ansai edited and published a number of texts, opened his own school in Kyoto (in 1655), and finished his

[42] In *Ben Rin Dōshun Honchō kōmoku* (Discussion of Hayashi Razan's *Honchō kōmoku* or Essentials of our dynasty). This document, which I could not locate, is quoted in Kobayashi, *Suika Shinto*, p. 607.
[43] Ozawa, *Kinsei shigaku*, p. 298.

first lecture cycle (spring 1655 through the end of 1656).[44] He lectured on his canon (the *Elementary Learning*, the *Reflections on Things at Hand*, and the *Four Books*, in that sequence) to which he added *Ch'eng Yi's Commentary on the Book of Changes*.

Chu Hsi's advice had been to follow a reading of the classics with a study of history. Two weeks after Ansai delivered his last lecture, we find him (on 1657/1/7) at the Kyoto shrine of Fuji no mori, dedicated to Prince Toneri, who in 720 compiled the *Nihongi*. There Ansai declared his intention to write a *Yamato kagami* (*Mirror of Japan*), and prayed for inspiration in understanding the mysteries of the *Nihongi*'s abstruse opening chapters, "The Age of the Gods."[45]

History writing as a new mode of intellectual activity in the early Tokugawa period was started for a variety of reasons. Tokugawa Mitsukini established his Mito historiographical office in his Edo mansion only a couple of weeks after Ansai's visit to the shrine, and after some of Razan's work was lost in the Meireki fire (1657/1/19). Mitsukuni was driven, it seems, not only by some sense of rivalry with the bakufu's historiographical project that was being executed by the Hayashi scholars, but also by the Neo-Confucian ideal of using history as a means for remonstrating with the rulers. It should be noted, however, that although Mito's *Dainihonshi* (Great History of Japan), dealt with problems of legitimate succession (in support of the Southern court), it was certainly not meant to convince the emperor (a successor of the Northern court) of bakufu legitimacy: the work was not presented to the court until 1819.[46]

Razan had started his historiographical work as an annalist for the bakufu. In 1641–1643, he compiled the *Kan'ei shoke keizuden* (The Kan'ei family genealogy of all houses), and in 1644, he was ordered to work on a *Japanese Annals* (*Honchō hennenroku*) which, except for the original manuscript, perished in the Meireki fire. The project was finally finished between 1664 and 1670, and its 310 fascicles came to be known as the *Honchō tsugan* (General mirror

---

[44] He also found time to get married and start writing his autobiography. Ansai's editorial work on sections of Chu Hsi's writings, between 1646 and 1657, concerns the following: the *Kankyōshi* (1646), the *Shūshisho* (1647), the *Hakurokudō gakuki shūchū* (1650), the *Keisaishin* (1655), the *Kōkyōgaiden* and *Kōkyōkango* (Misprints in the classic on filial piety) in 1656, and the *Daike shōryōshū* (Collection of discussions of the great Master; an anti-Wang Yang-ming work), sometime between 1652 and 1654.

[45] *Yamazaki kafu* (YAZ 2: 653). See also Ansai's *Yamato shōgaku* (NKB 9: 94).

[46] Nakai, "Domestication"; Kurihara, "Mitsukuni," p. 603 n58.

of Japan), a clear reference to its Chinese model, which turned out
to be Ssu-ma Kuang and not Chu Hsi. In 1652, Gahō also finished
his short *Nihon ōdai ichiran* or Overview of Japanese reigns; it was
printed in 1663.

Remonstrance to the rulers in Confucian fashion was certainly
not what prompted the bakufu to sponsor these historiographical
undertakings. Nor did the Tokugawa house seek to bolster its
legitimacy through these works. Kate Nakai writes that Razan and
Gahō

were keenly aware that ... the bakufu leadership was by and large far less
committed than they to the act of writing history as such. In the diary that
he kept during the process of compiling *Honchō tsugan*, Gahō recorded his
frustration over the tendency of influential figures within the bakufu to
regard the project as a decorative undertaking of secondary importance
that was taking too long and costing too much to complete.[47]

If there was little interest from the bakufu in the project, neither
was there an audience to which the monumental work was addressed. There were only three copies made of the *Honchō tsugan*:
one for the shogun, one for the Tokugawa library, and one for the
Hayashi library.[48] Access to this work was thus extremely restricted. The common argument that the bakufu patronized the
writing of history as an effort to convince others of its legitimacy
ought thus to be abandoned.

Razan, however, had had a lifelong interest in the project. As
with Ansai, the idea of tackling Japanese history from a Neo-
Confucian perspective was from the very beginning part of his
imagined identity as a would-be Confucian scholar. A reference in
a letter from Fujiwara Seika to Razan, written in 1604, indicates
that Razan hoped to one day write a *Kokuchō kōmoku* (Essentials of
our national dynasty) after Chu Hsi's *T'ung-chien kang-mu*. In his
miscellaneous writings of later years one finds sketches for its
execution; even the name *Yamato kagami* turns up.[49]

Historiography was thus less a medium of legitimation for the
rulers, who showed little interest in this aspect of Neo-Confucian
scholarship, than an idealistic part of the "professional activity"
that students of Chinese learning dreamt of engaging in—one that
was essential to their self-identity as *jusha* or Confucian scholars. To

[47] Nakai, "Domestication."
[48] Ozawa, *Kinsei shigaku*, p. 295.
[49] SGT 13: 92; RB 2: 210, 214.

call it idealistic is no exageration. These scholars did not have the raw material—an already complied history—they could mold to fit their cherished moral standards. Chu Hsi did not write history. He undertook a topical rewriting of Ssu-ma Kuang's *General Mirror of Government*. In Japan, no comprehensive history had been compiled since the mid-Heian period. An enormous task awaited anyone wishing to be a Japanese Chu Hsi, since there was no Japanese Ssu-ma Kuang. Indeed, Hayashi's *General Mirror of Japan* (*Honchō tsugan*) was modeled after Kuang's *t'ung-chien* (*tsugan*) rather than Chu Hsi's moralistic *kang-mu* (*kōmoku*). Such a "tsugan" enterprise, however, was well beyond the capacities of one man: teams of scholars were needed. When in 1664 Hoshina Masayuki approved the completion of the *Honchō tsugan*, a special magistrate was appointed, and a library and office constructed. Gahō worked on the project for six years with his two sons, two disciples, and a staff of twenty. Sources were a great problem. Those that were readily available, like the *Nihongi*, were untrustworthy and needed critical examination. Obstacles stood in the way of collecting new ones: Razan had stopped the *Japanese Annals* (*Honchō hennenroku*) at Emperor Uda's reign (887–897) because of the difficulty of obtaining documents later than the period for which official histories existed (the *Rikkokushi* or *Six National Histories* did not go beyond the mid-Heian period). In the introduction to *Honchō tsugan*, Razan complains of similar difficulties. Even the Hayashi scholars, backed by bakufu authority, ran into obstructionism on the part of the imperial court.[50]

The historiographical project Ansai had in mind was essentially a religious undertaking, for which he needed spiritual assistance. On 1657/2/26, one month after announcing his New Year's resolution to Prince Toneri at his shrine in Kyoto, he arrived in Ise—five traveling days from Kyoto—for his first visit to the Imperial Shrines. In one of the poems written on the occasion, Ansai alludes to the parallelism between the normative Way of Confucianism and the instructions of Yamato-hime, the foundress of Ise.[51] Two

[50] Ozawa, *Kinsei shigaku*, p. 207; Ikeda, "Ansaijugaku," p. 34; Kurihara, "Mitsukuni," p. 559.
[51] The poem translates roughly as follows: "*Praying at Kakure no yama* [a mountain in Ise]: On the mountain top, at the cremation ground, it is rare to [find one] weeping for unfulfilled filial duty toward one's deceased parents. [Yet,] a small Confucian with feeling for the past is briefly moved to tears: the Normative Way [*Great Learning* 10: 1–2] exists and is no different from Yamato-hime's instructions to make left what is left, and right what is right." (YAZ 2: 788; for other poems written during Ise pilgrimages, see *ibid.*, p. 751.)

weeks after his return from Ise, Ansai prayed at the Hachiman Shrine in Kyoto.[52]

What came of Ansai's dream? Nothing substantial in terms of history writing, but something very important for the scholarly orientation of the rest of his life, namely, a firm commitment to Shinto scholarship. Ansai's historiographical undertaking never proceeded beyond the conceptual stage: ten pages of *Notes on Japanese Era Names* (*Honchō kaigen-kō*) and a one-page *Table of Contents of the Mirror of Japan* (*Yamato kagami mokuroku*), listing the eighty-seven chapters (reigns of emperors) that would form the structure of his history.[53] In a later personal piece on Prince Toneri's shrine, written on 1671/11/23, the *Mirror of Japan* is no more mentioned.[54] By then Ansai had abandoned the project, but not without having spent a considerable effort in trying. His attempts in this direction may explain a curiously unproductive period in his career.

Before he declared his intention to write a *Mirror of Japan*, as we have seen, Ansai published a number of works. And again, during his seven-year service with Masayuki (1665–1672), he annotated or compiled, besides some six works for Masayuki, five volumes of his own. During the last ten years of his life (1672–1682), his production was frantic. Besides two large volumes on Shinto, he annotated, compiled, and/or published some fifteen tomes.[55] The eight years between 1657 and 1665, however, are a dead period. There is no public trace of any serious scholarly activity. The publication of two short texts (totaling thirty-two pages) has to be discounted, since they had been prepared earlier. There are also

---

[52] YAZ 2: 653.

[53] *Ibid.*, pp. 656–66 and 686–88. For an analysis of the historiographical significance of these two writings, see Ozawa, *Kinsei shigaku*, pp. 271–301.

[54] NNS 12: 272–74.

[55] Besides punctuating and publishing the *Four Books* and arranging for the publication of his own lecture notes (*Bunkai hitsuroku*), Ansai edited four compendia of the works of Chou Tun-yi, the Ch'eng brothers, Chang Tsai, and Chu Hsi; punctuated and published three works on the *Book of Changes* (besides one he only edited); and published, with his own punctuation, a work on the Elementary Learning. He also edited (with commentaries) a poem by Han Yü (768–824) on the unwavering loyalty of King Wen, called *Chü-yu ts'ao* (Jp *Kōyūsō*, Restraint in prison) (NST 31: 200–201). His two Shinto works are the *Nakatomi harai fūsuisō* (Wind and water draft on the Nakatomi purification), a compilation of past commentaries, interspersed with his own, on the text of the Nakatomi purification ritual (DNB 17: 2–298) and the *Jindai no maki fūyōshū* (Wind and leaves collection of the "Age of the Gods"), a work similarly composed of comments on the two opening chapters of the *Nihongi* (DNB 16: 9–224). This last work was not finished when Ansai died and was completed by his Shinto disciples.

two travelogues (thirty pages; 163 poems), and the *Yamato shōgaku* (Japanese Elementary Learning), written for a daimyo in Edo and based on the memory of his past readings—circumstances did not allow him to consult any reference works.[56] Moreover, in 1658/2, only a year after finishing his first lecture cycle at his new school and conceiving the writing of a *Mirror of Japan*, Ansai suddenly left for Edo for no immediately apparent reason. He stayed there for six months, and returned by way of Ise.[57]

According to Ozawa Eiichi, the slack period, as well as Ansai's first trips to Edo, are best understood in terms of his attempts to collect historical material. Ansai's two poetic travelogues, written en route to Edo in 1658 and 1659, reveal an interest in the history of the locales he traveled through—an interest which, as one would expect, was of a moralizing nature. Moreover, one of the contacts Ansai made in Edo seems to have been motivated by his efforts to obtain historical materials. Until he joined Masayuki in 1665, Ansai was doing sundry scholarly projects for two daimyo, Inoue Masatoshi, lord of Kasama (50,000 koku) and Katō Yasuyoshi, lord of Ōsu (the same size). Masatoshi was Master of Shogunal Cermonies when Ansai met him on his first trip in 1658, but was promoted that same year to Superintendant of Temples and Shrines. If Ansai was looking for documents, Masatoshi was certainly the person who could help him. In 1664, Gahō also turned to Masatoshi to help him collect post-Engi (901–923) records concerning the court nobility and the warrior class.[58] In this way Ansai was certainly made aware that he shared similar interests

[56] The two texts Ansai edited earlier are the *Kankyōshi kōchū* (Commentaries on [Chu Hsi's] *Kan-hsing* poems) and the *Bumei* ([Commentaries on King] Wu's precepts), a Chu Hsi selection on King Wu's ritual (ZYAZ 3: 14–45). The two poetic travelogues are the *Enyūkikō* and *Saiyūkikō* (Travelogue one and two of a far holiday) (YAZ 1: 22–52). Besides these works (and the *Yamato shōgaku*), Ansai produced during the eight-year span of 1657–1665 a few negligible pieces commissioned by daimyo. Thus he edited the *Gyōreki* (Ch *Yao-li*, Yao's calendar), a section from the *Book of Records*, which he provided with an introduction in which he compared the calendars of China and Japan. (For a description of the work, see Abe Yoshio, "Yamazaki Ansai chosho," pp. 108–109; for the introduction, see YAZ 1: 70–71). Ansai also wrote a postscript for a Korean edition of the *Analects* and the *Mencius* (*ibid.*, p. 84). The only reason why Ansai dealt with these works seems to be that these texts were in the possession of the daimyo Inoue Masatoshi (the *Gyōreki*) and Katō Yasuyoshi (the latter works). For Yasuyoshi, Ansai further composed an interpretive piece on the name Yasuyoshi (*Saisai no ki*; SGT 12: 132–34) and a family history (*Katōkaden*; YAZ 2: 648–50).

[57] YAZ 2: 653. For the next fourteen years, Ansai was to divide his time every year between Kyoto and Edo but after returning from Masayuki's funeral in 1673, he stayed in Kyoto for the remaining nine years of his life.

[58] Ozawa, *Kinsei shigaku*, pp. 210, 287–88.

with his rival Gahō (and Gahō, perhaps, learned of Ansai's low opinion of his scholarship).

In Ansai's voluminous notes from his readings, one finds a number of entries from Chinese histories that relate to Japan and Korea. It is unclear when these notes were taken, but they may have been related to his project to write a *Mirror of Japan*. In the end, not surprisingly, he gave up the whole idea and veered in a different direction. Ozawa surmises that Ansai may have understood that he had arrived at a crossroads.[59] Ideally, he should not have been faced with a dilemma, since in Neo-Confucian fashion one can study the Way through the Classics just as well as through the historical record. In Japan, however, that record did not exist and had to be put together first, which would have taken up all of Ansai's energies, as Gahō's experience clearly showed.[60] Ansai may thus have been confronted with a choice of either becoming a historiographer, and in this facing enormous difficulties, or pursuing his calling as a teacher of the Way, a *dōgakusha*. Ansai chose the later, with a twist. He abandoned Japanese history but became more and more involved in Shinto. If Japan's political history was beyond his reach, Japan's mythology and Shinto traditions provided him with an arena in which to discuss the Way embedded in Japanese society and human experience. He invaded this new territory for the first time in 1658 in his *Yamato shōgaku* (Japanese Elementary Learning).[61]

With this work, as the title indicates, Ansai had a publication for elementary education in mind, just as Chu Hsi had with his *Hsiao-hsüeh*. Ansai wrote his *Japanese Elementary Learning* for Inoue Masatoshi after they had discussed the inappropriateness of works such as the *Tale of Genji* and the *Tales of Ise*. In the introduction (25) Ansai also notes that he was forced to write the book without the help of any reference works. This explains many small inaccuracies, which are also one of the reasons why this work has been neglected by the Ansai school. Yet, the large number of allusions to Chinese and Japanese works testifies to Ansai's wide knowledge and reveals the salient aspects of his thought.

The *Japanese Elementary Learning* is a miscellany of teachings, advice, historical anecdotes, and discussions of social customs, but

[59] *Ibid.*, p. 290 (see YAZ 1: 352–58).
[60] For Gahō's difficulties in collecting historical materials, see *ibid.*, pp. 210–15.
[61] References in the text are to page numbers in NKB 9.

it is of interest primarily for its inclusion of numerous Shinto elements. The kinds of social customs Ansai discusses include funeral practices (mourning periods, memorial days, and services) (34–37, 69), the "well system" of land division and taxation (45), *junshi* (51–52), and marriage (including widowhood, divorce, and the behavior of wives and sisters) (56–67). Buddhism, of course, is singled out for special criticism (35, 78–79), as are "fake" Confucians (79) and their excessive obsession with things Chinese (88). There is also a brief, but interesting, critique of Christianity (85) which, like the one of Buddhism, focuses on doctrine. Ansai does not speak of Christianity the way the Japanese had experienced it. Instead, he attacks it by criticizing a Ming scholar, Hsieh Chao-che, whom he remembers as having praised the teachings of Matteo Ricci (1562–1610) because they were so similar to Confucianism.

Ansai is comfortable only with simple, clear categories. He abhors mixed genres: monks that marry and thus behave like laymen, or Confucians who shave their heads and thus posture as monks (79). Moral casuistry that guides one in ethical decision-making through the intricate web spun by particular circumstances is totally alien to Ansai's mind. This explains his predilection for extreme cases that involve unusual suffering or death; cases that unambiguously illustrate the operation of clear motives, principles, or virtues. Such cases not only exemplify the stark, uncompromising demands that the practice of virtue (especially loyalty) makes on human actors but also demonstrate that such norms are inborn and owe nothing to contingent circumstances.

The logic that constitutes these examples not merely as illustrations but also as proofs is simple. Extraordinary cases of heroism, self-sacrifice, uprightness, endurance, loyalty, and so on could not be explained by commonsensical reference to personal interests or social circumstances. Neither was such behavior to be reduced to the singular idiosyncrasies of the actors—an explanation that would have denied universality to the values expressed in such behavior. Instead, these exemplary actors constituted proof that man was born with innate ethical imperatives more powerful than the temptations of the flesh. Ansai's followers endlessly recited, discussed, and expanded upon the same examples. In this way these illustrations came to acquire the status of paradigms for behavior.

One of these examples celebrates King Wen's unflagging

loyalty, even during an unjust and cruel imprisonment, to King Chou, the last king-tyrant of the Yin dynasty.[62] King Wen was the father of King Wu, who overthrew the Yin and founded the Chou dynasty. Ansai points out, however, that, although both King Wen and King Wu were sages, Confucius praised King Wen (and his uncle T'ai-po, who also refused to rebel against the tyrant) as possessing a higher virtue than King Wu (41–42).[63] Ansai further cites Chinese and Japanese incidents of sons reporting the crimes of their fathers, thus exemplifying the priority of public duty (*kōgi*) over private obligation (*shion*) (40). On the absolute prohibition of widows from remarrying even if they had nobody to rely on, he quotes one of the Ch'eng brothers as saying that "starving to death is a small matter in comparison to the great matter of losing the Way" (57). His example of someone who had persevered in remonstrating with his lord is the historian Yü from Wei who, after failing during his life to communicate his criticism to his lord, designed his funeral in such a way that his criticism would be made clear to his lord (*Analects* 15: 6: 1; and 15: 8) (48). Treacherous Japanese vassals provide counterexamples (49–50), whereas Kusunoki Masashige (1294–1336) is praised for his dedicated loyalty and is compared to Chu-ko K'ung-ming (181–234 A.D.) (44).

With these dramatic examples, Ansai buttresses his main doctrinal points, which he already had laid out in *Heresies Refuted*. The innate virtues that constitute man's nature are the same as those that govern the life of the universe. Thus man "naturally" (*onozukara*) follows these innate virtues (25–26). Ansai stresses that even the obligation which binds minister-vassals to their lord (*kunshin no gi*) is part of a heavenly endowed nature, since—the familiar example—it is even present among the ants and bees (41), and he devotes the third and final fascicle of the work (70–93) to a discussion of the preeminence of *kei*, reverence.

The mind, lord of the house (or body), rules and coordinates man's mental life through *kei* (70). This virtue is the core of the mind-heart system of the orthodox transmission of the Way (*dōtō no shinpō*; Ch *tao-t'ung, hsin-fa*). Ansai establishes the cardinal position

[62] See, for example, Ansai's comments and those of his three leading students on Han Yü's *Chü-yu ts'ao* poem (together with a Naokata-Shōsai discussion on the legitimacy of revolt) in NST 31: 200–43.

[63] *Analects* 3: 25; 8: 1; and 8: 20: 4. For an analysis of the discussions of these texts in the Ansai school, see Maruyama, "Ansaigaku," pp. 658–60.

of this virtue through the whole of China's teaching, following closely the orthodoxy argument of Chu Hsi and his followers. Chu Hsi's "Extemporaneous Poems" (*Kan-hsing shih*; Jp *Kankyōshi*; lit. "Poems [I was] moved to write [while dwelling in the studio]") are cited in full (71–72). They illustrate that this virtue had been central since the time of the Yellow Emperor, when the word *ching* (*kei*) did not exist but its reality was expressed by Fu Hsi's Heaven and Earth hexagram. The tradition then passed through the Sage Kings to Confucius and Mencius, at which point it was lost, only to be repossessed by the Ch'eng brothers and Chu Hsi, who most succinctly expressed it in his "Exhortation for the Reverence studio" (*Ching-chai chen*; Jp *Keisaishin*). Ansai then deploys a redundant vocabulary (perpetuated by his students) that expresses the urgency and undivided energy with which one must preserve *kei*: without idleness (*uka to naku*), sternly (*kitto*), with a bouncy energy (*kappatsu hachi*) and single-minded concentration (*shuichi*; Ch *chu-i*) (72–73).[64] Constant vigilance is needed (90) because man's moral predicament is an all-or-nothing proposition: the slightest mistake leads to the greatest disasters, which are usually exemplified by the killing of one's lord (89). The mind, far from being empty, is the source of everything (90).

The Japanese references in the *Japanese Elementary Learning* are to literary, historical, and mythological works. Ansai uses *koka* (old poems) (47), the *Tsurezuregusa* and the *Manyōshū* (82–84). His most frequently used historical work is Kitabatake Chikafusa's *Jinnō shōtōki* (Chronicle of gods and sovereigns) (28, 40, 88, 89). This work is important to Ansai because it held a crucial place in his plan to rewrite Japanese history. Ansai was aware that the only classic on which Chu Hsi had not commented was the *Spring and Autumn Annals,* and that instead Chu Hsi had written his *Essentials of the General Mirror of Government* (*T'ung-chien kang-mu*), based on Ssu-ma Kuang's work.[65] Ssu-ma Kuang's was not an official history. Ansai, as always following Chu Hsi's path, also settled for a private

---

[64] *Kappatsu hachi*, is Chu Hsi's colloquial *huo-p'o p'o-ti* of his comment on the *Doctrine of the Mean* 12: 3 (See SGT 8: 27). *Shuichi* is discussed at length elsewhere by Ansai, Naokata, and Keisai (see NST 31: 90, 104, and 143–44, respectively). Keisai has another set of terms that express the keenness and urgency with which one has to stand watch over one's total self, and experience or savor one's ethical exertion: *shimijimi*, keenly (NST 31: 256), *shinobirarenu shinmi*, an unbearable true taste (p. 257), or a *yamarenai aji*, a savor that does not let up (p. 261). Ansai also contrasts two qualifiers: *tada* and *tsukusu* or *itaru*. Thus, for instance, *tada shiru* (pp. 30–31) or *tada zen* (p. 41) are insufficient because they are "mere" knowledge and "mere" good: the ideal is *tsukusu*, to "exhaust, complete, perfect" knowledge or goodness (*shizen, zen ni itaru*).

[65] SGT 12: 138, 185.

history of Japan, namely, the *Jinnō shōtōki*.[66] Most of the other historical works Ansai refers to in his *Japanese Elementary Learning*, as Ozawa has pointed out, testify to Ansai's interest in Japan's early history, especially Shinto.[67] Thus, due to the impracticality of the over-all project, the kind of sources available to him (the *Kojiki, Nihongi, Zoku Nihongi, Fudoki*, and so on), and his avowed determination to "crack" the "Age of the Gods," Ansai was drawn more and more to the study of Shinto. Although he eventually abandoned his intention to follow in Chu Hsi's "kang-mu" (*"Essentials"*) footsteps (as also Razan had), his Shinto enterprise, as will become clear, allowed him to see himself as performing a task very similar to Chu Hsi's main endeavor.

EMBODYING THE WAY IN JAPAN

Before Ansai's growing involvement in Shinto, as evidenced in his *Japanese Elementary Learning*, he had shared a commonly held view of Shinto that was inspired by a reaction against Buddhism. Like Razan, Yamaga Sokō, and Kumazawa Banzan, Ansai expressed the view that primitive Shinto before the arrival of Buddhism in Japan was the same as Confucianism. In 1651, on returning from the Confucian burial Nonaka Kenzan, his first patron, had given to his mother, Ansai wrote how Confucian funeral rites were the same as Shinto rites because the Ise teachings had always prohibited cremation.[68] The same year he opened his school he also wrote (on 12/9, his birthday) an introduction to the *Ritual of the Great Shrines at Ise* (*Ise Daijingū gishiki*), a work that dates back to 804. The world of *kami*, Ansai wrote, goes back to a preliterary time when even the character for *kami* did not exist. The word *kami* is a natural expression of the human voice. (For a similar view by Razan, see pp. 92–93) The unfathomably mysterious *kami* are the masters of yin and yang and the Five Evolutive Phases, which are embodied in the various gods. Amaterasu's promise to protect the imperial house forever is the beginning of the Kingly Way (*ōdō*), a way that, except in Ise, had been contaminated by Buddhism.[69]

[66] YAZ 2: 782. See also Ozawa, *Kinsei shigaku*, pp. 275–77, 282–83. Keizai mentions that Ansai abandoned his historiographic plans when he heard that the Hayashi were embarked on a similar project (NST 31: 352). On this complicated matter, see Ozawa, *Kinsei shigaku*, pp. 284, 292, 299–300.

[67] Ozawa, *Kinsei shigaku*, p. 289.

[68] YAZ 2: 771.

[69] NNS 14: 276, 278, 279.

As discussed earlier, Ansai filtered everything through beliefs that inclined him toward the construction of pure categories: the Way in its rudimentary simplicity, the tangible "metaphysics" of the *Book of Changes*, the concrete thought of Chu Hsi as reflected in his correspondence with his students, and the extreme paradigms of embodied virtues. Ise became for Ansai a pure enclave in which Japan's own teachings had escaped historical change, and where, within these teachings, the "Age of the Gods" held an even more privileged place.

Ansai visited Ise a total of six times.[70] These visits were undoubtedly religious pilgrimages. His first visit took place in 1657/2, after he decided to rewrite Japanese history. In 1663 he accompanied his two parents, sister, and brother to Ise. His four other trips were detours on his travels to and from Edo (1658 and 1659, 1668, and 1669). Ansai, however, probably had something else in mind besides worshiping at the Grand Shrines, because after 1669 he did not return to Ise: that year he received from Watarai Nobuyoshi and Ōnakatomi no Kiyonaga the *Nakatomi harai* (Nakatomi purification ritual) and Ise's sacred and secret traditions (which could be transmitted to no more than ten Shinto priests).[71] It seems, therefore, that an initiation into the Ise tradition had been Ansai's goal all along. His prestige as Masayuki's mentor was probably instrumental in his achievement of this aim. (The Ise priests may have seen in Ansai a valuable bakufu contact.) Two years later he received from Yoshikawa Koretaru the secret teachings of the Yoshida house. Thus by 1673, the end of Ansai's Edo period, he had acquired access to the teachings of the two most important Shinto schools of the time.

Let us return for a moment to Ansai's Shinto views prior to this time, as he expressed them in the *Japanese Elementary Learning*. There is no single theme that runs through the Shinto material, but among the miscellaneous information that Ansai provides throughout the text, a new points are worth noting. The random data include notes on important shrines, their history, and the identities of the deities worshiped there: Ise (87), Hachiman (88), Hiyoshi (90), and the history and meaning of the three imperial regalia (42). The mythology section on Susanoo's recovery of the sword from the tail of the dragon receives some attention (54–55), and

---

[70] YAZ 2: 653–54. For an analysis of Ansai's poems, written on these occasions, see Taira, *Kinsei*, pp. 181–82.

[71] Taira, *Kinsei*, p. 183 and p. 185 n8.

there are allusions to information not available in standard Shinto writings (85, 87). More important, the theme of Shinto as the Kingly Way (*ōdō*) is brought up (86) and its content is more specifically identified through the prophesies of Amaterasu and Yamato-hime. Amaterasu's promise of an uninterrupted rule for her descendants immediately follows the passage in which King Wen's unflagging loyalty to a corrupt ruler is praised (42): unconditional loyalty that preserves the continuity of the polity is the core of ōdō. Yamato-hime's famous teachings about keeping right what is right and left what is left—to be found in the *Shintō gobusho* and also in Kitabatake's writings—are connected with what one might call a position of ineluctable moral entropy: to give in even one inch to evil will only lead to total disaster (89) ("the initial mistake of a hair's breadth, resulting in an error of a thousand miles," according to a Chinese proverb).[72] Before concluding the work with some Shinto poetry and the poem he wrote on his visit to Prince Toneri's Fuji no mori shrine (94–95), however, Ansai touches on an important principle that became central to his approach to Shinto mythology.

The context is a discussion of the essence of the Way (unswerving loyalty and selflesness, guarded by an ever-vigilant mind) as expressed in Yamato-hime's prophecy. There he announces the principle (*ri*) that "the beginnings of Heaven and Earth are today's beginnings" (*tenchi no hajime wa kyō o hajime to suru*) (90). In other words, cosmogonic principles are still at work today, not simply in the historical sense that without an initial creation there would be no "today," but metaphysically as functional norms that govern man's life in the present. Because of this, Ansai argues, they must be studied, decoded, repossessed, and taught.

The same Shinto myths that intrigued Ansai as a source of the Way, as *more* than history, were dismissed by other Confucians of his time as rambling tales unworthy of scholarly scrutiny, precisely because they viewed them as *less* than history. In 1667, Hayashi Gahō argued that it is not easy to write about the creation of "the Age of the Gods" and that one had better not dwell upon it. Similarly, Mitsukuni wrote in 1684 that "all the matters pertaining to the Age of the Gods are by and large strange and rambling, which is why it was difficult to incorporate them into the 'Record of

[72] For Yamato-hime's teachings, see *Yamato-hime no mikoto seiki*, in *Watarai Shintō taisei* 1: 65; Kitabatake, *A Chronicle of Gods and Sovereigns*, p. 108. For the Chinese proverb, see Wang Yang-ming, *Instructions for Practical Learning*, p. 86.

Emperor Jinmu' [the third chapter of the *Nihongi*, the first historical chapter with exclusively human actors, following the two chapters on the 'Age of the Gods'].''[73]

Ansai, however, never doubted that the Way was also present in pure Shinto. Anything, therefore, that established a link or identity between the two was added to the growing amount of "evidence" which provided structure and content to this a priori belief. This raised a number of epistemological problems we will deal with later. At this point an illustration must suffice.

In the *Japanese Elementary Learning* (54), Ansai discusses the pillar around which Izanagi and Izanami concluded their nuptial ritual.[74] This pillar, he writes, is none other than the *shin no mihashira* ("mind-heart pillar") of the Ise shrines. This wooden pillar measures four *sun* (4/10ths of a foot) in circumference and is five *shaku* (feet) high; numbers corresponding to the Four Norms and Five Evolutive Phases.

It should be noted that this piece of imaginative architectural exegesis was not Ansai's. He himself acknowledged that he learned it from the *Shinto gobusho*.[75] To a believer attuned to symbolic resonances, the congruence of such centrally important phenomena as the Ise central pillar, its name, its measurements and cosmic virtues, is neither a coincidence nor a far-fetched fantasy but a reconfirmation through recognition of something one already holds true. Moreover, for someone as well-read as Ansai was in the Chinese tradition, including geomancy, such linkages were not as outrageous as they appear to the modern reader. After all, the imperial palace in China was laid out on a groundplan that reverberated with cosmological, numerological, and ethical significance.[76]

To return to Ansai's biography, it is certain that by 1665 Ansai had built a name for himself in Kyoto and Edo. In Kyoto, he writes in his *Japanese Elementary Learning*, some people after reading his *Heresies refuted* had wondered "who this man was who, with an air as if he were above Dharma, had done away with the Buddhas

[73] Hayashi Gahō, *Kokushikan nichiroku*, entry of Kanbun 7/3/3; and Tokugawa Mitsukuni, quoted in Fujita Yūkoku, *Shūshi shimatsu* (All about the practice of history), entry of Jōkyō 1/4/3. Quoted in Ikeda, "Ansaijugaku," p. 40.

[74] YAZ 1: 49. The same text is also found in one of the poems he wrote when visiting Ise in 1659.

[75] *Ibid.* This exegesis appears in the *Go-chinza hongi*, one of the Five Books of Ise Shinto (*Shintō gobusho*). See *Kojiki, Sendaikyūjihongi, Shintō gobusho*, p. 26.

[76] Granet, *Pensée*, pp. 178–80.

on one fell swoop" (79). In Edo, it may have been Inoue Masatoshi who contributed to Ansai's growing reputation. (In 1664, it will be recalled, Masatoshi was ordered by Hoshina Masayuki to assist Gahō with the collection of historical materials, and the next year Ansai was employed by Masayuki.)

Masayuki shared with Ansai a deep repugnance for Buddhism, a rigorous and dogmatic admiration for Neo-Confucianism, a growing interest in Shinto, and a concern for education. When Masayuki hired Ansai, he did so in his capacity as lord of Aizu. Ansai did not, like Yoshikawa Koretaru, receive a bakufu post. Most of Ansai's work for Masayuki had therefore to do either with Masayuki's own instruction in Neo-Confucianism or with domanial matters. By 1665, Ietsuna was twenty-four, and so Masayuki had not been functioning as shogunal regent for several years. He was nevertheless, a very powerful voice in the bakufu. The revised *Regulations for Military Houses* of 1663 was his work. In 1666 he prevailed against general disapproval within the bakufu when he banished Yamaga Sokō from Edo. The strict enforcement in 1668 of severe punishments for relatives of retainers who had committed *junshi* (outlawed since 1663) when the daimyo of Utsunomiya died, bears Masayuki's mark.[77] Yet much of Masayuki's attention during those years went to straightening out his own domain in Aizu before his retirement in 1669. Because this task did not require his presence in Aizu, however, Masayuki remained in Edo. It was not until the autumn of 1672 that Ansai visited Aizu with Masayuki. A few weeks later, Masayuki, whose health had been deteriorating for seven or eight years, died in Edo.

Unlike Razan, Ansai was hired specifically for his knowledge of Neo-Confucianism. Following the model of the Chinese literati, Ansai also insisted on maintaining a considerable degree of independence from those in power.[78] He was hired for approximately six months out of each year for the fee of 100 gold ryō, two seasonal garments, one *haori* coat for himself; 50 silver ryō and two garments for his father; and 30 silver ryō and one garment for his mother. But he refused to become Masayuki's vassal.[79] As a rule, Ansai's students, like ideal Confucians, prided themselves on their

[77] In 1668, retainers in the Utsunomiya domain committed ritual suicide (*junshi*) when their lord died. The punishment: transfer of the heir to Yamagata with a loss of 20,000 koku, the death penalty for two children of the dead retainers, and exile for other relatives. See Wajima, "Kanbun igaku," p. 147.

[78] See, for instance, the anecdote in Tsunoda et. al, *Sources* 1: 361–62.

[79] Yamada, *Yamazaki nenpu*, p. 7.

similar independence and scorned those Confucians who took permanent stipends as daimyo retainers.[80]

Ansai took on several assignments for Masayuki. He lectured on the classics and the *Reflections on Things at Hand* (which he punctuated and published in 1670). By the end of his second year, for example, Ansai had finished a cycle on the *Four Books*.[81] Masayuki, however, was intellectually an equal as much as a student. Together they compiled five works, two of which were gazetteers on the Aizu domain (*Aizu fudoki*, written before Ansai ever visited Aizu, and the *Aizu jinjashi*). (In addition, Ansai drafted a fifteen-point house rule for the domain.) The other three works were Neo-Confucian texts that were to be used in the newly founded domain school. They are: the *Gyokusan kōgi furoku* or Appendix to [Chu Hsi's] lecture at Yü-shan (contained in *Chu Hsi's Collected Literary Works*), the *Nitei jikyōroku* or Record of the two Ch'eng's political teachings (an anthology from the *Erh Ch'eng chüan-shi*) and the *Irakusanshiden shinroku* or Record of the mind-heart as transmitted through the Ch'engs and the three teachers. This last work is an anthology on the practice of *seiza* (Ch *ching-tso*) or quiet sitting as a means of self-cultivation, which Ansai accused many Confucian scholars of neglecting. The selections discuss the practice as it differs from Zen Buddhism's *zazen*, and are lifted from the works of the Ch'eng brothers and three other Sung scholars who form the link between the Ch'engs and Chu Hsi: Yang Shih, disciple of both Ch'engs and teacher of Lo Ts'ung-yen, who in turn taught Chu Hsi's mentor, Li T'ung.[82] It should be noted that during his years of service to Masayuki, Ansai also compiled the following works in Kyoto: the already-mentioned *Kōhanzensho* and other compilations from Chu Hsi's *Literary Works* and *Classified Conversations*: *Jinsetsumondō* (Questions and answers on explanations of "humaneness"), an important work to be discussed often in the Kimon school;[83] *Shōgaku mōyōshū* and *Daigaku keihatsu shū* (Collections of [clarifications by Chu Hsi] on the *Elementary Learning* and the *Great*

---

[80] On this matter, see Asami Keisai (*Satsuroku*, NST 31: 384) and Satō Naokata (*Gakudan zatsuroku, ibid.*, pp. 430, 439.

[81] Ikeda, "Ansaijugaku," p. 39.

[82] Within the Kimon school, Satō Naokata is the one who has expanded most on *seiza* and the cultivation of a mind that is "contemplativus in actione." (This is further discussed at the end of the next chapter.) For a good and very readable selection from his work, see SGT 12: 282–310.

[83] NST 31: 244–52. This text is followed by one of Keisai's many comments (pp. 253–304).

Learning); *Chūwa shūsetsu* (Collection of theories on "equilibrium and harmony" [from the *Doctrine of the Mean*]); and *Seiron meibiroku* (Record of the gradual illumination of the theory on nature), first formulated by the Ch'eng brothers and finalized by Chu Hsi.

For Ansai, the most important aspect of his years with Masayuki was the acquaintance he made with Yoshikawa Koretaru, who initiated him into Yoshida Shinto. Because of a lack of capable heirs in the Yoshida house, Koretaru had been entrusted with all Yoshida traditions and, due to a number of complicated circumstances, did not transmit all these teachings back to the Yoshida family in Kyoto but formally passed them on to Masayuki and Ansai.[84] These Yoshida teachings gave Ansai additional exegetical means of decoding the Way as embedded in the mythology chapters of the *Nihongi*. He could thus envision the possibility of repossessing the Way in the Japanese tradition.

Ansai did not stop at the study of Ise and Yoshida Shinto. After his final return to Kyoto in 1673, he collected from the Shinto priests who flocked to his lectures on the "Age of the Gods" half a dozen additional Shinto traditions such as Inari, Inbe, and Kamo. (Ansai was married to the daughter of the Shinto priest of the Kamo shrine in Kyoto.) Ansai's ambitions for Shinto were similar to those held by some of his contemporaries for other traditions: Suzuki Shōsan dreamt of streamlining Buddhism and, under shogunal patronage, making it the official teaching of the land; the Hayashi scholars claimed a monopoly on Neo-Confucian "orthodoxy" for the bakufu. The bakufu, it should be noted, throughout its entire history was never short of peddlers of ideology recommending their own wares as the best means to effective government.[85]

Ansai himself, however, his rigorous convictions about truth and heresy notwithstanding, never attempted to play the politics of ideology as Razan had done. His followers were the ones to foster national ambitions: the Kimon school during the Kansei Reform, and Suika Shinto in modern times. Ansai's interest lay in his religious commitment to the Way, which made him hope that he could reach Japan's pure tradition: the *tao-t'ung* (repossessing the Way) within Shinto. This desire explains Ansai's indiscriminate and uncritical reverence for all Shinto traditions, most of which

---

[84] For the historical details concerning the transmission of these commentaries from Koretaru to Masayuki and Ansai, see Taira, *Yoshikawa*, pp. 8–16, 24–51.

[85] See Ooms, "Neo-Confucianism."

were secret family traditions he endeavoured to make public, and which he meant to use to reconstruct a pure Shinto.[86] In this sense Ansai was also engaged in a "mirror" (*t'ung-chien* or *tsugan*) enterprise for Shinto, just as Razan, following Ssu-ma Kuang, was for Japanese history.

This growing identification with Shinto, the result of his efforts to retrieve the Way in Japan, profoundly affected Ansai's sense of self. On 1671/11/22, his new identity was ultimately expressed in a new Shinto name, *Shidemasu* or *Suika*, a reference to one of Yamato-hime's oracles, which stresses the importance of prayers to call the gods down and straightforwardness as a condition for receiving blessings.[87] Ansai was in Edo then. The next day he composed the *Record of the Fuji no mori Shrine* (*Fuji no mori yuzuemandokoro no ki*) as a substitute, one surmises, for a visit to Prince Toneri's Fuji no mori shrine in Kyoto.[88] The essay consists of a brief biography of the compiler of the *Nihongi* and the history of his cult at the shrine, and concludes with Ansai's view of Shinto and his own place within it. Ansai does not mention his *Mirror of Japan* project again; instead he is fully preoccupied with Japan's mythology. This text introduces in a succinct manner Ansai's approach to Shinto mythology and the sometimes baffling arguments that are further developed in his lectures on the "Age of the Gods."[89] The key sections read as follows:

The source of Shinto rests in [the two Evolutive Phases or Configurational Energies of] Earth and Metal. This tradition is already contained in the *Nihongi*. In the "Age of the Gods" chapters of the *Nihongi*, there are sections that speak only about Heaven and others that speak only about

---

[86] ZYAZ 1: 25–26. Asami Keisai also tells how Ansai complained about the jealous secrecy with which different houses guarded the traditions they, on the other hand, boasted of possessing. If these had to do with national ritual (*tenka ittō no rei*), they should be publicized, Ansai argued; all that is called secret is merely private (*Satsuroku*, NST 31: 368–69).

[87] See autobiography, YAZ 2: 654. The name comes from the following oracle (already paraphrased p. 103): "Humans are the divine beings under Heaven. They must do no harm to their heart-kami (*shinjin*). The gods COME DOWN (*shinSUI, kami SHIDEruru*) in/for those who first pray; divine protection (*myōGA, myōMASU*; lit. mysterious INCREASE) is for those who make uprightness their base. Thus, relying on one's original mind (*honshin*), everyone must obtain the Great Way. Therefore gods and humans (*shinjin*, or divine men) have to preserve the beginning of primeval chaos (*konton no hajime*) ..." in *Gochinza denki* of the "Shintō gobusho": *Kojiki, Sendaikyūjihongi, Shintō gobusho*, p. 14. Variants of the same important oracle appear in other books of the *Gobusho*, such as the *Hōki hongi* (ibid., p. 31) and the *Yamato-hime seiki* (ibid., p. 55).

[88] YAZ 1: 58–61. For an abbreviated version, see NNS 14: 272–74.

[89] For an example, to which I shall return, see Tsunoda et al., *Sources*, 1: 358–60.

man. There are passages that speak of Heaven in terms of man and others that speak of man in terms of Heaven. In this manner, the Way of the single unity of Heaven and man (*tenjinyuiitsu*) is made clear. However, among the explanations of the past, some are detailed and accurate while others are brief and simple; some agree with each other, others show discrepancies. Thus Prince Toneri collected all the old explanations and recorded them in detail without critically sorting them out. His effort at compilation stemmed from an attitude of respectful reverence (*tsutsushimi*), unlike the selective works by Shōtoku Taishi and Soga no Umako, the *Sendaikujihongi*, or Ōno Yasumaro's *Kojiki*. That is why the *Nihongi* is superior to all other works. . . .

I heard the following. Between Heaven and Earth the virtue/quality (*toku*) of Earth is gathered and occupies the position of the Center (*chū, naka*). The four seasons follow each other through this virtue; all things originate in it. In Japanese, this is expressed by the words *tsuchijimi, tsuchishimu* [written with the characters meaning "the earth-taste," "the earth-exertion"] which are none other than the Japanese readings for the character *kei* [reverence; Jp also *tsutsushimu*]. [The name of the river that flows through Ise,] the Isuzugawa [expresses the truth that] Earth produces Metal, and Metal produces Water. Ise is the Japanese reading for the two characters *itsu-se* [five narrows] and stems from the name Isuzugawa. Everywhere in Heaven and Earth the Five Configurative Energies [*goki*, the same as the Five Evolutive Phases] operate, [which results in] things pure and impure, beautiful and bad. Our country's superiority lies in its abundance of Earth and Metal [Configurative Energies, as in shown by] the long continuation of the direct blood-line of gods and emperors (*jinnō no shōtō*) since the time of creation. This is due [to three things]: the basic intention of Amaterasu's decree [to ensure the prosperity of her descendants to the end of times], the protection of the gods Koyane, Futodama, and Murakumo, and the guidance of Sarutahiko. This law, bequeathed from the Age of the Gods, is preserved in the Shrine of Prince Toneri who transmitted its mystery. Who else but a man [who embodies the spirit of] Suika would be able to understand these mysteries and clarify these secrets? . . .[90]

In this text, written at an important time in his life, Ansai makes several assertions and claims, and engages in a kind of logic that requires further explanation. The following points can be distinguished: first, Ansai privileges one part of one text of a bemuddled tradition. Second, he values the specific attitude of reverence with which the compiler, Prince Toneri, approached his texts. Third, the cryptic language of this text, with its criss-crossing of

---

[90] NNS 14: 272–74. See *Nihongi*, tr. Aston, pp. 77 ff.

heavenly and human reference points and subject matter, is said to express the general truth of the unity of Heaven and man. Fourth, this truth refers specifically to the divinely guarded imperial succession, which puts Japan above all other countries. Fifth, there is a subtext to the main text, one written with the cosmic concepts of Evolutive Phases, and decodable through etymology. We will deal with most of these points in the next chapter, but one requires our immediate attention. As in his *Heresies Refuted*, Ansai exudes confidence that he is a privileged commentator (in a long line) of a *tao-t'ung* or orthodox transmission of the Way. Why is it that Ansai somehow sees himself now, in 1671, as possessing the key to unlock these mysteries, when in 1657 he had requested divine assistance for the same task?

The core teaching of Yoshida Shinto, which had risen to prominence at the end of the fifteenth century, were transmitted in *den* (or *tsutae*, transmission). These are short exegetical commentaries, surrounded with graded restrictions on their permissible divulgation, concerning items such as names, sentences, or brief passages from the Shinto classics, especially the opening chapters of the *Nihongi*. All these *den* were transmitted to Yoshikawa Koretaru in 1656 by Ogiwara Kaneyori (1588–1660), the Yoshida heir and also at one time the officiant at Hideyoshi's Hōkoku shrine.[91] Koretaru returned the ceremonial *den* to the Yoshida house, but passed the doctrinal ones on to Hoshina Masayuki, on 1671/11/17. Ansai, who during his association with Koretaru had read most of these *den*, apparently persuaded the latter that it was wrong to keep these teachings secret and transmit them to only a single successor.[92] He received his formal initiation five days after Masayuki, on 11/12, the winter solstice.

The official transmissions of doctrine were accompanied by a bestowal of Shinto names on both Masayuki ("Hanitsu") and Ansai ("Suika"). It seems that this custom of bestowing Shinto names on the official transmittors of Yoshida orthodoxy, the carriers of a Shinto *tao-t'ung* (transmission of the Way) who thereby became "living shrines," had started with Koretaru and his teacher Ogiwara Kaneyori.[93] Many of Ansai's Shinto disciples re-

---

[91] SZS 22: 1a

[92] KSZH 5: 20a.

[93] On this custom of bestowing Shinto names at the time of the transmission of doctrine, see SZS 16: 1a; for its critique, see *ibid.*, 17: 12b and 18: 7b. See also Tani Seigo, " 'Suika' to iu reishago," pp. 166–70.

ceived such Shinto names, as did all of Hoshina Masayuki's daimyo successors. Many of these names allude to a *Nihongi* passage where Ō-ana-muchi, a god who pacified the land, is confronted with his own spirit.[94] The spirit appeared to him as a shining object from the sea and told Ō-ana-muchi that without him the work could not have been accomplished. Ō-ana-muchi then built a shrine to his own spirit on Mount Miwa.

This Ō-ana-muchi sequence of the ritual veneration of a spirit representing the self became, in the early Tokugawa period, the paradigm for a new Shinto concept of a sacred self. Its first application occurred in the Hōkoku cult of Hideyoshi. Then the single transmittors of Shinto's innermost doctrine (Ogiwara and Koretaru) were transformed into sacred vessels. With Ansai, the restriction to the single transmitter was broken, and several others were thus "sacralized." Ōgimachi Kinmichi (1653–1733), a member of the court nobility who became a student of Ansai's in 1680, even argued that every person, because he is a shrine that houses a spirit, was entitled to a Shinto "living shrine" name.[95]

The intensity and literal character of Ansai's belief took him one step further. In 1673 he organized in his home a ritual to the living shrine of his own person. Tani Seigo traces this idea of a cult to one's self back to the last weeks of Hoshina Masayuki's life, when Ansai was requested on 1672/11/21 to write a brief on a ritual for the living shrine of Masayuki.[96] Masayuki, however, died less than three weeks later (and the brief became a necrology). The last entry in Ansai's autobiography was his return to Kyoto in 1673/6 from Masayuki's funeral in Aizu, and he made no record of the remaining ten years of his life. The new sacred identity he had acquired may have had something to do with this silence. From his student Tamaki Masahide (1672–1736), however, we know that very soon after his return from his last trip to Edo, Ansai created a cult to his "self."

Ansai's cult to his "self" poses difficult problems of interpretation. Perhaps it constitutes his ultimate rejection of Zen Buddhism's view of the nonsubstantiality of the self. Neo-

---

[94] *Nihongi* (tr. Aston), p. 61. For a Japanese text, see *Nihon shoki* (Kokushi taikei, vol. 1), p. 48. Ogiwara Kaneyori's Shinto name was Kaumi (god-sea), Koretaru's was Aremi (see-[one's] self), Atobe Yoshiaki's (1659–1729) was Terumi (shining sea). See SZS 16: 1a. For the names of Hoshina Masayuki's successors, see Maeda, *Aizu-han ni okeru Yamazaki Ansai*, p. 230.

[95] DNB 16: 251; SZS 18: 7b.

[96] Tani Seigo, *Shinto genron*, pp. 198–99.

Confucianism had already countered this devaluation of the self by its emphasis on the cultivation of the self. In his peculiar ritual, Ansai took this notion, in his usual fashion, to an extreme by literally objectifying his self. Thus one ought to say that this was Ansai's cult not to "himself," but to his "self."

The symbols this cult activated all expressed the central values discussed in the *Fuji no mori* text: the *shintai* or sacred object consisted of a small pillar with the word *shin* (*kokoro*, mind-heart), whose numerical dimensions (four sides, each of five *bu*), like those of Ise's *shin no mihashira*, referred to the Four Norms and Five Relationships, sticking out of a copper metal box and rising out of red earth.[97] Metal and Earth are the most important of the Five Evolutive Phases, and Earth (*tsuchi*) is etymologically linked by Ansai to *tsutsushimi* (*kei*, reverence), the basis of a correct mind. Red is the color for purity (a red heart is a pure heart) in the *Nihongi*.[98] The *shintai* or sacred object was thus a composite of the physico-ethical normative coordinates that constitute man. It was that and more, since it also bore the name of Suika, the man who as a "living shrine" had become the embodiment of the Way in and of Japan.

On 1674/2/12, a separate shrine was built in a location within the compounds of a larger shrine that was administered by a Shinto priest, one of Ansai's students, who had been the officiant of the cult from the beginning. In 1681, however, members of the Yoshida house and the city magistrate, whose suspicion had been aroused by this strange worship of a living human being as a god, ordered an investigation. Consequently, just before Ansai's death on 1682/9/19, his shrine was dismantled and the cult was forced to relocate to a more modest place within the same compound: the side altar at a shrine dedicated to Saruta-hiko, the god who in Suika Shinto was held to be the founder of Shinto teachings.

For the last ten years of his life, Ansai was thus a living god to whom his Shinto students payed regular ritual tribute. These were also the years, it should be remembered, that Ansai recruited his most brilliant Neo-Confucian students. The next problem to consider is the friction among Ansai's followers generated by the coexistence of these two traditions.

[97] *Gyokusenshū*, DNB 16: 480–82, 496. A *bu* is 3 mm. or one-tenth of a *shaku*.
[98] On this point, see Ansai's lecture on the "Age of the Gods," NST 39: 153.

Seven. Suika and Kimon: The Way and Language

One should not bring reason to the explanation of Shinto.
—*Yamazaki Ansai*[1]

The *Nihongi* has no teachings like those of the Three Dynasties.
—*Satō Naokata*[2]

The concepts of Metal and Earth occupy a central position in Ansai's philosophy. They are physically present in the *shintai* of his Suika cult. In the *Fuji no mori* text, they account for Japan's ontological superiority and form the source of Shinto because they are already contained in the *Nihongi*. As such, however, they are absent from the "Age of the Gods" chapters. They are said to be "contained," imbricated (*sonawareri*) in the text as an ontological subtext.

Sonawaru is the verb Ansai also uses to speak of the quasi-physical arrangement of the Norms in the self.[3] The term thus refers to a presence, ontologically unquestionable but not readily perceivable. A superficial look at humans by one uninformed about the Way will not reveal the presence of the inborn Norms; a surface reading of the *Nihongi* will not detect the qualities of Metal and Earth. The certainty of belief posits their deep structuring presence. Belief, however, is rarely content with authoritative assertions. It often seeks the company of rationality, looks for persuasive arguments, and wants the most veridical proofs. Thus belief does not rest with positing its objects blindly. It also informs a hermeneutics that uncovers and verifies them. How then does Ansai demonstrate the all-importance of Earth and Metal and their correlatives, centrality and reverence? Why are these concepts so import? Finally, what is the source of Ansai's exegesis?

BENEATH MYTHOLOGY: A SUBTEXT ON A POLITICAL WAY

From the previous chapter we know how Ansai's historiographical ambition was structured parallel to Chu Hsi's rewriting

[1] KSZH 5: 9b.
[2] *Unzōrokushūi*, SNZ, p. 349.
[3] In the *Heresies Refuted*. See above, p. 202.

of Ssu-ma Kuang's private history of China. Ansai elevated Kitabatake Chikafusa's *Jinnōshōtōki* to a position parallel to Ssuma-Kuang's text. In a similar fashion, he ascribed analogical positions to two other texts from the Chinese and Japanese traditions: the *Book of Changes* and the "Age of the Gods" chapters (*Kamiyo no maki*) of the *Nihongi*. Ansai, one of his students reports, loved to repeat that the *I ching* was China's *Kamiyo no maki* and the *Kamiyo no maki* Japan's *I ching*. Furthermore, through this equation, Ansai identified with one of Chu Hsi's main undertakings, the restoration of the original meaning of the *I ching*. The *Kamiyo no maki* also had two layers of meaning: an open, surface meaning and a hidden, mysterious one.[4]

The parallelism of the two texts seems to have struck Ansai as a sudden insight in 1667. That year he was forced to cut short his stay in Edo because of an illness. While recuperating in Kyoto, he studied commentaries on the basic texts from which the *I ching* originated: the *Great Norm*, the *Lo Writing*, and the *River Chart*. Ansai had read these texts for the first time more than twenty years earlier. Now, he wrote, he suddenly understood them.[5] Before he even regained his health he edited and published them in the complicated and rather voluminous *Kōhanzensho*. In the preface to this work he wrote of his desire to step into Ts'ai Chen's footsteps and "study the gods, learn about creation and with a similar intention speak about these matters." Ansai concluded in his introduction,

In Japan at the time of the opening of the country, Izanagi and Izanami followed the divination teachings of the Heavenly Gods, obeyed yin and yang, and thus correctly established the beginnings of ethical teachings. In the universe there is only One Principle, [although] either Gods or Sages come forth depending on whether it concerns the country where the sun rises [Japan] or the country where the sun sets [China]. The [two] Ways [of Shinto and Confucianism] are, however, naturally and mysteriously the same (*onozukara myōkei suru*)."[6]

Ansai discussed the nodal point of this obscure link in another passage of the same work, where he commented on the *chū* (*naka*) numerical diagram, one of forty-one diagrams that explicate the content of the magic master diagram, the *Lo Writing*.

To understand the drift and import of Ansai's remarks, it is

[4] KSZH 5: 7a–8a.
[5] YAZ 2: 653.
[6] ZYAZ 2: 236, 237; NNS 14: 284–85.

IX	VIII	VII	VI	V	IV	III	II	I	lines/rows
9	6	3	8	5	2	7	4	1	a
8	9	6	7	5	3	4	1	2	b
7	8	9	4	5	6	1	2	3	c
6	3	2	9	5	1	8	7	4	d
5	5	5	5	5	5	5	5	5	e
4	7	8	1	5	9	2	3	6	f
3	2	1	6	5	4	9	8	7	g
2	1	4	3	5	7	6	9	8	h
1	4	7	2	5	8	3	6	9	i

Diagram 3

4	9	2
3	5	7
8	1	6

Diagram 1

Metal	Fire
Wood / Earth	
	Water

Diagram 2

necessary to recall that numbers were motivated symbols in the Chinese tradition. As Marcel Granet has admirably shown, they had more than mere ordinal or arithmetic value, and expressed cosmic and ontological interdependencies, hierarchized in equivalences and opposites. In this numerical ontology, the number five is the symbol of the center and is associated with the Evolutive Phase and the Configurative Force Earth.[7]

The *Lo Writing* is a magic diagram that arranges the nine primary numbers, which also have divinatory values, in such a way that the sum of each horizontal line, vertical row, or diagonal sequence is fifteen (see Diagram 1). In this disposition, the number five occupies the central square, balancing the other numbers at numerical equidistance from the center in pairs that total ten ($9 + 1 = 10$ and 9 and 1 are each four values removed from 5, the center; $3 + 7 = 10$ and 3 and 7 are each two values removed from 5, etc.). To these numbers correspond the Five Evolutive Phases as shown in Diagram 2.

One can further arrange these numbers into a larger magic

[7] Granet, *Pensée*, pp. 154, 162, 164–66, 168, 172, 208, 330, 331.

diagram of eighty-one squares, made up of nine lines and rows (see Diagram 3).[8] The first row (on the right) ranges the numbers in ordinal sequence from 1 to 9, whereas the last row (on the left) arranges them in reverse order from 9 to 1. The middle line and row form a cross of 5s. The rest of the diagram is filled in by balancing the numbers so that each pair at equidistance from these rows and lines of fives totals ten.

The effect of this arrangement is a perfectly balanced diagram that consists of inverted mirroring halves, whether one cuts it horizontally, vertically, or diagonally; halves within which each number's position, of which there are forty ([9 × 9) — the center position] ÷ 2), corresponds to its twin partner, except for the center number 5 (in position Ve). The corresponding place, however, is always inverted so that to each positive or good position (such as 7 in IId) corresponds a negative or bad position (7 in VIIIf), except again the central 5, which has no corresponding negative position and is perfect good. The center 5 (in position Ve) stands in another way for a balance of forces. There the two diagonal sequences of 1s (fullness of propitious forces) and 9s (fullness of nefarious forces) meet and are balanced, as is "proven" by the following operation: if one replaces the central 5 by a 1, then the vertical cross of the diagram (line V plus row e) adds up to 81, which is also the sum one arrives at if one replaces the central 5 by a 9 and adds up the diagonal sequences of 1s and 9s.

Forty-one other diagrams (one for each position) unfold and explicate the strikingly balanced good-and-evil structure of the cosmic order (represented in its simplest form in the original *Lo Writing*). They culminate in the forty-first *chū* diagram (not reproduced here), which even more dramatically proves the single centrality and perfect goodness of the number five (and the center). For Ansai this constituted overwhelming, tangible evidence that "*chū* [center, equilibrium; the virtue discussed in the *Doctrine of the Mean*] was fundamentally pure good without evil."[9] This, Ansai continues,

is the same *chū* as the one King T'ang spoke of [when he announced to his people, after overthrowing the Hsia and establishing the Yin dynasty in

---

[8] ZYAZ 2: 341–42. See also Granet, *Pensée*, p. 187. Although magic diagrams were very old in China, they were not used and studied until "very late" in Japan (Sugimoto, *Science in Japan*, p. 77). It seems that their study was in vogue during Ansai's time, especially in the emerging field of Japanese mathematics (Smith, *Japanese Mathematics*, pp. 57, 69, 116–22, 177–78). For a modern study of the subject, see W. S. Andrews, *Magic Squares* (Chicago, 1907).

[9] For the forty-first *chū* diagram and Ansai's commentary, see ZYAZ 2: 353.

1766 B.C. that "Shang-ti or the Lord in Heaven had conferred even to inferior people a moral sense (*chū*), compliance with which would show their nature invariably right"];[10] as the *tenchi no chū* or center of Heaven and Earth of which the *den* spoke; and as the *chū* that was transmitted by Yao, Shun and Yü.

Thus in China *chū* showed up in various teachings and was written with different characters (King T'ang's was not written 中 but 衷). In Japan, therefore, the same *chū*, as a central cosmic virtue and quality, must also be embedded in Shinto teachings; may also, as in China, appear in different guises; and be part of a transmitted tradition. Ansai thus proceeds by asserting that

in Japan worship of the Gods of Heaven and Earth created the name Amenom*inaka*nushi-no-mikoto [one of the first gods; his name means "Ruler-of-the-*Center*-of-Heaven].[11] Izanagi and Izanami succeeded him and erected the "kun*inaka*nohashira" [pillar-in-the-*center*-of-the-country], walked around it, had intercourse and produced children. Amaterasu-ōmikami, their child, shone over the whole universe and, as the sun, hangs in the *center* of the sky. She received dominion over Heaven. However, throughout the whole universe there is only One Principle. Thus, even without a priori forcing [a congruence], Shinto and Confucianism match perfectly. What a wondrous mystery!

The general parallel Ansai sets up between the beginnings of the Chinese tradition and those of Shinto was neither so novel nor so far-fetched that only Shinto exegetes subscribed to it. Even Ogyū Sorai, some forty years later, mentioned the similarities between Shinto and the age of the Sage Kings. Watarai Nobuyoshi, who gave Ansai the Ise teachings, held to the same independent, natural parallelism.[12] Ansai also stressed that the *Nihongi*'s opening chapters were not merely an explanation of the Five Evolutive Phases but an autonomous expression of the Way.[13] For Ansai, this *concordantia numinosa* came to occupy the central place in his teachings on Shinto. In his attempts at further unraveling the strands of

[10] *The Chinese Classics, III: The Shoo King.* Translated by James Legge. (Hong Kong: Hong Kong University Press, 1960), p. 185.

[11] *Nihongi* (tr. Aston), pp. 5, 12–13.

[12] Sorai wrote: "We do as was done in the three dynasties of Hsia, Yin, and Chou when we worship the ancestors of the imperial house together with Heaven, when we create teachings out of Shinto.... This is the Way of our country; it is nothing other than the ancient Way of Hsia and Yin" (quoted in Bitō, "Ogyū Sorai," p. 153). See also Yoshikawa, *Jinsai, Sorai, Norinaga*, pp. 244–51, especially p. 250. For Watarai Nobuyoshi, see his *Yōfukuki* (Record of the sun's return), written in 1650 and published in 1671 (NST 39: 87). The title refers to the winter solstice, the day when the work was finished. For a further discussion of the symbolic meaning of this day, see Chapter 6, note 28.

[13] NST 39: 145.

the Way that were common to Shinto and Confucianism, however, Ansai relied very heavily on the Yoshida tradition.

Since the 1370s, the Yoshida house had been organizing its exegesis of the *Nihongi* in a number of secret *den*, which ultimately came into Ansai's possession by way of Yoshikawa Koretaru.[14] Among the most important and secret of them was the *Dokon no den* (or *Tsuchigane no tsutae*), the Commentary on Earth and Metal. On various occasions Ansai proclaimed that it contained the essence of Shinto.[15] The information on Earth and Metal with which Ansai constructs his argument in the *Fuji no mori* text, discussed in the previous chapter—information preceded by the words "I heard the following"—probably comes from this *den*. This particular commentary, it should be noted, may not have been very old and may even have been the work of Koretaru. There exists a copy dated 1666/10/12. There is virtually no difference between Koretaru's *den*, Ansai's use of it in his lectures, and the *den* that became part of the more than one hundred such commentaries which, after Ansai, constituted the formal teachings of Suika Shinto.[16]

The *Dokon no den* establishes "reverence" as the heart of Japan's Shinto teachings, and thus gives this virtue the same central position as it held in the core of China's teachings since Sung times. Because the concept as such was totally absent from Japan's mythological accounts, it had to be read into or under the text, as words beneath words, to use Jean Starobinski's phrase.[17] The technique used was imaginative etymology that allowed the insertion, under a text replete with names of gods and cosmogonic events, of pertinent Chinese cosmic categories (especially the Five Evolutive Phases in their production sequence), all pointing to "reverence." We will follow Ansai in one such philological exercise, clarifying as we go relationships that he assumes are obvious.

Izanagi cut the *fire* god Kagu*tsuchi* (Fire produces Earth) into *five* (*itsutsu*) pieces.[18] *Tsuchi* (Earth) is the *center* in the diagram of the

---

[14] Taira, *Yoshikawa*, p. 139. For the classification of these commentaries in different categories of secrecy, see *ibid.*, pp. 149, 159, 172, 274 ff., 402.

[15] NST 39: 143; NNS 14: 283; see also KSZH 5: 8a.

[16] Ikeda, "Ansaijugaku," p. 47. For Koretaru's *den*, see NST 39: 67–72; for Ansai's use of it in his lectures, see *ibid.*, pp. 143–48, and Tsunoda et al., *Sources*, 1: 358–60; for Suika Shinto's *den*, see DNB 16: 386–88.

[17] For the centrality of *kei* in Chinese orthodoxy, see de Bary, *Orthodoxy*, pp. 68, 75–76, 79, 103–104, 127–28. See Starobinski, *Les mots sous les mots*.

[18] NST 39: 143–45; see also Tsunoda et al., *Sources*, 1: pp. 358–60. For the *Nihongi* text, see *Nihongi* (tr. Aston), pp. 28–29.

Five Evolutive Phases to which corresponds the number *five*. Fire, the origin of Earth, is associated with mind-heart, the place where the *kami* dwell (as "hokora" also proves: *hokora*, shrine, is the same as *hikura*, "fire storehouse").[19] Now *tsuchi* is also *tsuzumaru*, to harden, to gel, to be *jitto* or firm (with its moral overtones, like *kitto*, one of Ansai's favored words).[20] Thus when earth becomes hard, it is transformed into metal (Earth produces Metal). One way of hardening dirt is to moisten it (*tsuchi o shimuru*), a process that is none other than *tsutsushimu* or the Japanese reading for *kei*, "to hold in reverence." The place where this has to occur is the heart: without *tsutsushimu*, the *kami* will not dwell in one's heart. Japan is a country especially endowed with the Metal element, that is, a country where *tsutsushimu* (which produces Metal) is a way of life. These things, Ansai comments, are "omoshiroi koto," interesting, charming, meaningful.[21]

In the *Fuji no mori* text, it will be recalled, the name of Ise, where Amaterasu is worshiped, comes from *itsu-se*, *five* narrows, and stems from the river that flows through it, the Isuzugawa (written with characters meaning *fifty bells*, and bells are made of metal), which again links Five, Earth, Metal, and Water (Water is produced by Metal).[22]

Ansai's symbolic imagination was certainly as creative as that of Victor Turner's Ndembu exegete Mushona, or perhaps more correctly, both were articulate (and creative) spokesmen for a symbolic universe familiar to them but foreign to us.[23] It is not surprising that Ansai has not received much attention from modern scholars. Anthropologists may study lost worlds, but only those that have survived into some isolated present. They are thus able to pursue clarifications with live informants. Historians, on the other hand, study the frozen meanings of a past that has no survivors. The temptation is great to brush aside figures like Ansai with presentist arguments that only dimly veil a despair of ever understanding. Thus Ansai's arguments have been called "devious" and "tortuous rationalizations ... [which] later Shintoists were glad enough to dispense with."[24] The partial truth of this judgment, however, overlooks the long time that elapsed before Ansai's argu-

[19] See also NNS 14: 281.
[20] See above, p. 220.
[21] NST 39: 144, 145.
[22] See also DNB 17: 78.
[23] Turner, *The Forest of Symbols*.
[24] Tsunoda et al., *Sources*, 1: 354, 358.

ments were discarded. Moreover, it assumes that his type of discourse was definitively replaced by another presumably more rational, or at least less tortuous. As Hirata Atsutane and the prewar revival of Ansai's thought reveal, however, the discourse Ansai developed created a movement that may have been displaced but certainly not replaced. In fact, even today both the content and the procedures of this discourse are still very much alive in many so-called New Religions.

Rather than dismiss Ansai as a crank, it is our task to try to understand why his "tortuous arguments" were accepted by so many. A first question that thus arises is whether there was some method to Ansai's philological "madness." Did he himself speak of a method? A first point to be made is that the activity Ansai engaged in was not an "objective" inquiry into whether or not the *Nihongi* hid a subtext. From Neo-Confucianism he knew what Truth was, so it was just a matter of finding that universal Truth where it had to be. Its apparent absence was thus redefined as a hidden presence that had to be revealed. This effort to make a text render a subtext, to voice a silent truth, should not by itself alienate us from Ansai, since all interpretive sciences bring into play such hermeneutics. That Ansai found precisely what he knew had to be there should offend no one who understands the success, for instance, of Marxist historians, modernization theorists, or Lévi-Straussian structuralists. Ansai proved that he had mastered the essentials of Neo-Confucian "orthodoxy," a respected scholarly tradition imbued with great authority, and one that made claims to universal validity. He then rediscovered it, persistently and on a wide scale, in another cultural terrain. Thus, nothing was new and everything was new—as in the best modern scholarly tradition. Ansai did not, like his modern colleagues, find the class struggle, rational progress, or binary oppositions that their disciplines induce them to find. The scholarly tradition and the political environment he lived in authorized him to find "reverence."

Ansai's hermeneutic task was conditioned by the multivocal mode within which the Chinese tradition had been formulated. Through equivalences and correspondences, the same idea could be expressed through a number of signs: an evolutive phase, a divinatory combination, a number, a color, a physiological component, or simply a descriptive noun. Words in this tradition were thus animated with a signifying power similar to these other signs—a power that is maybe best spoken of as an embodying energy. Words were much more than transparent reference tools to a reality beyond themselves. They were emblems that almost magically embodied the reality they spoke of. Equivalent units from these different vocabularies (such as Earth, centrality, heart, the number five) were thus motivated by the same truth content.

Today we may be baffled by the disproportion between the broad ramifications of such multifaceted epistemology and the simple truths enunciated by this enormous discourse. When this symbolic discourse was alive and authoritative, however, modality redundance—the tendency of a discourse to fold over its truths additional layers of signs—provided cumulative assurance that indeed one had captured the truth. This helps explain why Ansai's new fold (mythological signs expressing a known truth) could find ready acceptance. He was simply adding a new chapter to "la prose du monde"; in a new mode but in an old vein.[25]

What was Ansai's procedure in this operation? One suggestion he makes should come as no surprise. Look for what you have to find, he says when he admonishes his students "to pay special attention to passages dealing with *tsuchi* (Earth)." Since etymology through phonetics could reveal words (realities) beneath the words of the *Nihongi*, Ansai had to go as much as possible not by the Chinese characters of the text but by their Japanese reading, which was, ironically, to reveal a Chinese or universal truth.[26] A few additional examples will illustrate these phonetic manipulations.

The name of the god Omohikane, who planned the scheme to entice Amaterasu back from the rock cave, is interpreted as *omoi* (meaning "think," but also "heavy") and *kane* (metal).[27] *Kami* is associated with *kami* (*ue*, above), *kagami* (mirror), *kangamiru* (consider together) and *kami miru* (to look above/from above, that is, to rule the earth below).[28] What is most important is that in this way Ansai cosmically grounded political ideas, as his discussion of *chū* (*naka*; Ch *chung*), center-equilibrium-harmony, indicates.

The Chinese or universal *chung* is found in Japan in the name of Amenomi*naka*nushi-no-mikoto. The *naka* refers to the keeping of the Way by both rulers and ministers (*shin*, *omi*). The ruler above overseas what is below and the ministers serve what is above. This

---

[25] Foucault, *The Order of Things*, ch. 2.

[26] NST 39: 144, 150; see also KSZH 5: 13b, 24a.

[27] NST 39: 147, 156. The scheme involved a striptease. I cannot resist making, in an Ansaian way, the "heavy" remark that indeed the god did some "heavy thinking."

[28] NNS 14: 280.

unity of the one ruler and his ministers is perfectly expressed in the family name of the *Naka*tomi (the oldest family of Shinto ritualists, also ancestors of the Fujiwara family of court ministers), which expresses the way of keeping *chū* or *naka*. This unity, moreover, was sealed by a common ancestry, since both rulers and ministers trace their genealogy back to Amenominakanushi, who is the same god, bearing a different name, as Kunitokotachi-no-mikoto (lit., "establish-the-country-forever"). (Elsewhere Ansai, like Koretaru, argues that Kunitokotachi, through Amaterasu, is the ancestor of the imperial line, and Amenominakanushi, through Kasuga daimyōjin, is the patron of the Fujiwara, the ancestor of the ministers.)[29] Hence the hierarchical relationship between rulers and ministers, resting on common blood ties, should never be disturbed. Rulers and ministers are one body, originally undifferentiated. This is a cosmic principle, since Kunitokotachi is the first god to spring from the primeval chaos (*konton*). He was a transformation of the reed-shoot that evolved from the chaos, and thus goes back to a time before Heaven and Earth were separated.[30] Thus we once again arrive, this time within an explicitly political argument, at the state of undifferentiatedness that was also privileged in the mind theories of Seika and Shōsan as well as the entire Neo-Confucian tradition.

The term *shin* (*omi*) of the compound *kunshin* (ruler-minister) is ambiguous because it may also include all subjects. It is not clear whether Ansai uses *shin* in this wider meaning. He apparently never explicated the term, as later Suika Shinto scholars did, to include *banmin*, all the people or even specifically the peasants. We will come back to this point later. For Ansai, who taught daimyo in Edo, the politically significant population was limited to the ruling class—at least he did not explicitly include "the masses." Thus *shin* is translated as "ministers" rather than "ministers-subjects." "Ministers" refers, in this context, to the "public servants" of Tokugawa Japan: daimyo and samurai.

A final example of political etymologizing comes from the most secret *den* Koretaru gave to Ansai, the *Commentary on Himorogi and Iwasaka*. It is a gloss on one line in the *Nihongi*, where some

---

[29] This paragraph summarizes several passages: NST 39: 137; DNB 16: 467–69; and DNB 17: 5. For Ansai, see DNB 16: 15; DNB 17: 5. For Koretaru, see DNB 15: 299; and a manuscript from the Cabinet Library: "Jindai no maki Koretaru kōsetsu" (Lectures on the "Age of the Gods" by Koretaru) (1670; 10 fascicles in 3 vols.), 1: 11.

[30] See *Nihongi* (tr. Aston), pp. 2–3.

secondary gods are ordered to set up "a heavenly divine fence and a heavenly rock-boundary [the meaning of the characters with which *himorogi-iwasaka* is spelled], wherein to practice religious abstinence on behalf of Amaterasu's descendants." [31] This "top secret" *den* contains the essence of Ōdō Shinto, Koretaru writes. [32] *Himorogi* is retransliterated with characters that change its meaning into "tree that keeps the sun" (Ansai) or "the sun has to be kept" (*gi* is not *ki* but *shiku*: Koretaru). This is the essence of the Way: that ministers keep and protect the Imperial Sun line, and that they do so in harmony (Ansai: *iwasaka* = *chū*) or forever unchanging, like rocks (Koretaru).

Punning, as one may call this play on words, was not for Ansai and Koretaru a parlor game, as it was in the poetry parties of their own time. Rather it provided them with a procedure to unearth fundamental truths in a new soil. The logic of this technique was not governed by what we call syllogistic logic. Their discourse received its cohesion from political realities. The political values they preached were commonplace and common sense in their day. Under the pretense of locating these values through an archeology of words, they were in reality revalidating them, and in a sense, by endowing old values with new persuasive power, they were re-creating them for their audiences. This persuasive force did not rest in the "logic" that strung words together. Rather it sprang from the last word that, sometimes in a string of many, unveiled the truth in an unexpected site. The more alien and epistemologically far that point of arrival was from where one started (from "reverence" to "dirt"), the more exhilarating, one presumes, the "discovery" and the more intense the rhetorical delight that in itself constituted the "proof."

Although Ansai rejected certain associations, he did not specify the reason. For instance, he viewed as spurious the following explanation of why the Nakatomi purification is divided into twelve steps. The source he quotes links the number twelve to the twelve generations of gods in the *Nihongi*, the twelve months of the year, twelve time periods of the day, twelve causes in Heaven (seven stars and the five Phases) and the twelve causes in man (seven openings in his head and the five viscera). These correspondences, according to Ansai, are *fukai*, strained connections of

---

[31] Koretaru: NST 39: 78–83; Ansai: *ibid.*, pp. 133, 135, 137 and DNB 17: 91, 144. See *Nihongi* (tr. Aston), pp. 81–82.

[32] DNB 15: 393, 394.

incongruent data, or *shigen*, private theories. He also rejects as *fukai* the interpretation of *chiki*, the ornamental crossbeams that jut out from the gables of the Ise Shrines, as *chigi* (wisdom-duty).[33] Ansai thus singled out certain meanings as truthful and rejected others as arbitrary. We (but not Ansai) would say that he acted arbitrarily both when he assigned and denied meaning.

The abundance and freedom of Ansai's etymologizing strategies may surprise us. The procedure, however, is still with us in the most learned circles. Heidegger's metaphysics is shot through with etymological reasoning that lodges itself in an epistemological interspace where proof and illustration blur.[34] As Jean Paulhan points out in an insightful essay, whole cultural theories have been based on linking the word "religion" with its alleged Latin root, the verb *religare*, "to bind" (religion *binds* men into a community), or by seeking the origin of culture in "cult."[35] Ansai grounded, through etymologizing, not a cultural theory but, in addition to a metaphysics, a politics and a very demanding ethics. Paulhan's essay is helpful in familiarizing us with Ansai's procedures.

Etymology, Paulhan argues, is not a knowledge or a science but a discursive procedure that uncovers meaning by allegedly pushing through to an original and motivated language. It tries to convince us by drawing sequences and consequences—illicit ones, in our eyes. Yet, the principles that direct one's choice are to be found only in oneself. Etymology justifies anything one wants it to without teaching us anything new: its logic is tautological. Like the proverbial Spanish inns, Paulhan writes, one does not find anything there but what one has brought along oneself. Yet, like a pun, etymology produces a sudden flash in the mind, a cutting insight that exudes an aura of proof.

First, Paulhan reasons, one starts with a pun, playing with similar sounding words, looking for "un petit drame." The greater the distance between the words (hence the search for old words), the stronger the flash of insight produced. (Here one is reminded of Ansai's *omoshiroi koto*, his remark that the theories he proposes are interesting.) Then one experiences, so to speak, the return of a

---

[33] DNB 17: 7–8, 56–57.

[34] Heidegger's philosophy is one that incessantly appeals to (is based on?) word plays. He breaks up words to reveal previously hidden meanings (Da-sein: being as spatially "being there;" Ex-istenz), plays on double meanings (Schuld: meaning both "guilt" and "debt" in German), or revives obsolete words (Bedingnis).

[35] Paulhan, *Alain*, first published in 1953 (Paris: Editions de Minuit). My references are to Paulhan, *Oeuvres complètes*, 3: 263–303. See especially pp. 265–86.

meaning that was initially overlooked. Through similarities in sound, paths are formed along which meaning can travel— linkages that seem fragile or amusing to some but quite reasonable and plausible to others. Finally, a projection occurs whereby the newly discovered meaning or idea, common to so many sounds and words, suddenly appears to have been the origin of those words and the primary reason for their existence. The result is not merely tautological in that we learn something that we knew. Rather, the idea now acquires a new dignity because it appears to have been the inspiration that originally formed the words and their linkages.

Paulhan's short phenomenological description appears to fit Ansai's verbal operations perfectly. The persuasive force of Ansai's etymological strategies may thus be nothing more than the rhetorical pleasure Aristotle talks about, that of "gathering the meaning of things": "people like what strikes them, and are struck by what is out of the way." [36] It is clear, however, that such proofs remain subjective. What is a pun for some, and legitimate only as fun— and that is the way many of Ansai's Neo-Confucian students took his Shinto theories, as we shall see—is infallible proof for others. It is a fine line that separates the punner from the etymologist, the cabalist from the phoneticist. In this context, it is instructive to recall the experience of a renowned French scholar, Ferdinand de Saussure.

The founder of modern linguistics, Saussure was for three years (1906–1909) engaged in an enterprise that produced a cabalistic exegesis that nobody else but he found in a voluminous and well-studied body of data that covered over two thousand years: all Latin poetry ever written. The only difference with Ansai is that after three years, for lack of any corroborating evidence for his findings, Saussure stopped discovering "des mots sous les mots." Meanwhile he had filled ninety-nine notebooks of evidence for the existence of such words beneath words. [37]

---

[36] *The Works of Aristotle Translated into English* (by W. D. Ross), vol. 2: *Rhetorica, De Rhetorica ad Alexandrum, De Poetica* (Oxford: Clarendon Press, 1946). See *Rhetorica*, p. 1404b 12; *De Poetica*, p. 1448b 16.

[37] Starobinski, *Les sous les mots*. Saussure assumed that Latin verses hid word-themes in the form of anagrams: names of gods, places, and persons. The letters forming the anagrams, he maintained, were apparently dispersed at random within the first few lines of every poem, as in the following two examples:

1. Taurasia *Ci*sauna Samn*io* ce*p*it;
2. M*ors* per*f*ecit *tua* ut essent—.

According to Saussure, the verse of the first example is an anagrammatic line hiding the name *Scipio*. The second example is an "anaphonic half-line, patterned after the vowels of

Although nowhere in the whole of classical and pre-modern Latin literature could any reference be found to the existence of anagrammatic rules, for three years Saussure continued to find internal evidence for his theory, and eventually asserted that all Latin poets, down to the nineteenth century, must have been aware of such rules. He even hypothesized an occult tradition, an anagrammatic *tao-t'ung* (transmitted tradition) if you will; or its opposite, a knowledge so common that it was never mentioned. The latter reduced the whole phenomenon to unconscious and natural dimensions:[38] mysteriously, Latin poets always communicated unconsciously through a text constructed from a subtext composed of word-themes—an idea akin to Ansai's *concordantia numinosa* between the Shinto text and a Neo-Cónfucian subtext. Ansai also said that the authors of the mythology did not intentionally write the Five Phases and so on into their text.[39] Rather, their writings unconsciously and mysteriously expressed the Way. Saussure's logic was identical to Ansai's, and so was his reliance on faith: Saussure admitted that a certain faith sustained the whole enterprise. Obviously he was constructing his data while thinking that he was merely isolating them.[40] He was aware of this possibility, and finally gave up after a fruitless search for outside evidence.

The fate of Saussure's anagrammatic studies raises two further points relevant to our discussion of Ansai. Saussure had good reasons for not publishing his findings, since he could not produce proofs others would accept as unassailable. One may also surmise that his world was not receptive to his particular interpretation of poetry. The motive force behind a poem, Saussure was suggesting, was not the creative subject or poet, but the inductive word.[41] (In that respect he did not change when later he concentrated his

---

Cornelius, reproduced in strict order; the *a* of *tua* is either a sign of interruption or an allusion to *Cornelia* (gens); the vocalism of *ut essent* remains in the anaphony" (p. 29).

These anagrams did not enunciate any new information since they usually related to the overt content of the texts. In other words, Saussure always knew what he would find in the subtext. During his voluminous readings he found anagrams everywhere. He even constructed rules of formation so complex that he once compared them to a Chinese game (p. 21)! Saussure maintained that these anagrammatic rules had for centuries governed the composition of poetry in Latin. The more he studied, the more skillful he became in discovering as many as four or five anagrams in one line (p. 153).

[38] *Ibid.*, p. 124–25.
[39] See above pp. 234, 237; see also KSZH 9: 21b.
[40] Starobinski, *Les Mots sous les mots*, pp. 123, 138.
[41] *Ibid.*, p. 152.

efforts on the study of *langue* as if *parole* did not exist.) Yet fifty years later, when the intellectual climate had changed and it had become fashionable in the 1960s to speak of "la mort du sujet," Saussure's notes were not only judged worth publishing, but were hailed as "la seconde révolution saussurienne." Roman Jacobson spoke of a genial intuition on Saussure's part.[42] For Saussure and Ansai, the plausibility or truth of their statements was determined by the prevailing system of values.

Second, Saussure's thesis, which minimized the presence of the creative subject behind the use of language, presents a great irony since Saussure himself was highly creative in his efforts to prove such a theory. A similar irony permeates Ansai's discourse. Posing as a "mere transmitter," he was actually very innovative. Furthermore, Ansai was writing a politics when he claimed instead to be formulating a mythological metaphysics.

There was, however, a politics that Ansai erased from his discourse and texts: that small part of the Chinese tradition where power and accountability were given a very circumscribed legitimacy, the theory of the change of Heaven's Mandate. The "killing of the lord" was the dreadful abomination that Ansai and his students evoked constantly as a theoretical possibility, but its reality and certainly its legitimacy were denied for Japan because rulers and ministers were existentially one through their sacred and cosmogonic origins. Man and Heaven were ontologically one. Any differentiation of that whole was seen as the beginning of a separation that could turn part against part—which meant, politically, party against party. Thus the unbroken and unconditional preservation of the imperial house was essential. In this respect, Ansai's position was more extreme than Koretaru's, who maintained that an unvirtuous lord should be replaced by another one, albeit from the same bloodline, chosen for his *chūtoku* or virtue of harmony, the quality needed to occupy the center.[43] For Ansai, rulers, whether virtuous or depraved, had to be served with blind loyalty.[44]

This rejection of violent political change as illegitimate (or even unthinkable), later became the subject of intense debate among Ansai's Neo-Confucian students within the Kimon school and

[42] See the dust jacket on Starobinski, *Les Mots sous les mots*.
[43] NST 39: 80.
[44] Ansai's paradigmatic text about unconditional loyalty is Han Yü's poem about King Wen (NST 31: 200–201).

between this school and Suika Shinto.[45] The only political action
that remained open for his followers, besides absolute loyalty to the
lord and his ministers was remonstrance and, as its precondition,
the maintenance of a certain economic independence from those in
power.[46]

This existential unity of the ruling class was to be fostered in all
its members by intense, untarnished, pure sentiments and attitudes. Duty (*giri*) was thus not enough, as Koretaru had already
preached: a full upright heart and empathy were also necessary.
Reverence, *kei*, was merely the mark that separated humans from
animals. Beyond reverence, total loyalty was required. Asami
Keisai pushed this imperative to its logical extreme: warm feelings
and total love (*ai, itoshii*) were to flow from the ministers to the
rulers.[47]

Around the Meiji Restoration and in the fourth decade of this
century, nationalists turned Ansai into an anti-bakufu imperial
loyalist. Their reading of Ansai was nothing but a distorted appropriation of his teachings. In Ansai's view, the bakufu partook of
the sacred character of the polity as much as the emperor did. On a
few occasions, however, he mentioned that the warriors had their
divine paradigm in Susanoo; that the shogun was like Susanoo or
Ō-ana-muchi; and that the sword (real, spiritual, or mythological)
was what kept order in the realm.[48]

By Ansai's time, however, the *bushi* or warriors did not need
further legitimation. They were part of normalcy, like the language one uses, so that questions of accepting or justifying them
were no longer salient in the collective consciousness. It is almost as
an afterthought that Ansai gives the warriors a mythologizing
legitimacy. Susanoo is much more important to him (and
Koretaru) as an exemplar of the conversion from a rebellious and
wild heart (with *too much* Metal) to a respectful heart (a return to
Earth;) of a god who had changed his passionate temperament
(*kishitsu*) and returned to his pure nature (*shō*).[49]

[45] KSZH 1: 3b. For the views of Keisai, Naokata, and Shōsai, see NST 31: 202–27; for
Kyōsai's critique of Naokata's views, see *ibid.*, pp. 467–69.

[46] For example, Keisai (NST 31: 384) and Naokata (*ibid.*, pp. 439, 441). Miyake Shōsai
served in the Oshi domain, Several times he attempted to resign because he was not allowed
to remonstrate. He was imprisoned for almost two years. (See on this, Abe Ryūichi, "Kimon
gakuha shoke," NST 31: 591–92; Maruyama, "Ansaigaku," *ibid.*, n21, pp. 671–72.

[47] NST 39: 82; DBN 15: 65; NST 31: 230–35.

[48] NST 39: 148, 170; DNB 17: 145, 146.

[49] For Koretaru, see DNB 15: 360. For Ansai, see NST 39: 148; DNB 16: 6, 120–21, 126,
208; and DNB 17: 251, 282.

If the activities of the *bushi* and their place in society went unquestioned in the late seventeenth century, the same cannot be said about the role of the warriors in pre-Tokugawa Japanese history. According to Asami Keisai, warriors in pre-Tokugawa times had not always kept their proper hierarchical place. He correctly accuses the Kamakura bakufu (Minamoto Yoritomo) of having gradually encroached upon imperial prerogatives without regard for *tenka* or the realm. Yoritomo "robbed imperial authority" by granting titles to people over whom he had no legal claims in order to make them his own private retainers. Such warriors expanded their power at the expense of the imperial house. Ieyasu, however, is totally blameless he says. Although quick to find fault with Yoritomo, Keisai is blind to Ieyasu's manipulation and emasculation of the imperial institution. He writes that Ieyasu and the warriors now showed respect for the emperor and the importance of the imperial line; they had been entrusted with authority over the realm, and ruled it in the emperor's name. He also identifies Ieyasu as a ruler who encouraged scholarship and thus enabled a genius like Ansai to come forward.[50] For Ansai and Keisai, Japan's polity showed no fissures. It was a perfect undifferentiated whole, in complete concordance (for Ansai, at least; Keisai does not deal with Shinto) with the mythological paradigm of sacred unity: the unity of Heaven and man (*tenjinyuiitsu*).

In his *Fuji no mori* text Ansai singled out this unity from a variety of possible interpretations as the fundamental truth of the Japanese myths. Koretaru had explained that the "Age of the Gods" could be talked about in various ways: in terms of *ki* and *shitsu*, *ri* and *ten* (primal energy and essences, principles and Heaven).[51] For Ansai, the "Age of the Gods" contains information about two categories of data: creation (*zōka*) and human affairs (*jinji*). More importantly, however, this text establishes the fundamental unity (*tenjinyuiitsu*) between these two categories of phenomena.[52] The discursive categories Ansai developed to construct this meaning are the three pairs:

(a) *zōka*, creation, and (b) *kika*, transformation of the cosmic energy;
(c) *shinka* (身化), physical, bodily transformation, and (d) *shinka* (心化), mind-heart transformation; and

[50] NST 31: 354, 355, 371, 388, 390, 408; see also KSZH 4: 10a–b.
[51] DNB 15: 301, 305.
[52] NST 39: 151, 156, 171; DNB 16: 383, 384.

(e) *mishō,* "unborn," like the Confucian concept of "unmanifest" (*mihatsu;* Ch *wei-fa*), and (f) *ishō,* "born, generated," (the Confucian "manifest," *i-fa*).[53] (It should be noted that the abstract "unmanifest-manifest" becomes the concrete "unborn-born".)

Ansai deploys these categories to demonstrate the ontological unity of human and spirit worlds and the beginning of creation. Through them he gives human affairs a mytho-metaphysical sacred character. Thus, human affairs are talked about in creative or godly terms and divine matters are talked about in human categories. The first seven generations of *Heavenly* gods are *zōka* (a) gods. The group of five generations of *Earthly* gods that succeed them are *shinka* (c) gods, signifying a *divine* transformation into *bodily* shapes. In the first group, starting with Kunitokotachi (= Amenominakanushi), a gradual concretization of primal energy occurs—*kika* (b). This passes through five generations that equal the productive cycle of the Five Evolutive Phases, and comes to rest in the seventh generation with Izanagi and Izanami (= yang and yin). This seventh generation forms the link between Heaven and Earth because in Heaven Izanagi and Izanami are still unborn (e), but when they descend to Earth they become born (f) by taking on the bodily form of male and female. Thus, they link *zōka* and *kika.* Izanagi and Izanami produce the physical world and the Earth gods, the most important of whom is Amaterasu, the sun goddess. The names of the *Heavenly* god *Kuni*tokotachi ("establish-the-*country*-forever") and the *earth* god *Ama*terasu ("deity shining in *Heaven*") are said to clearly indicate the imbrication of Heaven and Earth. Finally, examples for *shinka* (d) or mind-transformation, are provided by Susanoo and Ō-ana-muchi.

A MYTHO-ONTOLOGY

Once Ansai had established the intrinsically sacred character of human affairs, all the Confucian categories that Ansai (as to a great extent Koretaru) reads under the mythological narrative are affected by the character of the text from which they emerge. One can distinguish three ways in which they are thus affected.

Foremost, the metaphysical and ethical truths from the Chinese tradition are charged with additional religious authority and transformed into religious signifiers. The beginning of Heaven and Earth, Ansai writes, is relevant for the present because it is also the

[53] NNS 14: 290, 291; DNB 16: 28, 32, 384–86; DNB 17: 16.

beginning of today.[54] The beginning of creation is the pattern according to which thoughts in man's heart arise, says Koretaru; and what are in Heaven gods are sages (*hijiri*) on earth.[55]

Second, in Shinto these truths are rarely expressed in abstract terms (*ri*). To communicate them, the *Nihongi* relies more on concrete things (*ji* or *koto*) (Koretaru).[56] Thus there is a tendency to reify abstract notions (as we just saw with the notions "unmanifest-manifest.")

Finally, the thrust of the mythological discourse is to collapse different orders of reality into one, to stress undifferentiatedness as the root and fundamental character of phenomena common sense would see as different. This proclivity results in the playing down or outright negation of distinctions that were standard in the Chinese tradition. Or, to put it differently, the unitary tendencies that are also present in that tradition are pushed to further extremes. Epistemologically, this also means that arguments have to be forwarded to explain how one obtains knowledge. Knowledge here is not the common operation of differentiating among things and developing a vocabulary that reflects such differentiation. Rather it circumvents such operations.

Koretaru hints at such contrasting epistemologies when he writes that

Kunitokotachi, Izanagi and Izanami, by appearing together with Heaven and Earth, established the principles of the Way of Heaven and Earth; and they taught the principle of hierarchy between rulers and ministers by "using Heaven and Earth as a text, and the sun and moon as proof."[57] In their teachings *they did not use differentiations of the human mind* (*jinshin no funbetsu*).[58]

On the other hand, "discriminating knowledge (*funbetsu kakuchi*) is received from the Heavenly gods; all separation (*sabetsu*) was already contained in the primeval chaos; degrees of happiness or wealth are ordered by the gods."[59] One should thus, in reading the

[54] DNB 17: 150; *Yamato shōgaku*, p. 90.

[55] "Koretaru kōsetsu" (manuscript) 1: 8a; "Jindai no maki kaden kikigaki" (Verbatim notes on the [Yoshikawa] house commentary on the "Age of the Gods") (manuscript, Diet Library), 1: 1. On the mind/creation parallelism, see pp. 87, 89, 228, 260.

[56] DNB 15: 348, 385. The present vogue in Japan of the medico-cultural theory concerning the "left side of the brain" has its roots and antecedents in cultural statements like these.

[57] Ansai relies on the same statement from the *Myōbōyōshū* (see NNS 14: 288). See *Yuiitsu Shintō myōbōyōshū* by Yoshida Kanetomo (1435–1511) (NNS 14: 183). For a German translation, see "Yuiitsu Shinto Myōbōyōshū," translated by T. Ishibashi and H. Dumoulin, p. 238. See also p. 93, for Razan's use of this metaphor.

[58] DNB 15: 6.

[59] *Ibid*, p. 29.

Nihongi, beware of being trapped too easily by surface meanings: "the examples (*tatoe*) or metaphors do not simply illustrate a surface meaning (*kumen*); even casual metaphors (*karisome no tatoe mo*) are signs that are rooted [in deeper meaning] (*nezasu kiba aru zo*)."[60]

The pull of these discursive forces generated by the mythological field brings about the following "recoating" of Neo-Confucian elements. The return to one's original nature is a divinization process: a return to the gods of Heaven.[61] Men and women become, respectively, Izanagi or Izanami. Those with a true heart are even identified with the primeval god Kunitokotachi.[62] The divine world of undifferentiatedness is the homeland of the no-thought mind. If one reaches the no-thought state, one's chest empties and a shapeless pillar (*mihashira*) rises within it.[63] Mental states and categories thus become concretized as they are identified with mythical actors.

This reification is carried even further, however. Ansai and Koretaru make it clear that they are talking about the physical organ of the heart.[64] If Shinto had had a more developed icono-graphical tradition, this could very well have led to some version of a Sacred Heart cult. In the body, the heart is positioned over, or higher (*takai*) than, the abdomen (*hara*). Hence, man's body con-tains a *Taka*maga*hara* (the Heavenly Plain on High where the gods live): the heart which the gods will take as their abode if man first empties it.[65]

The mind-heart (*kokoro*) as the dwelling place for the gods was a widespread Shinto notion and was one that could also be found in Chinese philosophical writings.[66] Ansai and Koretaru, however,

[60] "Koretaru kōsetsu" (manuscript) 1: 10.

[61] DNB 15: 77.

[62] "Koretaru kōsetsu" (manuscript) 2: 19, 14. For a similar statement by Razan, see p. 90.

[63] DNB 15: 291, 309. On the *shin no hashira*, see pp. 224, 232.

[64] Koretaru: DNB 15: 14; Ansai: NST 39: 129.

[65] Koretaru: "Koretaru kōsetsu" (manuscript) 1: 11; DNB 15: 17–20. Ansai: DNB 17: 144, 16.

[66] See, for instance, in Yoshida Kanetomo's *Shinto taii* (Great Meaning of Shinto) (DNB 15: 42; this text is a line-by-line commentary by Koretaru on Yoshida's text); the *Shintō gobusho's Hōki hongi* (*Kojiki, Sendaikyūjihongi, Shintō gobusho*, p. 31); Hayashi Razan's *Shintō denju* (NST 39: 12); Watarai (Deguchi) Nobuyuki's *Yōfukuki* (*ibid.*, p. 106). Ansai (NST 31: 44) quotes Chu Hsi's comment on *Mencius* 7A: 1: 1 ("He who has exhausted all his mental constitution [heart] knows his nature. Knowing his nature, he knows Heaven"—Legge's translation). For Chu Hsi's full comment, see SGT 8: 381. For a selection of other passages where Chu Hsi discusses the heart-mind, see *Shushishū*, edited by Yoshikawa Kōjirō and Miura Kunio, pp. 106, 325–29. See also p. 253 n.70.

return explicitly to the physical meaning heart has in the Chinese medical tradition. They speak of *shinzō*, the physical heart.

Ansai, as we know from his *Notes*, was well acquainted with the *Yellow Emperor's Classic of Internal Medicine* (*Huang-ti nei-ching su-wen*), and his father was an acupuncturist. Many early Tokugawa scholars had studied medicine, and doctors were sometimes called to lecture on Neo-Confucian texts.[67] Ansai's attention is drawn, for instance, to passages that speak of the heart as the dwelling place of *shen* (Jp *kami*, gods) or of *shen-ch'i* (Jp *shinki*, divine energy) or of Specific Configurative Forces, *hun-p'o* (Jp *konpaku*, soul); and to those in which the heart is described as the sovereign ruler from whom emanate directing influence and clear insight, *shen-ming* (Jp *shinmei*, god, spirit).[68]

In the original text, the Chinese terms referred to psycho-physical realities that operated not through organs but through functional "orbs" (in Manfred Porkert's terminology), one of which was the "orbis cardialis," (in traditional terminology the viscerum of the heart).[69] Following Porkert then, the hackneyed Shinto phrase "mind (or body) as the dwelling place for the gods" referred in the Chinese medical classic to the presence in man, or in his *orbis cardialis*, of a Configurative Force (*shen* or *shen-ch'i*) whose polar energies (yin and yang) could not be sounded or localized.[70] The other terms also signify psycho-physical phenomena. In philosophical texts, however, in contrast to medical ones, these

[67] The fathers of Yamazaki Ansai, Ogyū Sorai, and Wakabayashi Kyōsai practiced medicine. Kaibara Ekken, Asami Keisai, and Miyake Shōsai were at one point studying to become doctors. Hoshina Masayuki studied Neo-Confucianism first with a bakufu doctor. Nakae Tōju relates how in 1624, at age sixteen, he was the only samurai to attend a lecture by a Zen monk from Kyoto on the *Analects*; the monk had been invited to Ōmi by a doctor (NST 29: 286–87). Also see Chapter 3, note 67, and Chapter 6, note 39.

[68] YAZ 2: 583.

[69] Porkert, *Chinese Medicine*. For pertinent passages, see the following pages: On "orbs," pp. 22, 107, 111; "orbis cardialis," p. 127; *shen*, pp. 175, 181, 192, 196; *shen-ch'i*, p. 173; *shen-ming*, p. 127; *hun-p'o*, pp. 27, 111, 184. Compare with *The Yellow Emperor's Classic of Internal Medicine*, translated by Ilza Veith, p. 133; p. 189 n11; p. 222 n14.

[70] Porkert, *Chinese Medicine*, pp. 19, 173, 192, 196. In an interesting passage of his *Classified Conversations* (fasc. 98; a reference I owe to Conrad Schirokauer), Chu Hsi discusses the inborn nature of principles in man in the following way: "All things have a heart (*hsin*, *kokoro*, not *hsin-tsang*, *shinzō*) and its inside is always empty. It is like the hearts (*hsin*) of chickens and pigs that are served as food dishes. If you cut those open, you will see [what I mean]. It is the same with man's heart (*hsin*). That empty space contains many principles (*dōri*), completes Heaven and Earth, and embraces the past and the future. [To say that,] extended, [the heart] covers Heaven and Earth, is nothing but this. One wonders whether this is what makes man's heart mysterious (*tz'u so-hsün jen-hsin chih miao; myōtaru yuen*). The principles (*ri*) in man's heart are called nature. Nature is like the basis [field] of the heart. What fills its central emptiness is nothing else but principles. The heart is the dwelling place

terms, *including heart* (that is, mind) expressed spiritual energies and supernatural entities that roughly correspond to the Japanese meanings of gods, spirit, soul, and so on. For Koretaru and Ansai, however, the gods dwelled in the heart in one's chest.

As Theodore de Bary has demonstrated, mind-and-heart learning formed the core of Chinese orthodoxy. Ansai had grasped the importance of *hsin-fa* (Jp *shinpō*), the "system of teaching and practice of mind-cultivation with its emphasis on mind in its a priori, undifferentiated state." [71] We have already seen how Ansai privileged this state. The locus in the *Nihongi* where he discovers this mind system is the passage, already referred to, where Ō-ana-muchi is confronted with his own spirit who appears before him as a shining object from the sea. [72] This episode took place immediately after the god had boasted that he alone (*are hitori*) had pacified the land. The spirit, however, admonished Ō-ana-muchi that without him such a great feat could not have been accomplished. The god then understood that his spirit was behind his achievement and built a shrine to it on Mount Mimoro (Mount Miwa).

In the lecture notes on the "Age of the Gods" that Asami Keisai took down, Ansai's explanations of this passage wax, not eloquently but redundantly, over four printed pages. The whole passage has the quality of an evangelical sermon. Ansai hammers home a few main points. One imagines that he underlined these points by striking his desk with his stick, as was his habit while lecturing. [73] An emphatic *zo*, as a coda, brought every phrase to a firm stop. Why Ansai's excitement?

This passage, he contends, reveals Ō-ana-muchi's insight into the "mind system" (*shinpō*). [74] What Ō-ana-muchi first assumed he

---

of directing influence and clear insight (*shen-ming, shinmei*); it rules the whole self" (*Shushishū*, pp. 325–26). In this text then, Chu Hsi also "grounds" the mind in the organ of the heart. However, he does so in a speculative manner. Moreover, the mind's activity is described in strongly psycho-cognitive terms (the mind can transcend space and time and generate direction and insight). In other passages, as Yoshikawa Kōjirō comments on p. 327, Chu Hsi clearly posits two different principles for the mind and the physical heart. With Ansai, however, the opposite is true. I know of no texts where he clearly differentiates the two, whereas on many occasions he stresses that they are the same.

[71] De Bary, *Orthodoxy*, pp. 128–30.

[72] For the text, see *Nihongi* (tr. Aston), pp. 60–61. For Ansai's exegesis, see NST 39: 166–70 (lecture notes taken by Asami Keisai); DNB 16: 141–47 *passim*; DNB 17: 262–64.

[73] Sagara, *Jukyō undō no keifu*, p. 63.

[74] NST 39: 166; the whole passage is on pp. 166–70.

had performed through his body alone (*hitori*, alone, written with the characters *isshin*, one-body, is explicitly interpreted by Ansai as *karada*, body—another instance of objectification) is revealed to him to have been achieved by something within his body, his *kokoro* or mind-heart. In other words, Ō-ana-muchi is not conversing with *a* spirit; he is talking to himself, or more precisely, his body is speaking to his spirit, his self. The "shining object above the sea plain (*unabara*)" is in fact "what is above one's abdomen (*wa-gahara*)." This passage thus proves that Ō-ana-muchi's body housed a mind-god (*shinshin*) which makes of our bodies the bodies of gods which must be kept pure.[75] (A visit to a Shinto shrine will purify both body and mind.) Ō-ana-muchi lost his original pride and thus ranks with Susanoo as a divine exemplar. They both return to their original virtue, which identified them with the virtue (*tokugi*) of the Sun Goddess in Heaven. Moreover, both were extremely useful gods, having pacified the country by the sword. Thus they expressed the essence of Shinto, which, for Ansai, was the same in mythological times as in his own time, when Heavenly affairs rested with the imperial court, and the shogun, who was one with the emperor, ruled the country he had pacified by the sword. In addition, Ō-ana-muchi, while still alive, worshiped his own *shintai* or divine substance when he built a shrine for his spirit on Mount Mimoro (according to the characters, "Three rooms/ houses," transliterated by Ansai to mean "body-house, self-house," or simply self). This last aspect, as we know, was taken literally by Ansai, for he, too, objectified his self in a cult; a Shinto ritual equivalent of Neo-Confucian moral self-cultivation.

The Way, the Teachings, and Nature are three fundamental categories within the Confucian tradition. Like the "mind-system," Ansai transposed these into a mythological key. We have already encountered two of them. Human nature, although characterized by the Five Norms with which man is born, is essentially *kei*, reverence, and (through an etymological sleight of

[75] The spirit reveals himself with two names: *sakimitama* and *kushimitama* (meaning, according to the characters, "good-fortune-spirit" and "mysterious spirit"—Aston: guardian spirit, wondrous spirit). Ansai, however, quotes past exegesis that identifies the two spirits with the Chinese double soul, *hun-p'o* (Jp *konpaku*), and he himself further associates *saki* and *kushi* with two other characters, meaning, respectively, "beforehand" and "comb" (= thing). Thus Ansai plunges into some typical epistemological comments: through our *sakimitama* we know beforehand the qualities of things (that they are white or black, and so on), while our *kushimitama* allows us to distinguish forms (clouds, flowers, and so on) (NST 39: 167; DNB 16: 417). Heidegger, in seventeenth-century Japan, could not have done better.

hand) is located in the Japanese texts as *tsutsushimu*. The Way in Japan is Amaterasu's Way. Ansai linked the third category, the Teachings, with another mythological figure, Saruta-hiko.[76] The commentaries that Ansai and his school construct around this god again bring to mind Levi-Strauss's "bricolage." They are a dizzying example of the imaginative procedures through which Ansai familiarized and sanctified basic Confucian values for his Japanese audience.

First Saruta-hiko, as transmitter of the teachings, is identified with their source by ascribing to him the same virtue as those of the Earth god Amaterasu and the Heavenly god Kunitokotachi (another pacifier of the land).[77] Thus Saruta-hiko's inner qualification as a guide for the Way is secured. His role in the *Nihongi* narrative is to function literally as guide to the August Grandchild, Ninigi (Amaterasu's grandchild and progenitor of the first emperor, Jinmu), when he descends from Heaven with the three imperial regalia to take charge of the land. Saruta-hiko led Ninigi to the upper waters of the Isuzu River in Ise, and thus became the predecessor of Yamato-hime, who much later built Amaterasu's Ise Shrine.[78] Saruta-hiko is thus linked backward to a primeval undifferentiatedness and to Amaterasu, and forward to Ise. His name, which contains the word *saru*, (monkey) opens other passages of meanings and linkages to the popular *kōshin* cult, iconographically represented by the hear-no-evil, see-no-evil, speak-no-evil squatting monkey (often pictured as three separate monkeys), covering up his ears, eyes, and mouth with his hands.

This cult has Taoist origins. It was believed that on *kōshin* night—*kōshin* is also a zodiacal and calendrical sign—the three worms that reside in people's bellies left the sleeping body to report on each person's behavior to the Emperor in Heaven. The Emperor then shortened each person's lifespan in proportion to the seriousness of his or her misdeeds. If one stayed awake, however, the three worms could not leave the body. Hence the custom of the *kōshin* wake, which took the form of poetry readings, to prevent the shortening of life. Ansai knew this tradition but, armed with a wealth of quotations from Chinese sources (such as poems by Hsü Hun and Chu Hsi, and the Ming encyclopedia *Pen-ts'ao wang-mu* by Li Shih-chen, who gives a medical explanation for the legend), he

[76] NNS 14: 293; DNB 16: 443.
[77] NST 39: 159.
[78] *Nihongi* (tr. Aston), pp. 77–79; KSZH 9: 37b.

dismissed the Taoist and Buddhist superstitions associated with the cult. Furthermore, he traced Japanese *kōshin* wakes as pure poetry sessions back to the Nara and Heian periods, and found in the poems allusions to Saruta-hiko; an association further confirmed for him by a commentary (*den*) from Ise. Ansai added, however, that in his own day popular belief had again surrounded the practice with Taoist and Buddhist fabrications.[79] In Suika Shinto, the cult was thus restored to its alleged pure origins.

The doctrinal associations with Saruta-hiko/*kōshin* pullulated. One has sometimes to marvel at the number of constructions Ansai and his exegetes were able to stack on a text the size of a pinhead. As god of the crossroads, in the *Nihongi* and in popular *kōshin* belief, and as guide for Amaterasu's Grandchild to Ise, Sarutahiko was the perfect candidate to preside over the teachings of the right Way. Saruta-hiko's very peculiar body shape expressed such identification. The *Nihongi* tells us that he had glowing eyeballs like an eight-hand mirror: such a mirror was the most important symbol of Amaterasu. A light shone from his mouth and from his anus: both his outside body (mouth) and his inner heart (anus—*sic*), that is, his total self, inside and out, were filled with the virtue/quality of the sun.[80]

Saruta-hiko's nose was seven *sun*, the length of his back seven *shaku*: seven is the number associated with the zodiacal sign *saru*, monkey (which equals the southwest direction). *Saru* is seven spaces removed from the northeast direction (*tora*) where the sun rises. Seven, by Japanese count, is half the spaces in the day and year division into twelve, and thus means fullness of growth and creation. According to the twenty-fourth hexagram of the *Book of Changes* ("Return") it also stands for return of young light. Saruta-hiko was waiting in the southwest for the sun's grandchild to appear in the northeast.[81] He embodied *himorogi*, keeping the sun.[82]

Saruta-hiko's virtue is also associated with *tsuchi*, Earth, and through the etymology of Ise and Isuzugawa, mentioned pre-

---

[79] YAZ 2: 666–67; DNB 16: 442.

[80] DNB 16: 443; see also "Kōshin no den," manuscript, dated 1776 (Seikadō bunko).

[81] "Koshin no den" (manuscript). See also a 1753 manuscript (Ōkura Institute) by Matsuoka Takefuchi (1702–1783), "Hōreki-ki" (Record from the Hōreki era [1751–1764]) (2: 97–99; my pagination); KSZH 8: 1a. On the number seven and its association with growth, young light (and the winter solstice), see the Judgment of the twenty-fourth hexagram in the *Book of Changes*. See also above Chapter 6, note 28.

[82] DNB 16: 441.

viously, to the number five and *tsutsushimu*, hold in reverence.[83] The *saru* in his name also can mean "to forgo." Thus he is the god who forswears evil (sometimes spoken of as the seven passions) and returns to his pure nature, namely, the primeval chaos where there is no thought, an embryolike state represented by the crouching position of the *kōshin* monkey.[84] Thus the covered eyes, ears, and mouth do not suggest an effort to block out the senses but the state of undifferentiatedness where the senses are not yet activated, the realm of unmanifest reverence, the perfection of the Way, the "harmony" (*chū*) of the *Doctrine of the Mean*.[85] The stone *kōshin* statues along the village paths become reminders of the ineffable undifferentiatedness of primeval chaos and the yet undisturbed no-thought mind permeated with *kei*.

In Neo-Confucianism, the primeval void was called the "Ultimateless yet also Supreme Ultimate." For Chou Tun-yi and Chu Hsi, this is a transcendental void that is not empty but contains all the principles that emanate from it in progressive differentiation (yin and yang, the Five Evolutive Phases, and so on). The "Ultimateless yet also Supreme Ultimate" is thus also immanent: it remains present at all levels of differentiation, in the multiple realities that evolve out of it. In Neo-Confucianism, however, the notions of "creation" from yin and yang on downward and the binary functioning of the various principles within natural and human phenomena are those that receive the greatest attention. The underlying ontological unity of the cosmos, while by no means neglected, was rarely the focus of discussion. Rather, this principle of unity functioned as a given, and was routinely referred to in the opening paragraphs of a treatise or essay. After all, the "Ultimateless yet also Supreme Ultimate" was dangerously close to the empty-void theories of Buddhism.

Ansai, however, never stops coming back to the One Principle, the source that penetrates everything, and he seems unconcerned with its proximity to Buddhist heresy. During his Zen days, Ansai must have believed in the emptiness of *mu*. His subsequent discovery not that there was no void but that the "void" was pregnant with the whole universe, programed with all the principles, was possibly an insight that retained its force throughout the rest of his

[83] *Ibid.*, p. 443.
[84] "Kōshin no den" (manuscript); KSZH 8: 1b; DNB 16: 443. For a photograph of a wayside stone *kōshin*, see my "Religion of the household," p. 246.
[85] DNB 16: 443; Matsuoka, "Hōreki-ki" (manuscript) (2: 101).

life. Whatever the reason, however, from the very beginning of his Confucian career, Ansai highly valued this view of the ontological oneness of things.

In his *Heresies Refuted* (1647), he stressed this One Principle that penetrates all and, although diversified in nature and in man, remains one. One year earlier, the year he left the monastery, he published an unannotated and unpunctuated collection of twenty poems by Chu Hsi called (*Chai-chū*) *kan-hsing* ("Extemporaneous poems"; Jp *Kankyōshi*). Ten years later, in 1656, he punctuated and annotated this text and wrote an introduction and commentaries that he published in 1658.[86] His comments consist almost exclusively of quotations from Chinese sources that stress this cosmic unity of the Way: Chou Tun-yi's *Explanation of the Diagram of the Great Ultimate* (*T'ai-chi-t'u shuo*), Chang Tsai's *Western Inscription* (*Hsi-ming*) and *Correcting Youthful Ignorance* (*Cheng-meng*), and others.

In the first poem, Chu Hsi writes how the two principles of yin and yang are mysteriously one and are penetrated by one undifferentiated principle (in Japanese: *konzen to shite ichiri tsuranuki*). Ansai comments that the Supreme Ultimate is the One Principle that penetrates Heaven and man.[87] A similar emphasis is found in poems Ansai wrote himself around that time and in his reading notes.[88] Ansai also published a work in which he collected scholarly commentaries, including his own, on a phrase in the *Reflections on Things at Hand*, a phrase attributed to Ch'eng Yi (*Chūbakumuchinsetsu*: Interpretations of *Ch'ung-mo wu-chen* or "Empty and tranquil, and without any sign [and yet all things are luxuriantly present]").[89] Ansai comments that this state of unperturbed fullness refers both to creation (*zōka*) and to man's mind (*jinshin*). The original text continues: "The state before there is

---

[86] NNS 17: 189–90; ZYAZ 3: 390, 14–29.

[87] ZYAZ 3: 17.

[88] See Ansai's first New Year's poem of 1654 (ending in "One origin, spring, penetrates the four seasons") (YAZ 1: 8), and another one from 1658 which emphasizes that the diagram representing the Supreme Ultimate (a white circle) penetrates the nine other diagrams that sketch the gradual unfolding of principles (YAZ 1: 26). In his notes as well, he marvels at the wondrous undifferentiatedness of what is already differentiated as *ri* and *ki* (YAZ 1: 169). I owe these references to Tomoeda, "Yamazaki Ansai no taikyokusetsu," pp. 1–3. In 1651, Ansai who so preoccupied with Chou Tun-yi's Diagram and Chu Hsi's interpretation of it that he had a dream where Chou Tun-yi confirmed that Chu Hsi's interpretation was correct (Yamada, *Yamazaki nenpu*, p. 4).

[89] ZYAZ 3: 78–86; see also SGT 12: 178. For the English text of the entry, see *Reflections on Things at Hand* (translated by Wing-tsit Chan), pp. 25–26.

any response to it is not an earlier one, and the state after there has been response to it is not a later one." Ansai again identifies this state with creation and man's mind. He felt that this aspect of the pre-existence of principles and norms, even before they manifest themselves in concrete situations, had not been sufficiently noticed in the past. It is for this reason that he compiled those interpretations that emphasized this point.

Elsewhere Ansai argues that it is reverence that fosters Heaven's will, embedded in one's body at a yet unmanifest level as the Three Bonds and the Five Relationships.[90] What this means is that reverence has to be fostered *even in the absence of a social or political context that would demand its expression.* How does one go about such practice? This cultivation of reverence is based on an unobjectified fear. Two classical texts are quoted: the image of the fifty-first hexagram and the introduction to the *Doctrine of the Mean.* The first reads: "Thunder repeated: the image of shock. Thus in fear and trembling the superior man sets his life in order and examines himself." The latter reads: "The path may not be left for an instant. If it could be left, it would not be the path. On this account, the superior man does not wait till he sees things to be cautious, nor till he hears things to be apprehensive. . . . Therefore the superior man is watchful over himself when he is alone."[91] Thus Ansai upholds the extreme ascetic ideal of uninterrupted self-watchfulness *even when circumstances do not require it*; a kind of red alert of the mind in a constant state of unmanifested reverence that is based on an interior terror (the "apprehension" of the *Mean* and the "fear and trembling" of the *Book of Changes* are written with the same characters: Ch *k'ung-chü*; Jp *kyōkū*).

We are dealing here with a fundamental dimension of Ansai's ethics. This is further corroborated by the following statement from a manuscript collection of Ansai's sayings:

In the *Great Learning*, the solitary watchfulness (*shindoku*) leads to a rectified mind; in the *Doctrine of the Mean*, caution and fear lead to solitary watchfulness [the *shin* of *shindoku* has the Japanese readings of *tsutsushimu*, restrain; *osoreru*, fear; *imashimeru*, admonish; *shitagau*, obey]. This is what it comes down to (*kō arō koto nari*). They are naturally the same.

---

[90] See Ansai's preface (1655) to Chu Hsi's poem "Exhortation for the Reverence studio" (which two years earlier had also deeply touched Itō Jinsai) (ZYAZ 3: 6–13; for the preface, see also SGT 12: 153–54), and to *Chūwashūsetsu*, published in 1672 (ZYAZ 2: 401–21; for the introduction, see also SGT 12: 170).

[91] *The I Ching* (translated by Wilhem & Baynes), p. 198; *Doctrine of the Mean* 1: 2 and 3 (Legge's translation). The last sentence also appears in the *Great Learning* 6: 2.

This statement is followed by:

The *Doctrine of the Mean* is higher than the *Great Learning*. In the latter, the essence of the Way is illustrious virtue. In the former, illustrious virtue is defined as the Will of Heaven, and man obtains it from Heaven. In this respect, the *Mean* is one step above the *Great Learning*. The latter [Text: 5] speaks of "the perfect achievement of the tranquillity of the realm." The former [1: 5] speaks first of a "Heaven and Earth being settled in their place and all things flourishing [where equilibrium and harmony are perfect]." In the end, the *Mean* is one step higher than the *Great Learning*.[92]

Ansai thus showed a clear preference for the more mystical view of cosmic unity as it is expressed in the *Mean* without reference to the political reality of pacifying the realm; a harmony produced by a nonobjectified "caution and fear." Whereas Seika, Shōsan, and Irin'an still felt the need to mention the threat of military power as a possible enforcer of morality, Ansai generates fear from within.

Furthermore, Ansai's analysis of the Neo-Confucian view of cosmic unity dovetails with his Shinto doctrine of the unity of Heaven and man (*tenjinyuiitsu*). The *yuiitsu* (single, one, unique, alone) is not meant to indicate Shinto's purity vis-à-vis other doctrines such as Buddhism. If refers, rather, to the interpenetration of Heaven and man. Heaven here refers to the world of the seven Heavenly gods, the pre-creation Heaven without shapes or forms, the primeval chaos, already programed with the principles of creation. Thus, the beginning of Heaven and Earth is still with us: it is the beginning of every day.[93]

Later, Matsuoka Takefuchi (1701–1783) argued that Ansai did not mean by this the micro-macrocosmic correspondences one finds in medical treatises which declare that man's head is round because the sky is round, and his feet form a square because the earth is square. Matsuoka pointed out that such explanations were supported by Ch'en Shun (1153–1217) and even by Chu Hsi, who believed that the Five Viscera (orbs) of man corresponded to the Five Evolutive Phases. According to Matsuoka, Ansai rejected these theories.[94]

In this respect, Matsuoka was wrong in his reinterpretation of

[92] "Yamazaki sensei goroku" (manuscript), p. 11.
[93] DNB 16: 383; 17: 150; *Japanese Elementary Learning*, p. 90.
[94] "Shodenshō" (Copy of all commentaries). Manuscript copy (Ōkura Institute) of Matsuoka Takefuchi's *den*, originally made in 1762, in 2 vols.; no pagination. The text is found in vol. 2, under "Tenjinyuiitsu no den." See also KSZH 8: 2a; 9: 21b.

Suika Shinto, for Ansai did not, in fact, reject all such theories. However, Matsuoka was certainly correct in suggesting that the thrust of Ansai's teachings lay elsewhere, namely, in Ansai's emphasis on the relevance of "pre-creation," unmanifest values for producing in man a fundamental disposition of respect, fear, and obedience.

LANGUAGE TENSION: A PARTING OF PATHS
OVER THE SAME WAY

Ansai was uncomfortable with anything that smacked of differentiation, duality, or dividedness. This proclivity informed detailed points of his teachings, and on another level drove him to collapse Shinto into Neo-Confucianism. It also led him to a controversial interpretation of Neo-Confucian categories. The *Great Learning* had codified a famous distinction between the inner and outer realms. Although separate, these two realms met in man. Ansai, however, moved the boundary between these realms, thereby giving man an undivided position within a single realm, the inner.

Traditionally, the first four categories in the *Great Learning* (from the investigation of things, to complete knowledge, to sincere thoughts, to rectified hearts) were thought to pertain to what was inner, while the remaining four (from cultivating the person or self, to regulating the family, to right government, to tranquillity in the realm) were associated with the outer realm.[95] Ansai instead included self-cultivation in the inner realm.[96] Thus, the individual was no longer split between inner dispositions and outward comportment. For Ansai, *keigi-naigai* meant first, respectful reverence inward, which included reverence toward the self and the body (the Chinese character for "self" or "person" in "cultivating the person" can also mean "body"), and second, the execution of one's duty in the outside world of the family, and so on.

This stark dichotomy between inner and outer is reminiscent of Seika's overemphasis on the inner and his severance of the self from

[95] *The Great Learning*, Text: 5.
[96] NST 31: 19, 29, 55; SGT 12: 175. For a full discussion of the *keigi-naigai* question, see Bitō, *Hōken*, pp. 68–74, and Taira, *Kinsei*, pp. 150–73. Ansai's argument was that Chu Hsi had deviated from the meaning *keigi-naigai* had been given in the *Book of Changes* (in the Commentary on the Lines—on six in the second place—of the second hexagram; Wilhelm & Baynes translation, p. 393).

the political world through a rejection of the "investigation of things." For Shōsan also, political reality is what it is; one abstains from judgments and simply performs one's assigned tasks. Ansai, in a similar way, seems to deny the possibility of any input of the self into the polity other than the execution of one's duty. Even the very important Neo-Confucian critical imperative of "remonstrance to the rulers" thus seems to be denied legitimacy. As with his preference for the *Mean* over the *Great Learning*, Ansai pushes the polity into the background, out of the focus of his concern. This does not mean that he is apolitical. He is profoundly political because there *is* a polity, and it is taken for granted.

This interpretation of inner and outer, which Ansai put forward around 1680, was one of the causes for a break with two of his leading students, Satō Naokata and Asami Keisai. The issue continued to be hotly debated even after Ansai's death.[97]

On the one hand, Ansai's position should come as no surprise, especially if one keeps in mind his selective emphasis on states of undifferentiatedness in the Neo-Confucian classics and Shinto myths. Koretaru had already declared that, in principle, inner and outer were not separated in Shinto.[98] Ansai also upheld that purity of the body was identical with purity of the heart.[99] His own cult shows how deeply anchored in his thought this belief was. On the other hand, it should also come as no surprise that some of his students refused to follow Ansai this far in his reinterpretation of Neo-Confucianism.

Ansai had achieved a highly personal synthesis of Shinto and Neo-Confucianism; a synthesis based on an unshakable belief in the degree to which the Way is embedded in man as inborn Norms and Relationships, which rested on a pervasive, non-objectified, fearful reverence as a basic human disposition. The single truth enunciated in this synthesis, however, was reached in quite different ways in Shinto and Neo-Confucianism. Althought faith and certainty guided Ansai's exploration of that truth in both traditions, two different epistemologies were involved.

A number of factors account for this difference in approach and epistemological strategy. One, notwithstanding Ansai's claim that

[97] In general, the Shintoists, like Tomobe Yasutaka (1667–1740), backed Ansai's *keigi-naigai* interpretation, whereas his Neo-Confucian students criticized it. For essays on this question, written by Asami Keisai, Satō Naokata, and Tomobe Yasutaka, see *Nihon jurin sōsho*, vol. 6.

[98] "Koretaru kōsetsu" (manuscript), 3: 47b.

[99] NST 39: 161; DNB 16: 95.

Shinto independently embodied the Way and that therefore no *fukai* or artificial transplants of associated Neo-Confucian meanings were needed, his repossessing of the Way in Shinto was artificial, clever, *omoshiroi*, or interesting. The nature of his etymological manipulations bears this out. The derivative character of Japan's Way in relation to China's was difficult to camouflage. This eventually became the critique Motoori Norinaga and his followers leveled at Ansai. The question, however, had already come up with Ansai's first- and second-generation students such as Satō Naokata and Wakabayashi Kyōsai (Asami Keisai's disciple).

Two, Shinto and Neo-Confucianism each had produced different discourses. This raised difficulties when attempts were made to represent one text, the mythological narrative, as a transposition of a subtext with a different character. The mythological text, constructed around supernatural events, actors, and objects, was forced to surrender a subtext of abstract arguments and principles. This could not be done without a proper theory of language, which did not exist and thus had to be produced, hesitantly, while the exegesis was being conducted.

Three, although such language theory was vague, the critical attitudes demanded by Shinto and Neo-Confucian materials were clearly different and stood in sharp contrast with one another. Ansai could reconcile the two in his mind, but most of his students could not. Thus it is quite understandable that many of his students, while subscribing to the same truth as Ansai, could not find it in both traditions at the same time. They resolved this epistemological tension by choosing either Suika Shinto or the Kimon school of Neo-Confucianism. As we shall see, pedagogical arrangements in his school show that Ansai was forced to acknowledge this tension. Ansai was fiercely exclusivistic with regard to the Truth, which could be only One although embedded in two traditions. Many of his students felt the same exclusivism not only concerning the Truth but also concerning its expression.

Finally, Ansai's fundamentalist, dogmatic approach created an intolerant and self-righteous atmosphere that resulted in a series of breaks, expulsions, and factional splits. These were for the most part triggered by disagreements on points of doctrine and interpretation, and further aggravated by personality conflicts. Ansai's own career is rife with strong disagreements with other scholars (Seika, Razan, Gahō), rejections of his own teachers (Nakano Kenzan, Watarai Nobuyoshi, and Yoshikawa Koretaru) and expulsions of his best students (Satō Naokata and Asami Keisai).[100] This pattern continued even after his death: Naokata and Keisai stopped speaking to each other, and Miyake Shōsai, who with them formed the "genial" trio of Ansai's star students, broke off relations with Keisai's successor, Wakabayashi Kyōsai (1679–1732).[101]

The question of language is central to these four points. Ansai sensed abstruse mysteries in the mythological texts, but access to these required the decoding of the *Nihongi*'s language. Koretaru compared the sacred writings to a cluster of tangled threads. To disentangle them, he wrote, one must first understand that thought is expressed differently in Japan than in China: the Chinese use principles (*ri*) only, whereas the Japanese also rely on concrete things (*koto*).[102] Wakabayashi Kyōsai similarly asserted that in Japan things were not explained by principles, but principles were explained through material things (*mono*). He therefore concluded that the surface reading one customarily applies to Confucian works will yield no meaning if applied to the *Nihongi*.[103]

Two other factors (themselves of an interpretive nature) deeply informed any exegetical effort: certain views on the nature of the Japanese language prior to the introduction of Chinese characters, and the blurring of categories in mythological narrative that was presumed to point to the fundamental truth of undifferentiatedness. It was assumed that the pristine spoken Japanese language was a "natural" language. The word *kami*, Ansai claimed, was a natural expression of the human voice; words in the mythological texts were like the words of young children.[104] Kyōsai encouraged

---

[100] For Ansai's criticism of Fujiwara Seika, see SGT 12: 139. Koretaru broke off relations with Ansai because of Ansai's urging that he accept Ise Shinto teachings and also that he return the Yoshida teachings to the Yoshida house (Taira, *Yoshikawa*, pp. 409–10). Watarai Nobuyoshi and Ansai had a falling out because Ansai urged Nobuyoshi to accept Urabe Shinto exegesis (*ibid.*, p. 409). The source for the rift between Ansai and Nonaka Kenzan was either a quarrel over the use of funds Ansai had received from Kenzan or, more in character, Ansai's scolding of Kenzan over the inappropriateness of the latter's trip to Edo (where he was summoned by his lord) while he was still wearing mourning garments for the death of his mother (Taira, *Kinsei*, p. 147).

[101] Details are lacking over Naokata's alienation from Keisai, but in their later years they only communicated in writing and refused to talk to each other. Similarly, Shōsai and Kyōsai, Atobe and Naokata, did not simply hold different opinions on certain issues (most important about Shinto) but they rejected each other's teachings quite passionately. On the three splits between these scholars, see Maruyama, "Ansaigaku," pp. 610, 613, 609, respectively.

[102] DNB 15: 158, 385.

[103] KSZH 8: 7a.

[104] NNS 14: 276, 288. For Razan on this subject, see p. 93.

his students to approach Shinto with a mental attitude like that of a child listening to fairy tales.[105] Such an approach, needless to say, is worlds apart from the Neo-Confucian enterprise of the investigation of things and the plumbing of principle.[106]

The emphasis on undifferentiatedness had certain consequences. The mythological narrative, like the Neo-Confucian Diagram of the Supreme Ultimate, traced the genesis of all phenomena from an original diffuse state. Such schemes emphasized, and indeed were predominantly preoccupied with, the process of creation through differentiation. Yet it was the original state of undifferentiatedness that the exegesis focused on. This raised problems of terminology. Words by their very nature individualize things and represent reality from limited perspectives. How does one speak, then, about an undifferentiated state where particularized things as we know them do not exist? This is the problem mystics in the West resolved through the *via negativa* of expression. In Japan too, a distrust of the written, frozen word developed. Thus Koretaru's groping formulation:

It is not the Way if one talks of it by simply producing words that are oriented to everyday affairs (*nichiyōmono ni mukatte, sono mama kotoba o hassuru*). However, one will have neither regrets nor failures if one produces words that articulate [or "patiently endure, give latitude to"— *kanben shite*] things on the basis of undifferentiatedness (*imada hassezaru ni kono yue o kanben shite kotoba o hassureba*).[107]

Koretaru identifies the poems of the "Age of the Gods" as a privileged textual locus where such expressions of the mind are minimally mediated by outside realities, and thus come close to being a pure language (of interiority). In this interpretation, it should be noted, he follows leads from Fujiwara Teika (1162–1241). These poems, Koretaru writes, unrestricted by

[105] KSZH 8: 5a.

[106] This is not to say that nothing escaped the application of Neo-Confucian rational investigation. Sorai wrote that "the evil of plumbing principle is that it lacks sufficient awe for Heaven and spiritual beings. . . . How could one plumb principle in exhaustion? People claiming such knowledge are deluded" (*Bendō*; NST 36: 30).

[107] DNB 15: 307. This and other statements concerning the privileged status of speech over writing are relevant to Jacques Derrida's thesis of logocentrism in the West (see especially his *Of Grammatology*, pp. 11–15, 97–98, 161–63). Derrida suggests that China, unlike the West, valorized writing over speech (pp. 91–93). Japan, however, clearly has a tradition of logocentrism in its theories of poetry, and, as we have seen, in the Shinto theories of Razan, Koretaru, and Ansai. This Japanese logocentric tradition was occasioned by an historical consciousness that Japan had an indigenous spoken language before the alien Chinese script was introduced.

metric rules, are not arty or florid, but direct expressions of thought. Poems are flowers produced from the seeds of the mind. The Way of the Gods is the essence (*tai*) and the way of poetry is its function or application (*yō*).[108] These themes (developed further by Kokugaku scholars) gave rise to questions concerning the appropriateness of a childlike language to discuss truth in a literate society where the latest fashion in learning was Neo-Confucianism.

Ansai summarized his own approach to the study of the "Age of the Gods" with two principles concerning form and content. He adopted these from a work written by Inbe Masamichi in 1367: "In antiquity, discussion of the Great Way [rested on two principles]: for terms, the words of infants were borrowed, and the content was about the mind of the *kami*."[109] This naive, uncritical, respectful attitude toward the Shinto texts contrasts sharply with Ansai's excellent text-critical approach to Neo-Confucian works, especially Chu Hsi's writings, where he distinguishes carefully between his earlier and his more mature works, traces shifts in Chu Hsi's thought, searches for parallel texts to clarify obscure passages, and completes unfinished works in line with Chu Hsi's intentions. Ansai's best students could not live with such epistemologically divergent approaches, applied not separately to different subjects (for example, poetry and philosophy) but simultaneously to the study of one subject, the Way. Their refusal to accept Ansai's Shinto was, in addition to the *keigi-naigai* controversy, one of the main reasons why Satō Naokata and Asami Keisai broke with Ansai around 1680. Miyake Shōsai also had difficulties with Shinto. Of Ansai's three leading disciples, however, the self-confident, cynical Naokata was the most uncompromisingly rationalistic and the most deeply offended by Ansai's Shinto teachings.

Naokata, who genuinely admired Ansai's genius with respect to Neo-Confucianism, bemoaned Ansai's infatuation with Shinto as a waste of scholarly talent. The reason, he thought, was that even

[108] DNB 15: 362, 381; "Koretaru kōsetsu" (manuscript), 6: 34.
[109] NST 14: 288. The phrase is from the introduction of Inbe Masamichi's *Jindaikan kuketsu* (Oral traditions of the "Age of the Gods"). In 1664/3, a volume was published that conveniently juxtaposed four interpretive traditions of the "Age of the Gods": the *Nihonshoki jindaikan gōkai* (Comprehensive interpretations of —). The four texts were Inbe's *kuketsu*; Yoshida Kanetomo's (1435–1511) *Jindaikanshō* (Copy of —); Kiyohara Nobukata's (1475–1550) *Nihonshoki kōgi* (Lectures on —); and Ichijō Kaneyoshi's (1402–1481) *Nihongi sanso* (Commentaries on —). Six months later, however, in 1664/9, Ansai edited and printed Inbe's *kuketsu* in a separate volume. See Tani, "Yamazaki Ansai ni yotte kōkan sareta *Jindaikan kuketsu*," p. 2.

Ansai did not know the true measure of scholarship.[110] Referring to his disagreement with Keisai and Shōsai concerning the affair of the forty-seven rōnin—Naokata, defending the bakufu, held strictly to the legal point that they had broken the law and should thus not be extolled as paragons of virtue—he stressed that once one has made a decision according to a single principle, one cannot switch to another even for the sake of the realm. This is why he viewed Keisai's famous work, *Seiken igen* (Last words on royal service with a peaceful mind—a work that extolls blind loyalty to Japan), as a bad book. In the same vein, Naokata criticized Yamazaki Ansai: "even a man of the stature of Ansai was blinded because he latched on to Shinto."[111]

Naokata attacked and ridiculed all efforts whereby the Way was rediscovered in Japan. The teachings of the *Nihongi*, he argued, were not on a par with those of the Sages of the Three Dynasties, and if China were to produce new sage kings whose virtue would spread over the four seas, Japan would have no choice but to accept them and submit.[112] He lambastes the idea that Japan is a divine country, as was supposedly proven by the *kamikaze* or divine winds that destroyed the Mongol fleets in the thirteenth century. This is most strange, Naokata writes. If Yao and Shun decided to attack Japan, the purpose was to punish evildoers and rescue the people, and there should not have been a bad storm. Therefore, if the Mongol fleet was destroyed, this does not prove that Japan is sacred and virtuous, but that the Mongols themselves were bad, had strayed from Heaven's principle, and deserved to be met by a bad storm. This rather convoluted argument was perhaps partly a riposte to Keisai's declaration (also ascribed to Ansai) that a true Japanese Confucian would have to defend Japan even if the agressor were Mencius; that to fight him and capture him would be in accord with true Confucian principles.[113]

Naokata also specifically rejected as *okashiki* (strange) the argument that Japan was a divine land because it had, in contrast to China, a creation theory. In a contemptuous reference to Ansai's etymological and numerological exegesis concerning the Isuzu river in Ise, Naokata also judged it strange "that the Kumozu river

[110] *Unzōroku*; SNZ, p. 246.
[111] *Unzōrokushūi*; SNZ, p. 312.
[112] *Ibid.*, p. 349.
[113] *Unzōroku zokushūi*; SNZ, p. 627; Tsunoda et al., *Sources*, 1: 360–61. For Keisai, see Maryuama, "Ansaigaku," p. 631, and "Asami sensei gakudan," p. 2a, in "Keisai sensei zatsuwa hikki" (manuscript).

[a river in the Ise region which Naokata, possibly on purpose, confuses with the Isuzu river] is said somehow to be a keeper of the number Five." [114] One final example of Naokata's Shinto critique that seems to have escaped the censor's black ink (his *Collected Works* were printed in 1941, but many "unpatriotic" passages were erased by official censorhip) relates to Amaterasu. "That Amaterasu, like a queen on a par with King Wen, would have said [to Ninigi], 'You are lord of Japan' is a theory that does not make sense. That is much like the mistakes [made in China] where [scholars] have made Confucius into an uncrowned king who supposedly wrote the *Spring and Autumn Annals* by using divination stalks." Naokata here correctly identifies the kind of exegesis Ansai was applying to Shinto: Ansai's methodology held more in common with the etymologizing and divinatory interpretations that prevailed in China during the Later Han and subsequent centuries than with the Sung Neo-Confucians. [115]

In a letter of 1700, Naokata answers some questions a student (Atobe Yoshiaki?) had asked about Yamazaki Ansai's career, intellectual background, and his involvement in Shinto, including his Suika cult. [116] Naokata was full of praise for Ansai's belief in Chu Hsi, and credited him with founding a pure Confucian tradition in Japan. He admitted, however, that he did not understand why Ansai in his later years—Naokata joined Ansai's school in 1671—seemed to have given more weight to Shinto than to Neo-Confucianism. Maybe, he speculated, it was because Ansai [in his last years in the monastery, before he turned to Neo-

[114] *Unzōroku zokushūi*; SNZ, p. 627. This is, of course, an oblique reference to Ansai's etymological theories concerning the Isuzugawa, Ise, and so on.

[115] *Unzōroku*; SNZ, p. 247. During the Later Han dynasty, a theory arose that made Confucius into a secret recipient of the Mandate of Heaven, and thus an "uncrowned king." (A T'ang emperor later officially bestowed upon Confucius the title of King Wen-hsüan: Naokata does not use the term "uncrowned king," but speaks of King Wen-hsüan.) This theory was linked to a prognosticative interpretation of the *Spring and Autumn Annals*. See Fung, *A History of Chinese Philosophy*, translated by Derk Bodde, 2: 18, 71–87, 129–30; and also Hsiao, *A History of Chinese Political Thought*, translated by F. W. Mote, 1: 525–27. Compare Ansai's interpretive strategies with what Tung Chung-shu (179?–104? B.C.) wrote: "In what may be numbered, there is a correspondence in number. In what may not be numbered, there is a correspondence in kind" (Fung, *A History* 2: 31); "Names are the representative symbols of great principles. One records the meanings of these representative symbols in order thereby to spy out the things that lie within them ... the standards for names and appellations are derived from Heaven and Earth.... The ancient sages emitted ejaculations which mimicked (the sound of) Heaven and Earth" (p. 85). See also Wang Pi's (229–249) theories on the relationship between the symbols of *Book of Changes*, ideas, and words (pp. 184–87).

[116] *Unzōroku*; SNZ, pp. 11–12.

Confucianism][117] believed in the unity of the Three Teachings.
But then, he continued, Ansai loathed Buddhism but firmly believed in Shinto. Once it is admitted, however, that Shinto also
holds the truth, then every teaching of every country could claim
the same. There is only one truth (*ichiri*) in the universe. Hence,
either Confucianism is correct and Shinto false, or the other way
around, but they cannot both be true at the same time. Since
Confucianism holds the truth, Naokata wrote, he did not understand the charge that reading Chinese books and following the
Chinese Way makes one a traitor to Japan, the country that feeds
and supports one.[118]

This last remark shows how Ansai's intellectual progeny had
become polarized between Shinto and Confucian followers. For
both sides, the demands of truth were total and exclusive: one
could not compromise on the truth—though both sides held that
the core of this truth was a pervasive and constant disposition of
fearful reverence.

Naokata believed that the truth was inextricably linked to the
language in which it was expressed. Thus, because he viewed
Shinto's mythologizing mode as an unacceptable and inappropriate medium for the representation of truth, he was led to deny
the existence of any ultimate truth in Shinto. Few, however, had
Naokata's majestic self-assurance in the logic of his own position.
His self-confidence is easily visible in the following striking words:

A scholar has no base (*hon, moto*) if he does not believe in the principle of
his own self (*jiko no ri*). It is all right to believe in the Sages, but it does not
measure up to belief in one's own principle (*wagari*). Look at Tseng Tzu
and Tzu-hsia. Ch'eng [Yi or Hao] said: "If you believe in people, you
don't believe in principles." Shintoists believe in gods, hold fast there, and
lose their base. For people, there is something more noble than the self,
and that is Heavenly Principle. Nothing can match this noblesse. Besides
one's mind, there is nothing powerful enough to rely on.[119]

Many of Ansai's students switched allegiance between Shinto and
Neo-Confucianism, but few were able to hold on to both. Asami
Keisai, toward the end of his life (1652–1711), became sym-
pathetic to Shinto. Atobe Yoshiaki (1652–1729), in 1698 received
the Suika Shinto *den*, but two years later became a Naokata student
and abandoned Shinto, only to revert to it in 1704. Wakabayashi

---

[117] See Ansai's reference to such a period in his life, in the *Heresies Refuted* (NNS 17: 247).
[118] For Wakabayashi Kyōsai's defense against a similar charge, see KSZH 8: 2b.
[119] *Gakudan zatsuroku*; NST 31: 462.

Kyōsai, who became Keisai's student in 1702, twenty years later clearly opted for Suika Shinto, which he then tried to recharge with a new dose of Neo-Confucianism.

One can thus surmise that the choice was more between two intellectual styles, tastes, and languages than between two radically different doctrines. At the time, however, things were not perceived that way. Shintoists and Confucians were accusing each other of missing the truth. Keisai complained that when Confucians heard what he had to say, they accused him of having been led astray by Shinto, whereas Shintoists accused him of having forgotten Shinto. Kyōsai criticized both schools for their ignorance of one another and attacked Shintoists when they refused to associate the *chū (naka)* of Amenominakanushi with the *chung* of the *Doctrine of the Mean*. Kyōsai, indeed, exerted himself to bring Neo-Confucianism back into Shinto: "the *kami* are nothing but living principles, *ri*." He denigrated the naive way of the pure Shintoists, and criticized the fact that the transmission of the Suika Shinto *den* had become an empty formality in which knowledge did not play any role. He even reported a case in which a *den* was sold for a thousand kan and an equal amount of koku.[120]

Through Kyōsai we know that similar tensions already existed in the late 1670s, when Ansai was still alive. He relates how by around 1680, Ansai's time was being monopolized by a priest from the Kamo shrine (whose Shinto teachings Ansai also received). Day after day, his students were made to wait, for Ansai invariably showed up late for his lectures whenever that priest was around. The Shinto babble of this man was hard to swallow for Naokata and Keisai. One day they took this priest aside and argued him into a corner. Ansai was quite upset about this incident, and from then on Naokata and Keisai were treated like outsiders (*tozama*). Naokata was finally expelled, and he took Keisai with him. They were not even allowed at Ansai's funeral.[121] The in-group thus came to consist, according to Kyōsai, of less intelligent Shinto fanatics who inherited Ansai's Shinto teachings, a development detrimental to the intellectual quality of Suika Shinto's future. Kyōsai specifically regretted that Keisai did not receive the *den*.[122] There was, however, a reason for this. Ansai considered Keisai too sharp and analytical to be entrusted with Shinto teachings.

[120] KSZH 8: 4b; 9: 7b, 27a; 10: 9a; 9: 36b; 3: 30b; 9: 28b.
[121] Maruyama, "Ansaigaku," p. 581.
[122] KSZH 3: 16a–b, 9: 21a.

On this matter, Kyōsai reports Keisai as saying:

One should not bring reason to the explanation of Shinto. Once Ansai told me: "If a man of your ability were to lecture on Shinto, everyone would stand in awe, bow his head, and submit. That would be extremely easy, but such would be merely playing up to the Shinto texts (*shinsho o aishirau*) and the essence would escape. The way to read Shinto texts is first to innocently and naively present the old explanations. It is very important that you borrow the words of children."[123]

"At the time," Kyōsai wrote elsewhere," Keisai was young [he joined Ansai's school in 1679/6 at age twenty-seven], talented, dapper, and very inquisitive, and could not in an innocent and naive way swallow whole the 'simple' explanations of Shinto." Thus the field was left to "Shinto worshipers of a lesser intellectual quality like Ōgimachi Kinmichi"[124] Kubota Osamu has found further evidence that Ansai indeed discriminated among his students as to who could study Shinto and who could not. Miyake Shōsai, who joined in 1679, expressed an interest in Shinto, but was told that "while he was deeply involved in studies, he did not need Shinto," whereas someone else was instructed that he "could reverently study Shinto because he was slow and simple." Thus Ansai himself understood that the package of the truth mattered greatly. Some would find the truth in Shinto, while others had better not even try. He also claimed that he himself kept the two separate and did not discuss Neo-Confucianism in his Shinto lectures, and vice versa.[125]

Wakabayashi Kyōsai's effort to steer the Shintoists away from what in his eyes were simplistic and unpersuasive explanations is worth examining, because he became totally committed to Ansai's Confucianized Shinto. From his arguments, one senses the direction in which some of the other Suika Shinto followers were drifting. It is not that Kyōsai lacks a nationalistic conviction of Japan's superiority. To the contrary, he offers numerous arguments as to why the Japanese emperor is the only real emperor in the world (in other countries emperors are only the top of a social hierarchy, whereas in Japan the emperor was associated with the sun, of which there is only one in the universe); or why Japan is the center

---

[123] *Ibid.*, 5: 9b.
[124] *Ibid.*, 5: 11b.
[125] Kubota, "Kimon gakuha to Shintō," pp. 12–13; or *id.*, *Shintōshi no kenkyū*, pp. 604–605.

of the world (Japan is to the world what the heart is to the body because both have large quantities of Metal Energy). He attacks, however, the jingoism of those who label the reading of Chinese works as a treasonous act.[126] He also tries to translate into more sophisticated terms the central tenet of the unity of Heaven and man that is spoken of in the *Nihongi* in a mythological language. This language, he argues, is no longer understandable to his contemporaries.

Kyōsai fully subscribes to the central concept of the interpenetration of Heaven and man. Thus he argues that one should not emphasize the difference between the age of the gods and the age of man (the latter starts with the first emperor, Jinmu). That we count reigns starting with Jinmu, Kyōsai writes, is merely a convenient counting device. We do not start before Jinmu because the data are fuzzy in the time that Heaven and Earth were not yet separated; but, properly speaking, Jinmu is the sixth ruler. Yet, while maintaining the unity of mythology and history, Kyōsai also stresses constantly that there are ways of talking about the unity of Heaven and man that do not make sense today. Again and again he comes back to this point.[127]

According to Kyōsai, one cannot speak indiscriminately of man in Heavenly categories and about Heaven in human categories. Heaven, man, and things have their own separate ways and principles according to the *li-i fen-shu* (Jp *riichi bunshu*) rule of the unity of principle and the diversity of its particularizations. Today's Shinto scholars, however, indiscriminately and in an artificial way (*jinsaku de*) reduce everything to the "Age of the Gods." They forget that the language within which these two chapters of the *Nihongi* were written was a language generated by a time when Heaven and man were not yet separated. In those days, there were no words as in later ages.

Now we live in an age of civilization, Kyōsai continues. The difference between our time and the age of the gods is like the difference in a man's life between his adult years and the time when he was one with his mother's body in the womb. The language of children also differs from that of adults. One cannot talk to or treat adults as if they were children. Hence to adopt the language of the "Age of the Gods" is artificial (*sakui*), like adopting the coquettish

[126] KSZH 9: 39a, 8b; 8: 2b.
[127] *Ibid.*, 10: 26a–b; 1: 2a–b (also NST 31: 466); 2: 16b–17b; 8: 1b–2a; 9: 21b, 37a.

(*amae*) talk of children. Kyōsai thus tries to maintain the normative importance of creation while accomodating the impact of historical change.

The Chinese, Kyōsai also points out, went beyond the *Book of Changes*, their "Age of the Gods." Many sages have appeared to clarify that book, and adapt it to a literate civilization. Ansai certainly said that the *Book of Changes* was China's "Age of the Gods" and vice versa, but he did not mean to reduce all discussion to the "Age of the Gods." His saying was a slogan to draw attention to Shinto at a time when everybody was fascinated with Confucianism.

Neither does the essence of the unity of Heaven and man lie in the correspondences between the gods and yin and yang, the Five Evolutive Phases, and so on. If one speaks of it in that way, one may create the impression that such interpretation was forced (*waza to*), or that it was the purposeful intention of the ancients to write these correspondences into the text. This impression should be avoided because the concordance is natural.

Instead of such interpretations, Kyōsai stresses the unmanifest (*wei-fa*; Jp *mihatsu*) state of the time of the age of the gods as an exemplar for man's fundamental attitude. This emptiness of mind, comparable to the primeval chaos, should be penetrated by fear and reverence.[128] In this sense, the chaos of the myths and the unity of man and Heaven express man's ontological condition in the world—a condition that can be warped, however, by the slightest thought of selfishness. Man's mind should thus always be fully alert for the slightest deviation. What Kyōsai in his renovated Suika Shinto advocates is thus no different from Ansai's moral imperative or from a point made again and again by Naokata and Keisai: there is a world of difference between total perfection and the slightest mistake, but the tiniest selfish thought is essentially no different from the most hideous crime ("the slaying of one's lord").[129]

In all of Ansai's writings, this extreme asceticism seems to be intended exclusively for rulers, especially ministers (*shin, omi*), that is, the daimyo and samurai. The term "ministers," however, is ambiguous and may include all subjects. Yet Ansai never spells out that he has the people—all subjects—in mind. His silence con-

---

[128] *Ibid.*, 8: 5a; 9: 20a, 33b; 10: 9b, 11b.
[129] For examples, see NST 31: Ansai, pp. 25, 27, 41, 61, 87, 91, 93–94; Naokata, pp. 110, 117–19, 169; Keisai, p. 230.

trasts sharply with early eighteenth-century writers who consciously widened the category to include all Japanese. Kyōsai, for instance, broadens the etymological interpretation Ansai gave to the Nakatomi name (ministers that keep harmony, *naka*) to the commoners: all the people of the realm should be *Nakatomi*. Sarutahiko's teachings are beneficial "even for the peasants."[130] Ōgimachi Kinmichi argued that not only the recipients of the *den* but all Japanese, because gods dwell in their hearts, ought to have a "living shrine" Shinto name.[131] *Kei* ought to be kept by all the people (*banmin*). *Himorogi* came to be interpreted as a word that stood for Shinto shrine ("all shrines are dedicated to the protection of the emperor") and for the civic duty of all Japanese ("those who, while living in Japan do not keep it, are not Japanese").[132]

DISCIPLINE, REVERENCE, AND PRACTICE

Ansai put his stamp on two major intellectual movements of the Tokugawa period, and his students brought his teachings to an ever wider audience. Naokata lectured to an impressive number of daimyo.[133] Later, during the Kansei Reform, Kimon scholars staffed the Bakufu College. Suika Shintoists reached others. Takenouchi Shikibu (1712–1767) taught Suika Shinto to Emperor Momozono. The numerous Shinto priests among Ansai's followers must have brought elements of Suika doctrine to the commoners. Institutionally speaking, however, what Ansai had brought together did not stay together. Disputes and rifts multiplied within both Suika Shinto and the Kimon school as well as between them. Seemingly minor issues often hardened into permanent divides in this fundamentalistic, all-or-nothing philosophical landscape. Yet on each side of these multiplying partitions that separated Suika from Kimon, caused hostility between Naokata and Keisai, alienated both of them from Ansai, and forced Kyōsai to distance himself from his Suika colleagues, we find

---

[130] KSZH 9: 26a; 10: 27a.

[131] SZS 18: 7b.

[132] Matsuoka, "Shodenshō" (manuscript), under "Himorogi"; Tamaki, "Himorogi iwasaka gokuhi no den; sanshu shinpo gokuhi no den" (Manuscript, Kyoto daigaku; no pagination). These two *den* (together with a third one) were not reprinted in 1935 in Masahide's *Gyokusenshū* (DNB 16: 377–498) because of their "top secret" character.

[133] They include daimyo from Fukuyama (Mizuno), Isezaki (Sakai), Nagashima (Masuyama), Dewa (Satake), Hikone (Ii) and others (Abe Ryūichi, "Kimon gakuha shoke," p. 578.).

the same uncompromising demands for total, undivided dedication to high-minded ideals, be they individual spiritual perfection or the purity of national identity. In this respect, Ansai's spiritual descendants followed the same ethical agenda: the one Ansai had formulated.

Ansai's ideology thus came to inform ethical and political ideals whereby the rulers, and later all subjects, were enjoined to cultivate a militant, vigilant, ever-abiding self-watchfulness against all signs of selfishness. This ideal of moral inner-centeredness was not very different from what Neo-Confucianists in China strove for. Yet, while the prescriptions were not different, the political contexts in terms of which ethical action was defined in the two cultures created a profoundly different ethos in each.

First of all, Neo-Confucianism was a doctrine that in China had been geared to the ruling cadres and not to the masses.[134] The moral subjects it purported to create were upright officials who were exposed to numerous pressures and who shouldered heavy responsibilities in the conduct of human affairs. Some held literally dozens of posts, one after another, all across China. Chu Hsi's vision of the ideal human being was informed by an image of the ideal official who, as the one in charge of a large population, had to make numerous weighty and just decisions. This "one-man-rule" prevailed not only at the very top of the political hierarchy, but at its lowest echelons as well, where district magistrates were encouraged to take initiative. These officials, appointed in unfamiliar territory and often totally ignorant of the local dialect, had only their learning and their authority to go by. In their assigned posts, they had to impress their underlings and the people in general with their forbearance and strength of character. They could not rely on blood ties, house rank, or the sword. At the higher level, they had the privilege of remonstrance. Moreover, since they had an economic base to fall back on, principled withdrawal and resignation were genuine possibilities for them. Finally, the formative centuries of Neo-Confucianism (the Sung and Yüan) were periods of deep national crisis for China. Against this political background, Neo-Confucianism in China takes on an ethical grandeur and practical applicability that is often overlooked when its philosophy is discussed.

The Tokugawa situation stands in sharp contrast to this. The rank-and-file samurai, and even the daimyo, were not burdened

---

[134]Watanabe, "Tokugawa zenki Jugakushi," pp. 67–75.

with the kind of administrative and judicial responsibilities Chinese officials shouldered. In sheer numbers, Japan's ruling class was about seven times as large as China's. Samurai constituted between six and seven percent of the population, whereas by the end of the Ching dynasty, Chinese officialdom amounted to between three quarters of one percent and one percent of the total population.[135] Many samurai did not hold any office. However, unlike the members of the Chinese gentry who were degree-holders without office or stipend but who played genuine local leadership roles, these samurai were rulers, drew stipends, and in their castle towns lived isolated from the people. Secure in their position of domination, they lived complacently (although not necessarily in luxury) in an era of undisturbed peace. They needed neither knowledge nor self-cultivation to acquire or maintain their position of privilege. Their duty of protecting domains or castle towns against nonexistent enemies or of ritual attendance in Edo had become empty formalities.

The alarmist ethical urgency that resounds throughout Ansai's teachings impresses the distant observer (as it did Ansai's Tokugawa critics) as shrill and unfounded. In vain one searches for signs of national or local emergencies that could justify such alarm. The result of teachings such as Ansai's was to instill in the Japanese what strikes outsiders even today as an overzealous, undivided commitment of body and soul to routine quotidian tasks and details; the kind of energized mental state elsewhere considered legitimate and sustainable only in national political emergencies. As we have noticed, similar traits also characterized Suzuki Shōsan's ethical teachings. Ansai's construction of ethical and ideological formulae that were being taught to more and more Japanese by far outweighs any other achievements with which Ansai and his school have been credited; achievements that were all, in one way or another, ultimately related to ideology.[136]

[135] *Ibid.*, p. 74.

[136] Japanese scholars have credited Ansai and his school with responsibility for a variety of historical developments, some of which has been called into question by Maruyama Masao ("Ansaigaku," pp. 607–608). The most obvious issue is the jingoistic nationalism that, from among all the traditions Japan had to offer, singled out Ansai's japanized Neo-Confucianism and his revitalized Shinto as the most appropriate for its own ideological formulations.

Further, questions that Ansai raised for the first time stayed alive throughout the Tokugawa period and beyond. These issues were generated by Ansai's rigid fundamentalism: his determination to adopt Neo-Confucianism faithfully and literally, or at least adopt certain elements of it, as a guiding beacon. One such issue, endlessly debated well into the Meiji period, was the question of the adoption of heirs (see McMullen, "Non-agnatic

As in China, this discourse activated cosmic categories, yet the real-life situations that were described in Japan as the privileged locus of their ethical application strike one as disproportionately diminutive because devoid of visible political dimensions. In this scenario, the first sprouts of evil were always portrayed as horrible abominations with enormous repercussions. Koretaru writes that one thought reverberates through the whole realm and nation.[137] Everything in the universe, Keisai warns, resonates in man, and everything in man resonates in the universe. Thus it is imperative that evil thoughts be nipped in the bud, even before they appear in words or actions and one recognizes them as faults.[138] The inclination toward good and evil never ceases, and takes place in that space between no-thought and the emergence of one thought.[139] One has thus to pay close attention to the emergence of the smallest thought. Not a hair's breadth of desire can be allowed, because an ineluctable law of moral entropy will turn the slightest fault into the most abominable evil (which is always political evil: the killing of one's lord).[140] Such injunctions based on a logic of moral entropy were certainly not alien to Chinese teachings, but there the thoughts and decisions of the Emperor did resound throughout the realm.

Adoption"). In Japan, no restrictions limited the choice of candidates for adoption when no heirs were available, whereas ideal practice in China was restricted to agnates with the same surname. Following the latter, the Kimon School as a rule rejected nonagnatic adoption, whereas Suika followers argued against such a prohibition. (Ansai, Keisai, and Kyōsai died without natural heirs or provisions for adoption; their family names became extinct.)

Ansai was also the first to publish Chu Hsi's writings on the emergency granary system, which several daimyo subsequently implemented (*Shushi shasōhō*, published between 1658 and 1660, ZYAZ 2: 492–507; SGT 12, 334–35. Another question was the legitimacy of the Northern Imperial Court during the fourteenth century. Ansai, in his scant historical writings, was the first since that time to raise the question in public, now not as a burning political issue but as a matter of principle (Ozawa, *Kinsei shigaku*, p. 285). The issue became central to the later Mito School and the bakumatsu loyalists. Finally, Ansai insisted that scholars maintain political distance from those in power. A good number of Ansai's followers took this rule to heart, and this ideal constituted a critique of the Hayashi house.

In these specific and limited ways Ansai gave shape to Japan. The prewar nationalists, however, claimed without qualification that Ansai *was* Japan, which is why in postwar Japan he is largely rejected as a representative of an oppressive past that is better forgotten. Such wholesale rejection admits to the important place Ansai occupied in that past, especially in relation to the formation of ideology.

[137] DNB 15: 319.

[138] NST 31: 120; SGT 12: 238.

[139] Koretaru, DNB 15: 312.

[140] Ansai, *Daigaku Suika sensei kōgi*, NST 31: 25, 27, 41, 61; Naokata, *Keisaishin kōgi, ibid.*, pp. 118–19; Keisai, *ibid.*, p. 169.

The concrete images Naokata used to communicate the necessary state of mental alert are metaphors of extreme situations that galvanize all one's energies: one's response to a house on fire, battlefield situations, or being in the presence of an important personage. Thus one cannot relax even if one is alone. One should always hold oneself *as if* an important guest is about to arrive. Everything should be treated as an important matter, with caution and circumspection, *as if* one were handling a jug of water filled to the brim.[141]

The behavior to which such high "reverence" is prescribed, however, is minute etiquette of a very private nature. The heavy responsibilities shouldered by Chinese officials were not shared by most of their Japanese counterparts. Thus these teachings come down to such prescriptions as: "one's step should never be either clumsy or hurried but light; one's hands should always be firm *as if* one were reporting to a superior; when writing, one's posture and the way one grinds the inkstone or holds the brush should express single-minded concentration."[142] The purpose of this behavior was not to signify authority during the exercise of public functions. In Japan, self-cultivation had little public bearing; its radius of emanation was mostly a private one.

These virtues, however, *were* political virtues. To the extent that they came to regulate the life of more and more people, more and more Japanese came to *act as* "officials"—unknowingly, since the ideology misrepresented these political values as universal ethical values, and the conditions were lacking in which they could *be* officials.

As these values were taught as natural ones, so their pursuit had to be natural. Even the asceticism this entailed, an artificial effort that might reveal the unnatural character of the values if not properly presented, had to be "natural": the pursuit of reverence in everyday life, Naokata writes, has to be undertaken as if it were second nature, otherwise one will never attain it, as one can never catch one's own shadow; one has simply [mindlessly] to apply oneself with an undisturbed inner peace to whatever matter one deals with.[143] Yet this natural, effortless effort was obviously strenuous. Naokata also writes: "Buddhism is a convenient and easy teaching. A man with a mind no matter how evil can become a

---

[141] *Keisetsu hikki*; *ibid.*, pp. 112, 117–18.
[142] *Ibid.*, p. 117; Ansai, *Keisaishin kōgi*, *ibid.*, p. 87.
[143] Naokata, *Keisetsu hikki*, *ibid.*, p. 110.

Buddha by simply chanting the *nenbutsu*. Confucianism is far from an easy matter. If you don't spend your energies to the point of spitting blood, you will never become a sage or a gentleman." [144]

This ascetic effort should thus be pursued in that mental state between quietude and movement where the mind has been moved but has not yet manifested itself outward: between the void (*mu*)—which it is not because the mind has been set in motion, and manifestation (*u*)—which it is not because no outside traces have appeared yet; in the space (*ma*) between wanting to move and not-yet-moving. Thus reverence should penetrate both movement and quietness, although it is primarily quietness. [145]

Neither Buddhism nor mere book learning will bring about this state of mind: to rely simply on books is like mounting a wooden horse. Only sincere and total personal experiential self-realization (*taininjitoku*; Ch *t'i-jen tzu-te*) can achieve this. The whole bodily self (*mi no ue*) has to be penetrated with that experience. The method through which this is achieved is *seiza*, quiet sitting. [146]

Seiza is the means to acquire the quiet, undifferentiated mind in the middle of worldly affairs. It produces, Naokata argues, the ideal man of the Way. This true Confucian stands between the Buddhist and the layman or vulgar Confucian. Buddhists cultivate a dead quietness. Buddhism is about *sei no sei*, quietness in quietude, or, one might say, being contemplativus in contemplatione. The vulgar Confucian is *dō no dō*, all scattered activity, activus in actione. The true Confucian, however, is *sei no dō*, quiet in action, contemplativus in actione. [147]

Naokata's succinct formula refers to the same inner-worldly asceticism that Seika, Irin'an, and especially Shōsan were preaching. In the West, the ideal of "contemplativus in actione" was one that was held to be accessible only to religious specialists. It was the spiritual ideal on which the Society of Jesus was founded, an order that posited itself midway between the world and the cloister, yet in the world. In Japan, however, this became the normative ideal that was upheld and propagated by and for men in the world. An ideal of militant alertness, appropriate for an army, and an ideal of worldly detachment and inner perfection, appropriate for religious

[144] *Gakudan zatsuroku*; *ibid.*, p. 454.

[145] Ansai, SGT 12: 173; Naokata, *Keisetsu hikki*, NST 31: 103–104, 107.

[146] Naokata, *Shuseisetu*, SGT 12: 282; Keisai, *Seizasetsu hikki*, *ibid.*, p. 293; on *seiza*, see Naokata, SGT 12: 282–310.

[147] For this paragraph, see SGT 12: 284–85.

virtuosi, is what eventually came to form the core of the discipline expected from every Japanese when this ideology became the national ideology in modern times. The Ansai schools were major contributors to the ideology that buttressed this discipline.

The praxis associated with Ansai's ideology was stern and demanding, but this did not keep followers away. They were as numerous as those of the most famous teachers of the period. In concluding this analysis of Ansai's teachings, one cannot avoid trying to account for their distinctive importance.

THE patient reader who has followed us through the lush semiotic flora generated by Ansai's hermeneutics will probably have noticed that much of the vegetation looked familiar. Indeed, what Ansai has to say about a great number of things (emptiness of mind, reverence, Buddhism, the pristine language of primitive Shinto, the parallelism between the *I ching* and the "Age of the Gods," specific equivalences between Shinto mythemes and Confucian ideologemes), had already been said by others. A quick perusal of the composite picture drawn in Chapter 3 will immediately reveal many points of similarity, if not outright identity, between Ansai's teachings and earlier writings, especially on Shinto matters and the relationship between Shinto and Neo-Confucianism. This is equally true for Ansai's Neo-Confucian writings themselves. Here his source is not Yoshida or Ise Shinto but the writings of the Korean scholar Yi T'oegye (who had also exercised some influence on Seika and Razan).

If an analysis of the content of Ansai's teachings reveals little that is significantly new, how is one then to account for their powerful impact? For Ansai's influence was more lasting than that of the other writers we have discussed. Fujiwara Seika did not found a school. Hayashi Razan may have provided a number of warrior-administrators with some education, but it was one that lacked vigor and inspiration. His school almost disappeared in the eighteenth century, and when revived in 1790 was staffed with Kimon scholars. Suzuki Shōsan left no intellectual progeny.

Yamazaki Ansai's eccentric personality cannot adequately explain his long-range impact, either. During his own time, there is little doubt that his intense sense of a demanding and single Truth, his reputation as an accomplished student of Chu Hsi's thought, and his prestigious connection with Hoshina Masayuki helped him gather students. But Suzuki Shōsan, also an eccentric, was no less than Ansai convinced that his teachings constituted the whole and only Truth, and unremittingly insisted on ethical practice. Moreover, whereas some students gathered around Ansai exactly for these reasons, others (like Kaibara Ekken) were driven away by these same traits.[148]

If it is not the content of his teachings, the intensity of his claims to truth, his insistence on practice, or his eccentric character that set Ansai apart from his contemporaries, what produced, then, the strong commitment of so many to the truths of Ansai's teachings, Suika and Kimon alike? I would argue that perhaps the most important factor is the systematic structure of his thought. This structure gives his teachings, especially Suika Shinto, the "ideological closure" lacking in the other ideological constructs of the time.

Ansai's hermeneutic operations on the Shinto texts bear a striking resemblance to the patristic and medieval system of scriptural hermeneutics in the West. On first sight, such a parallel may appear to be of interest only to students of comparative religion and to be irrelevant to a discussion of ideology. Recently, however, Tzvetan Todorov has drawn attention to the importance of that tradition for the interpretation of symbolism as such.[149] Patristic theology applied four different levels of interpretation to the scriptures, and Fredric Jameson has argued that these four levels of interpretation perform what he calls the "ideological closure" of a text. Texts that in this way become carriers of a quadruple meaning are endowed with an ideological power capable of creating political subjects. In Althusserian terms, such an ideology force-

---

[148] Kaibara Ekken paid a visit to Ansai in 1657/4 (Osawa, *Kinsei shigaku*, p. 272), but seems to have disliked Ansai's rigorism. In any event, it is clear whom he has in mind in a passage of his *Taigiroku* (Record of great doubts; 1713) when he argues against the central importance *kei*, reverence, has come to acquire since Sung times. If one extolls *kei* over *chūshin* (loyalty/trust), one turns the means into an end, Ekken writes. Then, he continues, "even if one has the outside appearance of earnestness and solidity, inside one is diseased with weakness and feebleness; because without sincerity (*makoto*), things are worthless." He laments the kind of people produced by such teachings: "People today, in their obstinate and blind narrow-mindedness, do not understand [correctly] the letter [concept] *kei*. Shackled by the letter *kei*, they are single-minded, cramped, bigotted, rigid, compulsive. That is what their mind is like. They are dry, dessicated, without harmony, without joy. That is how they relate to others. They know nothing of the reality of affection or deep amicability; they are set on cruel harshness and stern censuring. That is the kind of people they are. Without humaneness or tolerance, their demeanor is intended to restrict and suppress. By temperament they are not [capable of] pursuing a calm and relaxed composition" (NST 34: 49). For a German translation, see Graf, *Kaibara Ekiken*, pp. 442–43.

[149] Todorov, *Symbolisme et interprétation* (1978).

fully addresses individuals, "interpellates" them with a force similar to a policeman's shout "Hey, you!", and transforms them into subjects, that is, constitutes them as singled-out self-conscious individuals and as persons who conduct their lives in an imagined relationship as if they were *subjected* to a transpersonal reality.[150]

In Suika Shinto as a whole, and in many of its doctrinal particulars, one can easily identify four levels of interpretation like those that govern patristic hermeneutics. Together *and simultaneously*, these four levels of interpretation induce an ideological transformation of the textual heritage of Japan's indigenous tradition. Ansai's systematic textual intervention can be summed up by saying that he constructed a new overall allegorical system that nevertheless preserved the literality of the original texts. By looking at the four stages through which this was accomplished, we can demonstrate the ideological character of this operation.

First, Ansai maintained the *literality* of the texts through the belief that they reported the real, "historical" beginnings of creation. As already mentioned, this is what separated Ansai from other Confucian scholars, who rejected these texts because they were nonhistorical. For Ansai, however, the *kami* of the creation story were real, the divine origin of the imperial house genuine.

At the same time, Ansai like others before him, made the data of the "Age of the Gods" available for a second, properly *allegorical* interpretation by subscribing to the universality of ethico-political teachings from China. These teachings were cast in a polythetic mode that assumed the analogical equivalence of signs. For instance, the number Five = the Center = the element Earth. In a similar vein, Ansai extended such sequences through the application of etymologizing strategies: = Amenomi*naka*nushi (*naka*, center) = *tsuchi* (earth) = *tsutsushimu* (reverence). This open-ended, epistemological mode within which universal truth was expressed made possible the rewriting of mythological truth. Thus,

[150] Jameson, *Political Unconscious*, pp. 29–31. The four levels of interpretation are: literal (historical), allegorical, moral (focused on the individual), and anagogical (collective meaning of history). Dante's examples of such fourfold investment of meaning are: the escape of Israel from Egypt = redemption in Christ = conversion of the soul from sin to grace = the sanctified soul reaching everlasting glory. Thomas Aquinas identifies the quadruple content of theological hermeneutics as follows: the Old Law in itself; the things of the Old Law signifying things of the New Law; things done in Christ as signs of what we should do; things that lie ahead in eternal glory (these examples are borrowed from Todorov, *Symbolisme et interprétation*). For a brief introduction to Louis Althusser's concept of ideology, see Larrain, *Concept of Ideology*, pp. 154–64. For Althusser's views, see his "Ideology and Ideological State Apparatuses," especially pp. 170–77.

familiar divine actors and actions were valorized as exemplars of political and ethical values.

This allegorical rewriting of the texts, which amounted to discovering a subtext under the mythological narrative, opened up in these texts a third, *moral* level that established relevances the individual was enjoined to adopt as imperatives of behavior. These texts now addressed, grabbed, interpellated the individual and insisted on his ethical practice. For Ansai and his students, the undifferentiatedness of primal chaos was a normative state of mind; the *kami* dwelled in the empty mind; one was a living shrine—one could even become Kunitokotachi. It is at this level that Ansai systematized and intensified to a higher degree the traditions that constituted his raw material.

Finally, Ansai further articulated an *anagogical* interpretation whereby these teachings were rewritten in terms of the destiny of Japan, a country superior to all others. Using the cosmic categories of the Five Phases, Ansai and his followers argued for a privileged place of Japan in the world, a claim they further buttressed by the uniqueness of the unbroken line of imperial succession.

The sequence of the simultaneous significations these texts were made to produce form more than a series: they constitute a cycle that can be described as follows: the texts, as the story of creation and the origins of the imperial family, first signified a collective dimension. Through allegorical modulations they were then reduced to moral teachings for the individual's perfection. Subsequently they were reopened, bringing along and maintaining religiously charged imperatives for behavior, to a new collective dimension. Japan as the collective present and future thus became the focus of the individual's intense cathexis. Individuals could in this way conceive of their ethical behavior and live their lives in an imagined relationship to a transpersonal reality, the nation. A system of representations that enables one to conceive of experience in this way is what Jameson, following Louis Althusser, calls an ideology. Texts and teachings that have been reworked in this way have achieved ideological closure.

This is not to deny the ideological dimensions of writings such as those of Suzuki Shōsan or the Kimon School. It only draws attention to an additional characteristic of Ansai's teachings, one that can be called full ideological closure and that may help explain the energetic response Ansai's teachings provoked, nonwithstanding the toll on logic and rationality they exacted. The process just described is as much a japanization (or domestication) of Neo-Confucianism, as it often has been called, as an ideologization of Shinto teachings (which were previously the private property of Shinto families and thus lacked social impact).

The Kimon School's teachings were not structured along the above four levels of interpretation. Satō Naokata, indeed, rejected outright all japanization efforts. Yet he prescribed an equally intense and unbending dedication to the minutiae of daily comportment, discipline, and ethical ideals. At the collective level, his loyalty was not to the nation but to the state (bakufu stability), upholding as he did the primacy of bakufu law against the apologists for the forty-seven rōnin. Asami Keisai, also a Kimon scholar, in his *Seiken igen*, emphasized the need for absolute loyalty to Japan. There was a constant cross-over of students between the two schools (Wakabayashi Kyōsai, Atobe Yoshiaki). Although perhaps working with a different scheme that could not be said to effect a full ideological closure (Naokata and Keisai attached no significance to the Shinto myths of origins, yet they were deeply committed, respectively, to the "state" and the "nation"), the Kimon School could, to the same degree as Suika Shinto, absorb the individual without remainder into society.

Although Ansai's predecessors had occasionally performed a complete ideological operation on single Shinto mythemes, Ansai's particular contribution to this tradition is clear. He worked out a comprehensive and systematic articulation of all core tenets of the Chinese with the Japanese tradition (the allegorical level of interpretation); he stressed more intensely than others the imperative of ethical practice (the moral level or interpretation), and laid the groundwork for a full development of the "nationalistic" dimension (the anagogical level of interpretation). Most important, whereas prior piecemeal ideological transformations of Shinto were performed secretly within the established Shinto theological families of Ise and Yoshida (in their secret commentaries or *den*), Ansai performed his operation in public for rulers and a great number of students. One generation later, Japanese from all walks of life were being interpellated by his teachings.

During the early Tokugawa period Neo-Confucianism was liberated from the confines of the Buddhist monastic establishment and made available for broad ideological use. Shōsan, in turn, deinstutionalized and politicized Buddhism in the same way. And Ansai set Shinto free from its confinement to the circle of Shinto specialists, and made it also available for ideological investment. Thus, through Yamazaki Ansai's teachings, the *kami* and other items of the Shinto tradition came to be valorized in an ideologically and politically significant way, at a personal and national level, as ethical exemplars.

Early Tokugawa ideology, through both discourse and ritual, wrought a great transformation in Japanese society by constructing, more or less in succession, three new political realities: it transformed warriors into virtuous rulers; it signified a new society, clearly segmented and divided at the political and social level, as a sacred undifferentiated whole; and it created committed subjects out of the mass of the ruled.

Eight. Conclusion: History and Silence, Tokugawa Ideology Reconstructed

Ieyasu had conquered the nation on horseback, but being an enlightened and wise man, realized early that the land could not be governed from a horse. He had always respected and believed in the Way of the Sages. He wisely decided that in order to govern the land and follow the path proper to man, he must pursue the path of learning. Therefore, from the beginning he encouraged learning.—*Hayashi Razan*[1]

The enabling moment for this study consisted of calling into question what historiographical tradition had transmitted as an undisputed fact: that Neo-Confucianism was put to use by Tokugawa Ieyasu as a bakufu ideology. As we now know, this "fact" was itself an ideological construct. It thus became impossible to proceed unreflectingly to an analysis of Tokugawa ideology from a routine reference to the classic passage of the *True Tokugawa Records* (*Tokugawa jikki*) quoted above, which until now has located a historical beginning, the natural starting point of inquiry and exposition.

As we have seen, the emblematic links this text and others like it establish between Neo-Confucianism, the Hayashi house, and Ieyasu were in fact manufactured by Hayashi scholars in the 1660s. Such passages from the *Tokugawa jikki*, as it turns out, are actually quotes from Seika's biography, written by Razan, and from Razan's biographies, written by his two sons. The *Tokugawa jikki* were compiled in the first decades of the nineteenth century—by Hayashi scholars. By then, the question of a bakufu-enforced orthodoxy had become a genuine issue. Therefore, these texts reflect concerns with political realities in the 1660s and 1800s and cannot be considered accurate accounts of Ieyasu's policies. Early Tokugawa ideology thus came to constitute not a ready-made object of analysis, but a problematic, uncharted terrain to be explored.

In the course of this study, I have pusued a number of questions within this field and refurnished the landscape with new landmarks. This reconstruction is not without its own problems. The

---

[1] Quoted in the *Tokugawa jikki* (early 1800s) 1: 339, quoted in Maruyama, *Studies*, p. 15.

first question is a direct consequence of the inappropriateness of the "single actor/single doctrine" scheme. The recognition of the historicity and complexity of Tokugawa ideology exploded its unquestioned singularity of doctrine and intention into a multiplicity of objects and producers. What can one say, if anything, about the consciousness and motives of these producers? Broadly speaking, it seems that one is confronted by the dilemma of interpreting ideology either as a mask or as a veil.[2] Were these constructs consciously intended to hide the particular interests of the ruling class, or did they function as a subliminal veil that unconsciously refracts such interests? Are they the result of a plot to deceive, or, more innocently, are they expressions of a false consciousness?

In addition, we must address the question of why historians have spoken so spontaneously of a Tokugawa ideology, whereas they do not endow earlier epochs with analogous constructs. Have they merely fallen victim to Hayashi Razan's representation of the "facts," and should we therefore stop speaking of a Tokugawa ideology? Or, conversely, is there an Ashikaga or Kamakura ideology that has never been named? This traditional nomenclature and its absence in scholarship on pre-Tokugawa times suggests that seventeenth-century Japan witnessed the first emergence of ideology.

Let us start with the question of motivation. Ideology displays its most conspicuously binding force in the realm of political legitimacy.[3] It effects a social agreement, in thought and action, to view a system of government as legitimate and just. For Tokugawa Japan, this meant the preservation of the dominant position of certain warrior families over other warrior houses and the commoners, secured during the previous decades. This position had been obtained by force of arms. Although the aims of establishing legitimacy are the same as those of warfare, legitimacy, being a matter of assent not achieved through coercive force alone, calls for other means. Ideology can thus be seen as a continuation of warfare with other means and, indeed, only achieves its aims if it can relegate power to the background of public consciousness.

In this different kind of warfare, a particular type of weapon was used in a very deliberate manner: an armory of significations that were strategically directed against all contenders for power. Japan's supreme rulers, from Oda Nobunaga through Tokugawa

[2] Merquior, *The Veil and the Mask*.
[3] On this Weberian view, see *ibid.*, p. 1.

Iemitsu, consciously deployed signifying strategies by mythologizing their personae and their positions. They transformed their military power into sacred authority, their rule into an embodiment of the Way of Heaven. Nobunaga and Hideyoshi confronted other warlords and the commoners as their rivals for power, and their personal cults were aimed at both. The emperor, however, was still a resource that could be used in their struggle against these rivals. He was therefore more the object of political maneuvres than of symbolic manipulations.

The Tokugawa faced a different situation. The final annihilation of peasant resistance by force of arms had eliminated the commoners as challengers of Tokugawa power, and hence as targets for legitimizing efforts. The Tokugawa shoguns aimed their symbolic manipulations at those contenders who were left. All the daimyo and housemen, and now the emperor, formed the audience for the Ieyasu cult.

The broader ideological constructs that marshaled discursive argument for the correctness of the new political system were by and large, however, not commissioned by the bakufu. The misrecognition of the new system of domination as a regime of virtue was created primarily through the activity of a new class of schoolmen. Not only does power generate private interests (which it tries to hide by generalizing them); private interests also seek power. Thus a class of learned men that included doctors, monks, exmonks, déclassé warriors, and teachers, who were left outside the new power structure but who, unlike the peasants and other commoners, had a rich body of knowledge (Buddhist, Shinto, and Neo-Confucian) at their disposal, used this knowledge to draw themselves closer to the center. Their strategic "intentions" were private and possibly even unconscious—it is more difficult to discern their motives than those of the new rulers. What is important, however, is that they all contributed to a discourse that served these rulers.

By constructing a discourse about the warrior class, these men furthered the consolidation of that class. They provided the warriors with a clearer class identity than they had ever had before, simply by objectifying them in a discourse that excluded all others except marginally as the ruled. More specifically, their teachings stressed the need for maintaining the warrior class as the ruling class (through its monopoly on virtue) and maintaining the hierarchy within that ruling class (through the loyalty of ministers to the lord). Suzuki Shōsan is perhaps an exception. He preached not only to samurai but also to commoners. Yet he taught an analogous apolitical (work) ethic of selfless, dedicated productivity in the service of the whole society; one that was an extension of the samurai ethic.

Although this discourse was not constructed by bakufu order, it filled a space whose boundaries had been marked, for the bakufu had made it clear what could and could not be said. Those whose speech and practice were different were driven underground (*kakure*), as the suppression of Christianity and certain Buddhist sects demonstrates. In this respect, Kumazawa Banzan's harassment, and especially Yamaga Sokō's banishment, have been misapprehended by most historians, who have interpreted these incidents as proof of an enduring bakufu concern with orthodoxy. Rather, they were passing phenomena. The ban on Christianity and on the Ikkō and Fujufuse sects, however, constituted lasting policies. This suppression indicates that the discourse that *did* develop did not represent universal interests. The homogeneity of early Tokugawa discourse was the result of subtle (and not so subtle) limits set on discursive activity and practice. Neither did this homogeneity express a general consensus—even though the universal claims of this discourse projected the appearance of a consensus on truth—arrived at in a constraint-free atmosphere. For some groups, the special interests of the bakufu remained exactly that; they rejected the bakufu's representation of its own particular interests as generally beneficial to the whole society.[4] It is not surprising then, that some prominent daimyo and bakufu leaders (in the 1660s) showed an active interest in a discourse that had been constructed under such conditions. These two factors of selective suppression and semi-official interest have led to the assumption that one is dealing with a "state ideology" in early Tokugawa Japan.

Although the links between this discourse and power were more subtle than the term indicates, early Tokugawa discourse certainly constituted an ideology. It was eminently serviceable for political purposes precisely because, having homogenized knowledge within ethical and cosmic categories, it was silent on the subjects of power and domination.

Whether the propagators of this discourse plotted to obfuscate

[4]Jürgen Habermas discusses the question of generalizable interests in his *Legitimation Crisis*, p. 111.

the interests of the ruling class they often eagerly sought to serve; or whether, overwhelmed by the new order and peace in society, and habituated to the new limits this order imposed (and which they may not have recognized as limits), they were blinded and trapped in a false consciousness of the nature of domination of the new political system is irrelevant for our purposes. It is not necessary to measure the moral integrity or ironic perspicacity of these men, for whether they were trying to deceive or whether they themselves were among the deceived, the effect on society was the same. The public knowledge of society they constructed was a deception—a deception perhaps without deceivers but certainly with a large number of deceived. Their representations stood as a movement around and away from power, a substitution for it. This substitution, however, erased its own human, artificial, contingent character because it was presented under the guise of a natural knowledge about all of reality.

Finally, some sense must be made of the impression historians have given, perhaps unwittingly, that the construction of Tokugawa ideology constitutes the emergence of ideology *per se* in Japan. Are we dealing with—to use another metaphor—the birth of ideology in Japan? Part of the answer, which I believe is an affirmative one, is already contained in the way I have used the concept: as a continuation of warfare with other means, a warfare that pitted two identifiable social classes against one another. I shall try to demonstrate that I am not drawing a bull's eye around the hole in the fence after having fired the shots.

The thesis implies that pre-Tokugawa Japan, properly speaking, had no ideology because it had no class confrontation. In other words, the question becomes the following: what is it that characterizes pre-Tokugawa society if it is not class antagonism, and what can we call the discursive representations of society present in those periods if we cannot call them ideologies? To provide plausible answers to this double question in the form of concluding remarks is difficult. Nevertheless, one can argue as follows.

The place warriors occupied in Japanese society between their emergence in the Kamakura period and the end of the fifteenth century was not destructive of the prevailing social and economic arrangements that were structured around the *shōen* (manor) system. These warriors came to acquire a commanding position in society by inserting themselves into the network of legal land rights that constituted that system. They were an additional number of individuals who, together with others, shared profits from the land, and indeed saw to it that the others got their rightful shares. The *shōen* system consisted largely of a system of dues, a complicated patchwork of graded rights to products from the land—rights that were divided among the workers on the land, landowners, property managers (often samurai), and commendee-guarantors of these rights (temples, noble houses, and warrior leaders).

Although one can argue that any legal structure is not without its covert ideological dimensions, the *shōen* system certainly was not ideologically objectified. Its cohesion and universal character as a national system is only the product of the privileged gaze of the historian. The system was not generated, through legislation, by a political center. It developed locally as contingent arrangements that were protected by a higher authority. The warriors became part of these arrangements, no doubt encroaching on the interests of some, but not threatening the interests of a whole class. This may help explain the absence of any formal ideology, even of a warrior ideology, during those centuries. Any attempt at teasing one out of the meager writings of a few daimyo (mainly house rules) shows interpretive strain and fails to convince.[5]

The superimposition of rights in the *shōen* system prevented, at the local level, any group of persons from building a clear, exclusive relation to the land, and thus also hindered the development of autonomous local communities organized as genuinely bounded units. It is only when warrior bands began to cut into these legal relationships, and through force to build contiguous domains out of these legal estates that various structural changes took place: the commoners, freed from legal bondage, started to organize themselves into self-contained, self-managing local communities; these commoners now suddenly encountered a new, single enemy, the warriors; a conflict thus arose over legitimate control of the land between commoners and warriors; and a more comprehensive social unit, the contiguous domain, emerged victorious from this struggle: the domain that was a microcosmic society. This novel social creation, incorporating the new local community of the village, demanded a clarification of the status different classes of people would hold within it (witness the *Tako House Code*). Furthermore, this was the first time in Japanese history that commoners at the local level in such great numbers were involved in a

---

[5] See Steenstrup, *Hōjō Shigetoki*.

struggle for power against domination by another group, clearly perceived by them as an undesirable class: the warriors who sought to centralize power. These warriors, in turn, perceived and treated the commoners as a class different from their own—witness the differences in Nobunaga's methods of warfare and his treatment of the enemy when the enemy consisted of Ikkō commoners rather than other samurai. Finally, the very transparent, arbitrary character of this domination called for justification or rejection at the level of legitimizing arguments.

The peasants resisted by force of arms and by formulating their arguments in a world view that had no place for a warrior class, but only for themselves as direct servants of Buddha or the emperor. It was precisely to undercut this world view that Nobunaga arrogated for himself divine status and cast himself in the role of protector of the emperor and guarantor of supernatural blessings. The first ideological formulations of the period under study were thus put together as a counter-strategy to the world view of the peasants.

However, in the following decades Tokugawa ideology did not displace a pre-Tokugawa ideology. The peasant contruct, which I call a world view, was only prevalent in a few provinces, and it did not constitute a societywide ideology (meant for all classes of people and comprehensive in the scope of phenomena it addressed) that was displaced by analogous Tokugawa constructs.[6] The interests served by this world view, which was chiefly an appeal to higher authority against intruders, a refusal to pay taxes to the warriors, were still clearly visible as the interests of one class and were not generalized to include those of the intruders in any way.

Tokugawa ideology succeeded much better in obfuscating the class interests of the warriors within a discourse about the nature of society as a whole. This included the commoners, even if they were simply taken for granted as recipients of virtue. The Tokugawa, in order to stay in power, had to consign to oblivion the class conflict that lay in fact beneath the new system of domination. Watanabe Hiroshi has recently remarked that references one finds in the early Tokugawa writings to "the four classes" were stylistic conventions used to speak of "the people."[7] If this is correct, then such re-

---

[6] I am aware that I reverse Lucien Goldmann's distinction between world view and ideology; see his "Genetic Structuralism," p. 114, and his *Essays on Method*, pp. 12, 22–24, 111–15.

[7] Watanabe, "Tokugawa zenki Jugakushi," pp. 32–33.

ferences are not proof that the early discourse gave a clear identity to the various classes of the ruled: their identity was subsumed under the larger one of being nonrulers.

One can thus conclude that a novel situation necessitated the production of an all-embracing new discourse on society, that the production of a new knowledge became for the first time in Japanese history an integral part of the strategy for power. This power, of national dimensions, had to produce not a new truth about a society that was already there, but a truth about a society that was being fashioned for the first time along a clear line of demarcation separating a new class of rulers from the ruled.

That truth, however, was of the nature of a half-truth perceived as the whole truth. The truth about the new society that could not be told was that it was an arbitrary system of domination by a few over the many, with no intrinsic rationale. This system had to be signified through a distorted knowledge about itself.

Throughout this study, I have relied on this particular view of ideology, and I also have consistently characterized the Tokugawa system as a system of domination. Some may object to such historiographical practice as being informed by preconceived notions rather than by the historical reality it pretends to portray with some accuracy. And, indeed, much of my vocabulary comes from theoretical writings. In defense of my choice I can adduce the following argument that is partly inspired by Jürgen Habermas's model of the suppression of generalizable interests and his notion of an ideal speech situation.

Since ideology (for the most part in an inconspicuous yet systematic manner) limits social knowledge, it necessarily establishes silences that suppress generalizable interests that run counter to the particular interests the ideology serves. Because silences leave no record, Habermas proposes a counterfactual reconstruction of a hypothetical state of a system of norms that would be arrived at in a constraint-free setting. This construction should be guided by the question of "how members of a social system would in this way have collectively and bindingly interpreted their needs." Where would conflicts of interest have arisen? Habermas invites us to "conceptualize the non-events of suppressed, that is latent, claims and needs." [8] It would seem that if such a reconstruction can point in a convincing manner to silences as fields of buried needs and

---

[8] Habermas, *Legitimation Crisis*, pp. 111–17, esp. pp. 113, 114. See also Lukács, *History and Class Consciousness*, pp. 50–53.

interests, then our particular use of ideology to define early Tokugawa political thought is fully warranted.

In our case, we are not dealing with total silence. There are a number of indications that this silence was the result of pressures that have left traces and can be documented. Certainly, the tens of thousands of peasants who were slaughtered in the last decades of the sixteenth century and in the Shimabara rebellion, and the sudden disappearance of those voices representing their interests are proof of this.[9] The imperial institution was also slowly subjected to warrior authority, sometimes in humiliating ways. The signs of resistance and protest are there, however. Emperors Ōgimachi and Goyōzei used the meager means at their disposal to domesticate warrior power: the granting of court rank and office to warriors. But even that authority was taken away. As tensions grew between the bakufu and the court, Emperor Go-mizunoo resorted to the only means of protest left to him: abdication. In 1629, at age thirty-five, he surprised the bakufu by leaving the throne to his six-year-old daughter, who became Empress Meishō. The yearly pilgrimage of imperial emissaries to a substitute Amaterasu in the Nikkō mausolem, which was serviced after 1647 by the emperor's brother, is symbolic of the final subjugation of imperial authority to that of the bakufu.

Historiography is another discursive field that points to significant silences. Records pertaining to the origins of the Tokugawa family were, at the time, considered secret. Further, only those histories that did not name power but constructed events as the natural victory of the virtuous over the evil were printed, as we know from the existence of other histories that survived only in manuscript form. The Hayashi scholars carefully distinguished between their private opinions and what they could profess openly.

These intrinsic aspects of early Tokugawa history justify speaking of ideology as a representation that served a particular system of domination. From Tokugawa Japan there is another voice, however—one that barely survived to the present, and unambiguously spoke of ideology and society in an even more radical way.

[9] Bitō Masahide would disagree with this interpretation. Referring to the "Warring States" period, he writes, rather surprisingly, that the transition from the middle ages to the early modern period was "relatively smooth" and that the "soldier/peasant division" was "carried out with no resistance" ("Society and Social Thought," pp. 3, 6). On other points, we are in full agreement: the emphasis on functional usefulness for every member of society he finds in early Tokugawa (pp. 4–6), or his view that authority was not "legitimized through self-conscious theories" (p. 7).

This is Andō Shōeki (1703–1762?), about whom little is known and whose writings were not discovered until well into the Meiji period. He must have escaped the bakufu's attention; otherwise his work would have disappeared into the silence with which the bakufu surrounded itself. Shōeki, in speaking what should not have been said, was a voice from this silence:

The Way of the Sages functioned to make excuses for thieves. . . . Beginning with Fu Hsi, Shen Nung, the Yellow Emperor, Yao, Shun, Yu, T'ang, Wen, Wu, the Duke of Chou . . . and all the sages, saints, and Buddhas down through the generations in Japan, including Hayashi Razan . . . violated the Way of Heaven by robbing the common people.[10]

For Shōeki, all teachings were ideology, and ideology nothing more than an excuse to rob the people.[11] The system it served, according to him, was one not of domination but of outright exploitation. This is an indigenous voice from Tokugawa Japan, chronologically not far removed from our period (and closer to it than the *Tokugawa jikki*). Scholars have listened for too long to another indigenous voice, that of Hayashi Razan, for whom Neo-Confucianism was an orthodoxy and a truth. Andō Shōeki's views, like those of Razan (or any other writer), are partial views, but the time has come to look at Tokugawa ideology through Shōeki's eyes rather than Razan's. Shōeki's views are more to the point.

[10] Quoted in Maruyama, *Studies*, p. 255.

[11] For a Tokugawa story in which a genuine robber, caught by the police, defended his occupation as one ordained by Heaven, see *Toda Mosui zenshū*, pp. 198–99. I owe this reference to Watanabe, "Tokugawa zenki Jugakusi," p. 49.

Epilogue

EARLY Tokugawa ideology, as I have argued, was Japan's first ideology. In a sense, it is also the only one Japan has ever had. Social and political values in present-day Japan maintain the structure they received in the seventeenth century.

At that time, the professed aim of the new warrior ruling class was to protect society against the danger of social and political chaos. That obsession with order has continued undiminished, and still shows traces of the manner in which such an order was first institutionalized. By leading armies far greater than any Europe had ever known by that time, Tokugawa rulers learned to organize and manage great masses of people. They were able to transfer these skills from the military to the social and political realm. Military regimentation came to inform the model of social order. In their search for comprehensive stability, these rulers extended political control and social integration as far as they could: the villages became production brigades and everyone became an "official." To be useless was uncivic, and insubordination and separation were targeted as the principal forms of social disruption. These evils were fought by laws that gave shape to institutions, ideology that formed model citizens, and discipline that regulated behavior.

During the Tokugawa period, the threat of disruptive forces was internal. For the last century, that threat came both from within and from beyond Japan's borders. To this day, those in power in Japan have not lost an acute anxiety about an integrated whole without fissures. It is only within the constraints of this persistent concern for the whole that in Tokugawa and modern Japan a variety of ideas and practices were given room to develop. In Tokugawa Japan, these developments included ideological constructs formulated by all the major traditions, but also a market economy. During the last century, they have encompassed a variety of phenomena such as a constitutional monarchy, fascism, democracy, labor legislation, and capitalism. When, in the 1890s, the Japanese government needed to stipulate what values were to shape model citizens through the educational system, the state, in its role as educator, turned to those values that had proven effective since the early Tokugawa period. During the crisis of the 1930s, when an even sharper delineation of nationhood was needed, one that could mobilize the Japanese to the highest degree, the state turned to Yamazaki Ansai's ideology. In the last decades, the Japanese have once again become preoccupied with themselves, not in an atmosphere of anxiety or crisis, but with a sometimes arrogant sense of self-confidence. This time, the focus of their attention is Japan's economic success. And again, they have begun to praise the (capitalist) benefits to be drawn from a maintenance of "feudal" and quasi-military values.

Japan's future is intimately tied to the fate of this ideology. Its relative strength will help decide to what degree such values can be maintained, benefits accrued, and social problems addressed and resolved.

Character List

THIS list includes names, terms, phrases, and titles that are cited in the main text and the text of the notes, and that do not appear in the bibliography.

ai 愛
Aigo no waka 愛護の若
aishirau アイシラフ
Aizu 会津
Akamatsu Hiromichi 赤松広通
Akechi Mitsuhide 明智光秀
Akō 赤穂
amae 甘へ
Amakusa 天草
Amakusa Shirō 天草四郎
Amaterasu (Ōmikami) 天照 (大御神)
Amenominakanushi-no-mikoto 天御
　中主尊
Amida 阿弥陀
Andō Shōeki 安藤昌益
Arai Hakuga 新井白蛾
are hitori 吾身一ツ; 一身而己
Aremi 視吾
Asano Nagashige 浅野長重
Asano Yoshinaga 浅野幸長
Ashikaga 足利
Ashikaga Takauji 足利尊氏
Ashikaga Yoshiaki 足利義昭
Ashikaga Yoshimitsu 足利義満
Asuke 足助
Atobe Yoshiaki 跡部良顕
Azuchi-jō 安土城
Azuma kagami 東鑑
Azumateru kamumioya no mikoto
　東照神御祖命

bakufu 幕府
banmin 万民
batabata バタバタ
Ben Rin Dōshun Honchō kōmoku 弁林道
　春本朝綱目
Bonsan 盆山
Bonshun 梵舜
bu (measure) 分; (military) 武

budō 武道
Buke shohatto 武家諸法度
bun 文
buppō 仏法
buppōshōnin 仏法商人
bushi 武士
Bushi nichiyō 武士日用

Chai-chū kan-hsing shih 斎居感興詩
Chang Tsai 張載
Chan Ken-ch'ing 詹艮卿
chen-chi 真機
Ch'eng Hao 程顥
Cheng-meng 正蒙
Ch'eng Yi 程頤
Cheng-kuan cheng-yao, see Jōgan seiyō
Ch'en Shun 陳淳
Chieh (king) 桀
Ch'ien (hexagram) 乾
chigi 知義
Chikamatsu 近松
chiki 千木
chimatsuri 血祭
Ching-yen chiang-i (Jp *Kei'en kōgi*) 経筵
　講義
Chin-ssu lu (Jp *Kinshiroku*) 近思録
Chi Tzu 箕子
Chou (dynasty) 周; (king) 紂
Chou I Ch'eng chu'an 周易程伝
Chou I pen-i 周易本義
Chou Tun-yi 周敦頤
chū, *see* naka
Chūai (emperor) 仲哀
Chu Hsi 朱熹
chūkō 忠孝
Chu-ko K'ung-ming 諸葛孔明
chung, *see* naka
ch'ung-mo wu-chen, *see Chūbaku-*
　muchin(setsu) in bibliography under

Yamazaki Ansai
chūshin 忠信
Chu Shun-shui 朱舜水
chūtoku 中徳
Chu Tzu wen-chi 朱子文集
Chu Tzu yü-lei 朱子語類
Chü-yu ts'ao (Jp *Kōyūsō*) *see in bibliography under* Yamazaki Ansai

daibutsuden 大仏殿
daikan 代官
daimyo 大名
daimyōjin 大明神
Dainihonshi 大日本史
Daitokuji 大徳寺
Dajōdaijin 大政大臣
Date Masamune 伊達政宗
den 伝
Dewa 出羽
dō 堂
dōgaku 道学
dōgakusha 道学者
dokon 土金
dō no dō 動の動
dōri 道理
dōshin 道心
Dōshun 道春
dōtō, *see* tao-t'ung

Echizen 越前
Edo 江戸
eejanaika ええじやないか
emakimono 絵巻物
Engi 延喜
Engishiki 延喜式
Enryakuji 延暦寺
Erh Ch'eng chüan-shi 二程全集

Fabian (不干斎)ハビアン
fuda 札
fudai 譜代
Fuden 普伝
fudoki 風土
Fu Hsi 伏羲

Fuji no mori 藤森
Fujita Yūkoku 藤田幽谷
Fujiwara Kamatari 藤原鎌足
Fujufuse 不受不施
fukai 附合
Fukuoka 福岡
Fukuyama 福山
fumie 踏絵
funbetsu 分別
funbetsu no shioki subekarazu 分別ノ仕置スベカラズ
Fushimi 伏見
Futodama 太玉

gagaku 雅楽
gakumon 学問
gakuryo 学侶
Genji 源氏
genki 元気
Genna 元和
Genroku 元禄
geppō 月報
gi 義
Gifu 岐阜
gimin 義民
giri 義理
giri no ōyake 義理ノ公
Gobusho 五部書
Go-chinza denki 御鎮座伝記
Go-chinza hongi 御鎮座本紀
Godaigo (emperor) 後醍醐
gokenin 御家人
goki 五気
Gokomatsu (emperor) 後小松
Gokōmyō (emperor) 後光明
Gomizunoo (emperor) 後水尾
gomyōdai 御名代
gongen 権現
Gokurakuji 極楽寺
Goyōzei (emperor) 後陽成
Gozan 五山
gū 宮
gyō 行
gyōja 行者

Gyōnen (prince) 堯然
Gyōreki (Ch Yao-li) 堯暦
Gyūkōji 吸江寺

Hachiman 八幡
hajime 始
Hakurokudō shoin keiji, see Po-lu-tung shu-
  yüan chieh-shih
Hanitsu 土津
Han Yü 韓愈
haori 羽織
hara 腹
Harima 播磨
hatamoto 旗下
Hattori Ankyū 服部安休
Hayashi Hōkō 林鳳岡
hei 兵
Heian 平安
Heike 平家
hibun ni 非分に
Hie 日吉
Hiei 比叡
Higo 肥後
hijiri 聖
hikimawari sarashi 引廻晒
Hikone 彦根
hikura 火蔵
Himorogi 神籬
Hirata Atsutane 平田篤胤
Hiroshima 広島
hito no hitotaru 人の人たる
hitori 一身
hito to wa . . . kurai aru mono nari
  「人」トハ…位アルモノナリ
Hiyoshi 日吉
Hiyoshimaru 日吉丸
ho (Jp wa) 和
hōbōryō 宝坊領
Hōjō 北條
Hōki hongi 宝基本記
Hokke 法華
hōkō 奉公
Hōkōji 方広寺
Hōkoku 豊国

Hōkoku daimyōjin 豊国大明神
Hōkokuji 豊国寺
Hōkokusai zubyōbu 豊国祭図屏風
Hōkokuzan 豊国山
hokora ホコラ
hon, *see* moto
Hon'ami Kōetsu 本阿弥光悦
honchi 本地
Honda Masazumi 本多正純
Honganji 本願寺
honji-suijaku 本地垂迹
hon-matsu 本末
Honnōji 本能寺
honshin 本心
Hori Kyōan 堀杏庵
Hoshina Masayuki 保科正之
Hosokawa Gracia 細川ガラシア
Hosokawa Tadaoki 細川忠興
Hosokawa Tadatoshi 細川忠利
hōteki 法敵
hotoke 仏
Ho t'u 河図
Hsia 夏
Hsiao-hsüeh 小学
Hsieh Chao-che 謝肇淛
Hsieh Ching-hsien 薛敬軒
Hsi-ming 西銘
hsin-fa (Jp shinpō) 心法
Hsing-kung pien-tien tsou-cha (Jp
  Angūbenden no sōsatsu) 行宮便殿奏劄
Hsing-li wu-shu 性理五書
Hsin-sheng chih-chih 心聖直指
hsin-tsang, *see shinzō*
hsin t'u yeh 心土也
Hsü Hun 許渾
Huang Chen 黄震
Huang-ti nei-ching su-wen 黄帝内経素問
Hui-an 晦菴
Hui-neng 慧能
Hung fan 洪範
Hung fan huang-chi nei-p'ien 洪範皇極
  内篇
hun-p'o, *see konpaku*
hyō 俵

i 意

Ichijitsu Shinto 一実神道

ichijō 一条

Ichijō Kanera (or Kaneyoshi) 一条
　兼良

I ching 易経

ichirei 一霊

ichiri 一理

ichiza 一座

ie 家

Ienaga Saburō 家永三郎

i-fa 已発

I hsüeh ch'i-meng 易学啓蒙

Ii 井伊

ikan (Ch i-chien) 易簡

Ikeda Mitsumasa 池田光政

Ikegamiji 池上寺

ikki (the one ether/energy) 一気

ikki (uprising) 一揆

Ikkō 一向

Ikkō-ikki 一向一揆

Ikkyū Sōjun 一体宗純

Imagawa 今川

Imagawa Ryōshun 今川了俊

Inaba 稲葉

Inari 稲荷

Inbe 忌部

Inbe Masamichi 忌部正道

inkyo 隠居

Inoue Masatoshi 井上正利

iriban 入番

Ise 伊勢

Ise (furyū) odori 伊勢(風流)踊

Ise Nagashima 伊勢長島

Ise Sadatake 伊勢貞丈

Isezaki 伊勢崎

Ishida Baigan 石田梅岩

Ishiyama 石山

ishō 已生

Isuzugawa 五十鈴川

Itakura 板倉

itaru 至る

itoshii 愛シイ

itsu-se 五瀬

Iwasaka 磐境

Izanagi 伊弉諾

Izanami 伊弉冊

Izumo 出雲

Izusōkengyō En'ichi 伊豆惣検校円都

Jen-shuo (Jp *Jinsetsu*) 仁説

ji 事

jigyō 事業

jihi 慈悲

Jikkinshō 十訓抄

jiko no ri 自己ノ理

jin 仁

Jindai no maki, see *Kamiyo no maki*

jingi 仁儀

Jingū kōgō 神功皇后

jinji 人事

Jinmu (emperor) 神武

jinnō no shōtō 神皇の正統

Jinnō shōtōki 神皇正統記

jinsaku 人作

jinsei 仁政

Jinsetsu, see Jen-shuo

jinshin 人心

jinzai 人材

jitō 地頭

jitto ジット

Jōgan seiyō (Ch *Chen-kuan cheng-yao*)
　貞観政要

Jōkyō 真享

jufuse 受不施

junkenshi 巡検使

junshi 殉死

juntoku 順徳

Jurakudai 聚楽第

Kaemon 嘉右衛門

Kaga 加賀

kagami 鑑

kagura 神楽

Kagutsuchi 迦具士

kagyō 家業

Kaiho Seiryō 海保青陵

kakuchi 覚智

kakure カくれ

Kakure no yama 隠山

Kamakura 鎌倉
kami (above) 上; (god; Ch shen) 神
kamikaze 神風
"Kamiyo no maki" ("Jindai no
  maki," "Jindaikan") 神代巻
Kamo 賀茂
kan (roll of cloth) 疋; (weight) 貫
kanazōshi 仮名草子
kanben 勘弁
Kanbun 寛文
kane 金
Kan'eiji 寛永寺
Kan'ei shoke keizuden 寛永諸家系図伝
kangamiru 上観
Kang Hang 姜沆
Kan-hsing shih (Jp *Kankyō-shi*) 感興詩
kanjōkata 勘定方
Kanō 加納
kanpaku 関白
Kansai 関西
Kansei 寛政
Kanto 関東
kappatsu hachi (Ch huo-p'o p'o-ti)
  活溌々地
karada カラダ(体)
karisome カリソメ
karō 家老
Kasama 笠間
Kashiwahara Yūsen 柏原祐泉
kashoku 家職
Kasuga 春日
Kasuga daimyōjin 春日大明神
Katō kaden 加藤家伝
Katō Kiyomasa 加藤清正
Katō Yasuyoshi 加藤泰義
Kaumi 神海
Kawachi 河内
Kawagoe 川越
ke 仮
kei (punishment) 刑; (reverence; Ch
  ching) 敬
Keian 慶安
keigi (Ch ching-li) 敬義
keigi naigai 敬義内外
Keisaishin, see Ching-chai chen

ken (Ch chüan) 権
kenbutsu ni 見物に
Kenchōji 建長寺
kenjin 賢人
kenkai 見解
Kenmu 建武
Kenninji 建仁寺
Kennyo 顕如
ki (ether; energy) 気; (machine,
  loom) 機
kiba 牙
Kii 紀伊
kika 気化
kimi 君
Kimon 崎門
Kinai 畿内
kinban 勤番
Kinoshita 木下
Kinoshita Chōshōshi 木下長嘯子
Kinoshita Jun'an 木下順庵
Kirishitan 切支丹
kishitsu 気質
Kitabatake Chikafusa 北畠親房
Kitabatake Nobuoki 北畠信興
Kita'in 喜多院
Kitaniku yamabito 北肉山人
kiten 機転
kitto 屹度
kiyō 機用
Kiyohara 清原
Kiyohara Hidekata 清原秀賢
Kiyohara Nobukata 清原宣賢
kō (ōyake) 公
Kobayakawa Hideaki 小早川秀秋
kōgi (public authority) 公儀; (public
  duty) 公義
kōgi no onbyakushō 公儀の御百姓
kōgi no tame 公儀の為
kōgi shohatto 公儀諸法度
Kojiki 古事記
kōjin 行人
koka 古歌
kokoro 心
kokoro ni manbutsu o okazu shite
  kokū no naki ni totomarazu

心に万物をおかずして虚空のな
きにと々まらず
koku 石
Kokuchō kōmoku 国朝綱目
kokudaka 石高
Kokugaku 国学
kokuhō 国法
kokujin 国人
kokuō 国王
Kokura 小倉
kokusei 国政
kōmu 公務
konpaku 魂魄
konton 混沌
konzen to shite ichiri tsuranuki
　渾然一理貫
Kosaru 小猿
kōshin 庚申
koto 事
kouta 小歌
Kōya 高野
Koyane 児屋
Kōyūsō, see Chü-yu ts'ao
kū 空
Kugyō bunin 公卿補任
Kumagai 熊谷
Kumamoto 熊本
Kumaso 熊襲
Kumazawa Banzan 熊沢蕃山
kumen 句面
kumi 組
Kumozu 雲出
k'ung-chü 恐懼
kuni 国
kuninaka-no-hashira 国中柱
Kunitokotachi-no-mikoto 国常立尊
Kunō 久能 chi-no-mi
kunshi 君子
kunshin no gi 君臣義
kurai sōō 位相応
kushi 櫛
kushimitama 奇魂
Kusunoki Masashige 楠木正成
kuyō 供養
kyō (Ch ching) 経

kyōgen (Ch hsiang-yüan) 郷原
kyōkū, *see* k'ung-chü
Kyoto 京都
kyūri (Ch ch'iung-li) 窮理
Kyūshū 九州

Liang (dynasty) 梁
Li Chih 李贄
li-i fen-shu 理一分殊
Lin Chao'en 林兆恩
Li Shih-chen 李時珍
Li T'ung 李侗
Lo shu 洛書
Lo Ts'ung-yen 羅従彦
Lu Hsiang-shan 陸象山

ma 間
machishū 町衆
Manchu 清
Manyōshū 万葉集
Marubashi Chūya 丸橋忠弥
Masuyama 増山
Matsudaira Sadanobu 松平定信
Matsudaira sandaime no shogunsama
　松平三代目の将軍様
Matsunaga Shōsan 松永昌三
Matsunaga Teitoku 松永貞徳
meibun 名分
Meiji 明治
meikun 明君
Meireki 明暦
meishin 冥神
Meishō (empress) 明正
metsuke 目付
migoroshi 見懲
mihatsu 未発
mikoshi 神輿
Mimoro 三室
Minamoto Yoritomo 源頼朝
Minamoto Yoshisato 源義郷
Ming 明
Mino 美濃
Minobu 身延
mi no ue 身の上
mi no ue sōō 身上相応

miru 観る
mishō 未生
mitamamono 神物
Mito 水戸
Miwa 三輪
miya 宮
Miyake Kisai 三宅寄斎
Mizuno 水野
momme 匁
Momoyama 桃山
Momozono (emperor) 桃園
mono 物
monseki 門跡
Mōri 毛利
Mōri Motonari 毛利元就
Morikawa 森川
Moriyoshi 敬義
morokoshi no hijiri no miyo もろこし
　のひしりの御代
moto 本
moto no kokoro もとの心
Motoori Norinaga 本居宣長
mu 無
muga no kokoro 無我の心
Mujū Ichien 無住一円
mukyoku 無極
mune 指
munen mushin 無念無心
Murakumo 村雲
muri 無理
Muro Kyūsō 室鳩巣
Muromachi 室町
Musashi 武藏
myōga 妙加; 冥加
Myōkakuji 妙覚寺
myōkei 妙契
Myōshinji 妙心寺
myōtaru yuen, *see* (tz'u) sho-hsün
　(jen-hsin) chih miao

Nagasaki 長崎
Nagoya 名護屋
Naidaijin 内大臣
naka (chū; Ch chung) 中; 衷
Nakatomi harai 中臣祓

Namu-Amida-butsu 南無阿弥陀仏
Nanboku 南北
nanushi 名主
Nanzenji 南禅寺
Nara 奈良
Nawa Katsusho 那波活所
nenbutsu 念仏
nenryo 念慮
nen soō 年相応
nezasu 根サス
Nichiju 日樹
Nichiō 日奥
Nichiren 日蓮
Nihongi 日本紀
Nijō-jō 二條城
Nikkō 日光
Ninigi 瓊々杵
ninsoku yoseba 人足寄場
Nitta Yoshisada 新田義貞
Nō 能
Nokami 野上
Nonaka Kenzan 野中兼山
Nyorai 如来

ō 王
Ō-ana-muchi 大己貴
ōban 大番
ōbō 王法
ōbō ihon 王法為本
Oda Nobunaga 織田信長
Oda Nobutada 織田信忠
Odawara 小田原
ōdō 王道
Ōgimachi (emperor) 正親町
Ōgimachi Kinmichi 正親町公通
Ogiwara Kaneyori 荻原兼従
ōgosho 大御所
ohanashishū 御咄衆
Ōjin (emperor) 応神
ōjōya 大庄屋
okagemairi おかげまいり
okashiki 可笑; ヲカシキ
Okayama 岡山
Ōkubo (Hikozaemon) Tadataka
　大久保(彦左衛門)忠教

Ōmi 近江
omi (shin) 臣
Omohikane 思兼；思金
omoi (heavy) 重い；(thought) 思い
omoshiroi 面白い
on 恩
Ōnakatomi no Kiyonaga 大中臣精長
Ōnin 応仁
Ōno Yasumaro 太安万侶
onozukara 自ら
Onshinji 恩真寺
Osaka 大坂
Oshi 忍
Ōshio Heihachirō 大塩平八郎
ōson 王孫
Ōsu 大洲
Ōta Gyūichi 太田午一
otogishū 御伽衆
Owari 尾張
ōyake, *see* kō
Ōyamakui 大山咋
Ozawa Eiichi 小沢栄一
Oze Hoan 小瀬甫庵

Pen-ts'ao wang-mu 本草綱目
Po-lu-tung shu-yüan chieh-shih (Jp
　Hakurokudō shoin keiji) 白鹿洞書院
　掲示

Rankei Dōryū 蘭溪道隆
rei (spirit) 霊；(rites) 礼
reigi 礼儀
Reizei 冷泉
Rennyo 蓮如
ri 理
riichi bunshu, *see* li-i fen-shu
Rikkokushi 六国史
rikutsubuppō 理窟仏法
Rinnōji 綸王寺
Rinzai 臨濟
rōnin 浪人
ryō 両
ryōchi (Ch liang-chih) 良知
Ryōshun, *see* Imagawa Ryōshun
Ryūkyū 琉球

sabetsu 差別
Sado 佐渡
Saichō 最澄
Saisai no ki 省斎記
Saitō Dōsan 斎藤道三
Sakai Tadakatsu 酒井忠勝
Sakai Tadakiyo 酒井忠清
saki 先
sakimitama 幸魂
sakoku 鎖国
sakui 作意
Sanbō no tokuyō 三宝之徳用
Sanehito (prince) 誠仁
sankin kōtai 参勤交代
Sannō gongen 山王権現
Sannō ichijitsu 山王一実
santaisokuichi-isshinsankan 三諦郎一
　一心三観
sanyō 算用
Sanyō (Kanshitsu Genkitsu) 三要(閑
　室元佶)
sarashi 晒
saru (forego) 去る；(monkey-zodiac
　sign) 申；(monkey-animal) 猿
Saruta-hiko 猿田彦
Satake 佐竹
Sawada Gennai 沢田源内
sehō 世法
sei 性
Seifūruido 西風涙露
seijin 聖人
Seiken igen 靖献遺言
Seikyō yōroku 聖教要録
sei no dō 静の動
sei no sei 静の静
seiōseiji 聖王正治
seisei 惺々
seiza 静坐
seiza mihatsu no chū 静坐未発
　の中
seken no hō 世間の法
Sekigahara 関原
sengyō 賤業
senmon 専門
Sen no Rikyū 千利休

senshū 専宗

seppuku 切腹

sha 社

Shaka 釈迦

shaku 尺

Shang (dynasty) 商

Shang-ti 上帝

sharaku (Ch sa-lo) 洒落

Shasekishū 沙石集

shen, *see* kami

shen-ch'i, *see* shinki

Shen Nung 神農

shi (intention) 志; (private) 私

Shibata Katsuie 柴田勝家

shidan tomo ni mochisama hitotsu
  nari, gyō kawaritaru bakari nari
  四段共二用ヒ様ハーツ也。業替
  タル計也。

shigen 私言

shiki 死機

Shimabara 島原

Shimazu Yoshihisa 島津義久

shimijimi シミジミ

shimuru シムル

shin 心

Shinagawa 品川

Shinchōki 信長記

Shinchōkōki 信長公記

shindoku 慎独

Shingaku 心学

Shingon 真言

Shin Hiejinja 新日吉神社

shinjin (god-human) 神人; (god-
  mind) 神心

shinka (bodily transformation) 身化;
  (mind transformation) 心化;
  (ministers) 臣下

shinki 神気

shinkoku 神国

shinkun 神君

shinmei 神明

shin no (mi) hashira 心の(御)柱

shinobirarenu shinmi 忍ビラレヌ
  真味

shinpen 神変

shinpō, *see* hsin-fa

Shinran 親鸞

shinrei 神霊

shinryoku 神力

shinsho 神書

shinsui 神垂

shintai 神体

Shinto 神道

Shintō gobusho 神道五部書

shintoku 神徳

Shintō taii 神道大意

shintsū 神通

shinzō 心藏

shion 私恩

shitai sarashi 死体晒

shitsu 質

shiwaza しわざ

shizen (zen ni itaru) 至善

shō, *see* sei

shōen 荘園

shogun 将軍

shohatto 諸法度

shōjiki 正直

shōri 正理

shoshidai 所司代

Shoshihatto 諸士法度

Shōtoku Taishi 聖徳太子

shugo 守護

shugyō 修行

shuichi (Ch chu-i) 主一

shūjō 衆生

shūmon jinbetsuchō 宗門人別帳

Shun 舜

Shuo-t'ung 通書

shūshin (Ch hsiu-shen) 修身

Shūshi shimatsu 修史始末

Shushisho setsuyō 朱子書節要

shuso 首座

shusseken no hō 出世間の法

shutsuri 出離

Silla 新羅

Soga no Umako 蘇我馬子

Sōkenji 摠見寺

Sōkokuji 相国寺

Sōma 相馬

sonawaru 備る
sono ki 其の帰
sono mi ni semuru ni hitsuzen o motte
　其の身に責むるに必然を以て
sōō 相応
sōshi 双紙
Sōtō 曹洞
Ssu-ma Kuang 司馬光
Ssu-shu chi-chu 四書集注
Ssu-shu paio-che cheng-i 四書標摘正義
Sūden 崇伝
Sugawara Michizane 菅原道真
Suika Shinto 垂加神道
Suinin (emperor) 垂仁
sūkei 崇敬
Suminokura Soan 角倉素庵
Sumiyoshi daimyōjin 住吉大明神
sun 寸
Sung 宗
Sunpu 駿府
Sunpuki 駿府記
Susanoo 須佐之男
Suzuki Shigenari 鈴木重成
Suzuki Shigetatsu 鈴木重辰
Suzuki Shigeyuki 鈴木重之
Suzuki Shōsan 鈴木正三

tada タダ；只
tada shiru タダ知ル
tada zen タダ善
tai 体
T'ai-chi-t'u shuo 太極図説
taigi meibun 大義名分
taikō 太閤
Taikōki 太閤記
Taikō sujōki 太閤素生記
taininjitoku 体認自得
T'ai-po 太伯
tairō 大老
Taitokuin 台徳院
takai 高
Takamagahara 高天原
Takenouchi Shikibu 竹内式部
Tako 多胡
Tako Tokitaka 多胡辰敬

Takuan (Sōhō) 沢庵 (宗彭)
tameshi aru bekarazu ためしあるへ
　からす
T'ang (king) 湯
Tani Shinzan 谷秦山
tao-t'ung (Jp dōtō) 道統
tatoe タトヘ
ten 天
tenbatsu 天罰
tenchi 天地
tenchi no dōri 天地の道理
Tendai (Ch T'ien-tai) 天台
tendō 天道
tendō no ri 天道の理
tendō no tsune 天道の常
tenjinyuiitsu 天人唯一
tenka 天下
tenka fubu 天下布武
Tenkai 天海
tenka ittō no rei 天下一統ノ礼
tenkakokka 天下国家
tenka no seiji 天下の政治
tenmei 天命
tenri 天理
tenri no shizen 天理の自然
tenshu 天守
Tenshukyō 天主教
Terumi 光海
T'ien-tai, *see* Tendai
t'i-jen tzu-te, *see* taininjitoku
Tōbu 東武
Tōdaiji 東大寺
Tōdō Takatora 藤堂高虎
Tōkaiji 東海寺
toki no sōō 時相応
toku (explain) 説く；(virtue) 徳
Tokugawa Hidetada 徳川秀忠
Tokugawa Iemitsu 徳川家光
Tokugawa Ietsuna 徳川家綱
Tokugawa Ieyasu 徳川家康
Tokugawa Kazuko 徳川和子
Tokugawa Mitsukuni 徳川光圀
Tokugawa reimeikai 徳川黎明会
Tokugawa Tadanaga 徳川忠長
Tokugawa Tsunayoshi 徳川綱吉

tokugi 徳義

Tokyo 東京

Tomobe Yasutaka 友部安崇

Tomoeda Ryūtarō 友枝龍太郎

tomurau 弔う

Toneri 舎人

Tōnomine 多武峰

tora 寅

Tosa 土佐

Tōshō daigongen 東照大権現

Tōshō daigongen engi 東照大権現緑起

Toyoashihara no nakatsukuni 豊葦
  原中国

Toyokuni daimyōjin 豊国大明神

Toyotomi Hidetsugu 豊臣秀次

Toyotomi Hideyori 豊臣秀頼

Toyotomi Hideyoshi 豊臣秀吉

tozama 外様

Ts'ai Ch'en 蔡沉

Ts'ai Ch'ing 蔡清

Ts'ai Yüan-ting 蔡元定

Tseng Tzu 曽子

Tsu 津

tsubo 坪

tsuchi 土

tsuchigane, *see* dokon

tsuchi-ikki 土一揆

tsuchijimi 土味

tsuchishimu 土味

tsuchi wa ame no tasuke o ukuru ni
  kokoro nashi 地は天のたすけを清
  るに心なし

Tsuchiya Tomosada 土屋知貞

tsukusu 尽す

tsuminaku つみなく

Tsurezuregusa 徒然草

Tsushima 対馬

tsutae, *see* den

tsutsushimi 敬

tsutsushimu 敬む

tsuzumaru ツヅマル

T'ung-chien kang-mu (Jp *Tsugan
  kōmoku*) 通鑑綱目

Tung Chung-shu 董仲舒

Tzu-hsia 子夏

tz'u sho-hsün jen-hsin chih miao
  此所以人心之妙

u 有

Ube daimyōjin 宇倍大明神

Uchimura Kanzō 内村鑑三

Uda (emperor) 宇多

Uesugi 上杉

Uesugi Kagekatsu 上杉景勝

ujigami 氏神

ujiko 氏子

uka to naku 浮となく

unabara ウナバラ

Unpo irohashū 運歩色葉集

Utsunomiya 宇都宮

wagahara 我腹

wagari 我理

Wajima Yoshio 和島芳男

waka 和歌

Wakabayashi Kyōsai 若林強斎

Wakayama 和歌山

Wang Pi 王弼

Wang Yang-ming 王陽明

Watarai 度会

Watarai Nobuyoshi 度会延佳

waza (forced, purposeful) ワザ;
  (works) 業

Wei 衞

wei-fa, *see* mihatsu

Wen (king; Jp Bun) 文

Wen-hsüan 文宣

Wu (king; Jp Bu) 武

yakunin 役人

Yamaga Sokō 山鹿素行

Yamagata 山形

yamarenu aji ヤマレヌ味

Yamashiro 山城

yamatodamashii 大和魂

Yamato-hime 倭姫

yang 陽

Yang Shih 楊時

Yao 堯

Yen-p'ing ta-wen 延平答問

yin 陰
Yin (dynasty) 殷
Yi T'oegye 李退渓
yō 用
Yōfukuki 陽復記
yoku 欲
yokushin 欲心
Yonezawa 米沢
Yoshida 吉田
Yoshida Kanetomo 吉田兼倶
Yoshino mōde 吉野詣
Yü (king) 禹; (historian) 魚
Yüan 元
Yui Shōsetsu 由井正雪

yūmin 遊民
Yusa Bokusai 遊佐木斎
Yūryaku (emperor) 雄略

Zaō gongen 蔵王権現
zazen 坐禅
Zen 禅
zen-go 前後
Zenkōji 禅興寺
zo ゾ
Zōjōji 増上寺
zōka 造化
zokuju 俗儒
Zoku Nihongi 続日本紀

Bibliography

JAPANESE-LANGUAGE WORKS
NOTE: Place of publication is Tokyo, unless otherwise noted.

Abbreviations

DNB   Dai Nihon bunko 大日本文庫 (Great Japanese collection). 52 vols. Shunyōdō 春陽堂, 1934–1942.
       15: *Yoshikawa Shintō* 吉川神道. 1939
       16: *Suika Shintō* (1) 垂加神道. 1935
       17: *Suika Shintō* (2). 1937

IKNR   Iwanami kōza Nihon rekishi 岩波講座日本歴史 (Iwanami lectureship of Japanese history). 23 vols. (1962–1964); 26 vols. (1975–1977). Iwanami 岩波. All IKNR volumes referred to are entitled *Kinsei* 近世 (Early modern period):
       (1963) 9: *Kinsei 1*
       (1963) 10: *kinsei 2*
       (1975) 9: *Kinsei 1*
       (1975) 10: *Kinsei 2*
       (1977) 13: *Kinsei 5*

KSZH   *Kyōsai sensei zatsuwa hikki* 強斎先生雑話筆記 (Notes on casual talks by Master [Wakabayashi] Kyōsai). Edited by Oka Naonobu 岡直養. 12 fascicles plus appendices. Kobundō 虎文堂, 1937.

NKB   Nihon kyōiku bunko 日文教育文庫 (Japanese education library). 12 vols. Dōbunkan 同文館, 1910–1911.
       5: *Kunkai* (2) 訓誡・中 (Admonitions—vol. 2). 1910
       8: *Kakun* 家訓 (House rules). 1910
       9: *Kyōkasho* 教科書 (Textbooks). 1911

NNS   Nihon no shisō 日本の思想 (Japanese thought). 20 vols. Chikuma shobō 筑摩書房, 1968–1972.
       14: *Shintō shisōshū* 神道思想集 (Collection of Shinto thought). 1970
       17: *Fujiwara Seika, Nakae Tōju, Kumazawa Banzan, Yamazaki Ansai, Yamaga Sokō, Yamagata Daini shū* 藤原惺窩・中江藤樹・熊沢蕃山・山崎闇斎・山鹿素行・山県大弐集. 1970

NST   Nihon shisō taikei 日本思想大系 (Great collection of Japanese thought). 67 vols. Iwanami 岩波, 1970–1982.
       17: *Rennyo, Ikkō-ikki* 蓮如・一向一揆. 1972
       21: *Chūsei seiji shakai shisō* (*1*) 中世政治社会思想(上) (Medieval political and social thought—vol. 1). 1971
       26: *Mikawa monogatari, Hagakure* 三河語・葉隠. 1974
       27: *Kinsei buke shisō* 近世武家思想 (Early modern warrior thought). 1974
       28: *Fujiwara Seika, Hayashi Razan* 藤原惺窩・林羅山. 1975

29: *Nakae Tōju* 中江藤樹. 1974

31: *Yamazaki Ansai gakuha* 山崎闇斎学派 (The Yamazaki Ansai school). 1980

34: *Kaibara Ekken, Muro Kyūsō* 貝原益軒・室鳩巣. 1970

35: *Arai Hakuseki* 新井白石. 1975

36: *Ogyū Sorai* 荻生徂徠. 1973

39: *Kinsei Shintōron; zenki Kokugaku* 近世神道論・前期国学 (Early modern Shinto theory; early National Learning). 1972

48: *Kinsei shiron-shū* 近世史論集 (Early modern theories on history). 1974

51: *Kokugaku undō no shisō* 国学運動の思想 (Thought of the National Learning movement). 1971

59: *Kinsei chōnin shisō* 近世町人思想 (Early modern merchant thought). 1975

RB   *Razan sensei bunshū* 羅山先生文集 (Prose writings by master [Hayashi] Razan). 2 vols. Kyoto 京都: Heian kōkogakkai 平安考古学会, 1918.

SGT   Shushigaku taikei 朱子学大系 (Great collection of Neo-Confucianism). 15 vols. Meitoku shuppansha 明徳出版社, 1974–.

1: *Shushigaku nyūmon* 朱子学入門 (Introduction to Neo-Confucianism). 1974

7–8: *Shishoshūchū* (Ch *Ssu-shu chi-chu*) 四書集注 ([Chu Hsi's] Commentaries on the Four Books). 2 vols. 1974

12: *Chōsen no Shushigaku; Nihon no Shushigaku (1)* 朝鮮の朱子学・日本の朱子学(上) (Korean Neo-Confucianism; Japanese Neo-Confucianism (1)). 1977

13: *Nihon no Shushigaku (2)* 日本の朱子学(下) (Japanese Neo-Confucianism—vol. 2). 1975

SNZ   *Satō Naokata zenshū* 佐藤直方全集 (Collected works of Satō Naokata). Nihon koten gakkai 日本古典学会, 1941.

SZS   *Shinzanshū* 秦山集 (Collected writings of [Tani 谷] Shinzan [1663–1718]). Edited by Tani Tateki 谷干城. 49 fasc. Seishōdō 成章堂, 1910.

W   *Selected Writings of Suzuki Shōsan.* Translated by Royall Tyler. Cornell East Asia Papers. Ithaca, N.Y.: China-Japan Program, Cornell University, 1977.

YAZ   *Yamazaki Ansai zenshū* 山崎闇斎全集 (Complete works of Yamazaki Ansai). 2 vols. (consecutive pagination). Nihon koten gakkai 日本古典学会, 1936.

Z   *Suzuki Shōsan dōjin zenshū* 鈴木正三道人全集 (Complete works of Suzuki Shōsan, Man of the Way). Edited by Suzuki Tesshin 鈴木鉄心. Sankibō busshorin 山喜房仏書林, 1962.

ZYAZ *Zoku Yamazaki Ansai zenshū* 続山崎闇斎全集 (Complete works of Yamazaki Ansai: Continued). 3 vols. Nihon koten gakkai 日本古典学会, 1937.

Unpublished Manuscripts

Asami Keisai 淺見絅斎. "Keisai sensei bunshū" 絅斎先生文集 (Collected writings of Master Keisai). Prepared in 1955 for publication by Kondō Keigo 近藤啓吾.

―――. "Keisai sensei zatsuwa hikki" 絅斎先生雑話筆記 (Notes on casual talks by Master Keisai). Prepared in 1955 for publication by Kondō Keigo.

Hayashi Razan 林羅山. "Shintō hiden setchū zokkai" 神道秘伝折中俗解 (Plain explanation of secret Shinto eclecticism). Kokuritsu kōbunshokan Naikaku bunko 国立公文書館内閣文庫 (The Cabinet Library of National Archives). No. 143–493. No pagination.

"Kōshin no den" 庚申伝 (Commentary on *kōshin*). Signed Yamada Eikyō (?) 山田栄卿, 1776. Seikadō bunko 静喜堂文庫. 14 pp. No pagination.

Matsuoka Takefuchi 松岡雄渊. "Hōreki-ki" 宝暦記 (Record from the Hōreki era [1751–64]). Ōkura seishin bunka kenkyūjo 大倉精神文化研究所 (Ōkura Institute for Spiritual Culture), Yokohama 横浜. Man. No. ii–121 (second volume only).

―――. "Shodenshō" 諸伝抄 (Copy of all commentaries). 1762. 2 vols. Ōkura seishin bunka kenkyūjo 大倉精神文化研究所 (Ōkura Institute for Spiritual Culture), Yokohama 横浜. Man. No. ii–111.

Tamaki Masahide 玉木正英. "Himorogi iwasaka gokuhi no den; sanshu shinpō gokuhi no den" 神籬磐境極秘伝・三種神宝極秘伝 (Top secret commentary on *himorogi* and *iwasaka*; top secret commentary on the three divine treasures). Kyoto daigaku toshokan 京都大学図書館, Kyoto. Man. No. 1–05 sa 12.

"Yamazaki sensei goroku" 山崎先生語録 (Recorded sayings by master Yamazaki). Library of Ōkura Seishin bunka kenkyūjo 大倉精神文化研究所, Yokohama 横浜. Man. No. ii–76.

Yoshikawa Koretaru 吉川惟足. "Jindai no maki Koretaru kōsetsu" 神代巻惟足講説 (Lectures on the "Age of the Gods" by Koretaru). 1670. 10 fascicles in 3 vols. Kokuritsu kōbunshokan Naikaku bunkō 国立公文書館内閣文庫. Man. No. 143–401.

[―――.] "Jindai no maki kaden kikigaku" 神代巻家伝聞書 (Verbatim notes on the [Yoshikawa] house commentary on the "Age of the Gods"). Kokkai toshokan 国会図書館 (Diet Library). No. Wa 210.3 70.

Published Primary Sources

Arai Hakuseki 新井白石, see NST 35.

―――. *Hankanpu* 藩翰譜 (Account of the feudal domains). In *Arai Hakuseki zenshū*, vols 1–2.

―――. *Tokushi yoron* 読史余論 (Views on history). In NST 35: 183–431.

―――. *Arai Hakuseki zenshū* 全集 (Complete works of Arai Hakuseki). 6 vols. Kokusho kankōkai 国書刊行会, 1905.

Asaka Tanpaku 安積澹泊. *Dainihonshi sansō* 大日本史賛蔽 (A collection of exaltations for the *Dainihonshi*). In NST 48: 11–319.

Asakura Sōteki waki 朝倉宗滴話記 (Record of talks by Asakura Norikage 教景). In NKB 5: 126–43.

Asakura Toshikage. 朝倉敏景. *Asakura Toshikage 17 kajō* 朝倉敏景十七箇条 (The seventeen rules of Asakura Toshikage). In NST 21: 350–52 and in Kakei Yasuhiko, *Chūsei buke kakun no kenkyū*: "Sankō-hen," pp. 48–50.

Asami Keisai 浅見絅斎. His writings can be found in NST 31; SGT 12; see also manuscripts in previous section.

———. *Jinsetsumondō shisetsu* 仁説問答師説 (Explanations by the master on "Questions and answers on explanations of 'humaneness'"). In NST 31: 253–304.

———. *Kōyūsō shisetsu* 拘幽操師説 (Explanations by the master of [Han Yü's poem] "Restraint in prison"). In NST 31: 229–36.

———. *Satsuroku* 劄録 (Miscellaneous notes). In NST 31: 318–415.

Asayama Irin'an 朝山意林庵. *Kiyomizu monogatari* 清水物語 (The tale of Kiyomizu). In *Kanazōshi-hen*, pp. 11–48.

Chōsen no Shushigaku; Nihon no Shushigaku (1), see SGT 12.

Chūsei seiji shakai shisō, see NST 21.

Dai Nihon komonjo; Iewake 大日本古文書; 家わけ (Archives of Great Japan; By house). Edited by Tokyo daigaku shiryōhensanjo 東京大学史料編纂所. Tokyo daigaku, 1904– .

Dai Nihon shiryō 大日本史料 (Historical documents of Great Japan). Edited by Tokyo daigaku shiryōhensanjo 東京大学史料編纂所. Tokyo daigaku, 1922– .

Dokon no den. See under *Tamaki Masahide*, and *Yoshikawa Koretaru*..

Fujiwara Seika 藤原惺窩. His writings can be found in *Fujiwara Seika shū*; NST 28; SGT 13; NNS 17.

———. *Daigaku yōryaku* 大学要略 (Epitome of the *Great Learning*). In NST 28: 42–78.

———. *Suntetsu roku* 寸鉄録 (A record of pithy sayings). In NST 28: 10–39.

Fujiwara Seika, Hayashi Razan, see NST 28.

Fujiwara Seika, Nakae Tōju, Kumazawa Banzan, Yamazaki Ansai, Yamaga Sokō, Yamagata Daini shū, see NNS 17.

Fujiwara Seika shū 集 (The works of Fujiwara Seika), compiled by Kokumin seishin bunka kenkyūjo 国民精神文化研究所. 2 vols. N.p., 1939.

Gion monogatari 祇園物語 (The tale of Gion). In *Kanazōshi-hen*, pp. 51–116.

Hanitsu reishin gengyōroku 土津霊神言行録 (Deeds and words of Hoshina Masayuki). In *Zokuzoku gunsho ruijū* 続々群書類従 3: 260–93. Naigai insatsu 内外印刷, 1907.

Hayashi Gahō 林鵞峯. *Kokushikan nichiroku* 国史館日録 (Diary of the Office of National History). Vols. 16–17 of Hayashi Razan and Gahō, *Honchō tsugan*.

———. *Nihon ōdai ichiran* 日本王代一覧 (Overview of Japanese reigns). 1664.

Hayashi Razan 林羅山. His writings can be found in *Razan sensei shishū*; RB; NST 28 and 39; SGT 13.

———. *Hōtei shoroku* 庖丁書録 (Cook book). In *Hyakka setsurin* 百家説林 (Writings of the great masters), Zokuhen 続編 (Supplement), 1: 212–21.

Yoshikawa kōbunkan 吉川弘文館, 1905.

―――. *Santokushō* 三徳抄 (Selections of the three virtues). In NST 28: 151–86.

―――. *Seika sensei gyōjō* 惺窩先生行状 (Biography of master Seika). In NST 28: 188–98.

―――. *Shintō denju* 神道伝授 (Shinto initiation). In NST 39: 11–57.

―――. *Shunkanshō* 春鑑抄 (Selections called "Modeled after spring"). In NST 28: 115–49.

―――, and Gahō. *Honchō tsugan* 本朝通鑑 (General mirror of Japan). 17 vols. Kokusho kankōkai 国書刊行会, 1919.

Honsaroku 本佐録 (The Honsa record). In NST 28: 269–302.

Ikeda Mitsumasa nikki 池田光政日記 (Ikeda Mitsumasa's diary). Edited by Fujii Shun 藤井駿. Sanyō tosho 山陽図書, 1967.

Ikoku ōfuku shokan-shū; zōtei ikoku nikki-shō 異国往復書翰集；増訂異国日記抄 (Collection of foreign correspondence documents; supplemented by foreign diaries). Edited by Murakami Naojirō 村上直次郎. Yūshōdō 雄松堂, 1966.

Ise Sadatake 伊勢貞丈. *Sansha takusen-kō* 三社託宣考 (An essay on the oracles of the three shrines). In *Shintō sōsetsu* 神道叢説 (Shinto doctrines), pp. 413–15. Kokusho kankōkai 国書刊行会, 1911.

Jigen Daishi zenshū 慈眼大師全集 (Complete works of Tenkai). 2 vols. Kan'eiji 寛永寺, 1916.

Kaibara Ekken. *Taigiroku* 大疑録 (Record of great doubts). In NST 34: 9–64.

Kakei Yasuhiko 筧泰彦. *Chūsei buke kakun no kenkyū* 中世武家家訓の研究 (Studies in medieval warrior house rules). 3 parts with separate pagination, in 1 vol.: "Kenkyū-hen" 研究扁 (Study), 293 pp.; "Shiryō-hen" 資料扁 (Documents), 345 pp.; "Sankō-hen" 参考扁 (Additional material), 81 pp. Kazama shobō 風間書房, 1967.

Kana shōri 仮名性理 (Nature and principle discussed in kana script). In NST 28: 237–55.

Kanazōshi-hen 仮名草子篇. Tenri toshokanzō kinsei bungaku mikanbon sōsho 天理図書館蔵近世文学未刊本叢書 (Collection of unpublished literary works on the early modern period in the Tenri Library). Nara 奈良: Yōtokushakan 養徳社刊, 1947.

Kinsei buke shisō, see NST 27.

Kinsei chōnin shisō, see NST 59.

Kinsei nōsei shiryōshū 近世農政史料集 (Collection of historical materials on early modern agricultural administration), Edited by Kodama Kōta and Ōishi Shinsaburō 児玉幸多, 大石慎三郎. 3 vols. 1966–1972. Vol. 1: *Edo bakufu hōrei (1)* 江戸幕府法令（上）(Edo bakufu laws). Yoshikawa kōbunkan 吉川弘文館, 1966.

Kinsei shiron-shū, see NST 48.

Kojiki, Sendaikyūjihongi, Shintō gobusho 古事記・先代旧事本紀・神道五部書. Shintei zōho—Kokushi taikei 新訂増補—国史大系, vol. 7. Yoshikawa kōbunkan 吉川弘文館, 1966.

Kojiruien 古事類苑. 60 vols. Kojiruien kankōkai, 1931–1936.

Kyōsai sensei zatsuwa hikki, see KSZH.

Matsudaira Sadanobu 松平定信. *Kanko-dori* 諫鼓鳥 (Birds on the admonition drum). In *Rakuō-kō isho* 楽翁公遺書 (Literary legacy of Matsudaira Sadanobu), edited by Ema Seihatsu 江間政発, vol. 1. Yao shoten 八尾書店, 1893.

Miura Jōshin 三浦浄心. *Keichō kenmonshū* 慶長見聞集 (Collection of observations on the Keichō Era [1595–1614]). In *Nihon shomin seikatsu shiryō shūsei* 日本庶民生活史料集成 (Collection of historical materials on the life of common people in Japan), vol. 8, pp. 471–640. Sanichi shobō 三一書房, 1969.

Miyake Shōsai 三宅尚斎. His writings can be found in NST 31; SGT 12.

Nakae Tōju, see NST 29.

———. *Okina mondō* 翁問答 (Discussions with a venerable old man). In NST 29: 19–177.

Naoe Kanetsugu 直江兼続. *Naoe Kanetsugu shiki nōkaisho* 直江兼続四季農戒書 (Agricultural admonitions booklet for the four seasons by Naoe Kanetsugu). In *Dai Nihon shiryō*, vol. 12, fasc. 32 (1935), pp. 84–91.

Nihon dōgaku engen roku 日本道学淵源録 (Fountainhead of the Learning of the Way in Japan). Edited by Oka Jirō 岡次郎. 11 fasc. Kaimeidō 開明堂, 1934.

Nihon no Shushigaku (2), see SGT 13.

Nihonshoki 日本書記. Kokushi taikei 国史大系, (Great collection of national history), vols. 1–2. Second edition. Yoshikawa kōbunkan 吉川弘文館, 1966.

———. Nihon koten bungaku taikei 日本古典文学大系 (Great series of classical Japanese literature), vols. 67–68. Iwanami 岩波, 1967.

Nishikawa Joken 西川如見. *Chōninbukuro* 町人嚢 (Merchant bag). In NST 59: 85–173.

Ogyū Sorai, see NST 36.

———. *Bendō* 弁道 (Distinguishing the Way). In NST 36: 9–36.

———. *Seidan* 政談 (Political discourses). In NST 36: 259–445.

Ōkubo (Hikozaemon) Tadataka 大久保(彦左衛門)忠教. *Mikawa monogatari*, see NST 26.

Okuno Takahiro 奥野高広. *Oda Nobunaga monjo no kenkyū* 織田信長文書の研究 (A study of Oda Nobunaga documents). 2 vols. Yoshikawa kōbunkan 吉川弘文館, 1969–1970.

Razan sensei bunshū, see RB.

Razan sensei shishū 羅山先生詩集 (Poetic writings of master Razan). 2 vols. Heiankō kogakkai 平安考古学会, 1921.

Rennyo, Ikkō ikki, see NST 17.

Satō Naokata. His writings can be found in NST 31; SGT 12; SNZ.

———. *Gakudan zatsuroku* 学談雑録 (Miscellaneous record of talks on learning). In NST 31: 428–63.

———. *Keisaishin kōgi* 敬斎箴講義 (Lecture on [Chu Hsi's] "Exhortation for the Reverence studio"). In NST 31: 117–19.

———. *Keisetsu hikki* 敬説筆記 (Notes on explanations of "Reverence"). In NST 31: 100–16.

———. *Seiza setsuhikki* 静坐説筆記 (Notes on explanations of "Quiet sitting"). In SGT 12: 287–310.

————. *Shuseisetsu* 主静説 (Explanations on the centrality of "Quietness"). In SGT 12: 282–86.

————. *Tōjibun* 冬至文 (Winter solstice writing). In SGT 12: 274–75.

————. *Unzōroku* 韞藏録. In SNZ 1–299.

————. *Unzōrokushūi*— 拾遺 (Gleanings from —). In SNZ 300–608.

————. *Unzōroku zokushūi*————続————(Further gleanings from —). In SNZ 609–63.

————. *Satō Naokata zenshū*, see SNZ.

Sawada Gennai 沢田源内. *Warongo.* See next section under Katsube Mitake.

Shingaku gorinsho 心学五倫書 (Treatise on the Five Relationships in Mind Learning). In NST 28: 257–67.

Shintō shisōshū, see NNS 14.

Shinzanshū, see SZS.

Shisho shūchū, see SGT 7–8.

Shushishū 朱子集 (Chu Hsi collection). Edited by Yoshikawa Kōjirō and Miura Kunio 吉川幸次郎・三浦国雄. Vol 3 of *Chūgoku bunmeisen* 中国文明選 (Selections from Chinese civilization) (15 vols., 1971–76), edited by Yoshikawa Kōjirō and Ogawa Tamaki 小川環樹. Asahi shinbunsha 朝日新聞社, 1976.

Ssu-shu chi-chu, see SGT 7–8.

Suika Shintō, see DNB 16–17.

Suzuki Shōsan. His writings can be found in W; Z.

————. *Banmin tokuyō* 万民徳用 (Right action for all). In Z: 61–72 (English translation in W: 53–74).

————. *Fumoto kusawake* 麓草分 (Separating the grass at the foothill). In Z: 72–93.

————. *Ha Kirishitan* 破吉利支丹 (Christians countered). In Z: 131–37 (English translation in G. Elison, *Deus Destroyed*, pp. 377–89).

————. *Hogoshū* 反故集 (Collection of useless things). Compiled by Echū 恵中. In Z: 285–328.

————. *Mōanjō* 盲安杖 (A safe staff for the blind). In Z: 49–60 (English translation in W: 31–52).

————. *Roankyō* 驢鞍橋 (Donkey saddle bridge). Compiled by Echū 恵中. In Z: 138–284 (English translation of selections in W: 75–198).

Suzuki Shōsan dōjin zenshū, see Z.

Takeuchi Kakusai 武内確斎. *Ehon Taikōki* 絵本太閤記 (An illustrated *Taikōki*). 1797–1802.

Tako Tokitaka 多胡辰敬. *Tako Tokitaka kakun* 多胡辰敬家訓 (The Tako Tokitaka house rule). In Kakei Yasuhiko, *Chūsei buke kakun no kenkyū*: "Shiryō-hen," pp. 243–345.

Tamaki Masahide 玉木正英. *Dokon no den* 土金伝 (Commentary on Earth and Metal). In DNB 16: 386–88.

————. *Gyokusenshū* 玉籤集 (Collection of drawn pearls). In DNB 16: 377–498.

Tani Shinzan 谷秦山. His writings can be found in SGT 12; SZS.

Tenkai 天海, *Tōshō daigongen kana engi* 東照大権現仮名縁起 (The founding history in kana script of the "Great Avatar Shining in the East"). In *Jigen*

Daishi zenshū 1: 35–65.

———. See also *Jigen Daishi zenshū*.

Toda Mosui zenshū 戸田茂睡全集 (Complete works of Toda Mosui [1629–1706]). Edited by Hayakawa Junsaburō 早川純三郎. Kokusho kankōkai 国書刊行会, 1915.

Tokugawa jikki 徳川実紀 (The true Tokugawa records). Kokushi taikei 国史大系, vols. 38–52. Yoshikawa kōbunkan 吉川弘文館, 1964.

Tokugawa kinreikō 徳川禁令考 (Tokugawa law decrees). Edited by Ishii Ryōsuke 石井良助. 11 vols. Sōbunsha 創文社, 1959.

Tōshōgū goikun 東照宮御遺訓 (Ieyasu's testament). In NKB 8: 252–342.

Tsuchigane no tsutae 土金之伝 (Commentary on Earth and Metal), see Yoshikawa Koretaru, *Dokon no hiketsu*; and Tamagi Masahide, *Dokon no den*.

Wakabayashi Kyōsai. 若林強斎 His writings can be found in KSZH; NST 31.

Warongo, see next section under Katsube Mitake.

Watarai Nobuyoshi 度会延佳. *Yōfukuki* 陽復記 (Record of the sun's return). In NST 39: 85–117.

Yamada Omoihajime (?) 山田思叔. *Yamazaki Ansai nenpu* 山崎闇斎年譜 (A Yamazaki Ansai chronology). In *Nihon jurin sōsho* 日本儒林叢書 (Japanese Confucian writings), edited by Sekigi Ichirō 関儀一郎, vol. 3. Second edition. Hōshuppankan 鳳出版刊, 1971.

Yamato-hime no mikoto seiki 倭姫命世記 (Record of the age of Yamato-hime). In *Watarai Shintō taisei (1)* 度会神道大成 (Collection of Watarai Shinto, vol. 1) (Vol. 11 of *Daijingū sōsho* 大神宮叢書, Collected writings of the Great [Ise] Shrines). Edited by Jingū shichō 神宮司庁, pp. 61–92. Kyoto 京都: Ringawa shoten 臨川書店, 1976. Reprint of 1957 edition: Ōgaki 大垣, Kawase 川瀬.

Yamazaki Ansai. His writings can be found in: DNB 16–17; NKB 9; NNS 15; NST 31, 39; SGT 12; YAZ; ZYAZ.

———. *Bunkai hitsuroku* 文会筆録 (Notes). In YAZ 1: 91 to 2: 639 (consecutive pagination). Also in Tajiri Yūichirō 田尻祐一郎 and Maeda Tsutomu 前田勉. "Yamazaki Ansai *Bunkai hitsuroku* kan ichi 'Shōgaku' shakukō" 山崎闇斎『文会筆録』巻一「小学」釈稿 (Yamazaki Ansai's interpretive notes on the "Elementary Learning" from vol. 1 of his *Bunkai hitsuroku*). *Nihonshisōshi* 日本思想史 17 (1981): 105–14, and following issues.

———. *Daigaku Suika sensei kōgi* 大学垂加先生講義 (Lecture on the *Great Learning* by master Suika). In NST 31: 9–65.

———. *Enyūkikō* 遠遊紀行 (Travelogue of a far holiday). In YAZ 1: 22–35.

———. *Fuji no mori yuzuemandokoro no ki* 藤森弓兵政所記 (Record of the Fuji no mori shrine). In YAZ 1: 58–61; excerpts in NNS 14: 272–74.

———. *Hekii* 闢異 (Heresies refuted). In ZYAZ 2: 432–51; and NNS 17: 185–250.

———. *Honchō kaigen-kō* 本朝改元考 (Notes on Japanese era names). In YAZ 2: 656–66.

———. *Ise daijingū gishiki jo* 伊勢太神宮儀式序 (Preface to *The ritual of the Great Ise shrines*). In YAZ 1: 67–68; and NNS 14: 276–79.

————. *Jijushō* 持授抄 (Summary of the transmitted tradition [of the mind-system]). In NST 39: 129–39.

————. *Jindai no maki fūyōshu* 神代巻風葉集 (Wind and leaves collection of the "Age of the Gods"). In ZYAZ 1: 1–361; and DNB 16: 9–224.

————. *Jindai no maki kōgi* 神代巻講義 (Lecture on the "Age of the Gods"). Notes by Asami Keisai 浅見絅斎. In ZYAZ 3: 206–304; and NST 39: 141–88.

————. *Keisaishinkōgi* 敬斎箴講義 (Lecture on [Chu Hsi's] "Exhortation for the Reverence studio"). In NST 31: 80–95.

————. *Nakatomi harai fūsuisō* 中臣祓風水草 (Wind and water draft on the Nakatomi purification). In ZYAZ 1: 362–557; and DNB 17: 2–298.

————. *Saiyūkikō* 再遊紀行 (Second travelogue of a holiday). In YAZ 1: 36–53.

————. *Suikashago* 垂加社語 (Words by the Suika Shrine). In NST 39: 119–28; and NNS 14: 286–94.

————. *Yamato kagami mokuroku* 倭鑑目録 (Table of contents of the *Mirror of Japan*). In YAZ 2: 686–88.

————. *Yamato shōgaku* 大和小学 (The Japanese Elementary Learning). In ZYAZ 3: 157–205; and NKB 9: 25–95.

————. *Yamazaki kafu* 山崎家譜 (The Yamazaki lineage). In YAZ 2: 651–54, and also 761–64.

————, comp. and comment. *Bumei* 武銘 ([Commentaries on Chu Hsi's "King] Wu's precepts"). In ZYAZ 3: 30–45; preface in SGT 12: 158.

————, comp. and comment. *Chūbakumuchinsetsu* 沖漠無朕説 (Interpretations of "Empty and tranquil and without any sign" ["and yet all things are luxuriantly present" from the *Reflections on Things at Hand*]). In ZYAZ 3: 78–86; postscript in SGT 12: 178.

————, comp. and comment. *Chūwashūsetsu* 中和集説 (Collected interpretations of "equilibrium" and "harmony" [from the *Doctrine of the Mean*]). In ZYAZ 2: 402–21; preface in SGT 12: 170.

————, comp. and comment. *Hakurokudō gakukishūchū* 白鹿洞学規集註 (Collected commentaries on [Chu Hsi's] school regulations for the White Deer Grotto [Academy]). In ZYAZ 3: 1–5.

————, comp. and comment. *Kankyōshi kōchū* 感興詩考註 (Commentaries on [Chu Hsi's] "Extemporaneous poems"). In ZYAZ 3: 14–29.

————, comp. and comment. *Kōhanzensho* 洪範全書 (Complete writings on the *Hung Fan* or Great Norm). In ZYAZ 2: 236–371.

————, comp. *Daigaku keihatsushū* 大学啓発集 (Collection of [clarifications by Chu Hsi] on the *Great Learning*). In ZYAZ 2: 66–172.

————, comp. *Daike shōryōshū* 大家商量集 (Collected discussions of the great master [Chu Hsi]). In ZYAZ 2: 452–89. Foreword in SGT 12: 153.

————, comp. *Jinsetsu* 仁説 ([Chu Hsi's] Treatise on "humaneness"). In ZYAZ 3: 46–47.

————, comp. *Jinsetsu mondō* 仁説問答 (Questions and answers on explanations of "humaneness"). In ZYAZ 3: 50–58; and NST 31: 244–52.

————, comp. *Keisaishin* 敬斎箴 ([Chu Hsi's] Exhortation for the Reverence studio). In ZYAZ 3: 6–13; and NST 31: 74–79. Preface and postscript in SGT 12: 153–55.

———, comp. *Kōkyōgaiden* 孝経外伝 ([Chu Hsi's] Unofficial classic of Filial Piety). In ZYAZ 2: 173–85.

———, comp. *Mōshi yōryaku* 孟子要略 (*Mencius* compendium). In ZYAZ 2: 422–31; postscript in SGT 12: 176.

———, comp. *Seiron meibiroku* 性論明備録 (Record of the gradual illumination of the theory on nature). In ZYAZ 3: 59–76; preface in SGT 12: 171–72.

———, comp. *Shōgaku mōyōshū* 小学蒙養集 (Collection of [clarifications by Chu Hsi] on the *Elementary Learning*). In ZYAZ 2: 1–65.

———, comp. *Shūshisho* 周子書 (Chou [Tun-yi]'s work). In ZYAZ 2: 372–400.

———, ed. *Ekigaku keimō* 易学啓蒙 (Instructions to the young on the learning of the *I ching* [by Chu Hsi]). 1677.

———, ed. *Kōkyō kango* 孝経刊誤 ([Chu Hsi's] Misprints in the *Classic on Filial Piety*). 1656.

———, ed., *Shu-eki engi* 朱易衍義 (Extended meaning of the *I ching* by Chu Hsi). In ZYAZ 2: 186–235; preface in SGT 12: 172–73.

———, ed. *Shū-eki hongi* 周易本義 (Original meaning of the *I ching* [by Chu Hsi]). 1675.

———, ed., *Shushi shasōhō* 朱子社倉法 (Chu Hsi's emergency granary system). In ZYAZ 2: 492–507; preface and postscript in SGT 12: 156–58.

———and Hoshina Masayuki 保科正之, comps. *Aizu fudoki* 会津風土記 (Gazetteer of Aizu *han*). ZYAZ 3: 312–63; preface in YAZ 1: 72–73.

———, comps. *Aizu jinjashi* 会津神社志 (Gazetteer of Shinto shrines in Aizu *han*). Preface in SGT 12: 130.

———, comps. *Gyokusan kōgi furoku* 玉山講義附録 (Appendix to [Chu Hsi's] *Lecture at Yü-shan*). Postscript in YAZ 2: 743.

———, comps. *Irakusanshiden shinroku* 伊洛三子伝心録 (Record of the mind-heart as transmitted through the Ch'eng's 程 and the three teachers [Yang Shih, Lo Ts'ung-yen, Li Tung 楊時, 羅従彦, 李侗]). Preface and postscript in SGT 12: 163–66.

———, comps. *Nitei jikyōroku* 二程治教録 (Record of the two Ch'eng's political writings). Preface and postscript in SGT 12: 160–63.

Yamazaki Ansai gakuha, see NST 31.

Yamazaki Ansai zenshū, see YAZ (and also ZYAZ).

Yoshida Kanetomo 吉田兼倶. *Yuiitsu Shintō myōbōyōshū* 唯一神道名法要集 (Outline of Yuiitsu Shinto teachings). In NNS 14: 133–84.

Yoshikawa Korenaga (?) 吉川従長. *Himorogi iwasaka no daiji* 神籬磐境之大事 [Commentary on] the great matter of *Himorogi* and *Iwasaka*). In NST 39: 78–83.

Yoshikawa Koretaru, *Dokon no hiketsu* 土金之秘沢 (Secret law of Earth and Metal). In NST 39: 67–72.

———. *Jindaikan Koretaru-shō* 神代巻惟足抄 (Summary of the "Age of the Gods" by Koretaru). In DNB 15: 281–417.

————. *Shintō taii chū* 神道大意註 ([Koretaru's] comments on [Yoshida Kanetomo's] *The Great Meaning of Shinto*). In DNB 15: 38–48.

Yoshikawa Shintō, see DNB 15.

Zoku Yamazaki Ansai zenshū, see ZYAZ.

Secondary Sources

Abe Ryūichi 阿部隆一. "Kimon gakuha shoke no ryakuden to gakufū" 崎門学派諸家の略伝と学風 (The Kimon school's teachers: short biographies and notes on their styles). In NST 31: 561–600.

————. "(Ōkurayama bunka-kagaku kenkyūjo shozō) Kimon gakuha chosaku bunken kaidai" (大倉山文化科学研究所々蔵)崎門学派著作文献解題 (A bibliographical interpretation of works from the Kimon school—in the collection of the Ōkurayama Cultural Research Institute), *Ōkurayama ronshū* 大倉山論集, no. 6 (1957): 153–241.

Abe Yoshio 阿部吉雄. "Edo jidai jusha no shusshin to shakaigakuteki chii ni tsuite" 江戸時代儒者の出身と社会学的地位について (The social position and origins of Tokugawa Confucian scholars). *Nihon Chūkoku gakkaihō* 日本中国学会報, no. 13 (1961): 161–75.

————. *Nihon Shushigaku to Chōsen* 日本朱子学と朝鮮 (Japanese Neo-Confucianism and Korea). Tokyo Daigaku 東京大学, 1965.

————. "'Sharaku' dangi" 「洒落」談義 (A lecture on *sharaku*). *Jinbunkagaku kiyō* 人文科学紀要 (Humanities bulletin); Tokyo Daigaku kyōyōgakubu 東京大学教養学部 (University of Tokyo, College of General Education). [Kokubungaku-Kangaku 国文学・漢学 (National literature & Chinese learning), no. 11.] 39 (1966): 1–17.

————. "Yamazaki Ansai no chosho ni tsuite: shu to shite Shushigaku kankeisho no ryakukai" 山崎闇斎の著書に就いて：主として朱子学関係書の略解 (About Yamazaki Ansai's works: A brief interpretation mainly of his Neo-Confucian works), *Kangakkai zasshi* 漢学会雑誌 1 (1933), 1: 47–78, and 2: 85–116.

Akimoto Norio 秋本典夫. "Kinsei Nikkō Tōshōgū to minshū no sankei" 近世日光東照宮と民衆の参詣 (The early modern Tōshō shrine in Nikkō and popular pilgrimages). *Utsunomiya daigaku kyōyōbu kenkyū hōkoku* 宇都宮大学教養部研究報告 8 (1975), 1: 1–29.

Aomori Tōru 青盛透. "Suzuki Shōsan ni okeru kinsei Bukkyō shisō no keisei katei" 鈴木正三における近世仏教思想の形成過程 (The formation of early modern Buddhist thought in Suzuki Shōsan). *Bukkyōshigaku kenkyū* 仏教史学研究 18 (1976), 1: 1–33.

Asao Naohiro 朝尾直弘. "Bakuhansei to tennō" 幕藩制と天皇 (The bakuhan system and the emperor). In *Kinsei* 近世 (The early modern period): Taikei Nihon kokkashi 大系日本国家史 (Great collection of the history of the Japanese nation) 3: 187–222. Tokyo Daigaku 東京大学, 1975.

————. "Kinsei hōkenseiron o megutte" 近世封建制論をめぐって (About the theory of the early modern feudal system). In *Shokuhōseiken* 織豊政権 (Oda

Nobunaga and Toyotomi Hideyoshi's political authority): Ronshū Nihon rekishi 論集日本歴史 (Symposium: Japanese history) 6: 1–14. Yūseidō 有精堂, 1974.

――――. *Sakoku* 鎖国 (The closed country). Nihon no rekishi 日本の歴史 (Japanese history), vol. 17. Shōgakukan 小学館, 1975.

――――. "'Shōgun kenryoku' no sōshutsu" 「将軍権力」の創出 (The emergence of 'shogunal power'). In 3 parts. *Rekishi hyōron* 歴史評論, no. 241 (1970): 70–78; no. 266 (1972): 48–59; no. 293 (1974): 20–36.

――――. "Shōgun seiji no kenryoku kōzō" 将軍政治の権力構造 (The power structure of shogunal politics). In IKNR (1975) 10: 1–56.

――――. "Toyotomi seikenron" 豊臣政権論 (A theory of Toyotomi's political power). In IKNR (1963) 9: 159–210.

――――. "Toyotomi seikenron" 豊臣政権論 (A theory of Toyotomi's political power). In *Shokuhō seikenron* 織豊政権論 (Theories on Nobunaga and Hideyoshi's political power): Shimpojiumu Nihon rekishi シンポジウム日本歴史 10: 147–86. Gakuseisha 学生社, 1972.

Bitō Masahide 尾藤正英. *Nihon hōken shisōshi kenkyū* 日本封建思想史研究 (A study in the history of Japanese feudal thought). Aoki shoten 青木書店, 1961.

――――. "Sonnō-jōi shisō" 尊王攘夷思想 (Sonnō-jōi thought). In IKNR (1977) 13: 41–86.

Fujii Manabu 藤井学. "Kinsei shoki no seijishisō to kokka ishiki" 近世初期の政治思想と国家意識 (National consciousness and political thought in early modern Japan). In IKNR (1975) 10: 135–72.

Fujii Sadafumi 藤井貞文. "Kinseishi seiritsu no kadai: shūkyō-shisōshi no bawaai" 近世史成立の課題：宗教思想史の場合 (A task for early modern historiography: the case of the history of religious thought). *Kokugakuin zasshi* 国学院雑誌 62 (1961), 9: 173–86.

Fujiki Hisashi 藤木久志. "Tōitsu seiken no seiritsu" 統一政権の成立 (The establishment of unified rule). In IKNR (1975) 9: 33–79.

Fujitani Toshio 藤谷俊雄. "*Okagemairi*" to "*Eejanaika*" 「おかげまいり」と「ええじやないか」. Iwanami shinsho 岩波新書, no. 680. Iwanami, 1968.

Fukaya Katsumi 深谷克己. "Bakuhansei kokka to tennō: Kan'ei-ki o chūshin ni" 幕藩制国家と天皇：寛永期を中心に (Nationhood under the bakuhan system and the emperor, especially during the Kan'ei period [1624–1643]). In *Bakuhansei kakka seiritsu katei no kenkyū: Kan'ei-ki o chūshin ni* 幕藩制国家成立過程の研究：寛永期を中心に (Studies in the formative process of nationhood under the bakuhan system: especially during the Kan'ei period [1624–1643]), edited by Kitajima Masamoto 北島正元, pp. 221–74. Yoshikawa Kōbunkan 吉川弘文館, 1978.

――――. "Bakuhansei to tennō" 幕藩制と天皇 (The bakuhan system and the emperor). *Jinmin no rekishigaku* 人民の歴史学, no. 40 (1975), pp. 1–8.

――――. "Kōgi to mibunsei" 公儀と身分制 ('Public authority' and the status system). In *Kinsei* 近世 (The early modern period): Taikei Nihon kokkashi 大系日本国家史 (Great collection of Japanese history) 3: 149–85. Tokyo daigaku 東京大学, 1976.

Haga Kōshirō 芳賀幸四郎. *Chūsei Zenrin no gakumon oyobi bungaku ni kansuru kenkyū* 中世禅林の学問および文学に関する研究 (A study of medieval Zen scholarship and literature). Nihon gakugei shinkōkai 日本学術振興会, 1956.

Hori Isao 堀勇雄. *Hayashi Razan* 林羅山. Jinbutsu sōshō 人物叢書 (Biographies of historical personalities), vol. 118. Yoshikawa kōbunkan 吉川弘文館, 1964.

Ikeda Yukio 池田雪雄. "Ansaijugaku no tenkai" 闇斎儒学の展開 (The development of Ansai Confucian learning). *Rekishigaku kenkyū* 歴史学研究, no. 112 (1943): 23–54.

Imanaka Kanshi 今中寛司. *Kinsei Nihon seiji shisō no seiritsu: Seikagaku to Razangaku* 近世日本政治思想の成立：惺窩学と羅山学 (The establishment of early modern Japanese political thought: Seika and Razan's learning). Sōbunsha 創文社, 1972.

Ishida Ichirō 石田一良. "Zenki bakuhan taisei no ideorogii to Shushigakuha no shisō" 前期幕藩体制のイデオロギーと朱子学派の思想 (The ideology of the early bakuhan system and the thought of the Neo-Confucian schools). In NST 28: 411–48.

Ishige Tadashi 石毛忠. "'Shingaku gorinsho' no seiritsu jijō to sono shisōteki tokushitsu: 'Kana. shōri' 'Honsaroku' rikai no zentei to shite" 「心学五倫書」の成立事情とその思想的特質 ―「仮名性理」「本佐録」理解の前提として (Intellectual characteristics and the composition of the *Shingaku gorinsho*: A premise for understanding the *Kana shōri* and the *Honsaroku*). In NST 28: 490–504.

Ishii Ryōsuke 石井良助. *Edo jidai manpitsu* 江戸時代漫筆 (Essays on the Edo period). 5 vols. Inoue shobō 井上書房, 1959–1967.

——. *Tennō: tennō tōji no shiteki kaimei* 天皇：天皇統治の史的解明 (The emperor: a historical clarification of imperial rule). Kōbundō 弘文堂, 1950.

Kanaya Osamu 金谷治. "Fujiwara Seika no Jugaku shisō" 藤原惺窩の儒学思想 (Fujiwara Seika's Confucian thought). In NST 28: 449–70.

Kasahara Kazuo 笠原一男. *Shinshū ni okeru itan no keifu* 真宗における異端の系譜 (Genealogy of heresies in the New Pure Land sect). Tokyo daigaku 東京大学, 1962.

Katsube Mitake 勝部真長. "*Warongo*" no kenkyū 「和論語」の研究 (A study of the *Warongo*). Shibundō 至文堂, 1970.

Kawai Masaharu 河合正治. *Chūsei buke shakai no kenkyū* 中世武家社会の研究 (A study of medieval warrior society) Yoshikawa Kōbunkan 吉川弘文館, 1973.

Kawano Shozō 河野省三. *Shintō kenkyūshū* 神道研究集 (Collected Shinto studies). Saitama-ken jinjashō 埼玉県神社庁, 1959.

Kawazoe Shōji 川添昭二. *Imagawa Ryōshun* 今川了俊. Jinbutsu sōsho 人物叢書 (Biographies of historical personalities), vol. 117. Yoshikawa kōbunkan 古川弘文館, 1964.

Kinugasa Yasuki 衣笠安喜. "Bakuhanseige no tennō to bakufu" 幕藩制下の天皇と幕府. (The emperor and the bakufu under the bakuhan system). In *Tennōsei to minshū* 天皇制と民衆 (The emperor system and the people), edited by Gotō Yasushi 後藤靖, pp. 79–109. Tokyo daigaku 東京大学, 1976.

——. "Hōken shisō no kakuritsu" 封建思想の確立 (The establishment of feudal thought). In *Ōnin-Genroku* 応二元禄, edited by Nihonshi kenkyūkai 日本史研究会: Kōza Nihon bunkashi 講座日本文化史 (Japanese cultural history lectureship), 4: 247–305. Sanichishobō 三一書房, 1962.

Kitajima Masamoto 北島正元. "Tokugawa Ieyasu no shinkakuka ni tsuite" 徳川家康の神格化について (On Tokugawa Ieyasu's deification). *Kokushigaku* 国史学, no. 94 (1972): 1–13.

Kobayashi Kenzō 小林健三. *Suika Shintō no kenkyū* 垂加神道の研究 (A study of Suika Shinto). Shibundō 至文堂, 1940.

Kobayashi Yasumori 小林安司. "Hayashi Razan to Shintō" 林羅山と神道 (Hayashi Razan and Shinto). In *Shintō seishin kenkyū* 神道精神研究 (Research in the spirit of Shinto), edited by Nihon bunka kenkyūkai 日本文化研究会, 2: 245–66. Tōyōshoin 東洋書院, 1934.

Kōmoto Takeshi 甲元武士. "Nihon kinsei shoki ni okeru seiji to shisō: Tokugawa Ieyasu no seiji to Bukkyō" 日本近世初期における政治と思想—徳川家康の政治と仏教 (Politics and thought in early Tokugawa Japan: Tokugawa Ieyasu's politics and Buddhism). *Shichō* 史潮, no. 42 (1948): 43–62.

Kondō Keigo 近藤啓吾. *Asami Keisai no kenkyū* 浅見絅斎の研究 (A study of Asami Keisai). Shintō-shi kenkyū sōsho 神道史研究叢書, no. 7. Kyoto 京都: Shintō-shi gakkai 神道史学会, 1970.

Kondō Konomu 近藤喜. "Toyokuni daimyōjin no bunshi ni tsuite" 豊国大明神の分祀に就いて (On branch shrines of Toyokuni daimyōjin). In *Ueki hakase kanreki kinen kokushigaku ronshū* 植木博士還暦記念国史学論集 (National history essays: Festschrift for Doctor Ueki), pp. 357–77. Edited and published by Ueki hakase kanreki kinen shuku gakkai, 1938.

Kubota Osamu 久保田収. "Kimon gakuha to Shintō" 崎門学派と神道 (The Kimon school and Shinto), *Shintōgaku* 神道学, no. 7 (1955): 12–21.

———. *Shintōshi no kenkyū* 神道史の研究 (Studies in the history of Shinto). Ise 伊勢: Kōgakkan daigaku 皇学館大学, 1973.

Kurachi Katsumasa 倉地克直. "Suzuki Shōsan no shisō: bakuhansei seiritsuki no shihaishisō ni tsuite no hitotsu no kokoromi" 鈴木正三の思想: 幕藩制成立期の支配思想についての一つの試み (Suzuki Shōsan's thought: An essay on ruling ideas in the formative period of the bakuhan system). *Nihonshi kenkyū* 日本史研究, no. 155 (1975): 24–49.

Kurihara Shigeyuki 栗原茂幸. "Tokugawa Mitsukuni no seiji shisō" 徳川光圀の政治思想 (Tokugawa Mitsukuni's political thought). *Hōgakkai zasshi* 法学会雑誌 (Tokyo toritsu daigaku 東京都立大学) 18 (1978), 1–2: 547–628.

Kuroda Toshio 黒田俊雄. *Nihon chūsei no kokka to shūkyō* 日本中世の国家と宗教 (The medieval Japanese state and religion). Iwanami 岩波, 1975.

Kuwata Tadachika 桑田忠親. *Daimyō to otogishū* 大名と御伽衆 (Daimyo and otogishū). New augmented edition. Yūseidō 有精堂, 1969.

Maeda Kōji 前田恒治. *Aizu-han ni okeru Yamazaki Ansai* 会津藩に於ける山崎闇斎 (Yamazaki Ansai and the Aizu domain). Nishizawa shoten 西沢書店, 1935.

Mano Senryū 間野潜龍. "Mindai ni okeru sankyō shisō: toku ni Rin Chōon o chūshin to shite" 明代における三教思想: 特に林兆恩を中心として (The three-doctrines thought of the Ming with special reference to Lin Chao-en). *Tōyōshi kenkyū* 東洋史研究 12 (1952), 1: 18–34.

Maruyama Masao 丸山真男. "Ansaigaku to Ansaigakuha" 闇斎学と闇斎学派 (Ansai learning and the Ansai school). In NST 31: 601–74.

Matsuda Osamu 松田修. *Nihon kinsei bungaku no seiritsu: itan no keifu* 日本近世文学の成立: 異端の系譜 (The birth of early modern Japanese literature: The heterodox tradition). Sōsho Nihon bungakushi kenkyū 叢書日本文学史研究 (Collection of studies in the history of Japanese literature). Hōsei daigaku 法政大学, 1963.

Miki Seiichirō 三鬼清一郎. "Sengoku-kinsei shoki ni okeru kokka to tennō" 戦国・近世初期における国家と天皇 (Emperor and nation in the Warring States period and the beginning of early modern Japan). *Rekishi hyōron* 歴史評論, no. 320 (1976): 15–30.

———. "Taikō-kenchi to Chōsen shuppei" 太閤検地と朝鮮出兵 (The Taikō land survey and the Korean expedition). In IKNR (1975) 9: 82–116.

Minamoto Ryōen 源了圓. "Fujiwara Seika to Hayashi Razan" 藤原惺窩と林羅山 (Fujiwara Seika and Hayashi Razan). *Bungei kenkyū* 文芸研究 (Tōhoku daigaku 東北大学), no. 87 (1978): 1–10.

Miyata Noboru 宮田登. "Tōshō daigongen" 東照大権現. In *Nihon shūkyōshi no nazo* 日本宗教史の謎 (Riddles in the history of Japanese religions), edited by Wakabayashi Tarō 和歌森太郎 (2 vols). 2: 65–74. Kōsei 佼成, 1976.

Miyazawa Yoshikazu 宮沢誠一. "Bakuhan seiki no tennō no ideorogiiteki kiban: giseiteki minzokusei no mondai o chūshin ni" 幕藩制期の天皇のイデオロギー的基盤: 擬制的民族制の問題を中心に (The ideological basis for the emperor under the bakufu government, with special attention to the question of a fictitious national consciousness). In *Bakuhansei kokka seiritsu katei no kenkyū: Kan'ei-ki o chūshin ni* 幕藩制国家成立過程の研究: 寛永期を中心に (Studies in the formative process of nationhood under the bakuhan system: especially during the Kan'ei period [1624–1643]), edited by Kitajima Masamoto 北島正元, pp. 189–219. Yoshikawa kōbunkan 吉川弘文館, 1978.

Muraoka Tsunetsugu 村岡典嗣. *Nihon shisōshi gaisetsu* 日本思想史概説 (Outline of Japanese intellectual history). Nihon shisōshi kenkyū 日本思想史研究, vol. 4. Sōbunsha 創文社, 1961.

Nagura Tetsuzō 奈倉哲三. "Hideyoshi no Chōsen shinryaku to 'Shinkoku'" 秀吉の朝鮮侵略と「神国」(Hideyoshi's Korean invasion and the concept of 'The Country of the Gods'). *Rekishi hyōron* 歴史評論, no. 314 (1976): 29–35.

Naitō Akira 内藤昌. "Azuchi-jō no kenkyū" 安土城の研究 (A study of Azuchi castle). *Kokka* 国華, no. 987 (1976): 7–117; no. 988 (1976): 7–63.

Nakamura Hajime 中村元. *Kinsei Nihon no hihanteki seishin no ichi kōsatsu* 近世日本の批判的精神の一考察 (An essay on the critical spirit in early modern Japan). Sanseidō 三省堂, 1949.

Nakao Takashi 中尾堯. "Azuchi shūron no shiteki igi" 安土宗論の史的意義 (The historical significance of the Azuchi religious debate). *Nihon rekishi*

日本歴史, no. 112 (1957): 48–54.

Nishigaki Seiji 西垣晴次. *Eejanaika* ええじやないか Shinbutsu ōraisha 新人物往来社, 1973.

———. *Kamigami to minshū undō* 神々と民衆運動 (Gods and popular movements). Edo shiriizu 江戸シリーズ, no. 9. Mainichi shinbunsha 毎日新聞社, 1977.

Ōkubo Toshiaki 大久保利謙. "Bakumatsu seiji to seiken inin mondai: taisei hōkan no kenkyū josetsu" 幕末政治と政権委任問題：大政奉還の研究序説 (Bakumatsu politics and the problem of delegation of authority: An introduction to the study of the return of the system to the emperor). In *Bakuhantaisei* 幕藩体制 (The bakuhan system), edited by Ōdachi Uki 大館右喜, and Mori Yasuhiko 森安彦. Vol. 2: Ronshū Nihon rekishi 論集日本歴史, vol. 8: 287–304. Yuseidō 有精堂, 1973.

Okuno Takahiro 奥野高広. "Oda seiken no kihonrosen" 織田政権の基本路線 (Oda's route to power), *Kokushigaku* 国史学, no. 100 (1976): 29–58.

Ōkuwa Hitoshi 大桑斉. "Bakuhantaisei to Bukkyō: kinseishisōshi ni okeru Bukkyōshisōshi no ichizuke no kokoromi" 幕藩体制と仏教：近世思想史における仏教思想史の位置っけの試み (The bakuhan system and Buddhism: An essay on the place of the history of Buddhist thought in early modern intellectual history). *Bukkyōshigaku kenkyū* 仏教史学研究 17 (1974), 1: 94–117.

Ono Shinji 小野信二. "Bakufu to tennō" 幕府と天皇 (The bakufu and the emperor). In IKNR (1963) 10:313–56.

Ozawa Eiichi 小沢栄一. *Kinsei shigaku shisōshi kenkyū* 近世史学思想史研究 (A study in the history of early modern historiography). Yoshikawa kōbunkan 吉川弘文館, 1974.

Ozawa Hiroshi 小沢浩. "Bakumatsuki ni okeru minshūshūkyō undō no rekishiteki igi: ikigamishisō no seiritsu o megutte" 幕末期における民衆宗教運動の歴史的意義：生き神思想の成立をめぐって (The historical meaning of late Tokugawa popular religious movements; with special reference to the emergence of the idea of living gods). *Rekishigaku kenkyū* 歴史学研究, no. 11 (1973): 95–106.

Sagara Tōru 相良享. *Kinsei Nihon ni okeru Jukyō undō no keifu* 近世日本における儒教運動の系譜 (Genealogy of the Confucian movement in early modern Japan). Risōsha 理想社, 1965.

Sakurai Katsunoshin 桜井勝之進. *Ise jingū* 伊勢神宮 (The Ise shrines). Gakuseisha 学生社, 1969.

Sasaki Junnosuke 佐々木潤之介. *Daimyō to hyakushō* 大名と百姓 (Daimyo and peasants). Nihon no rekishi 日本の歴史, vol. 15. Chūōkōron 中央公論, 1966.

Shibusawa Eiichi 渋沢栄一. *Rakuō-kō den* 楽翁公伝 (Biography of Matsudaira Sadanobu [1758–1829]). Iwanami 岩波, 1937.

Shingyō Norikazu 新行紀一. "Ikkō ikki no shisō kōzō ni tsuite no ichi shikiron" 一向一揆の思想構造についての一試論 (An essay on the thought structure of the Ikkō ikki). In *Nihon rekishi ronkyū* 日本歴史論究 (Controversies in Japanese history), edited by Tokyo kyōiku daigaku shōshikai 東京教育大学昭史会, pp. 261–78. Ninomiya shoten 二宮書店, 1963.

Shintō jiten 神道辞典 (Shinto dictionary). Edited by Anzu Motohiko 安津素彦, and Umeda Yoshihiko 梅田義彦. Hori shoten 堀書店, 1968.

Suzuki Yoshijirō 鈴木由次郎. "Shushi to Eki" 朱子と易 (Chu Hsi and the *Book of Changes*). In SGT 1: 213–32.

Taira Shigemichi 平重道. *Kinsei Nihon shisōshi kenkyū* 近世日本思想史研究 (Studies in the intellectual history of early modern Japan). Yoshikawa kōbunkan 吉川弘文館, 1969.

———. *Yoshikawa Shintō no kisoteki kenkyū* 吉川神道の基礎的研究 (Basic research into Yoshikawa Shinto). Yoshikawa kōbunkan 吉川弘文館, 1966.

Takagi Shōsaku 高木昭作. "Edo bakufu no seiritsu" 江戸幕府の成立 (The establishment of the Edo bakufu). In IKNR (1975) 9: 118–53.

Tamamuro Fumio 圭室文雄. *Edo bakufu no shūkyō tōsei* 江戸幕付の宗教統制 (The Edo bakufu's administration and regulation of religion). Nihonjin no kōdō to shisō 日本人の行動と思想, vol. 16 Hyōronsha 評論社, 1971.

———. "Kakure daimoku" かくれ題目. In *Kinsei no chika shinkō: kakure kirishitan, kakure daimoku, kakure nenbutsu* 近世の地下信仰: かくれキリシタン・かくれ題目・かくれ念仏 (Underground beliefs in early modern Japan: Hidden Christians, hidden Nichiren, and hidden New Pure Land), edited by Kataoka Yakichi 片岡弥吉; Tamamuro Fumio 圭室文雄; and Oguri Junko 小栗純子: Nihonjin no kōdō to shisō 日本人の行動と思想, vol. 30: 115–205. Hyōronsha 評論社, 1974.

———. "Sūden to Tenkai" 崇伝と天海 (Sūden and Tenkai). In *Nihon shūkyōshi no nazo* 日本宗教史の謎 (Riddles in the history of Japanese religions), edited by Wakabayashi Tarō 和歌森太郎 (2 vols). 2: 53–63. Kōsei 佼成, 1976.

Tani Seigo 谷省吾. *Shintō genron* 神道原論 (Shinto theories). Ise 伊勢: Kōgakkan daigaku 皇学館大学, 1971.

———. "'Suika' to iu reishago" 「垂加」といふ霊社号 (The Shinto spirit-shrine name of 'Suika'). *Geirin* 芸林 21 (1970), 4: 166–77.

———. "Yamazaki Ansai ni yotte kōkan sareta *Jindaikan kuketsu*" 山崎闇斎によって校刊された「神代巻口訳」(*The Oral Traditions of "The Age of the Gods"* printed by Yamazaki Ansai). *Shintōshi kenkyū* 神道史研究 24 (1976), 3: 2–10.

Tokushi biyō 読史備要 (Historical reference book). Edited by Tokyo daigaku shiryō hensanjo 東京大学史料編纂所. Kōdansha 講談社, 1966.

Tomoeda Ryūtarō 友枝龍太郎. "Yamazaki Ansai no taikyokusetsu" 山崎闇斎の太極説 (Yamazaki Ansai's explanation of the Supreme Ultimate). In *Nihon shisō taikei geppō* 日本思想大係月報 (NST monthly bulletin) 63 (March 1980), insert to NST 31: 1–3.

Toyoda Takeshi 豊田武. "Eiyū to densetsu" 英雄と伝説 (Heroes and legends). In *Rekishi to jinbutsu* 歴史と人物 (History and personalities), edited by Nihon rekishi gakkai 日本歴史学会 (The Japanese historical association), pp. 1–24. Yoshikawa kōbunkan 吉川弘文館, 1964.

Tsuji Tatsuya 辻達也. *Kyōhō kaikaku no kenkyū* 享保改革の研究 (A study of the Kyōhō Reform). Sōbunsha 創文社, 1963.

Tsuji Zennosuke 辻善之助. *Nihon Bukkyōshi* 日本仏教史 (History of Japanese

Buddhism). Vol. 5: *Chūsei* 中世 (The middle ages) 4. Iwanami 岩波, 1960.

Tsushi-shi 津市史 (A History of the city of Tsu), edited by Umehara Mitate, and Nishida Shigetsugu 梅原三干・西田重嗣, Tsu 津: Tsushiyakusho 津市役所, 1959.

Umezawa Isetada 梅沢伊勢三. "Kodai shakai ni okeru dōtoku to shūkyō: Heian shoki no 'shōjikishin' to Shintō seishin" 古代社会における道徳と宗教: 平安初期の「正直心」と神道精神 (Ethics and religion in antiquity: "straightforward mind" in early Heian and the Shinto spirit). In *Nihon ni okeru rinri shisō no tenkai* 日本における倫理思想の展開 (Changes in Japanese ethical thought), pp. 269–95. Yoshikawa kōbunkan 吉川弘文館, 1965.

Wajima Yoshio 和島芳男. *Chūsei no Jugaku* 中世の儒学 (Medieval Confucianism). Nihon rekishi sōsho 日本歴史叢書 (Japanese history series), vol. 11. Yoshikawa kōbunkan 吉川弘文館, 1965.

———. "Hoshina seiken to Rinke no gakumon" 保科政権と林家の学問 (Hoshina Masayuki's policies and the learning of the Hayashi house). *Ōtemae joshidaigaku ronshū* 大手前女子大学論集, no. 9 (1975): 82–93.

———. "Kanbun igaku no kin: sono Rinmon kōryū to no kankei" 寛文異学の禁—その林門興隆との関係 (The Ban on Heterodoxy of the Kanbun era [1661–1672] and the fortunes of the Hayashi School). *Ōtemae joshidaigaku ronshū* 大手前女子大学論集, no. 8 (1975): 137–50.

———. "Kinsei ni okeru Sōgaku juyō no ichimondai: Razan no kōsho ni kansuru kokuso ikken o megutte" 近世における宋学受容の一問題—羅山の講書に関する告訴一件をめぐって (A problem concerning the introduction of Sung Learning in early modern Japan: The incident of the lawsuit concerning Razan's public lectures). In *Shigaku ronshū: Taigai kankei to seiji bunka* 史学論集—『対外関係と政治文化』(Historical essays: political culture and foreign relations), edited by Mori Katsumi hakase koki kinenkai 森克己博士古稀記念会 (The committee for the Festschrift in honor of Doctor Mori Katsumi), 3: 361–85. Yoshikawa kōbunkan 吉川弘文館, 1974.

———. "Kinsei shoki Jugakushi ni okeru ni-san no mondai" 近世初期儒学史における二三の問題 (A couple of problems in the history of early Tokugawa Confucianism). *Ōtemae joshidaigaku ronshū* 大手前女子大学論集, no. 7 (1973): 90–102.

Wakaki Taichi 若木太一. "Suzuki Shōsan no shisō to kyōka: Shimabara-Amakusa no ran sono to" 鈴木正三の思想と教化: 島原・天草の乱その後 (Suzuki Shōsan's thought and proselytization after the Shimabara rebellion). *Gobunkenkyū* (Kyūshū daigaku) 語文研究(九州大学), no. 31–32 (1971): 135–48.

Watanabe Hiroshi 波辺浩. "Tokugawa zenki Jugakushi no ichi jōken (1): Sōgaku to kinsei Nihon shakai" 徳川前期儒学史の一条件(上): 宋学と近世日本社会 (A conditioning factor for the history of early Tokugawa Neo-Confucianism (1): Neo-Confucianism and early modern Japanese society). *Kokka gakkai zasshi* 国家学会雑誌 94 (1981), 1–2: 1–82.

Yoshikawa Kōjirō 吉川幸次郎. *Jinsai, Sorai, Norinaga* 仁斎・徂徠・宣長. Iwanami 岩波, 1975.

(*Zōho*) *Yamazaki Ansai to sono monryū* (増補) 山崎闇斎と其門流 (Yamazaki Ansai and his school; Supplemented and augmented edition). Edited by Denki gakkai 伝記学会. Meiji shobō 明治書房, 1943.

WESTERN-LANGUAGE WORKS

Works on Japan and China

Asao Naohiro. "Shogun and Tennō." In *Japan before Tokugawa*, edited by John W. Hall et al., pp. 248–70. Princeton: Princeton University Press, 1981.

Bellah, Robert N. "Baigan and Sorai: Continuities and Discontinuities in Eighteenth-Century Japanese Thought." In *Japanese Thought in the Tokugawa Period: 1600–1868. Methods and Metaphors*, edited by Tetsuo Najita and Irwin Scheiner, pp. 137–52. Chicago: University of Chicago Press, 1978.

———. *Tokugawa Religion: The Values of Pre-Industrial Japan*. Glencoe, Ill.: The Free Press, 1957.

Berling, Judith A. *The Syncretic Religion of Lin Chao-en*. New York: Columbia University Press, 1980.

Berthelot, René. *La pensée de l'Asie et l'astrologie*. Paris: Payot, 1949.

Bitō Masahide. "Ogyū Sorai and the Distinguishing Features of Japanese Confucianism." In *Japanese Thought in the Tokugawa Period, 1600–1868: Methods and Metaphors*, edited by Tetsuo Najita and Irwin Scheiner, pp. 153–60. Chicago: University of Chicago Press, 1978.

———. "Society and Social Thought in the Tokugawa Period," *Japan Foundation Newsletter* 9 (1981), 2–3: 1–9.

Bloom Irene. "On the Matter of the Mind: The Metaphysical Basis of the Expanded Self." In *Individualism and Holism*, edited by Donald J. Munro. Ann Arbor: Center for Chinese Studies, University of Michigan, forthcoming.

Bolitho, Harold. *Treasures among Men: The Fudai Daimyo in Tokugawa Japan*. New Haven: Yale University Press, 1974.

Boscaro, Adriana, ed. *101 Letters of Hideyoshi*. Tokyo: Sophia University Press, 1975.

Brown, Delmer M., and Ichirō Ishida. *The Future and the Past: A Translation and Study of the Gukanshō, an Interpretive History of Japan Written in 1219*. Berkeley and Los Angeles: University of California Press, 1979.

Chu Hsi, and Lü Tsu-Ch'ien, comps. *Reflections on Things at Hand*. Translated, with notes, by Wing-tsit Chan. New York: Columbia University Press, 1967.

Collcutt, Martin. *Five Mountains: The Rinzai Zen Monastic Institution in Medieval Japan*. Harvard East Asian Series. Cambridge: Harvard University Press, 1981.

Cooper, Michael, ed. *They Came to Japan: An Anthology of European Reports on Japan, 1543–1640*. Berkeley and Los Angeles: University of California Press, 1965.

Crasset, Jean. *Histoire de l'église au Japon*. Paris: Estienne Michelet, 1689.

Davis, David. "The Kaga Ikkō-ikki, 1473–1580." Ph.D. dissertation, University of Chicago, 1978.

de Bary, Wm. Theodore. "Individualism and Humanitarianism in Late Ming

Thought." In *idem, Self and Society in Ming Thought*, pp. 145–247. New York: Columbia University Press, 1970.

———. *Neo-Confucian Orthodoxy and the Learning of the Mind-and-Heart*. New York: Columbia University Press, 1981.

———. *The Unfolding of Neo-Confucianism*. New York: Columbia University Press, 1975.

———, and Irene Bloom, eds. *Principle and Practicality: Essays in Neo-Confucianism and Practical Learning*. New York: Columbia University Press, 1979.

Elison, George. "The Cross and the Sword: Patterns of Momoyama History." In *Warlords, Artists and Commoners: Japan in the Sixteenth Century*, edited by George Elison and B. L. Smith, pp. 55–85. Honolulu: University Press of Hawaii, 1981.

———. *Deus Destroyed*. Harvard East Asian Series. Cambridge: Harvard University Press, 1973.

———. "Hideyoshi, the Bountiful Minister." In *Warlords, Artists and Commoners: Japan in the Sixteenth Century*, edited by George Elison & B. L. Smith, pp. 222–44. Honolulu: University Press of Hawaii, 1981.

———, and B. L. Smith, eds. *Warlords, Artists and Commoners: Japan in the Sixteenth Century*. Honolulu: University Press of Hawaii, 1981.

Fujiki Hisashi. "The Political Posture of Oda Nobunaga." In *Japan before Tokugawa*, edited by John W. Hall et al., pp. 149–93. Princeton: Princeton University Press, 1981.

Fung Yu-lan. *A History of Chinese Philosophy*. Translated by Derk Bodde. 2 vols. Princeton: Princeton University Press, 1953.

Graf, Olaf, O.S.B. *Kaibara Ekiken: Ein Beitrag zur Japanischen Geistesgeschichte des 17. Jahrhunderts und zur Chinesischen Sung-Philosophie*. Leiden: Brill, 1942.

Granet, Marcel. *La pensée Chinoise*. Evolution de l'humanité. Paris: La Renaissance du livre, 1934.

Grossberg, Kenneth. *Japan's Renaissance: The Politics of the Muromachi Bakufu*. Harvard East Asian Monographs, no. 99. Cambridge: Harvard University Press, 1981.

Hall, John Carey. "Japanese Feudal Laws. III: The Tokugawa Legislation." *Transactions of the Asiatic Society of Japan* 38, IV (1911): 269–331.

Hall, John W., et al., eds. *Japan before Tokugawa: Political Control and Economic Growth, 1500–1650*. Princeton: Princeton University Press, 1981.

———, and T. Toyoda, eds. *Japan in the Muromachi Age*. Berkeley and Los Angeles: University of California Press, 1977.

Hammitzsch, Horst. *Yamato-hime no mikoto seiki: Bericht über den Erdenwandel ihrer Hoheit der Prinzessin Yamato*. Leipzig: Richter, 1937.

Harootunian, Harry D. "The Consciousness of Archaic Form in the New Realism of Kokugaku." In *Japanese Thought in the Tokugawa Period, 1600–1868: Methods and Metaphors*, edited by Tetsuo Najita and Irwin Scheiner, pp. 63–104. Chicago: University of Chicago Press, 1978.

———. "*Jinsei, Jinzai* and *Jitsugaku*: Social Values and Leadership in Late Tokugawa Thought." In *Modern Japanese Leadership: Transition and Change*, edited by Bernard S. Silberman and H. D. Harootunian, pp. 83–119. Tucson:

University of Arizona Press, 1966.

Hayashiya Tatsusaburō. "Kyoto in the Muromachi Age." In *Japan in the Muromachi Age*, edited by John W. Hall and T. Toyoda, pp. 15–36. Berkeley and Los Angeles: University of California Press, 1977.

Hsiao Kung-chuan. *A History of Chinese Political Thought*. Translated by F. W. Mote. (One vol. published.) Princeton Library of Asian Translations. Princeton: Princeton University Press, 1979.

The I Ching or the Book of Changes. Translated by Richard Wilhelm, Cary F. Baynes. Bollingen Series XIX. Princeton: Princeton University Press, 1967.

Kato Genchi. "The Warongo." In *Transactions of the Asiatic Society of Japan* 45, II (1917): 1–138.

Kawai Masaharu. "Shogun and Shugo: The Provincial Aspects of Muromachi Politics." In *Japan in the Muromachi Age*, edited by John W. Hall and T. Toyoda, pp. 65–86. Berkeley and Los Angeles: University of California Press, 1977.

Kitabatake Chikafusa. *A Chronicle of Gods and Sovereigns*. Translated by H. Paul Varley. Translations from the Oriental Classics. New York: Columbia University Press, 1980.

Malm, William P. "Music Cultures of Momoyama Japan." In *Warlords, Artists and Commoners: Japan in the Sixteenth Century*, edited by George Elison and B. L. Smith, pp. 163–85. Honolulu: University Press of Hawaii, 1981.

Maruyama Masao. *Studies in the Intellectual History of Tokugawa Japan*. Princeton: Princeton University Press, 1974.

Matsumoto Shigeru, *Motoori Norinaga, 1730–1801*. Harvard East Asian Series. Cambridge: Harvard University Press, 1970.

McCune, George M. "The Exchange of Envoys between Korea and Japan during the Tokugawa Period." *Far Eastern Quarterly* 5 (1946), 3: 308–23. Reprinted in *Japan: Enduring Scholarship*, edited by John Harrison, pp. 83–100. Tuscon: University of Arizona Press, 1972.

McMullen I. J. "Non-agnatic Adoption: A Confucian Controversy in Seventeenth- and Eighteenth-century Japan." *Harvard Journal of Asiatic Studies*, 35 (1975): 133–89.

Miyagawa Mitsuru. "From Shōen to Chigyō: Proprietary Lordship and the Structure of Local Power." In *Japan in the Muromachi Age*, edited by John W. Hall and T. Toyoda, pp. 89–105. Berkeley and Los Angeles: University of California Press, 1977.

Muraoka Tsunetsugu. *Studies in Shinto Thought*. Japan National Commission: Ministry of Education, Japan, 1964.

Nakai, Kate Wildman. "The Domestication of Confucian Historiography: The Hayashi, the Early Mito School, and Arai Hakuseki." In *Confucianism and Tokugawa Culture*, edited by Peter Nosco. Princeton: Princeton University Press, 1984.

———. *Arai Hakuseki: Politics and Ideology in the Mid-Tokugawa Bakufu*. Cambridge: Harvard University Press, forthcoming.

Nakamura Hajime. "Suzuki Shōsan, 1579–1655, and the Spirit of Capitalism in Japanese Buddhism." *Monumenta Nipponica* 22 (1967), 1–2: 1–14.

Nihongi: Chronicles of Japan from the Earliest Times to A.D. 697. Translated by W. G. Aston (2 vols. Japan Society, 1896.) 2 vols. in one. Rutland, Vt.: Charles E. Tuttle Co., 1972.

Ogyū Sorai. *Bendō: Distinguishing the Way.* Translated by Olof G. Lidin. Tokyo: Sophia University Press, 1970.

Okada Takehiko. "Practical Learning in the Chu Hsi School: Yamazaki Ansai and Kaibara Ekken." In *Principle and Practicality: Essays in Neo-Confucianism and Practical Learning,* edited by Wm. Theodore de Bary and Irene Bloom, pp. 231–57. New York: Columbia University Press, 1979.

Ooms, Herman. *Charismatic Bureaucrat: A Political Biography of Matsudaira Sadanobu, 1758–1829.* Chicago: Chicago University Press, 1975.

———. "Neo-Confucianism and the Formation of Early Tokugawa Ideology: Contours of a Problem." In *Confucianism and Tokugawa Culture,* edited by Peter Nosco. Princeton: Princeton University Press, 1984.

———. "The Religion of the Household: A Case Study of Ancestor Worship in Japan." *Contemporary Religions in Japan* 8 (1967), 3–4: 201–333.

———. Review of Mary Elisabeth Berry, *Hideyoshi,* in *Journal of the American Oriental Society* 104 (1984), 2: 351–55.

———. Review of Robert J. Smith, *Ancestor Worship in Contemporary Japan,* in *Japanese Journal of Religious Studies* 2 (1975), 4: 317–22.

Porkert, Manfred. *The Theoretical Foundations of Chinese Medicine: Systems of Correspondence.* M.I.T. East Asia Science Series, vol. 3. Cambridge: MIT Press, 1978.

Sadler, A.L. *The Maker of Modern Japan: The Life of Shogun Tokugawa Ieyasu.* 1937. Rutland, Vt.: Tuttle, 1978.

Sansom, George. *A History of Japan, 1334–1615.* Stanford: Stanford University Press, 1961.

———. *A History of Japan, 1615–1867.* Stanford: Stanford University Press, 1963.

Sasaki Junnosuke. "The Changing Rationale of Daimyo Control in the Emergence of the Bakuhan State." In *Japan before Tokugawa,* edited by John W. Hall et al., pp. 271–94. Princeton: Princeton University Press, 1981.

Selected Writings of Suzuki Shōsan. Translated by Royall Tyler. Cornell East Asia Papers. Ithaca, N.Y.: China-Japan Program, Cornell University, 1977.

Smith, David Eugene, and Yoshio Mikami. *A History of Japanese Mathematics.* Chicago: Open Court, 1914.

Steenstrup, Carl. "The Gokurakuji Letter." *Monumenta Nipponica* 32 (1977), 1: 1–34.

———. *Hōjō Shigetoki (1198–1261): and His Role in the History of Political and Ethical Ideas in Japan.* Scandinavian Institute of Asian Studies Monograph Series No. 41. London: Curzon Press, 1979.

———. "The Imagawa Letter." *Monumenta Nipponica* 28 (1973), 3: 295–316.

Sugimoto Masayoshi, and David L. Swain. *Science and Culture in Traditional Japan: A.D. 600–1854.* Cambridge: MIT Press, 1978.

Toby, Ronald P. "Reopening the Question of *Sakoku*: Diplomacy in the Legitimation of the Tokugawa Bakufu." *The Journal of Japanese Studies* 3 (1977), 2: 323–63.

Totman, Conrad. *Politics in the Tokugawa Bakufu, 1600–1843.* Harvard East Asian Series. Cambridge: Harvard University Press, 1967.

Tsunoda Ryusaku, Wm. Theodore de Bary, and Donald Keene, comps. *Sources of Japanese Tradition.* 2 vols. Introduction to Oriental Civilizations. New York: Columbia University Press, 1964.

Tyler, Royall. "Reply to Winston L. King." In *Japanese Religions Newsletter* 2: 1 (October 1980), Appendix.

Walthall, Anne. "The Ethics of Protest by Commoners in Late Eighteenth Century Japan." Ph.D. dissertation, University of Chicago, 1979.

Wang Yang-ming. *Instructions for Practical Learning and Other Neo-Confucian Writings by Wang Yang-ming.* Translated, with notes, by Wing-tsit Chan. New York: Columbia University Press, 1963.

Wheelright, Carolyn. "A Visualization of Eitoku's Lost Paintings at Azuchi Castle." In *Warlords, Artists and Commoners: Japan in the Sixteenth Century,* edited by George Elison and B. L. Smith, pp. 87–111. Honolulu: University Press of Hawaii, 1981.

The Yellow Emperor's Classic of Internal Medicine: Huang ti nei ching su wên. Translated by Ilza Veith. New Edition. Berkeley and Los Angeles: University of California Press, 1966.

"Yuiitsu-Shintō Myōbō-yōshū: Lehrabriss des Yuiitsu-Shintō." Translated and explained by T. Ishibashi, and H. Dumoulin, S. J. *Monumenta Nipponica* 3 (1940), 1: 182–239.

General Works

Althusser, Louis. "Ideology and Ideological State Apparatuses." In *Lenin and Philosophy and other Essays* by L. Althusser. New York: Monthly Review Press, 1971.

Barthes, Roland. *Mythologies.* New York: Hill & Wang, 1972.

Biese, Alfred. *Die Philosophie des Metaphorischen.* Hamburg and Leipzig: Leopold Voss, 1893.

Bourdieu, Pierre. *Outline of a Theory of Practice.* Cambridge: Cambridge University Press, 1977.

———— and Jean-Claude Passeron. *Reproduction in Education, Society & Culture.* London: Sage Publications, 1977.

Conger, George P. *Theories of Macrocosms and Microcosms in the History of Philosophy.* New York: Columbia University Press, 1922.

Delbrück, Hans. *Geschichte der Kriegskunst in Rahmen der politischen Geschichte: IV. Neuzeit.* Berlin: Georg Stilke, 1920.

Derrida, Jacques. "La mythologie blanche: le metaphore dans le texte philosophique." In *id., Marges de la philosophie,* pp. 247–324. Paris: Editions de Minuit, 1972.

————. *Of Grammatology.* Baltimore and London: Johns Hopkins University Press, 1976.

Douglas, Mary. *Natural Symbols: Explorations in Cosmology.* New York: Vintage Books, 1973.

————. *Purity and Danger: An Analysis of Concepts of Pollution and Taboo.* London:

Routledge & Kegan Paul, 1966.

Durand, Gilbert. *Science de l'homme et tradition: Le "Nouvel Esprit Anthropologique"*. Paris: Tête de Feuilles, Sirac, 1975.

————. *Les structures anthropologiques de l'imaginaire: Introduction à l'archétypologie générale*. Collection Études Supérieures. Bordas, 1969.

Erickson, Carolly. *The Medieval Vision: Essays in History and Perception*. New York: Oxford University Press, 1976.

Foucault, Michel. *The Archeology of Knowledge*. Pantheon Books. New York: Random House, 1972.

————. *Discipline and Punish: The Birth of the Prison*. New York: Vintage Books, 1979.

————. *The Order of Things: An Archeology of the Human Sciences*. New York: Vintage Books, 1970.

————. *Power/Knowledge: Selected Interviews and other Writings 1972–1977*. New York: Pantheon, 1980.

Goldmann, Lucien. *Essays on Method in the Sociology of Literature*. St. Louis: Telos Press, 1980.

————. "Genetic Structuralism." In *The Sociology of Literature and Drama*, edited by Elisabeth and Tom Burns, pp. 109–23. Penguin, 1973.

Gramsci, Antonio. *Selections from the Prison Notebooks*. Edited and translated by Quentin Hoare and Geoffrey Nowell Smith. New York: International Publishers, 1971.

Habermas, Jürgen. *Communication and the Evolution of Society*. Boston: Beacon Press, 1979.

————. *Legitimation Crisis*. Boston: Beacon Press, 1975.

Hirsch, E. D. *Validity in Interpretation*. New Haven: Yale University Press, 1967.

Horton, Susan R. *Interpreting Interpreting: Interpreting Dickens's Dombey*. Baltimore: Johns Hopkins University Press, 1979.

Jameson, Fredrick. *The Political Unconscious: Narrative as a Socially Symbolic Act*. Ithaca, N.Y.: Cornell University Press, 1981.

Larrain, Jorge. *The Concept of Ideology*. Athens: University of Georgia Press, 1979.

Lévi-Strauss, Claude. *The Savage Mind*. Chicago: University of Chicago Press, 1966.

Lukács, Georg. *History and Class Consciousness: Studies in Marxist Dialectics*. Cambridge: MIT Press, 1968.

Merquior, J. Q. *The Veil and the Mask: Essays on Culture and Ideology*. London: Routledge & Kegan Paul, 1979.

Moore, Sally F. "Epilogue: Uncertainties in Situations; Indeterminacies in Culture." In *Symbol and Politics in Communal Ideology*, edited by *id.* and Barbara Myerhoff, pp. 210–39. Ithaca, N.Y.: Cornell University Press, 1976.

Needham, Rodney. *Belief, Language and Experience*. Chicago: University of Chicago Press, 1972.

————. *Reconnaissances*. Toronto: University of Toronto Press, 1980.

Palmer, Richard E. *Hermeneutics*. Evanston: Northwestern University Press, 1969.

Paulhan, Jean. *Alain ou la preuve par l'étymologie*. In *id.*, *Oeuvres complètes*. Vol. 3: *Le don des langues*, pp. 263–303. Paris: Cercle du Livre Précieux, 1967.

Piaget, Jean. *Structuralism*. New York: Basic Books, 1970.

Polanyi, Michael and Harry Prosch. *Meaning*. Chicago: University of Chicago Press, 1975.

Redlich, Fritz. *The German Military Enterpriser and his Work Force: A Study in European Economic and Social History*. 2 vols. Wiesbaden: Franz Steiner Verlag, 1964.

Said, Edward. *Beginnings: Intention and Method*. Baltimore: Johns Hopkins University Press, 1975.

Sperber, Dan. *Rethinking Symbolism*. Cambridge Studies in Social Anthropology. Cambridge: Cambridge University Press, 1975.

Starobinski, Jean. *Les mots sous les mots: Les anagrammes de Ferdinand de Saussure*. Le Chemin. Paris: Gallimard, 1971.

Temkin, Owsei. "The Elusiveness of Paracelsus," *Bulletin of the History of Medicine* 26 (1952), 3: 201–217.

———. "Metaphors of Human Biology." In *Science and Civilization*, edited by Robert C. Stauffer, pp. 170–94. Madison: University of Wisconsin Press, 1949.

Todorov, Tzvetan. *Symbolisme et interprétation*. Paris: Editions du Seuil, 1978.

Turner, Victor. *The Forest of Symbols*. Ithaca, N.Y.: Cornell University Press, 1967.

White, Hayden. *Metahistory: The Historical Imagination in Nineteenth Century Europe*. Baltimore: Johns Hopkins University Press, 1973.

———. *Tropics of Discourse: Essays in Cultural Criticism*. Baltimore: Johns Hopkins University Press, 1978.

Index

Library of Congress Cataloging in Publication Data

Ooms, Herman.
Tokugawa ideology.

Bibliography: p.
Includes index.
1. Political science—Japan—Philosophy—History.
2. Japan—Politics and government—1600–1868.   I. Title.

JA84.J3055 1985   320.5′5′0952   84-42897
ISBN 0-691-05444-4 (alk. paper)